Achieving Extreme Performance with Oracle Exadata

Rick Greenwald
Robert (Bob) Stackowiak
Maqsood Alam
Mans Bhuller

New York   Chicago   San Francisco
Lisbon   London   Madrid   Mexico City
Milan   New Delhi   San Juan
Seoul   Singapore   Sydney   Toronto

The McGraw·Hill Companies

Cataloging-in-Publication Data is on file with the Library of Congress

McGraw-Hill books are available at special quantity discounts to use as premiums and sales promotions, or for use in corporate training programs. To contact a representative, please e-mail us at bulksales@mcgraw-hill.com.

Achieving Extreme Performance with Oracle Exadata

1 2 3 4 5 6 7 8 9 0   DOC DOC   1 0 9 8 7 6 5 4 3 2 1

ISBN   978-0-07-175259-6
MHID   0-07-175259-5

Sponsoring Editor Wendy Rinaldi	**Technical Editors** Kevin Closson Maria Colgan Tim Shetler	**Production Supervisor** Jean Bodeaux
Editorial Supervisor Janet Walden		**Composition** Glyph International
Project Manager Anupriya Tyagi, Glyph International	**Copy Editor** Lisa McCoy	**Illustration** Glyph International
	Proofreader Susie Elkind	**Art Director, Cover** Jeff Weeks
Acquisitions Coordinator Stephanie Evans	**Indexer** Karin Arrigoni	**Cover Designer** Pattie Lee

For Elinor Greenwald, on her way to many successes; Josephine Greenwald, author of the forthcoming book *Frog on a Log;* and Robin Greenwald, who keeps things interesting along the way. For my wife, LuAnn Greenwald, who has made this wonderful family possible. And for my longtime best pal, Bailey Greenwald—we miss you.
—*Rick Greenwald*

For Jodie, my wife of over 30 years, who has always been there for me and has learned to say impressive technical phrases to my friends without having a full understanding of how to translate them.
—*Robert Stackowiak*

To my parents, who are the reason for my being here; to my father-in-law, a professor and an author whose dedication and commitment inspired me to write; to my wonderful wife, Suraiya, who fully supported me in this ordeal and gave excellent input despite not knowing the Oracle jargon; and finally, to my wonderful children, Zuha and Firas, who are the inspiration of my life.
—*Maqsood Alam*

For my parents, who taught me the value of education and hard work. For my brother, who stood by my shoulder guiding me through life's tribulations (and without whom I would still be selling music and stacking frozen chickens!). For my dear wife, Ladi, and for our bundle of joy, Pavan.
—*Mans Bhuller*

About the Authors

Rick Greenwald has been active in the computer industry for more than 25 years. He is currently Director of Partner Enablement at Oracle, where he has worked for more than 10 years. He is also the author or coauthor of more than 15 books, including the best-selling *Oracle Essentials* for O'Reilly & Associates, now in its fourth edition; *Beginning Oracle Application Express* from Wiley; *Professional Oracle Programming* from Wrox; and *Oracle Data Warehousing and Business Intelligence Solutions* from Wiley.

Robert (Bob) Stackowiak, vice-president of Business Intelligence and Data Warehousing in the Enterprise Solutions Group at Oracle, has worked for more than 20 years in the IT industry. His roles have included software development, management of software development, systems engineering, sales and sales consulting, and new business innovation and development. Bob has spoken at numerous computer-related conferences and has conducted briefings with companies around the world. He has coauthored several books, including *Oracle Essentials: Oracle Database 11g (4th Edition)* by O'Reilly and *Oracle Data Warehousing and Business Intelligence Solutions* by Wiley. In addition, his papers regarding data warehousing and computer and software technology have appeared in publications such as The Data Warehousing Institute's *Journal of Data Warehousing*.

Maqsood Alam, senior manager of product development at Oracle, is a software professional with more than 15 years of experience working with Oracle technologies, specializing in databases, maximum availability architectures, data warehousing, database migrations, and business intelligence. His current initiatives are focused on evangelizing Oracle Exadata, performing customer Proof-Of-Concepts and benchmarks, promoting best practices for migrations to Oracle from Oracle and non-Oracle databases, and also providing support to customers undergoing large Exadata implementations. He is an Oracle Certified Professional and holds a master's and a bachelor's degree in computer science.

Mans Bhuller, senior director of Database, Operating Systems and Management, Enterprise Solutions Group, Oracle, has worked at the forefront of emerging technologies at Oracle Corporation for the last 14 years. In this role, he has been paving the way for the Oracle Exadata Database Machine and other foundational technologies, such as Real Application Clusters (RAC), Grid, and Private Cloud. Mans is active in the Oracle Enterprise Architect community and has visited hundreds of customers. Recently, he has been building internal teaching classes around Exadata and Private Cloud and training others.

About the Technical Editors

Kevin Closson is a performance architect in Oracle's Systems Technology Group focused on Exadata and future platform solutions. His 24-year career has included engineering, technical marketing, support and application development positions specializing in Oracle, and clustered platforms. Prior to his tenure with Oracle, Kevin held positions within HP, PolyServe, IBM, Sequent Computer Systems, and Veritas where his main engineering focus was throughput and scalability enhancements of the Oracle server on high-end Unix SMP and clustered systems. Kevin holds patents in SMP-locking algorithms and database caching methods. He is a frequent speaker at industry trade shows such as Oracle OpenWorld, IBM PartnerWorld, IOUG-A, and regional Oracle user groups. In addition to book collaborations, Kevin's written works have appeared in *IBM Redbook, Oracle Magazine, Oracle Internals Magazine, SELECT,* and *CMG.* He is a charter member of the OakTable Network Organization. Kevin maintains a popular technical blog at http://kevinclosson.wordpress.com.

Maria Colgan is a principal product manager at Oracle Corporation and has been with the company since version 7.3 was released in 1996. Maria's core responsibilities are data warehouse best practices and the Oracle Optimizer. Based on Maria's extensive experience in Oracle's Server Technology Performance Group—where she conducted competitive customer benchmarks and tuning sessions—Maria creates and lectures on data warehouse best practices and in-depth insights into the Oracle Optimizer and the statistics it relies on.

Tim Shetler leads product management for the Systems Technology Group at Oracle. His product responsibilities include the Exadata Storage Server, database high-availability, database performance, compression, backup, and archiving. He has spent most of his career working with database management products, initially developing applications with Andersen Consulting (Accenture), and subsequently in product management and marketing roles at Hewlett-Packard, Informix Software, TimesTen, InQuira, and Oracle, with a primary focus on parallel processing and ultra-high-performance systems.

Contents

PART I
Features and Foundations

Foreword

Exadata has consumed much of my attention and the attention of a significant portion of my development team here at Oracle since the early 2000s. This project began when we saw our customers struggling with Oracle database implementations on hardware platforms that were inadequate to meet the demands of growing data sizes and workloads. In particular we found that Oracle performance was limited by the inability to move data from disks into the database fast enough. There was plenty of throughput in the disks themselves, and plenty of processing power in the servers, but the architecture for moving data from disks to processors was severely limited. Since inadequate throughput was clearly the cause of most performance bottlenecks, we started an effort to develop software to move database processing directly into intelligent storage. Later, it became clear to us that we needed to focus all our efforts on a specific storage platform to achieve the best performance and reliability.

When we first productized the Exadata platform, we offered two options. One option was to attach intelligent storage to customer purchased and configured database servers. The other option was to purchase a complete optimized Database Machine from Oracle, including servers, storage, and networking. We thought that many customers would find it more convenient to add storage to their existing standard configurations than to adopt a completely new platform. We could not have been more wrong. Almost no customers bought the storage only solution. Instead, we found huge interest in our customers for a completely integrated and optimized full database solution from Oracle. Thus, Oracle entered the integrated systems business.

We have come a long way since Larry Ellison introduced the first version of the Oracle Exadata Database Machine in 2008 at Oracle OpenWorld. Today, Exadata is used in production to run an incredible variety of applications. Exadata runs everything from enormous telecom data warehouses to response-time-critical financial trading applications. We have a growing number of deployments of Exadata running the most sophisticated applications in the world—Oracle E-Business Suite, Siebel, and PeopleSoft.

Many lessons were learned along the way as we worked with this fast-growing customer base. This book takes you through some of the history of the Oracle Exadata Database Machine and some of the best practices we developed. After you read this book, you should have a better understanding of fundamental Exadata concepts and how to leverage Exadata's benefits in your applications. My hope is that you find this book useful as you deploy and manage your Oracle Exadata Database Machine. I sincerely hope that the extreme performance you experience will take your business or organization to a new level of success.

Juan Loaiza
Redwood Shores, CA
October 2010

Juan Loaiza is senior vice-president of systems technologies at Oracle and manages the "systems" aspects of Oracle's database development organization, including Exadata, high availability and Data Guard, Oracle Secure Backup and RMAN, Flashback, performance, data and index management, and platform-specific development. He has worked in the database development organization since 1988 and contributed to every release since Oracle version 6. Juan has a bachelor's and master's degree in computer science from M.I.T.

Acknowledgments

Rick, Bob, and the entire author team would like to acknowledge the excellent review process managed by our editorial director, Wendy Rinaldi, and our acquisitions coordinator, Stephanie Evans. The technical editors, Maria Colgan, Kevin Closson, and Tim Shetler, provided more thorough reviews than any previous book we have been associated with—we feel confident that this book is highly accurate, but accept sole responsibility for any errors that may have slipped through the cracks. Rick and Bob would like to especially call out the work of Kevin, who often provided direction at a level that is not documented or widely known within Oracle.

Rick Greenwald would also like to thank his longtime collaborator, Bob Stackowiak, for his contributions and friendship for more than 15 years— quite an outcome from that initial meeting in line, and Maqsood Alam, who really delivered on his first book. The process of writing this book has been a process of almost continual learning and discovery, which would not have been as rich and complete without the help of many (in no particular order), including Robert Pastijin, Mark Townsend, Ron Weiss, Peter Wahl, Pete Sharman, Andrew Babb, Kodi Umamageswaran, Miroslav Lorenc, Herman Baer, Mahesh Subramaniam, Christian Craft, Mark Scardina, Kevin Jernigan, George Spears, Phil Stephenson, Alex Tsukerman, Jenny Tsai-Smith, Dan Norris, and all the many folks who contribute to internal Exadata mailing lists. And a special thanks to both Maria Colgan and Kevin Closson, who provided valuable insights over the course of the entire project.

Finally, a sincere shout-out to Nick Kritikos, my boss, who encouraged the creation of this book in many ways.

Bob would also like to acknowledge Rick Greenwald's extensive efforts on this book, including where he filled in gaps in some chapters when needed and his review of the book's content for consistency. Juan Loaiza provided important support for this project early in the process as the authors considered whether the time was right for a book covering Exadata. Of course, having the support of management at Oracle is critical, and Bob would like to acknowledge the support of Mark Salser and David O'Neill in the Oracle Enterprise Solutions Group and Kate Johnson in the Oracle Exadata Program Management Office in North America. Bob would also like to acknowledge the contributions and guidance offered over the years by George Lumpkin, Hermann Baer, Ron Weiss, Tony Politano, Joe Rayman, Rob Reynolds, Warren Dagenbach, Louis Nagode, and Alan Manewitz.

Maqsood Alam would like to acknowledge the coauthors for making this project a success, with a special thanks to Rick Greenwald for accepting this project and being a mentor along the way. A sincere token of appreciation goes out to all the reviewers, especially to Kevin Closson, who provided invaluable technical insights. Lastly, to my colleagues at Oracle Platform Technology Solutions, Henry Byorum, Aalok Muley, Milton Wan, and others, who time and again provide exciting opportunities that allow me to work with the latest and greatest technologies.

Mans Bhuller would like to send a big thank-you to the Oracle Exadata development team and executive management, in particular, Ron Weiss, Phil Stephenson, Mahesh Subramaniam, Kevin Jernigan, Tim Shetler, Juan Loaiza, and Kevin Closson (more for his sardonic wit rather than his galactic intellect). Mans would also like to recognize Andrew Holdsworth from the Real World Performance Team and Maria Colgan from the DW/SQL team, as well as his manager, David O'Neill, and SVP Mark Salser from the ESG team. Over the years I have benefited from the warmth of true friendship from Peter Sharman and Holger Kalinowski and would like to honor those mentors who have guided me in the past and those that still continue to guide me to this day: Mark Ashdown, Mark Large, Graham Wood, and Paul Cross.

Introduction

You are holding the first comprehensive book covering the Oracle Exadata Database Machine. You might be holding this book because of your desire to know more about exactly what this technology can do for you, but you and your fellow readers have come to this place from different starting points. You could be investigating the Exadata Database Machine because you are a longtime Oracle user who is curious as to the new capabilities you will get with this platform. Your curiosity may have been sparked by the large amount of publicity around the Exadata Database Machine, from Oracle, the press, and industry analysts. Or you might be approaching Exadata with a fair amount of skepticism, since new platforms that can deliver orders of magnitude of performance improvement are rare, to say the least, in a mature market like the relational database market.

This book should help you understand Exadata technology in a way that will extend your knowledge, validate the publicity (well, at least some of it), and show you how these vaunted performance improvements are actually delivered.

What Is Exadata?

This most basic question will require much of this book to fully explain, but the Exadata Database Machine is a bit like an elephant being approached by blind men. Is Exadata a new type of storage hardware? Is Exadata similar to an appliance built with the latest and greatest hardware components? Is Exadata primarily software that uses hardware components in some new ways? Is Exadata simply an optimally configured Oracle-complete hardware and software stack?

The answer to the question "Which of these is Exadata?" has a simple answer—"Yes." The Exadata Database Machine has been described in all of these ways, and more.

One facet of the Exadata Database Machine that we want to make sure to recognize is its simplicity. The Exadata Database Machine comes preconfigured and optimized, designed to implement best practices for Oracle software and hardware that have been decades in the making. For the most part, the Exadata Database Machine just works.

This simplicity has been the cause of much curiosity in the user community, since the internal operations of Exadata technology—the *way* it just works—have been somewhat shrouded in mystery. We believe that this book will go a long way toward removing these shrouds, while still leaving you with a real appreciation of just how innovative, powerful, and cool the Exadata Database Machine is.

The remainder of this book is our attempt to deliver on this promise.

PART

I

Features and Foundations

CHAPTER
1

Oracle and Tightly Integrated Hardware and Software Platforms

n 2008, Oracle introduced its first "Database Machine" with Exadata storage and promoted the new Machine as a breakthrough product. Only a year later, Oracle rolled out a set of major enhancements to the original offering in the form of the Sun Oracle Database Machine.

In 2010, new node configurations for the Oracle Exadata Database Machine were announced. Extraordinary levels of customer interest and demand led Larry Ellison, Oracle Chief Executive Officer, to call Exadata "the most exciting product [from Oracle] in many, many years." Today, the Oracle Exadata Database Machine is available for deployment as a platform dedicated to single data warehousing and online transaction processing databases, and for consolidation where multiple Oracle database servers are deployed.

Since Oracle is building and supporting database features designed for this specific platform, including the Oracle Exadata Storage Server Software, this offering raises some new considerations. Throughout most of Oracle's history, the Oracle database was designed to deploy and perform equally well on a variety of server platforms and storage devices. In this book, we'll cover what makes the Oracle Exadata Database Machine a unique platform as an integrated Oracle software and hardware combination, and how you can take advantage of its capabilities when you deploy it.

Despite introducing a shift in Oracle's platform strategy, the Oracle Exadata Database Machine builds upon previous lessons the Oracle community learned when deploying and managing Oracle databases on other platforms. So, we'll also cover how those earlier strategies and previously acquired skills can be utilized for this platform. When you finish reading this book, you should understand thoroughly the software, hardware concepts, and many of the best practices associated with the Oracle Exadata Database Machine and Exadata Storage Server technology.

If you think of the Oracle Exadata Database Machine as an "appliance," you are not correct in your understanding of the platform. Oracle has been careful to avoid that tag, though the platform is sometimes described as "appliance-like." The reason for this is simple. Some of the characteristics we will describe, such as the specific prebalanced configurations and rapid installation services, remind one of an appliance. But other characteristics, such as the need for database administrators (DBAs) to manage patches (updates to the database and also operating system versions), are decidedly familiar to those managing Oracle on traditional platforms. So throughout the book, we'll be careful to describe exactly how and why this platform is a combination of both of these entities.

In this first chapter, we'll briefly describe why we are seeing appliances and appliance-like platforms emerge now, and we'll start by describing the history of such platforms. This chapter also introduces the Oracle Exadata Database Machine and Exadata concepts that we'll cover in much more detail throughout the remainder of the book.

A History of Appliance-like Computing Solutions

The birth of appliance-like computing solutions is difficult to pin down. Computer systems were designed to store and retrieve data from their inception, and in the early days of computing, all underlying systems consisting of servers, storage, and software were designed, assembled, and supported by single vendors. Following on this design philosophy, early databases of varying types were optimized for specific hardware provided by those same vendors.

The 1970s saw the introduction of a new type of database, the relational database. Some of these early database vendors continued to develop and support specific hardware platforms. To speed up data warehousing performance (then called decision support), Teradata was founded in 1979 based on the concept of massively parallel processing systems and featuring a tightly coupled Teradata database, operating system, and server and storage platform. Another team of developers, originally involved in the creation of the Ingres database, formed Britton Lee in 1979 and introduced a hardware and software platform that served as database accelerator, optimizing performance on client platforms that surrounded other popular back-end servers. IBM introduced support of relational databases for large-scale transaction processing in 1983 with a database specifically designed for their mainframes, DB2 for MVS. In 1988, IBM introduced the AS/400 with its own relational database, SQL/400 (also known as DB2/400), targeting transaction-processing applications ideal for mid-sized companies and providing a platform noted for its ease of deployment and management.

One of the relational databases introduced in the late 1970s was Oracle, but Oracle (and many of Oracle's competitors) created database engines that were deployable on a variety of hardware vendors' platforms. In the 1980s, these databases gained popularity and were being developed using portable programming languages such as C. Support of multiple hardware platforms also became easier because of the growing popularity of Unix-based operating systems on many of these platforms. The growing popularity of database servers drove pricing for servers and storage downward and further escalated the rapid evolution of hardware components as vendors raced to differentiate from each other based on performance and other characteristics. The hardware components became more modular and open, and enabled IT organizations and vendors to mix and match servers, storage, and other devices. Throughout the 1990s, the tradeoff that most companies considered was the benefit of aggressive open systems pricing versus incremental value provided by tightly integrated solutions. For common workloads in many businesses and organizations, database performance differences were negligible when making this choice, making the lower cost of commodity hardware more attractive.

At the turn of this century, some factors emerged that caused IT organizations deploying and integrating their own software and hardware components to reconsider both the benefits and challenges of a modular strategy. First, all sizes of businesses began to experience a massive growth in data volume well beyond what they had previously experienced. Very large data volumes especially became common when deploying business intelligence and data warehousing solutions that produced significant business value by solving ad hoc business questions or providing deeper analysis for strategic decision making. Business analysts using such systems often required more detailed data, longer histories, and added data from external sources to uncover solutions to their business problems. The changing workloads and growing data volumes on these systems made the sizing and integration of system components more challenging. These systems also evolved from serving as "nice-to-have" strategic management systems to becoming tactical business management systems, thus introducing the need for better reliability, availability, and serviceability more commonly associated with transaction processing.

Some of the platform solutions from an earlier generation continued to service this need. But the need for shorter time-to-deployment and more predictable performance also led to the appearance of new platform choices from vendors such as Netezza, Greenplum, and DATAllegro that provided more out-of-the-box "appliance" solutions. These preintegrated and predefined solutions were assembled using a combination of commodity components and innovative packaging and integration. By tightly defining the entire platform, integrated hardware and software optimizations could be introduced on these systems, pushing the execution of some database intelligence into storage systems. Typically, these new vendors started with "open-source" databases that were customized for the hardware. Such platforms demonstrated exceptional performance for executing ad hoc queries, because the predefined hardware was balanced and because of integrated optimization of the software. As is common in growth markets where start-up vendors appear, some thrived while others disappeared or were acquired.

Meanwhile, the platform flexibility provided by a database such as Oracle was no longer always seen as a deciding factor, or even desirable, when selecting a database technology to be deployed. In some organizations, speed, ease of deployment and management, and more predictable performance became the deciding factors. It was time for a shift in Oracle's database platform strategy. But as you'll see, this shift was already years in the making before the release of the first Oracle Exadata Database Machine. Oracle was already taking the steps needed to transform it into a systems company.

Oracle's Evolution Towards Integrated Hardware and Software

When Oracle was founded in 1977 as Software Development Laboratories (SDL), relational databases were largely the subject of research papers. It was thought that relational databases would be too demanding for the hardware platforms that were available at the time. Nevertheless, SDL began Project Oracle for the CIA by creating a database based on IBM Research's System R4 model. Among other things, the early database was technically noteworthy for its early support of SQL. By 1983, Oracle had released a version of the Oracle database written in the C programming language to better enable portability to heterogeneous hardware platforms in that fast-growing market. Thus, began a mantra that Oracle ran equally well on and was optimized for a wide variety of hardware platforms.

Though initially targeting departmental minicomputers, Oracle had its eyes on enterprise-class servers for the computing market as early as the 1980s. Oracle saw that the means to get there was through clustering such systems to support large-scale databases and released its first product of this type for VAX clusters in 1986. A version of this product for Unix-based platforms, Oracle Parallel Server, followed in the early 1990s and was primarily deployed for scaling parallel queries in data warehouses or providing high availability in transaction processing. A breakthrough occurred in the introduction of the re-architected Oracle 9*i* database featuring Real Application Clusters (RAC) in 2001. "Cache Fusion" in Oracle9*i* RAC reduced traffic over the cluster interconnect, resulting in the ability for RAC to provide linear performance improvements as nodes and appropriate storage and throughput were added to cluster configurations. For the first time, Oracle was able to scale data warehousing and transaction-processing workloads on a variety of clustered systems.

Shortly after, Oracle signaled a move toward providing deeper infrastructure software capabilities and support that was formerly provided by partners or was simply lacking. Oracle Database 10*g* Enterprise Edition was introduced in 2003 with Automatic Storage Management (ASM) and embedded cluster management software, eliminating the need for third-party software that provided those capabilities. ASM virtualizes storage resources and provides advanced volume management, thus enabling the database and DBA to manage tasks such as striping and mirroring of data. The Automatic Database Diagnostics Monitor (ADDM) also first appeared in this release and provided advisory alerts and suggestions for tactics to improve performance based on periodic snapshots of performance in a production environment. These suggestions are displayed to DBAs by Enterprise Manager's Grid Control, whose enhanced alerting and management capabilities are critically important when deploying Oracle for large-scale databases and for "grid computing."

In 2005, penguins appeared on stage at Oracle OpenWorld in what was seen as a curious announcement at the time but would have important implications in establishing a complete Oracle platform. Oracle announced it would provide support for Red Hat and SUSE Linux and deliver an "unbreakable Linux" support model. Oracle later introduced Oracle Enterprise Linux, which has roots in Red Hat Linux from the open-source community to which Oracle had long provided technology. Meanwhile, Oracle had begun work on establishing reference configurations for data warehousing on Linux-based and other platforms from a variety of platform vendors.

Taken together, these moves by Oracle and the changes in the deployment strategies at many of Oracle customers led to Oracle's decision to launch a tightly integrated hardware and software platform. The initial platform, the HP Oracle Database Machine with Exadata storage, became available in 2008. In 2009, Oracle announced a second generation of the Oracle Exadata Database Machine and a new hardware platform—the Sun Oracle Database Machine. The acquisition of Sun by Oracle Corporation in 2010 completed the transition of Oracle to a vendor that can design, build, and support complete database hardware and software solutions that are deployed as systems. In September 2010, Oracle announced new X2-2 and X2-8 nodes for the Oracle Exadata Database Machine and also announced Solaris 11 as an alternative to the Oracle Enterprise Linux operating system for database server nodes. The "Unbreakable Enterprise Kernel for Linux" was announced at this time to provide support for the large number of processing cores made available in the Exadata Database Machine.

We'll discuss some implications of the Sun acquisition later in this chapter and some of the likely future directions. Table 1-1 summarizes some of the important events and timing that led to the Oracle Exadata Database Machine.

Year	Event
1977	Software Development Labs (SDL), later known as Oracle, is founded.
1979	Teradata is founded and creates a tightly integrated decision support system. Britton Lee is founded and creates a database accelerator platform.
1983	Oracle is rewritten in C programming language for portability across platforms. DB2 for MVS on IBM mainframes is introduced.
1986	Oracle database is introduced for VAX clusters.
1988	IBM introduces the AS/400 with DB2/400 for mid-range transaction processing.
1992	Oracle Parallel Server for Unix-based systems scales large data warehouses.
2000	Netezza is founded with the intention of creating a data warehouse appliance.
2001	Oracle9i with Real Application Clusters can scale any Oracle-based application.
2003	Oracle Database 10g enables grid computing and features Automatic Storage Management and the Automatic Database Diagnostics Monitor.
2005	Oracle announces support of Red Hat and SUSE Linux.
2006	Oracle announces Oracle Enterprise Linux.
2007	Oracle announces Optimized Warehouse Initiative reference configurations (described below).
2008	Oracle announces the HP Oracle Database Machine and Exadata Storage Servers especially for data warehousing.
2009	Oracle announces the Sun Oracle Database Machine (Exadata Version 2) for data warehousing, transaction processing, and consolidation of databases.
2010	Oracle completes the acquisition of Sun; Oracle announces Exadata X2-2 and X2-8 nodes, Solaris 11 support for Exadata, an "Unbreakable Enterprise Kernel for Linux," Oracle Exalogic, and the Exalogic Elastic Cloud.

TABLE 1-1. *Key Events in the Evolution Toward the Oracle Exadata Database Machine*

Next, we'll take a closer look at the fundamental concepts behind the Oracle Exadata Database Machine. These concepts will set the stage for what follows in this book.

Oracle Exadata Database Machine Fundamental Concepts

Prior to the availability of Oracle's Exadata Database Machines, most systems deployed by IT organizations to host Oracle databases were customized configurations designed by those organizations, their systems integrators, or by the server and storage vendors. The process of configuring such a custom platform solution requires a series of steps, each of which tends to be complicated, time consuming, and offers opportunities to make mistakes.

Such designs start with pre-implementation system sizing based on real and anticipated workloads. Once the servers and storage are determined for the platform, the components are acquired, installed, configured, tested, and validated. Individuals involved in this process often include systems and storage architects, database administrators, hardware and storage vendors, network vendors, and systems integrators. Delivered configurations can be problematic if proper balance is not provided in the design, most often occurring when the throughput delivered by the storage subsystem and storage-to-system connections and networks are not balanced with what the server-side CPUs and memory are capable of handling.

Oracle began to explore solving the problem of lack of proper balance in data warehousing systems through the Oracle Optimized Warehouse Initiative, and publicly announced that initiative in 2007. A series of reference configurations provided balanced server and storage configuration recommendations and eliminated much of the pre-implementation system-sizing guesswork. Developed with a number of Oracle's server and storage partners, the reference configurations were defined in charts that contained a variety of recommended server and storage combinations. The optimal platform for deployment was selected based on workload characteristics and required storage capacity. When closely adhered to, the reference configurations could deliver optimal performance for generic server and storage platforms.

Some organizations continued to struggle in deploying balanced platforms even where reference configurations were initially used. In some situations, the recommended storage was not purchased but was replaced by cheaper storage with similar capacity but inferior performance. In other situations, the server and storage platforms were initially configured and deployed as described in the reference configurations, but later upgrades and additions to the configuration were not made in a balanced fashion.

The introduction of Oracle's Exadata Database Machines eliminated much of this risk by offering a limited set of server and storage configurations within predefined racks. The systems scale a combination of database server nodes, Exadata Storage Server cells, and I/O throughput (including internal networking) in a balanced fashion as the system grows. So, as user workloads and data volumes grow, you can scale the systems to maintain constant response times. The Exadata Storage Server Software further enhances this scalability by minimizing the volume of data retrieved from the Exadata Storage Server cells to database server nodes, thus mitigating a typical throughput bottleneck.

The Oracle Exadata Database Machine thus shares the appliance characteristic of containing fixed components that assure a balanced hardware configuration. The multistep pre-implementation sizing, configuration, and integration process is reduced to understanding the planned workload and ordering the right standard rack configuration that will support the workload.

The first generation of this platform, the HP Oracle Database Machine, was configured specifically to handle data warehousing workloads. The ratio of database server nodes to Exadata Storage Server cells was set at 4:7, with each storage cell containing 12 disk drives for user data. The switch providing the fabric for database server node–to–Exadata Storage Server cell communications and RAC node-to-node communications was a high-speed InfiniBand switch rated at 20 Gb per second. For queries tested on this platform in combination with the Exadata Storage Server Software, Oracle would claim query performance speed-up of ten times or more as typical when compared to performance on other Oracle-based but non-Exadata data warehousing platforms. Platform upgrades were available in fixed configuration increments when Half-Racks and Full Racks needed to be scaled to meet increased workloads or storage demands. Key components were prepackaged and configured such that single points of failure were eliminated.

When Oracle introduced the second-generation Sun Oracle Database Machine in 2009, the ratio of database server nodes to Exadata Storage Server cells remained fixed at 4:7 in Half-Racks and Full Racks and for multiple Full Racks (and 2:3 in Quarter-Racks). As before, there were 12 disks for user data in each storage server cell. However, performance characteristics of key components were improved across the board.

The Intel Xeon 5540 CPUs in the database server nodes and Exadata Storage Server cells were about 80 percent faster than the CPUs in the earlier-generation Database Machine. The DDR dynamic access random memory (DRAM) was improved from DDR2 to DDR3, and memory capacity was increased in each database server node from 32GB to 72GB. Though a Full Rack also contained 168 disks for user data in this platform, disk throughput increased by 50 percent and storage capacity increased with the introduction of 600GB and 2TB disk drives. The addition of Exadata Smart Flash Cache to the Exadata Storage Server cells (384GB of Flash per cell) added a new dimension to speeding up I/O operations and database performance. To complete the balanced performance improvements, Oracle doubled the throughput of the InfiniBand switch to 40 Gb per second. The increased power and flexibility enabled Oracle to extend the applicability of the configurations beyond just data warehousing to also support transaction processing and consolidation of multiple database servers to a single Sun Oracle Database Machine.

The Oracle announcement in September 2010 of the Oracle Exadata Database Machine X2-2 systems featured configured database server nodes to Exadata Storage Server cells in the ratios previously mentioned. Nodes in the X2-2 systems had two sockets for CPUs per node but now contained six core Intel Xeon 5670 processors and 96GB of memory. At that time, Oracle also introduced large symmetric multiprocessing (SMP) nodes paired in new Oracle Exadata Database Machine X2-8 full-rack systems. Each node in the X2-8 configuration contained eight sockets holding eight core Intel Xeon 7560 processors along with 1TB of memory.

Figure 1-1 illustrates where the key components in the Oracle Exadata Database Machine X2-2 configurations reside in a Full Rrack. The X2-2 configurations are typically deployed where smaller but more numerous nodes are more appropriate for workloads and to meet high-availability performance needs (since an individual node failure would have less impact on overall system performance than loss of a larger SMP node). Oracle Exadata Database Machine X2-8 systems are deployed where workloads scale better on large SMP nodes and/or where larger memory footprints are required.

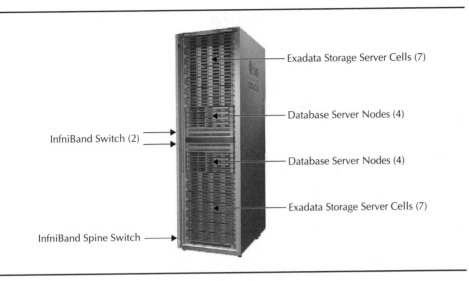

Exadata Storage Server Cells (7)

Database Server Nodes (4)

InfniBand Switch (2)

Database Server Nodes (4)

Exadata Storage Server Cells (7)

InfniBand Spine Switch

FIGURE 1-1.   *Oracle Exadata Database Machine X2-2 Full Rack*

The specifics of this hardware will continue to change over time. But the fundamental balanced design concepts continue with each subsequent release of the product. As new designs emerge, capacities and performance levels continue to improve across these key components in a balanced fashion.

Software Integration and the Oracle Exadata Database Machine

Though understanding the hardware concepts is important, it is equally important to understand the implications of Oracle's software integration to this platform. Oracle's platform support includes the operating system, Oracle Enterprise Linux, as the foundation for the database server nodes and Exadata Storage Server cells. As an alternative, Oracle also offers the Solaris 11 operating system for the database server nodes. Upon this platform, Oracle tightly integrates Oracle Database 11*g* Enterprise Edition and extends database functionality into storage with the Exadata Storage Server Software. Other Oracle database software components on the platform that are central to a typical deployment are RAC and the Oracle Partitioning Option.

One example of the tight integration of the hardware and database is the leveraging of Exadata Smart Flash Cache as a database cache. Supported in the Oracle Exadata Storage Server Software available with Oracle Database 11*g* Release 2 Enterprise Edition, Oracle provides a caching algorithm that is more than simply the "last recently used" data to avoid frequent flushing of the cache. The Exadata Storage Server Software thus leverages the Flash as a cache and automatically manages it by default. The DBA can designate usage of the Flash Cache for specific application tables and indexes by using an ALTER command with the CELL_FLASH_CACHE attribute set to KEEP.

The Oracle Exadata Storage Server Software really provides two key functions—managing Sun servers as disk arrays and pushing key database functionally into storage to speed up performance. The Exadata Storage Server Software performance speed-up capabilities are transparent to Oracle SQL and optimizer. This approach is beneficial, since applications can run unchanged on the Oracle Exadata Database Machine and also because as new Exadata Storage Server Software releases introduce new optimization techniques, these will also provide their benefits transparently. For example, users of early HP Oracle Database Machines that later installed database upgrades to Oracle Database 11*g* Release 2 and the corresponding Exadata Storage Server Software gained benefits from transparently having access to new underlying features such as storage indexes and data-mining model scoring.

Because the optimization is transparent, there is no certification process for applications specifically tied to their support of the Oracle Exadata Database Machine. Rather, the applications simply need to be supported on the necessary Oracle database version (Oracle Database 11*g* Enterprise Edition Release 2 or later on the Sun versions of the Oracle Exadata Database Machine), scale well when deployed on RAC, and should not have unusual storage characteristics that preclude the use of Automatic Storage Management.

Management of the platform is provided by Oracle Enterprise Manager Grid Control. Strategies for backups, disaster recovery, user management, security, and other common DBA tasks remain unchanged from other Oracle deployment platforms. Certainly, the balanced nature of the platform and better integrated optimization of database and hardware does simplify the DBA's role to some degree. In addition to standard Oracle database management capabilities, Grid Control adds capabilities specific to managing Exadata Storage Server cells through a plug-in. A DBA has the ability to view how queries are resolved and see certain Exadata Storage Server optimizations, such as smart scans and Bloom filters, in their Explain Plans.

When managing multiple databases or mixed workloads, I/O resource management through the Database Resource Manager and Exadata Storage Server Software can ensure that users and tasks will have the resources they need. Databases can be designated to run on certain database server nodes, but a more flexible means of sharing the resources of a single database node can be achieved through the use of instance caging and setting a "CPU count" per database instance in the Database Resource Manager. Enterprise Manager provides a single point of management for Quality of Service (QoS) where policies are defined and enabled, performance is monitored, and resources can be reallocated when needed.

For the more technically advanced, there is an Exadata Storage Server cell command-line interface (CELLCLI) available for managing the cells. Management Services provided by the Oracle Exadata Storage Server Software deployed on the cells enables administering, managing, and querying the status of the cells from either Grid Control or the CELLCLI interface. Cell Services provide the majority of other Exadata storage services needed, while Restart Services are used to update the Exadata software and ensure storage services are started and running.

Impact of the Platform on Personnel

Traditionally, platform determination, deployment, and maintenance tasks are delegated to many individuals. As you might have gathered from the description of the Oracle Exadata Database Machine thus far, a platform like this can affect the roles of your enterprise architects, storage architects, development and deployment DBAs, and network and systems administrators. For an enterprise system of this type, having the right business sponsor also engaged in the process is often key to gaining funding to buy the system and claiming success after deployment.

The role of enterprise architect has gained in popularity and breadth of responsibility. Enterprise architects often evaluate the ability of a platform to meet technical architecture requirements and standards, as well as their appropriateness in meeting business requirements as defined by business sponsors. A platform like the Oracle Exadata Database Machine can introduce new considerations into such an evaluation. The potentially rapid speed of deployment and predefined balanced configuration help eliminate potential errors and risk of project delays that often occur when platforms are custom designed. More focus can be placed on matching the value of such a platform in delivery of solutions that meet business goals and provide real business return on investment. On the other hand, organizational standards for certain hardware and storage components might not align and might need to be overlooked in cases where the value of a complete integrated system outweighs the benefits of conflicting technical component standards. In fact, technical component specialist roles, such as the role of storage architect, typically change from one of selection of components to evaluating more advanced deployment considerations, such as planning for disaster recovery.

The DBA's role also can change in fundamental ways. The Oracle Exadata Storage Server Software minimizes certain design and management considerations, such as the need to apply extensive indexing typical on other Oracle-based platforms. Striping and mirroring are handled through ASM, so basic storage management tasks often move to the DBA's area of responsibility. DBAs for the Oracle Exadata Database Machine also typically monitor patch releases for not only the Oracle database and Exadata software, but also for the operating system. Other basic tasks remain unchanged. For example, high availability and disaster recovery can be enabled using Data Guard and Flashback. Backups are handled using Oracle's Recovery Manager (RMAN).

Networking the system into the current IT infrastructure is performed during the installation process. Oracle and some Oracle partners offer rapid installation services that usually are completed within two or three days after system delivery, and include the configuration of the Oracle Exadata Database Machine InfiniBand switch. Once configured, the Oracle Exadata Database Machine appears much like any other Oracle database server on a network.

As you might gather, the consolidation of system and database management roles has implications for speed of change once the system is deployed, given that its management is much more centralized. Organizations that have deployed such platforms often find their ability to respond to new configuration needs within IT are greatly enhanced, and there are new opportunities for architects to focus on more difficult and challenging problems common in any enterprise deployment situation.

Future Directions

Upon the completion of the acquisition of Sun by Oracle Corporation, Oracle executives began to outline a platform system vision of the future. Key in that vision is the emergence of integrated software and hardware solutions. The Oracle Exadata Database Machine represents the first such platform.

In this initial chapter, we've outlined at an introductory level what this platform is. Oracle has been pretty clear that the vision for the future extends into the realm of end-to-end hardware and software solutions, going beyond simply databases and eventually including applications. The transaction processing and data warehousing data models of those applications reside in Oracle databases and hence, can reside on the Oracle Exadata Database Machine today. There is great potential for Oracle to further package and bundle such solutions, easing deployment and use, speeding up performance, and assuring even better security and availability.

Of course, most applications also rely on middle-tier components. While the discussion of deployment of such components is outside the scope of this book, Oracle's extensive array of Sun servers can certainly also meet those needs. With the continued introduction of other tightly integrated Oracle software and Sun hardware configurations such as Exalogic, a platform designed to speed WebLogic and Java-based applications, end-to-end solutions from Oracle promise to move deployment strategies from custom design, build, and integration to rapid assembly of well-defined components.

Oracle is clearly evolving the administration and maintenance of its software toward being more self-tuning and self-managing. Enterprise Manager Grid Control continues to complement this direction by providing a monitoring and management interface not only for the database but also for middleware and applications. Where organizations do not want to do the maintenance themselves, there are initiatives underway within Oracle and among its partners to provide managed services for these platforms. Oracle also positions these platforms to fill critical roles in "private cloud" or "public cloud" deployment scenarios, where organizations can obtain the benefits of Software-as-a-Service (SaaS) when deploying their own hardware and software platform infrastructure or when accessing the infrastructure of an Oracle platform services provider. The Oracle Exalogic Elastic Cloud includes Exalogic and Exadata as key middleware and database platforms linked via InfiniBand that are deployed for such cloud-based solutions.

The server and storage platforms that make up the Oracle Exadata Database Machine themselves will continue to evolve too. For databases, having large volumes of frequently accessed data closest to the CPUs has always been a desirable method for speeding up performance. Many predict that over coming generations, you will come to expect ever larger capacities of Flash and memory and will also see large footprints of physical disk storage disappear from the data center. The impact of such changes in server and storage configurations should improve the performance of all workloads and also result in dramatic reductions in floor space, cooling, and electrical power required. These advances could lead to solutions of new classes of business problems that can't be practically solved today.

Summary

Now that you've read this introductory chapter, it should be clear to you that the Oracle Exadata Database Machine builds upon Oracle database capabilities familiar to an immense worldwide technical community, but also adds new innovative integrated software and hardware that could have a profound impact on your organization. Having the benefit of looking back, we can see how this platform evolved from development efforts at Oracle that took place over a period of years. The acquisition of Sun now enables Oracle to entirely develop, build, sell, and support pre-engineered and integrated software and hardware solutions.

Given how the evolution took place, we structured the book to next review some Oracle database topics that might be familiar to you. Those topics will lay the groundwork for gaining a full understanding of the Oracle Exadata Database Machine platform as we cover it in detail in later chapters.

CHAPTER
2

Oracle 11g Enterprise
Edition Features

o doubt about it, the Exadata Database Machine and Exadata technology offer a unique combination of hardware and software to create a whole new value proposition for IT. But many of the components of this unique combination are far from new. In fact, you could see the Database Machine as a simple extension of features and functionality that have been developing in the Oracle database for more than 25 years.

This chapter will introduce you to the key features of the Oracle database, available in Oracle Database 11g Enterprise Edition either as standard features or additional options. The chapter will not cover the full breadth of functionality available with Oracle Database 11g, but simply highlights those features with particular relevance to the Exadata environment.

The depth of coverage in this chapter will, of necessity, not be comprehensive. Detailed examinations of these features are far beyond the scope of this single chapter. Instead, the chapter will cover the basics of these capabilities, as well as some of the particulars that you will need to understand to appreciate both the features of Exadata software described in the next chapter as well as the best practices that are covered in the remainder of the book.

Of course, you may choose to skip this chapter if you are already very familiar with the material covered, but, as authors, we would hope that you would find the limited time you spend reading this material to be a worthwhile investment, as a review if not a completely new learning experience.

Data Integrity and Performance

Data integrity is the rock upon which all databases must be built. You expect that your data will retain the values you create despite any number of complications, from machine or component failure to the constant potential for one user's changes to unknowingly overwrite changes to the same data by another user.

All mature relational databases use a system of logging to allow you to recover the database in the event of hardware failure. The scope of this type of recovery is bounded by the *transaction.* A transaction is an atomic unit of database work that can contain one or more statements that insert, update, delete, or select data. In terms of changes, a relational database guarantees that a transaction is either completely written to the database—committed—or entirely removed from the database—rolled back. If a relational database crashes, the recovery process ensures that all committed transactions are represented in the recovered database, while any transactions that have not been committed are rolled back.

The transaction is also used to protect threats to data integrity caused by the actions of multiple users. The power of a database like Oracle is that a single data store can support access for hundreds or thousands of users simultaneously. One of the truly amazing things about the Oracle database is that not only can all these users access the data, but they all think that they are the only user of the database. Each of these many users is isolated from the actions of all other users.

To protect integrity, a database must be able to prevent one user's changes to an individual row from modifying that data at the same time that another user is modifying the same data. In order to accomplish this, databases use a system of locks. A lock prevents a particular type of access to data.

The key goal of locks is to protect the consistent integrity of data. However, just like a lock in a door, a lock on data, of necessity, prevents other users from accessing that data, so databases typically have two types of locks. An exclusive lock normally prevents all access to a piece of data. Exclusive locks are also known as write locks, since they are obtained by users trying to write data.

When users are reading data, they typically use a shared lock. Many users can have a shared lock on the same piece of data, since many users can read that same data simultaneously without posing any threat to the integrity of the data. But a writing user cannot obtain an exclusive lock on a piece of data when there are shared locks on that data, since changing data when a user is reading it could result in a reader getting a data value that had been changed but not yet committed.

This scenario means that a user may end up waiting for a lock to be released before they can complete their work. A writing user, with an exclusive lock, prevents all users from accessing the data being modified. And readers can prevent writers from obtaining the exclusive lock they need to perform their modifications.

The challenge is to use a system of locks to guarantee data integrity—a quality that can never be compromised—without the lock and locking system causing performance to degrade. This type of performance issue is called contention, as users wait on locks while contending for the same piece of data as other users.

Although contention may seem somewhat unlikely, usage patterns in most databases result in a fair amount of contention, based on the relative amount of writes to the database. Online transaction processing (OLTP) databases, the core operational databases in most organizations, frequently see a fair amount of contention, which gets worse as the number of users increases.

Oracle has long been the leader in the area of OLTP databases because of the technology the database uses to deliver data integrity while significantly reducing contention and its performance impact.

Locks and Lock Management

Oracle reduces the potential impact of contention in two basic ways. The first way is to reduce the scope of locks and the overhead required to manage those locks.

The atomic unit for standard I/O operations in the Oracle database is the block. All standard reads from and writes to Oracle data access at least one block of data. Blocks are typically 2 to 32KB, so each block usually contains multiple data rows. Despite this fact, Oracle does not place locks on an entire block of data, which would result in having some rows that were not being modified or read being locked. This feature is called row-level locking.

Oracle is certainly not unique in this approach, as many modern, robust databases also lock at the row level. Most other databases use a lock manager to hold active locks and to limit access to rows based on these locks. Having row-level locks can result in a lot of locks being used by the database, which can mean a lot of resources used by the lock manager. For this reason, some other databases have a policy of *lock escalation.* Lock escalation occurs when the overhead of managing a lot of row-level locks becomes resource intensive, so the lock manager converts a group of locks on one entity to a single lock on a larger entity. For instance, if the lock manager detects that a significant percentage of rows in a block are locked, it would release the row-level locks and place a lock on the block. If many blocks were locked, a lock manager could swap these locks for a lock with a larger scope, such as a table. In these cases, the efficient route for the lock manager can have the effect of increasing contention and reducing overall throughput.

The Oracle database avoids this problem by removing the lock manager from the overall process. Instead of storing locks in a lock manager, Oracle simply stores locks in the same block as the data being locked. Since a data block has to be in memory for any access to occur, the locks for rows in that block are also memory-resident. Without a lock manager consuming resources, there is no need to escalate locks to save those resources.

These features are good ways to prevent contention by reducing the scope and resource requirements of locks. But there is an even better way to provide great performance while still protecting data integrity. The method used by Oracle for this purpose also provides an even higher level of data integrity by ensuring a consistent view of data at all times. This feat is accomplished by one of the core features of the Oracle database that goes by the somewhat unwieldy name of multiversion read consistency, or MVRC.

MVRC

Multiversion read consistency (MVRC) has been a part of the Oracle database for more than 20 years, and for this reason, the feature is sometimes overlooked when discussing Oracle. But don't let this occasional lack of focus mislead you. MVRC is the most important feature for ensuring great performance in an Oracle OLTP database.

MVRC has the effect of completely eliminating the need to use shared locks in the Oracle database. Remember, a shared lock is required to prevent a writer from changing data while it is being read.

Oracle solves this potential problem by maintaining multiple versions of a row that has been changed. There is no need for a writer to block a reader, since the consistent data required by that reader still exists in a previous version of the row.

Figure 2-1 illustrates MVRC at work. When a query encounters a row that has an exclusive lock, the query simply uses an earlier version of the data.

Compare this with the alternative offered by most other databases. These databases also avoid write locks, but they do this by simply ignoring them and reading the changed value, even though that value has not been committed to the database. This approach may not lead to a problem, but what if those changes are never committed, if they are rolled back instead? When this situation occurs, you have a crucial loss of data integrity; a query has read a value that *never* was part of the data.

But MVRC goes farther than simply avoiding the contention caused by write locks. Consider the following example of a long-running query

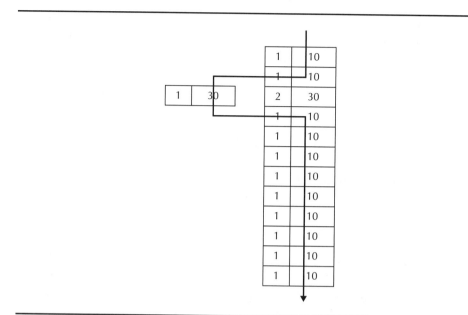

FIGURE 2-1. *MVRC at work*

performing a summary aggregation, as shown in Figure 2-2. The query begins to read through the data at a particular time. At that time, the sum should return the value of 140. A few milliseconds later, a row with a column value of 30 is deleted, and the deletion is committed. Since the deletion occurs after the row was read by the query, the previous value for the row is included in the sum.

A millisecond after this, another user updates a later row, increasing the value from 10 to 20. This change is committed before the query gets to the row, meaning that the newly committed value is included in the query. Although this action is correct, keep in mind that this change means that the final sum for the query will be 150, which is not correct. In fact, the sum of 150 was never correct. When the query began, the correct sum would have been 140. After the row is deleted, the correct sum would have been 110. After the subsequent update, the correct value would have been 120. But the sum would never have been 150. The integrity of the data has been lost. In a busy database with long-running queries, this could happen frequently.

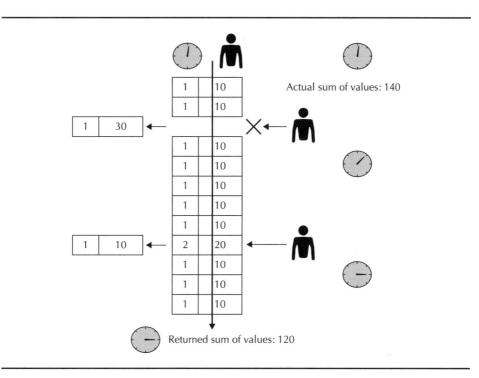

FIGURE 2-2.   *Summaries without MVRC*

If you have a busy database (and who doesn't), you could be getting a wide variety of incorrect data in your query—not a desirable outcome, to say the least.

Figure 2-3 shows that MVRC handles this scenario correctly. When a query begins, it is assigned a system change number, or SCN. If the query encounters a row with a larger SCN, the query understands that the row has been changed since the query began, so Oracle uses an earlier version of the row to deliver a consistent view of data at a particular point in time. Oracle always delivers a consistent snapshot view of data, all without the overhead of read locks, lock management, and the contention they can cause.

To sum up, with MVRC, readers don't block writers, writers don't block readers, and queries always deliver a consistent view of data. Other major database vendors cannot deliver these benefits seamlessly, giving Oracle a significant advantage for the past two decades.

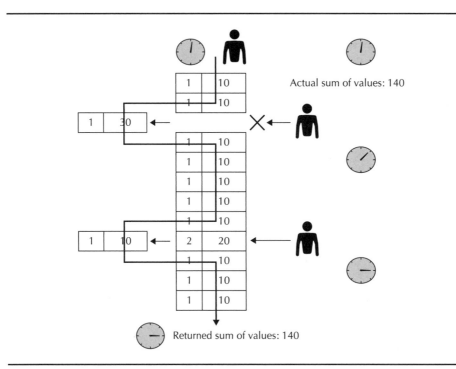

Actual sum of values: 140

Returned sum of values: 140

FIGURE 2-3. *A consistent view of data with MVRC*

Flashback

Before leaving this discussion of MVRC, you should understand that Oracle has leveraged the internal processes and structures used to implement MVRC to add a set of flashback features to the database. As the name implies, flashback is the ability to deliver a view of the database at an earlier point in time. A number of flashback features are available in Oracle 11*g*:

- Flashback query allows users to run queries as if they had taken place in the past with the use of a couple of keywords in a standard SQL statement.

- Flashback database gives administrators the ability to roll back an entire database to an earlier point in time.

- Flashback drop gives you the ability to remove the effects of one of those unfortunate "oops" moments, when you mistakenly drop a database object.

In addition, many other varieties of flashback are used for different types of operations, including error diagnosis and corrections. Although flashback might just be along for the ride, provided by the infrastructure that supports MVRC, the flashback features can prove to be extremely useful.

Flashback also points out one of Oracle's great strengths. Since MVRC has been a part of the Oracle database for so long, the supporting technology is robust enough to provide additional functionality with little additional development effort, extending Oracle's feature advantages.

Real Application Clusters

As mentioned earlier, Exadata technology cannot be seen as springing fully formed from the brow of Oracle. Exadata technology is built on Oracle features that have been shaping the capabilities and direction of the database for many years. The best example of this progression is how Real Application Clusters, almost always referred to by the less unwieldy acronym of RAC, provides the basis for the eventual hardware/software synergies in the Exadata Database Machine.

RAC is the foundation of the Oracle grid story, both figuratively and literally. RAC gave users the ability to create a powerful database server by grouping together multiple physical servers. This capability provides an unmatched value proposition for database servers. That value proposition, and how it is implemented, is explored in the following pages.

What Is RAC?

RAC was the marquis feature of the Oracle 9*i* release, so most readers will probably be familiar with the general capabilities of this feature. But since RAC and grid are really the first big steps towards Exadata and the Exadata Database Machine, it's worthwhile to spend a few paragraphs reviewing the exact definition and architecture of RAC.

The official name of the feature does make sense. When introduced, the defining characteristic of RAC was that it could be used transparently with existing, or real, applications. There was no need to rewrite or refactor existing applications to take advantage of the benefits of RAC, a virtue that is common to most new Oracle features.

The second part of the name points to what made RAC different. Normally, an Oracle database is only associated with a single instance—a single running copy of the Oracle database software—which was in turn

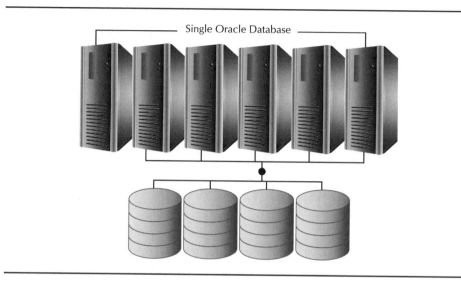

FIGURE 2-4. *Architecture of Real Application Clusters*

associated with a single physical server. An Oracle database with RAC could run across multiple instances and servers, as shown in Figure 2-4.

You can see multiple servers, or nodes, which work together through the means of a layer of software called *clusterware.* Clusterware acts to coordinate the operation of the member nodes as well as to monitor and maintain the health of these nodes. Oracle has its own clusterware, which is bundled with Oracle Database Enterprise Edition.

You can also see that each node has an instance running and that all instances access the same shared storage. This shared storage and the software portion of RAC means that a user can connect to any of the nodes in the cluster and access the same database transparently. The resources of all the nodes in the cluster are combined into a single pool of resources.

The architecture of RAC introduced significant benefits in two key areas—availability and scalability.

RAC and Availability

A single RAC database can include instances on more than one node, which has dramatic implications for the overall availability of an Oracle RAC database. If any single node goes down, the failure has virtually no impact on any of the other nodes, which continue to operate as normal.

This continuous operation means that even if a server node fails, the database continues running and does not have to be recovered. And every node acts as this type of hot backup for every other node, so the more nodes added to the cluster, the more reliable the cluster becomes.

To be absolutely accurate, the loss of a server node will affect some RAC users—those who are attached to that node. Just as with a single instance, these users will lose their connection to the database and all in-flight transactions will be rolled back. Users of the failed node will normally have to reconnect to another node, although another Oracle feature, Transparent Application Failover (TAF), can automate this process. The Oracle software stack also offers Fast Application Notification, which sends messages when an instance is not available, and Fast Connection Failover, which automatically reacts to these messages.

In addition, RAC includes distributed resources to manage tracking of data blocks across nodes, which we describe in the section on Cache Fusion later. If a node becomes unavailable, there is a brief pause for all users as the portion of the distributed management database is reassigned to existing nodes, but this pause is typically only a few seconds.

These particulars are minor, but the overall availability advantages are significant—an Oracle instance can disappear without requiring the shared database to be recovered, providing hot standby capability across all the nodes of a RAC cluster.

RAC and Scalability

RAC provides more than just hot standby for an Oracle database. As mentioned previously, a RAC database is completely transparent to the user and their application. This transparency means that administrators can add nodes to a RAC cluster without any changes to applications or user configurations.

This simple statement has fairly profound implications. Assume that you are running out of horsepower with a non-RAC Oracle database. At this point, you will need to acquire a bigger server that you will migrate your database to. This will require administration effort, some downtime, and a fairly large expenditure.

Compare that with RAC. If you have a two-node cluster, you can simply add another server to the cluster to increase the horsepower of the overall database by about 50 percent—without even bringing down the overall database.

RAC does offer linear scalability, in that adding a node to a two-node cluster will increase the horsepower by about 50 percent, or adding a node to a three-node cluster will add 33 percent to the overall power of the cluster. Don't mistake this type of linear scalability for perfect scalability, in that a two-node cluster will not produce 200 percent of the throughput of a single-node server. However, you will not find decreasing efficiency as you add more nodes to the cluster, crucial to the use of larger clusters.

The scalability of RAC has significant implications for your database budget. With a single database server, you would typically size the server to handle not only today's demands; instead, you will size the server to handle the anticipated load a couple of years in the future to avoid the overhead of a server upgrade too soon. This approach means that you will end up buying more servers than you need, increasing cost and forcing excess server capacity in the initial stages.

With RAC, you can simply buy the number of nodes you need to handle your near-term requirements. When you need more power, you just buy more servers and add them to the cluster. Even better, you can buy smaller commodity servers, which are significantly less expensive than larger machines. And to top it all off, the server you buy in nine months will give you more power for your money than a similar server today.

All of these benefits are part of the common Oracle liturgy, but there is one other advantage that RAC scalability provides. Even experienced administrators are frequently wrong when they try to estimate the requirements for a database server two years out. If they overestimate future needs, their organizations end up buying excess hardware and software—the lesser of two evils. If they underestimate, they will find themselves having to upgrade their database server early, because the database services it provides are more popular than they expected. So the upgrade, with its concomitant overhead and downtime, affects a popular service.

With RAC, you are never wrong. You won't overestimate, since you will plan on buying more servers when you need them, whether that is in nine months or five years. And you won't be plagued by the penalties associated with underestimation.

Cache Fusion

Up to this point, we have been looking at RAC from a fairly high level. You could be forgiven for not appreciating the sophistication of RAC technology. The really interesting part comes when you understand that the instances spread across multiple nodes are not just sharing data—they are also sharing their data caches, which is the key to the performance offered by RAC.

The diagram shown in Figure 2-5 is a slight expansion of the architecture shown in Figure 2-4. The difference is that you can now see the shared cache, implemented by technology known as Cache Fusion.

Although all instances share the same database files, each instance in a RAC database, since it is located on physically separate servers, must have its own separate memory cache. Normally, this separation could lead to all kinds of inefficiencies, as data blocks were cached in the data buffers of multiple machines. Part of the RAC architecture is an interconnect, which links caches on separate servers together and allows transfers directly between different memory caches. This architecture allows the database cache to grow as more nodes are added to a cluster.

When a SQL operation looks for a data block, the instance looks first in its own database buffers. If the block is not found in those buffers, the instance asks the cluster management service if the block exists in the buffer of another instance. If that block does exist in another instance, the block is transferred directly over the interconnect to the buffers of the requesting node.

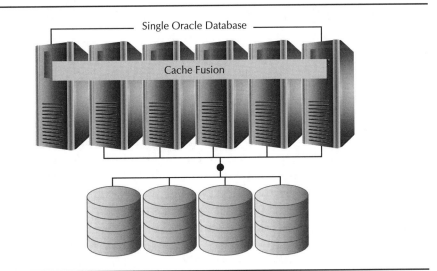

FIGURE 2-5.   *RAC and Cache Fusion*

Cache Fusion uses a global service, where the location of every data block in every cached is tracked. The tracking is spread over all the nodes; this tracking information is what has to be rebuilt in the event of a node failure. RAC uses some intelligence in assigning ownership of a particular block. If the block is usually used on a particular instance, that instance is given the responsibility of tracking that block, cutting down on the interconnect traffic and the transfer of blocks between nodes, reducing any potential bottlenecks caused by flooding of the interconnect.

There may be times when you want to limit the way that a particular application or instance uses the resources of the entire cluster, and RAC provides a number of options, which are described in the next section.

Cache Fusion and Isolation

Did you notice something that was not mentioned in the discussion of Cache Fusion? In the first section in this chapter, you read that the smallest unit of standard data movement is the data block and that a data block can (and usually does) contain more than one row. So what happens if one row in a block is being modified by a transaction on one instance and another instance wants to modify a different row in the same block? Good question, and one that Oracle, unsurprisingly, has covered.

A single row in a data block can be part of an active write transaction and have an exclusive lock on that row. If the block containing that row is requested for a write operation on another row in the block, the block is sent to the requesting node, as expected. However, the node that originates the transfer makes a copy of the block, called a past image, which can be used for instance recovery in the event of a failure or to construct a consistent image of the row, part of the overall operations used to implement multiversion read consistency. When the row is committed on the requesting node, the block is marked as dirty and eventually written to the database. Once this version of the block is safely part of the database, the past image is no longer needed. Metalink (MOS) note 139436.1 explains how instances interact in different locking scenarios in greater detail, if you are interested.

Allocating Resources and RAC

Up to this point in the discussion of RAC, we have been looking at the architecture of RAC as if the cluster were supporting a single database. In fact, RAC is frequently used as a consolidation platform, supporting many databases and instances.

Once you start supporting multiple databases on a RAC architecture, you may find that you want to allocate the computing resources to appropriately serve the different uses of the database—or even modify those allocations, depending on a variety of factors. This section will describe some of the RAC-centric ways to accomplish this task.

Load Balancing, Part One

To a connecting session, a RAC database appears as a single, monolithic database. This key feature is what allows existing applications to take advantage of RAC without modification. But the underlying implementation of RAC involves physically separate servers, and each session will be connected to only one of those servers. How does RAC decide which instance to assign to an incoming connection request?

When RAC was introduced with Oracle 9*i*, the software determined the connection target by the CPU utilization of the different member instances. A new connection was assigned to the instance running on the server with the lowest level of CPU utilization.

This type of connection assignment did provide more efficient usage of the overall RAC cluster than a random allocation, but the end result was balancing the load for the overall cluster. The process assumed that the entire RAC database was being used equally by all instances. As larger clusters went into production, and as users started implementing RAC to consolidate multiple databases on a single cluster, this single-minded approach was not flexible enough to allocate computing resources appropriately. Enter services.

Services

Services, introduced with Oracle Database 10*g* Release 2, are a way to provision nodes in a RAC database for specific applications, as shown in Figure 2-6.

You can define which instances handle requests from a service. In this way, you can segregate the processing power provided by an instance to

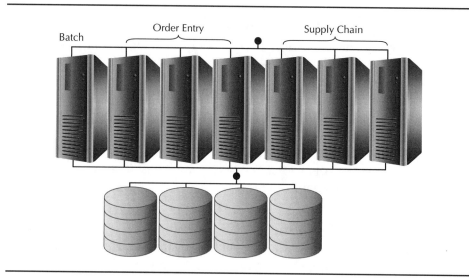

FIGURE 2-6. *Services and RAC*

one or more services, as you can assign more than one service to a particular instance.

You can dynamically adjust which instances handle which services, either in response to external conditions, such as time of day, or to designate which nodes should take on a service in the event of a failure of a node designated for that service.

The configuration of services and nodes is done as part of the RAC configuration, and clients simply connect to a service, rather than the RAC database or an individual node.

Load Balancing, Part Two
Once you define services, you can use a more sophisticated method of allocating resources between different nodes associated with a service.

You can still use the traditional method of allocating connections based on CPU utilization for the service, the same approach that has been used for RAC since its introduction.

You can also assign connections based on more advanced metrics of runtime performance delivered through the means of a Load Balancing Advisory. These advisories are sent to the listeners for each instance involved in a service.

When you use the Load Balancing Advisory, you configure whether you want to determine the connection load balancing based on throughput for an instance or the service time, representing the speed of response, for an instance. The Load Balancing Advisories deliver the information required to determine the appropriate connection assignment based on real-time workload conditions. The dynamic nature of this approach helps to ensure a more balanced workload across service instances, resulting in better utilization of resources automatically.

Load Balancing Advisories can also be delivered to clients so that environments that support client-side connection pooling can benefit from this type of intelligent connection allocation.

Server Pools

The concept of services gives you the ability to assign operations to a specific set of nodes within a RAC database. With Oracle Database 11*g* Release 2 came the introduction of server pools and quality of service measurements, which take this concept even further.

Services used to be assigned to specific nodes, which was a good way to divide up resources, but this approach required services to be explicitly assigned to one or more instances, which could create an increasing management overhead as the number of configuration options multiplied. A server pool is a collection of nodes, and services are assigned to a pool rather than a set of specific nodes.

RAC uses server pools to allocate resources between different services assigned to a pool. You can define a quality of service policy, described in more detail in Chapter 8, which specifies the performance objectives for an individual service, as well as the priority of that service. If a high-priority service is not getting sufficient CPU to deliver the defined quality of service, RAC makes a recommendation to promote the scheduling priority for that service with the CPU scheduler.

This remedy will improve the performance of the promoted service, which very well may not affect the qualities for the other services in the pool. If multiple services for a pool are all failing to meet their quality-of-service goals, the server pool can implement a different scenario to share resources, using Database Resource Manager (described later) or grab a node from another pool to remedy the problem, although the transfer of this node may take some time, depending on the specific implementation scenario.

The RAC database also uses feedback on the amount of memory used for a single server node in a server pool. If there is too much work for the memory on the node, that node will temporarily stop accepting new connections until the demand for memory is decreased.

Additional Provisioning Options

The Oracle Database includes other ways to provision database server resources, such as Database Resource Manager, which is described later in this chapter, and instance caging, implemented through Database Resource Manager, which allows you to specify how to allocate CPU resources between different database instances that may be sharing a single physical server.

RAC One

A RAC database gives you the ability to take a pool of resources and use them as if they were a single machine. In today's computing environment, virtualization provides a different approach—the ability to share a pool of resources offered by a single physical machine among multiple virtual machines.

RAC One is a flavor of RAC that delivers the same type of benefit. An instance using RAC One runs on a single node. If that node should fail, the RAC One instance fails over to another node. Since the RAC One database was only running on a single instance, the underlying database will still need to be recovered, but the RAC One software handles this recovery, as well as the failover to another node, transparently, reducing downtime by eliminating the need for administrator intervention.

You can think of RAC One as a way to implement virtual database nodes rather than virtual machines. The purpose-driven nature of RAC One makes administration easier, and the elimination of a layer of virtual machine software should deliver better performance with the same hardware.

RAC and the Exadata Database Machine

Although RAC was introduced before the advent of the Exadata Database Machine, and although there is no absolute requirement that you use RAC on the Machine, the two offerings are made for each other. In fact, the Database Machine is sometimes referred to as a "grid in a box," and RAC is the foundation of that grid.

The Exadata Database Machine includes a number of physical database servers in the same cabinet, so using RAC to pool the resources of those servers is a natural complement. The Database Machine is also configured for optimal RAC performance as it provides a high-bandwidth interconnect between the database servers.

In addition, since the Exadata Database Machine can be used as a platform for consolidation, there may be scenarios when RAC One is appropriate for this environment.

Automatic Storage Management

Real Application Clusters was a big step forward for the Oracle database. With RAC, you could combine multiple physical database servers together to act like a single database, offering a new way to deploy and scale database servers.

Automatic Storage Management, or ASM, extends a similar capability for storage. ASM was introduced with Oracle Database 10*g*, and provides a way to combine multiple disks into larger logical units, reducing storage costs and simplifying management. In addition, like RAC, ASM delivers additional benefits, such as improving performance and availability and simplifying a number of key management tasks.

What Is ASM?

ASM is storage management software, providing a single solution for a cluster file system and volume management. ASM manages a collection of storage disks, simplifying the interface to those disks for database administrators. ASM eliminates the need for third-party software like volume managers and file systems for Oracle database environments.

ASM runs as an instance, just like an Oracle database, and the ASM instance has some of the same organization as a database instance. Each database server that will use ASM must have a single ASM instance, which can manage storage for one or more database instances on the node.

The ASM instance maintains metadata about storage. The ASM instance uses this information to create an extent map that is passed to the database instance, which removes the necessity of the database instance to go through the ASM instance for access. The database instance interacts with ASM when files are created or modified, or when the storage configuration is modified by adding or dropping disks. This implementation gives ASM the flexibility to dynamically expand and contract storage, to implement mirroring and striping transparently, without affecting performance.

With ASM, you first build grid disks out of cell disks, which are built on top of LUNs, or logical units, as shown in Figure 2-7.

All management of storage is done at the level of disk groups by the ASM instance. An individual database file must be stored within a single disk group, but a single disk group can contain files from many different database instances. ASM provides a file system interface to the files stored in each disk group.

ASM is included with all editions of the Oracle Database that support Real Application Clusters, which includes Standard and Enterprise Editions. ASM comes with the Oracle database rather than with the RAC option, so you can use ASM for single-instance databases as well as Real Application Cluster databases, providing many of the same benefits for the single instance.

NOTE
ASM relies on Oracle Clusterware to manage multiple nodes in a cluster and synchronization between database instances and ASM, so ASM always requires Oracle Clusterware.

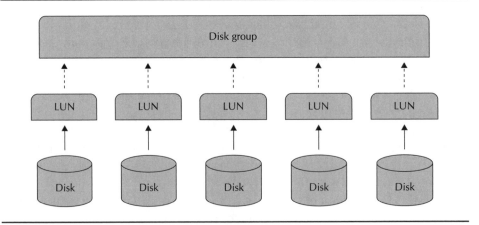

FIGURE 2-7. *Automatic Storage Management*

ASM and Performance

ASM automatically stripes files across multiple physical disks, which increases the access performance by spreading I/O over multiple disk heads. This placement avoids excessive hot spots in disk files, and also contributes to better I/O performance. ASM normally creates stripes based on the size of the allocation unit (AU) assigned to a disk group, but for some files, such as redo logs, ASM stripes are smaller to reduce I/O latency on these crucial files.

The I/O performance produced by ASM is roughly equivalent to the performance of a raw partition, without having the more extensive management overhead of raw storage.

In some cases, such as a stretch cluster, where nodes of a cluster are widely separated, ASM can give better performance by reading from a more local mirrored copy of data, rather than trying to access the primary copy at a more distant location. This capability is configured by means of an initialization parameter.

Oracle Database 11*g* Release 2 introduced a new performance feature for ASM called Intelligent Data Placement. A disk is circular, which means that the outer tracks of the disk are moving faster than the inner tracks, resulting in faster read times for data on the outer tracks. You can specify that data for a file or an entire disk group is either on the outside or inside of the disk, providing better performance for the outer sections. This Intelligent Data Placement works well with two disk groups, one for data and one for the Fast Recovery Area (FRA), which is used for backups. The FRA can go on the inner tracks of the disk, ceding the better-performing sections to the data disk groups that are in active production use.

ASM and Availability

In terms of disk storage, ASM provides an availability solution by automatically *mirroring* data in a disk group. Mirroring data means making an extra copy of the data in the event of a block or disk failure, similar to the functionality provided by redundant arrays of inexpensive disks (RAID) disks. You can choose to mirror data once, to assure reliability if a single point of failure occurs, or twice, to assure reliability even if a second failure should occur. You also have the option of not mirroring data, which you might choose if you are using ASM with a RAID disk that already provided mirroring, although ASM mirroring is specifically designed to support database access. You can assign mirroring on the basis of individual files to implement different levels of redundancy for different scenarios.

You want to make sure that the mirrored image of the data is kept separate from the primary copy of the data so that a failure of the disk that holds that primary copy will not also affect the mirrored copy. To implement this protection, ASM uses the concept of a failure group. When you define a disk group, you also define a failure group in relation to that disk group. Mirrored data is always placed in a different failure group, which ensures that a mirrored copy of the data is separated from the primary copy of that data. If a block fails or is corrupted, ASM will automatically use a mirrored copy of the data without any interruption in service. You can direct ASM to actually repair bad blocks from either a command-line interface or Enterprise Manager.

Normally, a read request will use the primary copy of the data. If the read request for that primary copy fails, ASM will automatically read the data from a mirrored copy. When a read fails in this way, ASM will also create a new copy of the data, using the mirrored data as the source. This approach is automatically used whenever a read request for data is executed and a bad data block is discovered. You can force this type of remapping on data that has not been read by means of an ASM command.

Frequently, disk failures are short-lived, or transient. During a transient disk failure, changes can be made to the secondary copy of the data. ASM keeps track of these changes, and when the disk comes back online, performs an automatic resynchronization to make the now-available copy of the data the same as the copy of the data that was continually accessible. This tracking means the resynchronization process is fast.

ASM and Management

There has always been overhead associated with managing storage for an Oracle database, such as determining which blocks have free space. ASM takes care of all of these issues, removing them from the DBA workload.

In fact, ASM manages much more than these basic tasks. The striping and mirroring discussed in the previous sections is done automatically within a disk group.

You can also dynamically resize a disk group by adding more disks to the group, or take disks out of a disk group. Both of these operations can be performed without any downtime. If you add new disks to a disk group, ASM will rebalance data across the new disks. ASM does an intelligent rebalance, only moving the amount of data necessary to ensure an even balance across the new set of disks, and rebalancing is done, by default, asynchronously, so as to not impact online performance. ASM includes a parameter that gives you the ability to control the speed of rebalancing, which, in turn, has an impact on the overhead used by the operation.

Since ASM manages most administrative details within a disk group, you would normally create a small number of disk groups. In fact, Oracle recommends creating only two disk groups—one for data and the other for the Flash Recovery Area used to hold database backups.

ASM itself can be managed through SQL*Plus, Enterprise Manager, or a command-line interface.

Partitioning

Computing hardware is, in the broadest sense, made up of three basic components—a computing component (CPU), memory, and storage. Over the course of the history of computing systems, different components have been the primary culprits in the creation of bottlenecks caused by insufficient resources. For the last ten years, the main source of performance bottlenecks has been the storage systems that service I/O requests.

To address this area, the Oracle database has continually implemented strategies to reduce the overall demand for I/O operations, such as indexes and multiblock reads for table scans. Partitioning is another of these strategies.

NOTE
As you will see in the next chapter, the Exadata Storage Server takes this approach of reducing I/O to a whole other level.

What Is Partitioning?

A partition is simply a smaller segment of a database object. When you partition an object, you break it into smaller pieces, based on the value of a *partition key*, which consists of one or more columns.

All SQL statements interact with the partitioned object as a single unified entity, but the Oracle optimizer is aware that an object is partitioned and how it is partitioned. The optimizer uses this information to implement a strategy of partition pruning. A query that needs to implement some type of selection, either with a predicate or a join, can simply avoid reading partitions whose partition key indicates that none of the data in the partition will pass the criteria. In this way, the execution path can avoid accessing a large portion of an object, reducing the overall I/O requirements. The performance gain, like the partition, is implemented transparently.

You can partition both tables and indexes with any of the partition methods that are described in the next section. Three different relationships are possible between a partitioned table and an index, as shown in Figure 2-8.

- The index and the partition can be partitioned on the same partition key. This relationship, known as equipartitioning or a local index, means a separate portion of the index for each partition in the database. If most of the queries running against your partitioned table will result in partition pruning, equipartitioning amplifies the benefits of this approach.

- An index could be global and partitioned on a different partition key than the associated table. This scheme will deliver benefits for some queries where the index partition key can be used for partition pruning, and other benefits for queries where the table partition key can be used.

- An index can also be global and unpartitioned, and the table is partitioned. Although this relationship may not produce as large a benefit as equipartitioning, some types of random access will work better this way, as a global index can be accessed with a single read rather than having to probe each index partition.

Partitioning Types

Partitioning provides benefits by dividing up a larger table into smaller portions, based on the value of the partition key. A table or index can only be partitioned once at the top level, of course, since partitioning dictates the logical storage of the object, but the partitioning scheme used must correspond with the way that a query will be requesting data in order to provide performance benefits. Because of this, Oracle has continually expanded the ways that you can partition tables since the introduction of this feature with Oracle 8.

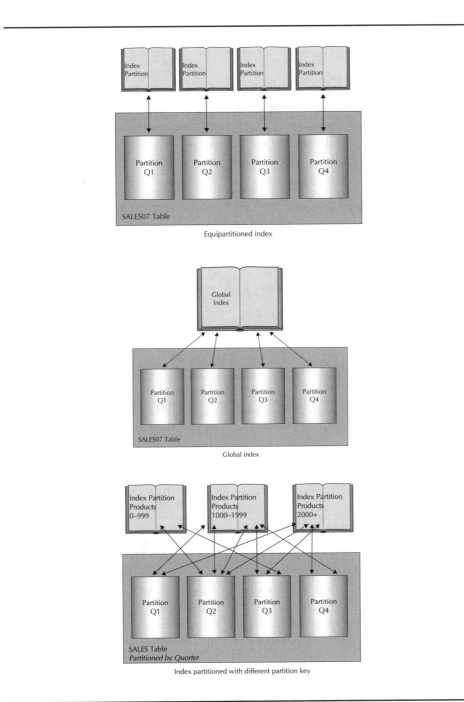

Equipartitioned index

Global index

Index partitioned with different partition key

FIGURE 2-8.   *Index and table partitioning*

Oracle Database 11*g* Release 2, the current release of the database at the time of this writing, supports the following types of partitioning:

- **Hash**   The partition key for hash partitions is created by running a hash function on the designated partition column. The hash calculation is used to ensure an even distribution among partitions, even when the distribution of the actual values of the partition column is uneven. A hash-partitioned table cannot use partition pruning when the selection criteria include a range of values.

- **Range**   Range partitioning uses the actual value of the partition key to create the partitions. Range partitioning is described with a low value and a high value for the partition key, although you can have one partition without a low value for all values lower than the specific value and one partition without a high value for a similar function at the high end. Range partitions can be used for partition pruning with a range of values, either specified or implied through the use of the LIKE operator.

- **List**   In a list partition, you assign a specific list of values for a partition key to indicate membership in a partition. The list partition is designed for those situations where a group of values are linked without being consecutive, such as the states or territories in a sales region. List partitions can be used for partition pruning with the LIKE operator.

- **Composite**   Composite partitioning is a way of adding a subpartition to a table, giving the table two levels of partitioning, as shown in Figure 2-9. Composite partitioning allows Oracle to go directly to a partition with specific values in two dimensions. With Oracle Database 11*g*, you can have any mix of composite partitions that include range, hash, or list partitions.

- **Interval**   An interval partition is a way to reduce the maintenance overhead for range partitions that use a date or number as the partition key. For an interval partition, you define the interval that specifies the boundaries of a partition. The Oracle Database will subsequently create partitions as appropriate without any further intervention. If the value for a partition key requires a new partition to be created, that operation is performed automatically. You can

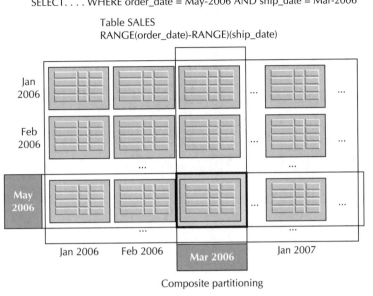

SELECT. . . . WHERE order_date = May-2006 AND ship_date = Mar-2006

Table SALES
RANGE(order_date)-RANGE)(ship_date)

Composite partitioning

FIGURE 2-9. *Composite partitioning*

change an existing range-partitioned table into an interval-partitioned table, as long as the ranges fall into a specific pattern, or you can extend an existing range–partitioned table into an interval table in the future. You can also merge partitions at the low end of an interval-partitioned table to create a single-range partition. This last option is particularly useful for gaining the benefits of an interval partition while implementing an Information Lifecycle Management (ILM) strategy for reduced storage costs.

■ **REF**   A REF partition is another form of partitioning that reduces overhead, as well as saving storage space. Having parent and child tables in a foreign key relationship is a common implementation practice, especially since this architecture allows for partition-wise joins, described in the next section on parallel execution. A REF partition on the child simply points back to the parent and instructs Oracle to use the same partition scheme as the parent, as shown in Figure 2-10. Any changes made in the partitioning scheme in the

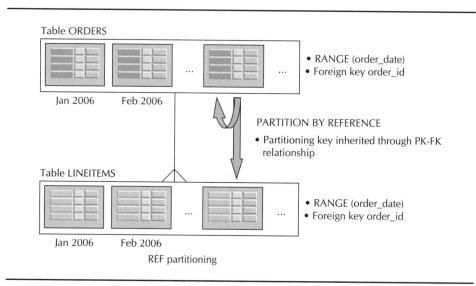

FIGURE 2-10. *REF partitioning*

parent table are automatically implemented in the child table. REF partitioning has an additional benefit with regard to storage. Since both tables are using the same partition key, there is no need to store the key value in the child table, eliminating redundancy and saving storage space.

■ **Virtual** Virtual partitioning allows you to partition a table on a virtual column. The virtual column is defined as the result of a function on existing columns in the table. The virtual column is treated as a "real" column in all respects, including the collection of statistics, but does not require any storage space.

Other Benefits

Partitions can produce performance benefits by reducing the I/O needed for query results, but partitioning delivers other benefits as well.

To Oracle, partitions are seen as individual units for maintenance operations. This separation means that a partition can be taken off-line independently of other partitions, that maintenance operations can be performed on individual partitions, and that the failure of an individual partition does not affect the availability of the remainder of the table.

TIP
One exception to this availability advantage occurs if a partition has a global index. The global index will be unusable and will have to be recovered if even one partition becomes unavailable.

The ability of partitions to act as separate units means that you can use partitions to reduce storage costs through an ILM approach, moving less frequently accessed partitions to lower-cost storage platforms.

Partitions come with their own set of maintenance operations, including the ability to drop and add partitions to a table without taking the table offline, as well as the ability to merge partitions together or split a single partition into two.

Partitioning and the Exadata Database Machine

The key performance benefit provided by partitioning is a reduction in the amount of I/O necessary to satisfy a query. This key benefit is dramatically expanded with a number of Exadata features, such as Smart Scan and storage indexes, which are described in the next chapter.

But these features simply amplify the approach of partitioning. All the benefits of partitioning still apply to the use of the Exadata Database Machine. In this way, partitioning is the start of the performance enhancement continuum delivered by the Exadata Database Machine and, as such, is as integral to the overall benefits provided as RAC is for the use of the database servers.

Parallel Execution

Parallel execution, or *parallelism,* has been a part of the Oracle database for more than a decade. This long-time feature has become even more important in the context of the Exadata Database Machine, where multiple nodes, CPUs, and intelligence in the storage systems can increase the speed of individual parallel tasks as well as handle more of these tasks at the same time.

What Is Parallel Execution?

Normally, SQL statements are executed in a serial fashion. A statement comes to the Oracle database and is assigned to a server process to execute. A database server has many user processes active at any point in time, and each statement was assigned to a single server process.

NOTE
This description applies to a dedicated server, where there is a one-to-one connection between a user request and a user process on the server. Oracle also supports shared servers, where one server process is shared between multiple user requests, but that technology is outside the realm of this chapter.

Parallel execution is a way to reduce the overall response time of a statement by having multiple processes work on the statement together. By dividing the work up among these multiple processes, or *parallel servers*, each server does less work and finishes that work faster.

As you will read shortly, there is some overhead involved with this distribution of work, as well as with the re-aggregation of the results of the parallel work, but the overall performance benefit of the parallel operations provides benefits for longer-running operations in most cases.

What Can Be Parallelized?

The Oracle Database can parallelize a range of SQL statements. Table 2-1 lists the SQL tasks that can be executed in parallel.

The tasks listed in Table 2-1 are not all SQL statements. The actual implementation of parallelism takes place at the level of the subtasks that make up the overall execution of a statement. As an example, the query listed next has four subtasks that can be run in parallel—a table scan of each of the two tables, the join operation, and the aggregation requested.

```
SELECT customer_name, sum(order_total) FROM customers, orders WHERE
customers.customer_id = orders.customer_id
```

Task	Operation
SQL access method	Table scans, fast full-index scans, partitioned index range scans, sorts, aggregations, set operations, external table access
Joins	Nested loop, sort-merge, hash, partition-wise joins
DDL	CTAS (CREATE TABLE . . AS SELECT . .), CREATE INDEX, REBUILD INDEX
DML	INSERT-SELECT, UPDATE, DELETE, MERGE

TABLE 2-1.   *Parallel Tasks*

How Parallelism Works

In order for parallelism to be implemented, a database has to divide the data that is the target of a task into smaller groups for each separate parallel process to work on. The Oracle Database uses the concept of granules. Each granule can be assigned to a single parallel process, although a parallel process can work on more than one granule.

NOTE
In fact, parallelism can be more efficient if each parallel process works on more than one granule. When a process finishes its work on a granule, the process can get another granule to work on. This method of distribution avoids the potential problem of the convoy effect, when the completion of the overall task is only as fast as the slowest parallel process. If a parallel process completes its work, rather than sit around waiting for its peers, the process simply begins work on another granule.

With Oracle, a granule can either be a partition or a range of data blocks. The block-based granule gives the Oracle Database more flexibility in implementing parallelism, which can result in more SQL statements and tasks that can benefit from parallel operations.

The Architecture of Parallel Execution

When the Oracle Database receives a SQL statement that can be executed in parallel, and when parallelism is enabled for that instance, the parallel execution process begins, as shown in Figure 2-11.

In first step of parallel processing, the server process running the statement becomes the *parallel query coordinator,* shown as QC in the diagram. The QC is responsible for distributing and coordinating work among the *parallel server* processes, shown as PX in the diagram.

The query coordinator communicates with the parallel servers through a pair of buffers and, in most cases, the parallel servers communicate with each other through another set of buffers.

Parallelism at Work

Now that you know the basics of parallelism in Oracle, we can walk through a couple of examples of parallelism in action.

The first example is a simple table scan, as shown in this SQL statement:

```
SELECT * FROM customers;
```

The query coordinator divides the target data up into granules and assigns a granule to each parallel server in a set of parallel servers. As a parallel server completes the table scan of a granule, the results are returned

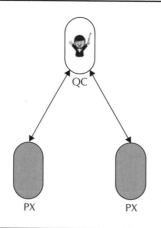

FIGURE 2-11. *The architecture of parallel execution*

to the query coordinator, who combines the accumulated results into a result set to return to the user. That example is simple enough.

The process gets a little more complicated when there are multiple tasks within a query that can benefit from parallel processing. Let's return to the SQL statement originally mentioned in the previous section:

```
SELECT customer_name, sum(order_total) FROM customers, orders WHERE
customers.customer_id = orders.customer_id
```

The query coordinator will assign granules for scanning one table to one set of parallel servers, the producers. Once the producers complete scanning that table, they send the resulting rows to the second set of parallel servers, the consumers, and begin to scan the second table. Once the consumers start to receive rows from the second table scan, they will begin doing the join. As the producers start to send rows to the consumers, they will have to redistribute the rows to the appropriate consumer process in order to complete the join.

The query coordinator has a number of options for redistributing the data, as shown in Table 2-2.

Redistribution Method	Use
HASH	Provides equal distribution of work across servers
BROADCAST	Used when one result set is much smaller than the other, so sending the smaller result set to the larger set is more efficient
RANGE	Used for parallel sort operations so further sorting is not required
KEY	Used for some types of joins so that only one side of the join needs redistribution
ROUND ROBIN	Typically used as the final redistribution before data is returned, when the order of access does not matter

TABLE 2-2. *Redistribution Methods*

The results of the join are sent to a set of parallel servers for sorting, and finally to a set of parallel servers for the aggregation process.

Although this discussion has mentioned several different sets of parallel servers, any SQL statement can only use two sets of parallel servers at a time. These two sets of servers can act together, as *producers* and *consumers*. In this example, the set of parallel servers that was going to perform the sort act as consumers of the results from the parallel servers that were doing the join operation.

Partition-wise Parallel Joins

The reason why the previous pages went into some depth on the mechanics of parallel processing is to allow you to understand one of the great goals of parallel execution: partition-wise parallel joins.

Parallel processing is whizzing around in the Oracle database, with loads of parallel processes working together, completing tasks in a fraction of the time of a single serial process. Allowing parallelization for subtasks is a great way to amplify the overall gains from parallelism, but this method can also add some overhead. In the previous description, you may have noticed one particular type of overhead that could be significant—the redistribution of data in order to perform a join.

There is a way you can completely avoid this overhead through the use of parallelism in coordination with partitioning. Figure 2-12 illustrates the difference between a standard parallelized join operation, which requires redistribution of data, and a partition-wise parallel join.

In order to accomplish a partition-wise parallel join, both tables have to be equipartitioned using the same partitioning method, and both tables have to have an equal number of partitions.

In the join illustrated on the right in Figure 2-12, the two tables that are to be joined are both partitioned on the key value used in the join. The underlying partitions ensure that the results of a table scan from a partition on one table will only ever be joined with the results of the table scan on the matching partition in the other table.

By eliminating the need to redistribute data, a partition-wise parallel join can deliver better response time than queries that require standard joins. The superior performance of the partition-wise parallel join can influence

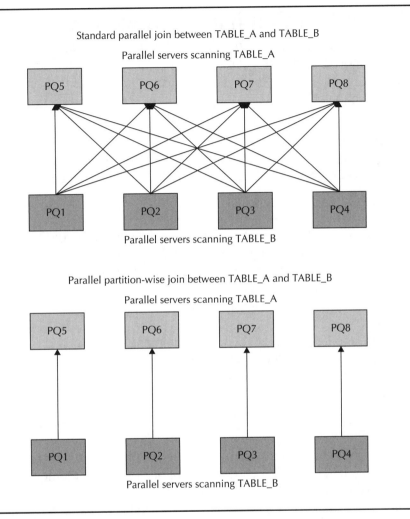

FIGURE 2-12. *Standard parallel join and a partition-wise parallel join*

the partitioning schemes you put in place for your overall database, depending on the usage scenarios for your data. In fact, partition-wise parallel joins only need a single set of parallel servers—there is no need for a set of producers and another set of consumers.

How Do You Configure Parallel Execution?

At this point, you understand how the Oracle Database uses parallelism to improve response time. The database does all of this work transparently. But obviously, you have to configure the resources that will be used for implementing parallelism.

Enabling Parallel Execution

Parallel execution is enabled for the Oracle Database by default. However, you can turn parallelism off for a session with the following command:

```
ALTER SESSION DISABLE PARALLEL (DML | DDL | QUERY);
```

This command allows you to disable parallel execution for DML, DDL, or query operations. The command can also be used to turn on parallelism for any of these types of operations by replacing the keyword DISABLE with the keyword ENABLE.

NOTE
The ALTER SESSION . . . PARALLEL statement has a third option, FORCE, which you will learn about in the next section.

There are two more places where you can specify the use of parallelism. You can define a particular object with the PARALLEL *n* clause, which indicates that the object will use parallel execution, with *n* representing the degree of parallelism (which you will learn more about in the next section). You can also include a PARALLEL hint in your SQL statement.

These three methods are used to allow parallelism for different types of SQL statements. For queries and DDL, you need to have any one of these methods in action—an ALTER SESSION ENABLE command, a PARALLEL clause on an object in the SQL, or a hint in the SQL.

For DML, you will need to have issued the ALTER SESSION command and either have a hint in the SQL statement or have created one of the objects in the statement with a PARALLEL clause.

Enabling Parallel Servers

Enabling parallelism is the first step in its configuration. As you read previously, the query coordinator gets a set of parallel processes, but from where? Oracle uses a pool of parallel processes to serve the needs of parallel execution across the database.

The number of parallel servers you have on an instance has two potential effects. You want to have enough parallel servers to properly service the requests for parallel execution, which delivers the performance increase, but you don't want to have too many parallel servers, since these servers use resources whether they are in use or not.

There are two initialization parameters you can use to allocate the pool of parallel servers. The PARALLEL_MIN_SERVERS parameter specifies the number of parallel servers to initially allocate when the instance starts up. The PARALLEL_MAX_SERVERS parameter indicates the maximum number of parallel servers to allocate. If your PARALLEL_MIN_SERVERS is less than your PARALLEL_MAX_SERVERS, Oracle will spin up additional parallel servers in response to demand until the maximum number is allocated to the pool.

NOTE
Why so much detail? In the other sections of this chapter, you basically learned about the capabilities of a feature, but not this type of drill down on configuration and the like. The reason for this increased focus on administration is so that you can understand the options you have for implementing parallel execution, options that will become more relevant in the rest of this chapter.

At this point, you know how parallel execution works, how to enable parallelism for an instance, and how to configure a pool of parallel servers. But how does Oracle know how many parallel servers to allocate for any particular statement? The answer lies in the next section.

Degree of Parallelism

You can configure the number of parallel servers to handle all the parallel execution requests for the entire instance, but how do you control how many parallel servers are used for a particular statement? The number of parallel servers used for a statement is called the degree of parallelism for the statement, commonly abbreviated to DOP.

Setting the DOP

You can set the default degree of parallelism at four different levels. First of all, the default DOP for a database is calculated with the following formula:

```
CPU_COUNT * PARALLEL_THREADS_PER_CPU
```

The CPU_COUNT parameter is normally set by the Oracle database, which monitors the number of CPUs reported to the operating system, and the PARALLEL_THREADS_PER_CPU also has a default, based on the platform, although the normal default is 2. You can set either of these parameters yourself if this default allows for too many parallel servers, or if the system is I/O bound, which could represent the need to split I/O operations further with parallel execution. Default DOP will be used when the parallel attribute has been set on an object explicitly or via a hint but no parallel degree was specified.

You can also set a specific DOP for an individual table, index, or materialized view, either when you create the object or subsequently modify it. If a SQL statement includes objects with different DOPs, Oracle will take the highest DOP as the DOP for the statement.

The ALTER SESSION command was discussed earlier in this section with regard to enabling parallelism. This command has another format that allows you to specify the degree of parallelism:

```
ALTER SESSION FORCE PARALLEL (DML | DDL | QUERY) PARALLEL n;
```

where *n* is the DOP for the duration of the session.

Finally, you can include a hint in a SQL statement that specifies the DOP for the statement.

A particular SQL statement may have multiple defaults that apply to the statement. The order of precedence for the DOP is hint, session, object, database, so the DOP indicated in a hint will be used instead of any other DOP that is present.

DOP in Action

The last step in understanding how the degree of parallelism affects parallel operations is to understand exactly how this value is used in the runtime environment.

If your Oracle instance has parallelism enabled for a particular type of statement, the optimizer will calculate the degree of parallelism for that statement. A statement can only have a single DOP, which will dictate the number of parallel servers used for all subtasks.

When the statement execution begins, the query coordinator goes to the parallel server pool and grabs the number of parallel servers that will be required for execution—either the DOP or twice the DOP, if the execution will involve both producers and consumers. If no parallel servers are available, the statement will be run serially.

But what if some parallel servers are available in the pool, but just not enough to satisfy the full request? In this case, the query coordinator will take as many parallel servers as it can and adjust the DOP for the statement accordingly—unless the initialization parameter PARALLEL_MIN_PERCENT is set, in which case the statement can fail to execute at all, as explained later in this section.

Modifying DOP

That last statement may have caused you some concern. Here you are, carefully calculating and setting the DOP for objects, sessions, and statements in order to produce the best performance from your Oracle instance. But an instance can support many users, applications, and SQL statements, so you may have a situation where there are not enough parallel servers to go around at a particular point in time. You may not want to populate the parallel server pool with enough servers to guarantee a full DOP during times of peak demand, since this may waste resources most of the time. What will you do?

Oracle has provided several different ways to address this situation dynamically.

One method is adaptive parallelism, enabled by setting the PARALLEL_ ADAPTIVE_MULTI_USER parameter. When this parameter is set to TRUE, the Oracle instance will adjust the DOP for statements while taking into account the workload at the time of execution. The goal of adaptive parallelism is to ensure that there will be enough resources available for all parallel executions, so the Oracle instance will reduce the DOP when appropriate.

Adaptive parallelism takes a fairly aggressive approach to ensuring that there are sufficient parallel resources, and this approach may lead to different DOPs being set for the same statement at different times. If you choose to use this approach to limiting parallelism, you should make sure to test its effect on your true runtime environment.

Another method of limiting the DOP is through the use of the Database Resource Manager, which you will learn more about later in this chapter. With Database Resource Manager, you can limit the DOP of all statements, depending on which consumer group is executing the statement. Since membership in consumer groups can change based on runtime conditions, this method gives you the ability to only limit DOP when conditions require it. The DOP specified by Database Resource Manager also takes precedence over any other default DOP, so the limitations of your resource group are always enforced.

Oracle Database 11g Release 2 has an even better solution for addressing this problem, called Automatic Degree of Parallelism, or Auto DOP. Auto DOP does more than just guarantee that a statement will run with a certain DOP—it gives you much more flexibility to control parallelism across the board.

With Auto DOP, Oracle follows the decision process shown in Figure 2-13.

The first step in the process is when the optimizer determines if a particular statement will even benefit from parallel execution by comparing the estimated execution time with the PARALLEL_MIN_TIME_THRESHOLD parameter, set to ten seconds by default.

If the execution time exceeds this threshold, the next step is to calculate the ideal DOP, which is accomplished in the standard way of determining the DOP from different levels of defaults. Once this ideal DOP is calculated, the value is compared with the PARALLEL_DEGREE_LIMIT parameter, which can be used to limit the overall degree of parallelism for the instance, normally set based on the number of CPUs in the system and the parallel

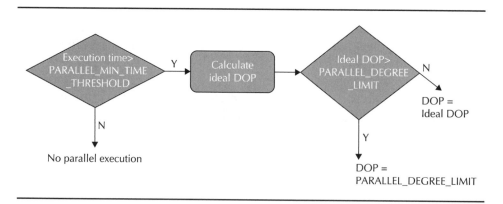

FIGURE 2-13. *The Auto DOP decision process*

threads allowed per CPU. The default value for PARALLEL_DEGREE_LIMIT is default DOP or CPU_COUNT X PARALLEL_THREADS_PER_CPU.

All of these methods will reduce the DOP, depending on environmental conditions. Although this approach prevents your system from slowing down, due to excessive demands for parallelism, it creates another problem. Assuming you assigned a DOP for a reason, such as ensuring that a statement ran with a certain degree of performance, simply toning down the DOP will not give you the desired results. So must you always accept a reduction in performance for the good of the overall environment?

Ensuring DOP

Reducing the DOP for a statement can be more than an inconvenience. Take the example of creating a table and loading data, which is done on a nightly basis. The statement has a DOP of 16, uses both producers and consumers, and completes in three hours with this degree of parallelism in our example. When the statement goes to execute, the parallel server pool only has eight parallel servers available. The statement grabs them all, but ends up with a DOP of 4, due to the need for two sets of parallel servers. Oops—the job now takes 12 hours, and runs over into your production window, which interferes with business operations.

This outcome is especially annoying when you consider that the number of available parallel servers is constantly changing and that the scarcity of parallel servers may have been a transitory phenomenon, with a full complement of parallel servers becoming available seconds or minutes later.

There are two features in Oracle Database 11*g* that can protect you from this outcome. The first method, which is not new to Oracle Database 11*g*, is blunt, but effective. The PARALLEL_MIN_PERCENT parameter dictates the minimum percentage of parallel servers that must be available for a statement to execute. With the previous example, you could set the PARALLEL_MIN_PERCENT for the session to 50, which translates to 50 percent. This setting would require the assigned DOP to be at least 50 percent of the default DOP. In the previous example, the statement would actually return an error. You would have to handle this error in your script or code, but at least you would avoid a scenario when a simple lack of parallel server processes affected your production environment. A little bit more code, and a slight tolerance for slower execution, in return for protecting your overall production environment.

Once again, Oracle Database 11g Release 2 has a better solution in the form of parallel statement queuing. As its name implies, statement queuing puts statements into an execution queue when they need a degree of parallelism that cannot be satisfied from the currently available pool of parallel servers. The decision tree process for statement queuing is shown in Figure 2-14.

Once a statement is put into the parallel statement queue, it remains there until enough parallel server processes are available to run the statement with the proper DOP. The queue uses a first-in, first-out scheduler, so parallel statements will not be delayed by other statements with a smaller DOP placed in the queue later.

If you do not want a statement placed into this queue, you can use a hint on the statement itself.

Statement queuing will only kick in when the number of parallel servers in use is greater than a number you specify—a value less than the total number of parallel servers, but one that prevents this process from proceeding in environments where this type of alternative is not necessary. You can also force a statement to be queued, even if the parallel server limit has not yet been reached, with a hint in the statement.

Please keep in mind that the best solution for implementing the proper DOP is always to do a thorough analysis of your parallel execution needs and your environment and set the DOP appropriately. Even the Auto DOP feature will not ultimately deliver the same benefits produced from this measure of planning and foresight.

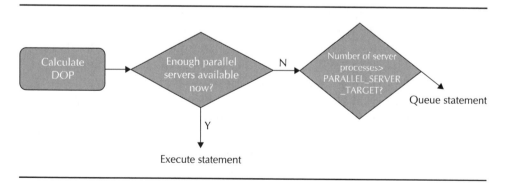

FIGURE 2-14. *Decision tree for statement queuing*

Parallelism and RAC

In a RAC database, parallel server pools act as a shared resource for all nodes. If there are 64 parallel servers on each node in a four-node cluster, the RAC database sees an overall pool of 256 parallel server processes. This abundance is, in many ways, a good thing, but with some potential downside.

As the previous explanations showed, quite a bit of communication can take place during the parallel execution of a statement, both between the query coordinator and different parallel processes. This communication can have an impact in a RAC environment.

Suppose you had parallel servers spread over all the different nodes and these servers had to redistribute the results of a subtask. Internode communication takes place over the interconnect between nodes, and a flood of traffic could affect the performance of this crucial resource.

NOTE
The Database Machine uses InfiniBand as the interconnect, which can normally handle this type of traffic.

Oracle Database 11*g* uses an intelligent default approach to distributing parallel server processes. When the database goes to execute a statement in parallel, Oracle will first try to run the statement with parallel servers on the node that is executing the statement. If this cannot be done, the RAC database will look for another node that can supply enough parallel server processes to execute the statement with the calculated DOP. When these two options are not available, parallel servers from multiple nodes will be used.

CAUTION
There is one caveat to this default approach. If the DOP used is the default DOP for the database, RAC will simply grab processes from across all nodes—yet another reason to spend some time analyzing the usage patterns for parallel execution and setting DOP defaults more specifically.

In addition to this default approach, you can specifically limit the allocation of parallel servers to one or more nodes. By setting the PARALLEL_FORCE_LOCAL parameter to true, you only allow the use of parallel processes on the node where the statement is executing. You can also define instance groups, a collection of nodes, and limit the use of parallel servers to the nodes in a particular instance group.

In-memory Parallel Execution

In-memory parallel execution is another new feature introduced in Oracle Database 11*g* Release 2. This enhancement is another way that Oracle combines the benefits of parallel execution with a RAC environment.

When a RAC database executes a statement with parallel processes, the database checks to see if the objects referenced by the statement could be cached in the aggregated data buffers across all nodes in the server. (This decision is based on a set of heuristics, rather than a simple size calculation.) If there is enough cache available, the granules created for parallel execution are stored in memory on separate nodes, and all operations on those granules are executed on those nodes. This arrangement delivers the benefits of caching entire objects in memory without needing to have the entire amount of memory on a single node.

The data remains cached on the specific node, so if subsequent SQL statements run with parallel execution require this data, the request is sent to the node and the end results returned to the requesting node.

Parallelism and Exadata

Parallel execution, like RAC and partitioning, is designed to work very well in a grid environment. Since the Exadata Database Machine is engineered to be a tightly connected grid, parallelism is ideal for producing great results on this platform. But the Exadata Storage Server provides even more parallelism.

Exadata Storage Servers, which will be covered in detail in Chapter 5, consist of an array of storage systems, and these systems use parallel operations to speed performance.

This storage parallelism does not in any way negate the power of parallel execution for SQL statements. Rather, the parallelism in storage acts as an I/O speed-up for all SQL statements, even for statements that execute serially on database server nodes. The end result is that you may not see as large a difference between serial execution of a statement and the parallel execution of the same statement, but the parallel execution will still provide a significant performance improvement.

Data Guard

A significant part of the overall Exadata Database Machine value proposition is the high availability provided by redundancy throughout the box. Data Guard is a way to supplement this high availability with a disaster recovery solution to provide protection against all types of failures.

What Is Data Guard?

High availability is a quality that, at its core, refers to the absence of a condition. A highly available solution is one where there is little or no downtime.

Traditionally, high availability has been implemented through redundant components in hardware and supporting software capabilities. Real Application Clusters, for instance, allows for the use of multiple servers, with each server acting as a hot failover for the others, without requiring any application changes to take advantage of this feature.

But there are scenarios where even this type of redundancy is not sufficient to avoid downtime, scenarios where a failure affects all the components of a redundant solution, such as a broad power failure or structural issue in an entire building, neighborhood, or region. These occurrences are appropriately referred to as disasters.

Data Guard is used to protect against these disasters by means of a standby database. The standby database can be virtually any distance from the primary database. Data Guard is used to keep the contents of the standby database in sync with the primary database. If the primary database fails, users can reconnect to the standby database after a brief recovery operation and continue their work.

The scenario described is termed a failover, where the standby database takes over for the primary database after that database fails, usually unexpectedly. Data Guard can also be used for a switchover, where the standby database takes over for the primary database intentionally, for situations such as maintenance work on the primary database that require downtime.

How Can Data Guard Be Implemented?

The basic function of Data Guard is to provide a standby database for failover or switchover. Data Guard implements this functionality by shipping redo log information from the primary database to the standby database.

Once the redo arrives at the standby database, the records are applied to that database to synchronize it with changes on the primary database.

Modes of Redo Transmission

Although the redo is used to synchronize changes on the standby database, you have options on how the primary database interacts with this operation. You can specify that the redo stream is written to the standby database synchronously, which means that the transaction is not committed until the redo data is written to both the primary redo log and the standby redo log. This option can result in delays on the primary database, but guarantees that no data will ever be lost in the event of a primary failure.

You can also specify that the redo stream is written asynchronously to the standby database, which means that there is no performance impact on the primary database. However, with this mode, the standby database is usually a little behind in getting redo data, so a failure on the primary database could result in some data loss.

Data Guard also gives you the option of the best of both worlds. Redo data is written synchronously to the standby database as long as the redo transmission stream is not causing any delays. Once delays occur, the primary database switches to asynchronous redo data transmission. If the cause of the delay is transient and redo transmission can again be performed synchronously, Data Guard switches back to that form of operation. Although you cannot guarantee zero data loss with this method, you will get this level of integrity in normal conditions with little or no impact on the performance of the primary instance.

Standby Database Types

You also have three choices for configuring the Data Guard standby database, shown in Figure 2-15.

The implementation shown at the top of the figure is called a physical standby database where the redo data comes to the standby database and is then applied to the physical standby. Since the redo is being directly applied to the standby database, this database must be identical to the primary database. Redo information is normally only applied to a database while the database is in the process of recovery from a failure, so a physical standby database is in an ongoing state of recovery. This state means that the standby database is not available for use.

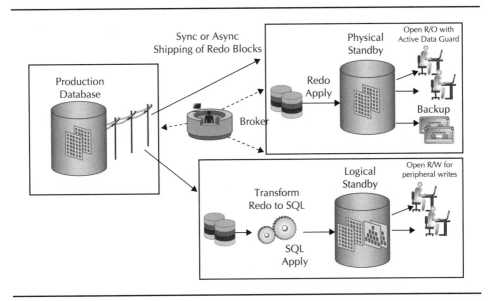

FIGURE 2-15.   *Data Guard implementations*

The implementation shown in the lower half of the figure is called a logical standby database. In this option, the redo data is converted into SQL statements that implement the changes made on the primary database. The SQL statements are then run against the standby database. Since changes are being made through SQL statements, the standby database is available for users. The use of SQL for updates means that there is no need for the standby to be an exact copy of the primary database—the standby can have additional structures, such as indexes, on tables used for standby as well as additional tables that are not on the primary database. Users can access the data in the standby database, and even perform write operations to the tables that are not in the primary database.

Logical standby does have some limitations, including a delay in the application of the redo, since the SQL conversion takes some time, and some limitations on what sorts of changes can be mined from the redo data.

Standard Data Guard, which supports both physical and logical standbys, comes as a part of the Enterprise Edition of the Oracle Database. Oracle also offers an option called Active Data Guard. Active Data Guard works on a physical standby, but allows that standby to be open for read activity even while the redo information is being applied. This capability means that the standby database can be used to offload some of the operations of the primary database, such as reporting or acting as the source of backup operations. Active Data Guard also delivers other benefits, such as detecting bad data blocks on either the primary or standby databases and correcting these blocks with valid copies from the alternative source.

Data Guard also gives you the ability to create a snapshot standby database. A snapshot standby database begins as a physical standby. At a point in time, you discontinue the application of redo information to the standby, allowing the database to be opened for both read and write operations. The redo data continues to stream to the standby, but is not applied. You can change the snapshot standby database back into a physical standby database by applying the accumulated redo data.

Data Guard Broker

Figure 2-15, shown earlier, includes a component that has not been discussed. The Data Guard Broker is a helper application that can be used to automate many of the maintenance operations required for Data Guard, including setting up and managing Data Guard configurations and, more importantly, handling switchover and failover operations with a minimum of operator intervention.

Data Guard and Exadata

As mentioned already, an Oracle database running on the Exadata Database Machine is, in virtually all respects, just a normal Oracle database. This fact means that any application that works against the proper version of a standard Oracle database will work on an Oracle database on the Database Machine with no changes, and that all the standard tools and utilities will work on these Oracle databases.

This statement is also true for Data Guard, with one exception. You will learn in the next section about Exadata Hybrid Columnar Compression. If you used this type of compression, Data Guard will still work properly, sending redo data to the standby database and applying it. However, if the standby target is not an Exadata Database Machine, data that used Exadata Hybrid Columnar Compression will not be available on the standby database. You can still use Data Guard, but to ensure the ability to fail over to the standby, you will have to forego the use of the data that used Exadata Hybrid Columnar Compression, at least until you perform an ALTER statement on the compressed data to decompress it on the standby server.

Compression

The Exadata Database Machine produces fairly dramatic performance improvements for an Oracle database. Part of this improvement comes from improved speed and capacity for all components of the machine, from CPUs to the network to the disk drives. Another part of the improvement comes from reducing the demand for resources, which contributes to improved throughput. Compression, in various options, has been a part of the Oracle Database for more than a decade, and compression can improve overall resource utilization by reducing the size of data, which reduces storage costs and I/O operations, in return for some CPU costs for the compression and decompression operations.

What Types of Compression Does Oracle Support?

Compression was first introduced with Oracle 9*i*. This initial compression option is known as table compression. With table compression, data was compressed with direct load inserts, which typically are only used with batch operations.

Oracle Database 11*g* Release 1 introduced a new form of compression referred to as OLTP compression. This new compression differed from table compression in several ways. First of all, Oracle Database 11*g* can read data in compressed blocks directly, meaning that read operations would not be affected by OLTP compression.

OLTP compression comes as a part of the Advanced Compression option, which also includes a variety of other compression technologies used to compress SecureFiles (large objects), backup sets, and network traffic.

Most importantly, OLTP compression provides compression for data that is inserted after the initial load without affecting write performance. The method used by OLTP compression to accomplish this is shown in Figure 2-16.

Data is compressed within a block on the initial load of data. Data added to a block is initially stored without compression, but when a block contains a sufficient amount of uncompressed data, the block is added to a compression queue, which performs compression as a background process. With this method, data added or changed after an initial load is eventually compressed without affecting the real-time write operation for the data.

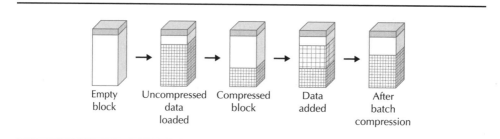

FIGURE 2-16. *OLTP compression*

SecureFiles

Oracle Database 11*g* also introduced SecureFiles, which provides compression for large objects stored in the database. SecureFiles gives you the option of three different levels of compression, where the effectiveness of the compression is balanced against the impact on CPU overhead.

Just as compression increases the effectiveness of storage by reducing the space requirements of data, SecureFiles goes an extra step by offering deduplication of large objects. Deduplication computes a hash value for stored large objects so that these objects can be uniquely identified. If an operation attempts to insert another copy of an existing object, SecureFiles simply adds a pointer to the already existing copy of the object. By reducing the number of large objects stored, SecureFiles improves storage efficiency, with no impact on read or write operations.

Benefits of Compression

Of course, compressing data means that you either need less storage for your data or you can store more data in the same storage. In either case, you will save money on storage.

But keep in mind that compressed data means that a compressed data block contains more data, which can mean fewer I/O operations to retrieve a set of rows. In addition, compressed data takes up less space in memory, which means more data blocks in the buffer cache and an improvement in the utilization of this cache. Taken together, these benefits can result in improved performance for some I/O operations, such as table scans, as well as increased overall query performance, based on a higher utilization of data in the buffer cache.

All the benefits delivered by table compression and OLTP compression are also produced by Exadata Hybrid Columnar Compression, which is exclusive to the Exadata platform and which you will learn about in the next chapter.

Remember that all types of compression do require some CPU and memory resources to compress the data when it is added or loaded to the database.

Database Resource Manager

Up to this point, most of the focus of our discussion concerning Oracle Database 11g features has been about providing better performance and scalability through reducing resource requirements. But, fortunately for our job security, there seems to be no end to the increasing requirements for computing services, which means we will all be forced to reckon with the situation where demand is greater than supply.

It is at times like these that we have to remember that performance is really not about resources at all—it's about expectations. Good performance is the result of user expectations of performance being met. And expectations build on consistency. If the responsiveness of an application varies wildly based on differing specific characteristics of an enterprise-wide workload, you can't really get away with saying that the performance is good sometimes and even better at other times.

The Database Resource Manager is a tool you can use to ensure consistent performance for critical groups of users and critical tasks to the business. Database Resource Manager not only helps to satisfy users with consistent performance, but also ensures an efficient allocation of oversubscribed resources.

What Is Database Resource Manager?

A database does many things, including manage resources between a group of users. In this way, the database server is responsible for some of the same tasks that an operating system performs. An operating system can allocate resources based on priorities, but the underlying operating system cannot allocate these resources differentially based on individual database users, since these users are not discernable to that software.

Database Resource Manager gives you the ability to prioritize resources to different users. You can specify how computing power is shared among different groups of users and guarantee that some groups will be able to use a fixed percentage of CPU time.

How Does Database Resource Manager Work?

There are three basic components used by Database Resource Manager, as shown in Figure 2-17.

The first component is the consumer group. A consumer group is a collection of sessions. A session is associated with a consumer group when the session is first created, either through mapping rules for sessions, which are defined as part of the resource plan, explained in the next paragraph, or a default consumer group associated with a particular user. Sessions can change resource groups in response to changing conditions, such as demand for resources, but each session can only be a member of a single consumer group at a time. The resources assigned to a consumer group are shared equally with all sessions within the group.

A resource plan is a scheme for sharing the overall resources available to an Oracle instance. The resource plan is made up of directives, which implement the sharing and limitations of resources between consumer groups.

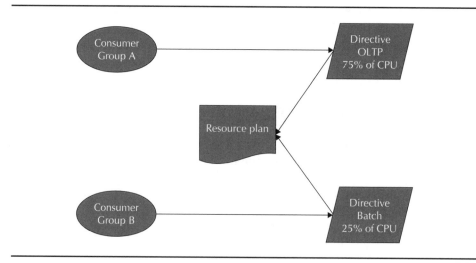

FIGURE 2-17. *Components of Database Resource Manager*

These three components work together at runtime, where each consumer group is assigned to one or more directives. As shown in Figure 2-17, the OLTP group is guaranteed 75 percent of CPU resources in scenarios where Database Resource Manager directives are in force, while the REPORTING consumer group is guaranteed 25 percent of CPU resources in the same circumstances.

What Can Database Resource Manager Affect?

Resource plans in Database Resource Manager can be used to allocate or limit a number of different resources, including:

- **CPU usage**   You can create a directive that limits the percentage of CPU resources for a consumer group. You can have multiple levels of directives, or subplans, for CPU allocation. Each level in a subplan can allocate up to 100 percent of resources, with any remaining resources passed on to the next level for further allocation. You can have up to eight levels of subplans.

- **Number of active sessions**   A directive can limit the number of active sessions for a consumer group. If this limit is reached, subsequent session requests are placed into a queue to wait for a currently active session to end. You can designate a timeout period to eliminate sessions that wait in the queue too long.

- **Degree of parallelism**   You can specify the degree of parallelism (DOP) for a consumer group. At runtime, this DOP is compared with the DOP calculated for an operation, and the lower of the two numbers is used.

- **Sessions**   You can specify that a session is to be terminated, based on a number of measures, such as the overall execution time for the session, the amount of idle time the session has used, or the amount of undo used by the consumer group. If the undo limit is reached, the DML statement currently executing is terminated and no other DML is allowed until undo space for the consumer group is freed.

Other Factors

There are a number of conditions that apply to the runtime operation of a resource plan. The overriding condition is that a resource plan and its associated directives only start to operate when the CPU is 100 percent utilized. If there is enough CPU to satisfy all requests, there is no need to allocate that resource.

NOTE
The latest release of Database Resource Manager includes the ability to set an upper limit for CPU resources, which is enforced whether this resource is oversubscribed or not.

You should also understand that the limit specified in a directive is the upper limit for a consumer group associated with that directive. In the resource plan shown in Figure 2-17, the OLTP consumer group is granted a maximum of 75 percent of CPU resources. If the OLTP group is only requesting 50 percent of CPU, the remaining consumer groups will simply divide up the remaining CPU resources.

You can have more than one resource plan for an instance, and you can switch resource plans at runtime. To switch resource plans, you use a function in the DBMS_RESOURCE_MANAGER PL/SQL package, included with the Oracle database, which also includes many other management options for resource plans and their use.

When you create a resource plan directive, you can include conditions that will cause an individual session to switch to another resource group at runtime. These conditions include the amount of CPU time used or the amount of I/O in terms of requests or the amount of data requested. You would use this type of switching to perform tasks such as moving a long-running query to a consumer group with a lower priority.

How Does Database Resource Manager Work with Exadata?

As with all the other capabilities discussed in this section, you can use Database Resource Manager with an Exadata Database Machine, just as you would with a single instance of Oracle or a RAC implementation. But the generic capabilities of Database Resource Manager—the ability to provision resource utilization between different consumer groups—are extended into the world of Exadata to the allocation of I/O resources, as you will learn about in the next chapter.

Analysis Capabilities

The Exadata Database Machine can be used for both data warehouse and OLTP workloads. Data warehouse workloads usually include some type of analysis of the existing data. Oracle Database 11*g* includes two capabilites that simplify the process of performing this analysis.

Analytic Functions

Oracle Database 11*g* comes with a rich set of analytic functions, such as the ability to calculate rankings and percentiles, moving window calculations, lag/lead analysis, first/last analysis, and linear regression statistics. Syntax for these analytic functions is used just like any other function, embedded in standard SQL. All these functions can be run with parallel execution.

In addition, business analysts can leverage the OLAP Option for the Oracle database for trending and forecasting functions and other analyses. The OLAP Option enables multidimensional cubes to be stored as objects in the Oracle database.

Data Mining

Data mining is the process of performing advanced analysis on large amounts of data in order to recognize trends and predict future events. Effective data mining can produce some of the highest value available in your data stores.

With data mining, you create a model, based on historical data, that identifies a behavior you are looking for in the future. You then apply this model to another set of data for scoring, which produces a value indicating the likelihood of the same behavior for members of the new set of data.

In the past, users would export data from a database to a separate server to perform this resource-intensive work. The Oracle Database gives you the option of performing data mining within the Oracle database, which reduces both the set of tasks needed to perform the mining and the overall resources needed to export the source data and import the results from another server.

Oracle Data Mining uses Generalized Linear Models, which build the models used for data mining analysis inside the Oracle database, based on one of a number of different algorithms that come with this feature. Once these models are created, you can score the data with the models to capture classifications, regressions and clustering in the models, and much more.

Enterprise Manager

If you have been involved in the world of Oracle database technology at any time over the past decade or so, you have probably heard of, and used, Enterprise Manager. Enterprise Manager is the tool that most customers use as their primary management interface to the Oracle Database. But if you have not looked at Enterprise Manager recently, you may be (pleasantly) surprised to discover that the functionality and the user interface have been significantly improved, as shown in Figure 2-18, which depicts a screenshot of the main management page for an Oracle instance.

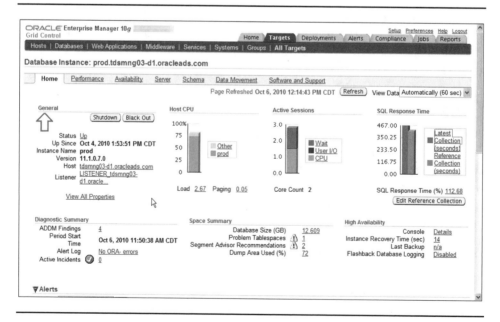

FIGURE 2-18. *The home page for an Oracle instance in Enterprise Manager*

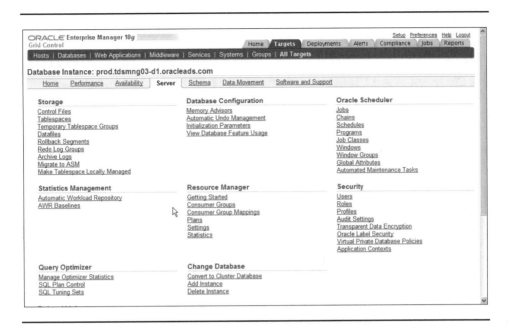

FIGURE 2-19. *Management areas for an Oracle database in Enterprise Manager*

In terms of functionality, Enterprise Manager has now grown to the point where you can do practically anything with this tool that you can do with any other management tool, even basic command-line utilities. The screenshot shown in Figure 2-19 shows a simple list of the areas that you can view and modify for an Oracle database instance through Enterprise Manager.

In both of these figures, you can see another key facet of Enterprise Manager. The user interface for Enterprise Manager is browser-based, and much of the information displayed also acts as a link to more detail on the area summarized by the information. To show one more example, Figure 2-20 illustrates the type of detail you can get about a SQL query, which can be reached from many different pages that display information about SQL, from a historical listing to a list of the SQL statements that have used the most resources.

With this depth of functionality, Enterprise Manager has also greatly expanded the breadth of management coverage. With Enterprise Manager, you can now manage software in the middle tier, applications and business

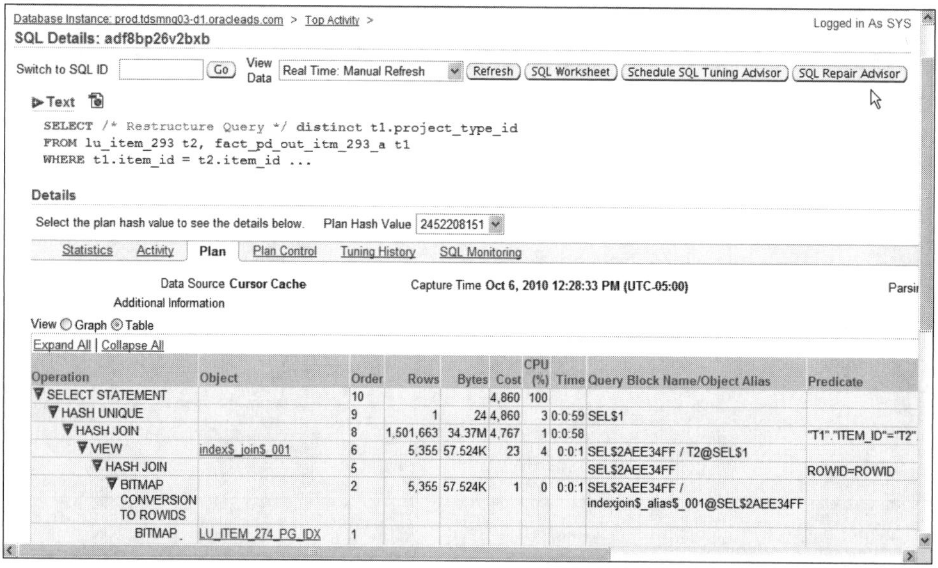

FIGURE 2-20. *SQL detail in Enterprise Manager*

transactions, network performance, operating systems, and even some types of hardware.

This last area of focus, hardware management, has been significantly expanded through the recent Sun acquisition. Sun's management tool, Operations Center, is being integrated into the standard Enterprise Manager framework. Quite a few of Oracle's acquisitions over the recent past have been components that are being integrated into the Enterprise Manager arena.

Enterprise Manager is even expanding its role in time, moving from managing a runtime IT environment to tools and helpers that can manage many parts of the software development process, including testing.

The capabilities of Enterprise Manager are so rich that no attempt to summarize them in a few pages would do justice to the product. Entire books have been written on the product, with more needed. For the purposes of this book, you should just understand that you will use Enterprise Manager to monitor and manage the activity of the Oracle software on the Exadata Database Machine in the same way that you would use Enterprise Manager with a standard Oracle database. Many scenarios on the Database Machine are no different from those of an individual instance. For example, if an ASM disk group goes down, Enterprise Manager recognizes this failure and can send an alert to an administrator. Whether this ASM group was built with disks on Exadata storage or not makes no difference in the way that Enterprise Manager will operate.

Enterprise Manager does include a plug-in that provides some extra capabilities relating only to the Database Machine, and the operation of this plug-in will be covered in the next chapter, as well as in Chapter 5.

Data Movement

The Exadata Database Machine is a real leap forward in performance and capability, and most customers already have a set of applications that can benefit from this new level of operation. Since these applications run on existing data stores, you will usually have to move data from those existing stores to the new platform.

Chapter 10 is focused on migration, but there are a few utilities and features of Oracle Database 11*g* that come into play when you are moving data onto the platform.

Utilities

Two basic utilities are used to move data into an Oracle Database. SQL*Loader is used to load data from standard external files into the database. SQL*Loader can be used to do more than simply put a complete file into a table, giving you the options to use multiple files as sources, multiple tables as targets, select the data to be loaded, and manipulate data being loaded through the use of SQL functions.

The other utility is Data Pump. Data Pump can export data from an Oracle database into a proprietary file format, which can be used as a source for the Data Pump import process. Data Pump can also load data directly from one Oracle database into another.

Best practices for the Exadata Database Machine call for the use of external tables for loads, rather than the use of these utilities, as described next.

Features

Three features of the Oracle database are also used in the process of moving data into an Oracle database. The first feature is used in conjunction with partitioning, which was discussed in a previous section. To move data into a partitioned table, you can create a temporary table with the same characteristics as a partitioned table and load the data into the table. Once the table is loaded, you create matching indexes on the table and calculate statistics on the table and its columns. At this point, you can add the table as a partition to the partition table target with a single operation, EXCHANGE PARTITION. This operation simply modifies the meta-data for the partitioned table, which causes a minimal interruption in production work.

As Exadata Database Machines are frequently used for data warehouse work, where large volumes of data are regularly added to existing databases, the EXCHANGE PARTITION method, along with the advantages of parallelism for loading, can come in handy.

Another feature that gives you the ability to add data to an existing Oracle database with very little interruption in service is the transportable tablespace. The tablespace is a logical storage unit that underlies all Oracle data structures.

Normally, when you migrate data, you have to extract data from the source database and load it into the target database. But transportable tablespaces, like the partition exchange explained previously, give you a faster way to migrate data from one Oracle database to another. With a transportable tablespace, you simply export the meta-data about the tablespace from the source database, move the files that are used by the tablespace to the target machine, and then load the meta-data into the data dictionary of the target machine.

You can even create a transportable tablespace from a backup set with Recovery Manager and have the tablespace reflect the state of the database at a specific point in time or SCN (system control number).

Finally, Oracle Database 11g includes a feature known as the Database File System, or DBFS. DBFS is built on SecureFiles, the feature used to store large objects, but builds on this storage capability by adding a file system interface, which allows a user to access the files through standard file system calls.

DBFS is used for moving data in conjunction with another Oracle feature known as external files. An external file, as the name implies, lives outside of the standard Oracle database. When you define an external table, you point to the external data source but create meta-data about that file, which allows users to access the file as if it were a table using standard SQL syntax.

One of the fastest ways to perform an actual import into Oracle tables is using a method known as CREATE TABLE AS SELECT . . ., or CTAS, which both creates a table using the structure defined by the SELECT statement and then loads the result set from the statement into the table.

TIP
You can use a similar method, INSERT AS APPEND, to add data to an existing table with similar benefits.

CTAS can use parallel execution to write data into tables very rapidly. Couple this with external tables, which can be read in parallel with the CTAS method, and you have an import method that takes full advantage of parallelism.

With DBFS, you can store external tables in the Oracle-based file system. This storage gives all the standard advantages of DBFS. Files stored in DBFS can be shared among multiple users of the Oracle database. File load operations are frequently performed using a RAC database as the target, which means that the source files have to be available on shared storage. Placing external tables in the DBFS meets this condition.

Operating Systems

Up until Oracle OpenWorld 2010, there wasn't much to say about operating systems as they related to the Exadata Database Machine. But the event featured several announcements about the operating systems that support the Database Machine, which make this a topic worthy of some discussion.

Solaris Support

Oracle announced that they will support the Solaris operating system with the release of Solaris 11 Express, which should be available by the time you read this book. The X2-8 version of the Exadata Database Machine will come with both Solaris and Oracle Linux installed, and you can choose which operating system you want to run on the database server nodes when the Machine is installed.

In fact, you could even run Solaris on one node of the X2-8 and Oracle Linux on the other node of the X2-8, although you could not, of course, combine these nodes into a single RAC cluster if they were running different operating systems.

Oracle Linux

Oracle also announced that the newly renamed Oracle Linux will now support two different Linux kernels. One kernel is designed to be 100 percent compatible with Red Hat Linux. Another kernel, termed the Unbreakable Enterprise Kernel (UEK), includes a wide range of enhancements that contribute to significant performance gains, such as 1.8 times more OLTP transactions per second, as claimed by Oracle.

These enhancements were added to the Linux kernel in order to support the type of high-performance, modern components that make up the Exadata Database Machine. For instance, the UEK supports memory affinity, which ensures that a particular server node will use the co-located memory rather than memory on another node—a change that could mean a performance benefit of an order of magnitude. The Unbreakable Enterprise Kernel includes many other enhancements, such as better support for Infiniband and flash memory, which also contribute to improved performance.

You can choose either Linux kernel when you install Linux for the Exadata Database Machine, although the Unbreakable Linux Kernel will initially only be available for database nodes in the X2-8 version of the Database Machine. With the improved performance delivered by the new kernel, it is a natural choice for use on the X2-8 database nodes.

Please note that the features that make the Unbreakable Enterprise Linux Kernel different have all been submitted for inclusion in the open-source version of Linux. Oracle Linux, with either kernel, is still completely open source.

Other Oracle Database 11*g* Features

Oracle Database 11*g* is probably the most feature-rich database product available today. The main sections already described in this lengthy chapter cover some of the large areas of functionality that either contribute to the overall performance of the Exadata Database Machine or will be used as part of the implementation of the Database Machine. There are a few other features that also play a role in addressing the same issues as the Database Machine that deserve a brief explanation.

Materialized Views

Data warehouses are used to extract additional value from an organization's data store by using that data for additional analysis. This analysis usually involves aggregation of the underlying data, a process that can take a significant amount of time in the production environment.

Materialized views are one way to reduce the runtime cost of these aggregations. A materialized view allows you to precalculate summary information, which not only avoids the need to perform these resource-intensive tasks at runtime, but also allows multiple queries looking for the same aggregation to reuse the same summaries. Materialized views come with their own set of refresh management options. You can choose to completely refresh the summaries in a materialized view, to perform an incremental refresh, or even to refresh summaries in materialized views every time an underlying table is updated. This last option gives you absolutely up-to-date summary information, but does impose overhead on every write operation to a table with one or more materialized views.

There are a set of views in the Oracle data dictionary that provide information on how much the data underlying a materialized view has changed, so you can determine if a materialized view needs a refresh based on this information.

Precomputed summaries can save runtime resources and enhance performance, and the flexible management of the refresh process is also a time-saver, but at this point you may wonder what is so special about materialized views. How is their functionality different from a summary table you build yourself?

The answer to this question lies with the Oracle optimizer. The optimizer recognizes the existence and composition of materialized views and can perform an operation known as query rewrite. When the optimizer receives a query requesting summary information that could be retrieved from a materialized view, the optimizer transparently rewrites the query to use this precomputed data. With query rewrite, you don't have to modify any SQL in any application to take advantage of a materialized view.

Oracle OLAP

Oracle OLAP gives you the ability to embed complete OLAP cubes within the Oracle database. These cubes are managed just like any other data in an Oracle database, included in the same backup and recovery procedures and able to use the same security capabilities as the Oracle database. You can also access data in an Oracle OLAP cube with the same SQL as you use with a standard Oracle schema structure, with the different aspects of the cube being exposed as cube-views.

An Oracle OLAP cube, like a materialized view, contains precomputed summary information. And like materialized views, the summaries in the Oracle OLAP cube are used in the query rewrite process.

If you find yourself using a load of materialized views to precompute a large number of potential aggregates on the same set of tables, you might find that using an Oracle OLAP cube could lower your overall maintenance, since you can refresh all the cells in a cube with a single refresh operation.

Star Transformation

A star transformation is another type of query rewrite performed by the Oracle optimizer. The star transformation is performed as a way to significantly improve the performance of queries directed against a standard star schema, which includes a fact table and a large number of dimensions.

To understand how a star transformation works, consider the following query, typical in a data warehouse scenario:

```
Select SUM(quantity_sold)
  From Sales s, Customers c, Products p, Times t
Where s.cust_id   = c.cust_id
And     s.prod_id  = p.prod_id
And     s.time_id  = t.time_id
And     c.cust_city = 'BOSTON'
And     p.product  = 'UMBRELLA'
And     t.month    = 'MAY'
And     t.year      = 2008;
```

Normally, the optimizer would start out by looking to perform a four-way join in the most optimal way, between the SALES, CUSTOMERS, PRODUCTS, and TIMES tables. Although the dimension tables are much smaller than the SALES fact table, performing a multiple-way join can still be costly, especially since the point of the join is simply to use the Cartesian product of the dimensional join to identify the rows in the fact table for the SUM operation.

Before you can understand the true power of the star transformation, you will have to understand a type of index called a bitmap index. This index differs from a normal B*-tree index in that the bitmap index includes a string of bits that represent individual rows in the underlying table for each value in the index. If the index column in the row has a particular value, that bit is set to 1 (turned on) for that row in the string of bits for that index value. Bitmap indexes are particularly suited to data warehouse scenarios, where the cardinality of the index is very low.

The beauty of the bitmap is when the index is used for selection or joins. Because the values are indicated by individual bits, the server can use a bitwise operation to compare two bitmap indexes, and bitwise operations are extremely fast. So if you have a query that is looking to use multiple selection criteria and each of these criteria is represented in a bitmap index, the server simply does a few fast operations instead of multiple selection operations.

When a star transformation is performed, the optimizer recognizes that the targets of the query are tables that exist in a star schema, with a bitmap index on each of the dimension values. The optimizer rewrites the query to include subselects that take advantage of these bitmap indexes, resulting in this query:

```
Select SUM(quanity_sold)
From Sales s
Where s.cust_id  IN
(Select c.cust_id From Customers c Where c.cust_city = 'BOSTON')
And     s.prod_id  IN
(Select p.prod_id From Products p where p.product  = 'UMBRELLA')
And     s.time_id   IN
(Select t.time_id From Times t Where t.month ='MAY' And  t.year =
2008);
```

The end result is an execution plan that is much faster than the execution plan that would have been required for the original query.

The query used in this example only uses the dimensions as a method to select rows from the fact table. But the optimizer can also use a star transformation to transform queries that need additional information from some or all of the dimension tables. The optimizer simply uses the interim result set from the star transformation as the driving table to join back to the dimension tables for the additional information. And, of course, the optimizer calculates the total cost of the star transformation versus the cost of running the query untouched to determine whether the star transformation will result in a faster execution plan.

Although star transformations are not unique to the Exadata Database Machine, this feature can provide significant performance benefits for data warehouse implementations on this platform.

Encryption

There is nothing about encryption as implemented in Oracle Database 11*g* software that is uniquely applicable to the Exadata Database Machine. Oracle Database 11*g* Advanced Security Option includes Transparent Data Encryption, so named because you can use this encryption without any changes to your application code. The encryption is implemented transparently.

However, the newest versions of the Oracle Database Machine use the X5600 (Westmere) chip in the Exadata Storage Server, as well as the database nodes in the X2-2 models. This chip supports AES-NI hardware-based encryption and decryption, which means these operations can be offloaded to these chips for much faster performance as well as relieving the database or storage server CPUs from the overhead of performing this task. Both the X2-2 database nodes and the storage server nodes will use this capability to decrypt data, with the goal of using the chip for encryption in future releases.

Since this capability is transparent, as is the encryption itself, you don't really have to concern yourself with it, although this enhancement will help the Exadata Database Machine perform even better with encrypted data than before the advent of this hardware for offloading operations.

Summary

In this chapter, you learned about the foundation that the features of Oracle Database 11*g* provided for Exadata technology. These capabilities have been built up over decades of development and include these major features:

- Multiversion read consistency, which prevents locking contention between writers and readers, removing one of the key factors in performance degradation

- Real Application Clusters, which allow you to increase the horsepower and availability of your Oracle database by combining multiple database server nodes into a single Oracle database

- Automated Storage Management, which delivers complete volume and storage management, providing scalability, performance, and reliability for database storage

- Partitioning, which helps to eliminate portions of data from consideration in supplying results to queries, a precursor to some of the features in Exadata software

- Parallel execution, which allows the use of multiple CPUs to address the needs of individual tasks and subtasks that are part of a SQL request, delivering greater performance in some scenarios and environments

- Data Guard, which provides a disaster-resilient configuration to provide for the highest levels of availability

- Compression, which is available in different flavors in Oracle Database 11*g* and an additional variety in Exadata

- Database Resource Manager, which is used to allocate oversubscribed resources among different groups of database users

- A variety of other features and functionality used in the Exadata world, including Enterprise Manager for management, tools for data movement, and different operating systems used on the Exadata Database Machine

This extensive list demonstrates that Exadata technology did not spring from the Oracle development organization as an entirely new entity, but rather as a continuation of progress that has been going on since the early days of Oracle.

The next chapter will cover the software that is unique to the Exadata Database Machine.

CHAPTER
3

Exadata Software
Features

s mentioned in the previous chapter, the Oracle Exadata Database Machine solution did not just spring into being from nothingness—this machine is built on a foundation laid by decades of software development at Oracle. But there are some software features that are new and unique to the Database Machine. This chapter will cover these features, as well as discussing the software used to manage the Exadata Storage Server.

Before diving into a discussion of these features, we should start by dispelling a fairly widespread misconception about the Oracle Exadata Database Machine, as stated in the following quote:

> "The Oracle Exadata Database Machine delivers extreme performance through the use of the latest and fastest hardware components."

There are parts of this statement that are correct. The Oracle Exadata Database Machine does use fast hardware components throughout. And the Database Machine does deliver extreme performance. But to credit the hardware exclusively for this performance is entirely off base.

In fact, the Oracle Exadata Database Machine is a complete solution, where the software and the hardware are tightly integrated and configured in a complementary fashion. But the real secret sauce for the Database Machine lies in its software. This software, at the highest level, aims and achieves a single goal—to use the resources of the Database Machine with as close to maximum efficiency as possible. It is this efficiency, designed and delivered by the Exadata software features, that leverages the performance capabilities of the hardware for maximum effect.

As you will see in the rest of this chapter, the Exadata software looks to implement efficiency across the three main resources used by databases—CPU, memory and storage—as well as reducing storage I/O operations. The Database Machine uses two basic strategies to optimize this efficiency. First of all, the software looks to allocate demand for resources in such a way that all resources are being fully utilized, reducing bottlenecks that can cause performance degradation. This allocation also helps to ensure that you can set performance expectations properly and continually satisfy those expectations.

Second, the software looks to diminish the demand for resources by cleverly eliminating usage that can be discarded without affecting the overall integrity of the database processes. After all, once you have squeezed all the efficiency you can out of the hardware, the next step is to reduce the need to utilize as many resources for any particular operation.

You will revisit these two foundation concepts again and again as you learn about the Exadata software in this chapter.

Smart Scan

Smart Scans are usually the place where discussions of Exadata software begin, mainly because of the dramatic effect these operations can have on performance. This section will contrast the operation of Smart Scans with the normal operations of the Oracle database, describe how Smart Scans are implemented, look at join filtering, and examine how to monitor the savings this feature delivers.

How Standard Queries Work

An Oracle database instance is the process that handles SQL statements, requests and receives data from the storage system, and delivers results back to the requesting process. For Oracle instances running on non-Exadata servers, the process of executing a simple query that selects from a single table proceeds like this:

- A query is submitted to the instance.

- The query is parsed, and an execution path is determined by the Oracle optimizer.

- The execution path is used to identify the extents and request data blocks from the storage system. A block is the smallest amount of data that can be transferred from the storage system to the instance.

- The blocks are used to retrieve the rows and columns for that table from the storage system to the database instance.

- The database instance processes the blocks, eliminating the rows that do not meet any selection criteria and assembling the requested columns to return to the user in a result set.

One particular point of potential inefficiency should leap out at you from this description—the requirement that all the potential blocks be read by the database instance. The database instance must implement selection criteria, which means many blocks are returned that are not needed to satisfy the query.

In addition, complete blocks are sent back to the instance. A block, of course, could contain rows of data that are not relevant for satisfying a particular query. And most queries only request a subset of columns from an entire row, making for even more inefficiency.

Blocks are served up from storage systems over internal pathways, which typically operate rapidly, but as database workloads scale, both in numbers of users and in the amount of data requested, even these pathways can become saturated, creating performance bottlenecks.

The Oracle database has a number of features that can reduce the number of blocks returned from the storage system, from the use of indexes for random reads, to partition pruning to eliminate large groups of blocks from consideration, to materialized views to eliminate the need to return large numbers of rows to perform aggregations. One of the main points of query optimization is to find the optimal execution path, which means, among other considerations, reducing the amount of I/O necessary to produce the desired query results. But the Oracle instance, outside the world of Exadata technology, is still bound to retrieve all potential data blocks, ensuring inefficiency in its use of I/O resources, because this method was the only one available for interacting with the storage system.

How Smart Scan Queries Work

Smart Scan, like most Oracle technology enhancements, works transparently. A query that can benefit from Smart Scan in the Exadata environment will use the feature without any changes or tuning. But the way that the data is requested and returned to the database server is significantly different from the way these tasks are accomplished with a standard query, resulting in potentially large performance gains for eligible queries. Smart Scan techniques can work on individual tables as well as tables that will be used in a join.

Individual Tables

The initial step in executing a query that will use Smart Scan is the same as with a standard query—the query is parsed and the Oracle optimizer determines an optimal execution plan. This similarity means that queries that use Smart Scan can still benefit from retrieving execution plans from the shared pool of the SGA.

Like a "standard" query, the Oracle database instance requests data from storage. Since the Exadata Database Machine always uses Automatic

Storage Management (ASM, explained in Chapter 2), the request is for allocation units gathered from the ASM extent map. If the access method for the table uses a full scan for the table or the index, the database node also includes meta-data, which describes predicate information used for the query.

The Exadata Storage Server Software retrieves all the data from the disks (and may also use the Exadata Smart Flash Cache, as described later in this chapter) and uses the predicate information to reject all of the data that does meet the conditions imposed by the predicate.

A query will not use Smart Scan if the columns being requested by the query include a database large object (LOB), or if a table is a clustered table or an index-organized table. If a query would normally qualify for Smart Scan but doesn't because the query contains a LOB, it's easy to work around this restriction by breaking the query up into two queries—one without a LOB that can take advantage of Smart Scan, and another to retrieve the LOB based on the results of the first query.

If a query does not require a full scan, the Exadata software works as a normal data block server, sending blocks back to the requesting database instance, just as a standard Oracle database would return data.

But if the query can use Smart Scan, the Exadata software goes to work. The Smart Scan process reads data blocks and keeps the relevant rows to return to the database instance. The relevant rows are identified by filtering based on selection criteria specified in the query. Smart Scan filters on predicates that use most comparison operators, including >, <, =, !=, <=, =>, IS [NOT] NULL, LIKE, [NOT} BETWEEN, [NOT]IN, EXISTS, IS OF type, NOT, and AND, as well as most SQL functions. The 11.2.0.2 release of the Exadata Storage software allows for the use of OR predicates and IN lists.

You can get a list of comparison operators that support Smart Scan with the following SQL query:

```
SELECT * FROM v$sqlfn_metadata WHERE offloadable = 'YES';
```

In addition, Smart Scan performs column projection, meaning that only the columns required for the query are sent back to the database instance.

As data is identified through the Smart Scan process, it is returned back to the Oracle database instance. But remember, Smart Scan queries are no longer returning standard data blocks to the instance, but a more concentrated set of rows and columns. Because of this, the results are sent back to the Program Global Area (PGA) of the requesting process rather than the normal

SGA destination of the data buffers. Once the data arrives at the PGA, the normal processing of the query continues to create the result set to send back to the requesting client.

Sending data directly to the PGA without placing blocks into the buffer cache in the SGA is the same way that parallel servers operate, so Smart Scan queries work appropriately with all other types of Oracle features.

NOTE
You may have noticed something here. If the results of a Smart Scan are not returned to the data buffers, then those results cannot help to populate those buffers for performance improvements in other queries. However, later in this chapter you will learn about the Exadata Smart Flash Cache, which can be used to cache data blocks from tables used for Smart Scan queries.

Join Filtering

Smart Scan uses predicate filtering and column projection on individual tables to reduce the amount of data sent back to the database instance. In addition to these single-table techniques, Smart Scan does join filtering.

Oracle has already been using a technique utilizing a *Bloom filter* to determine which rows may be needed to implement a join. A Bloom filter allows determination of membership in a set of values without requiring the space to store all the values. In the case of join filtering, a Bloom filter is created with the values of the join column for the smaller table in the join, and this filter is used by the Exadata Storage software to eliminate row candidates from the larger table, which will not be required to satisfy the join condition.

Bloom filters are uniquely suited to this task since they never return false-negative results, although they may have some false positives. In other words, using a Bloom filter to eliminate rows will never eliminate a row that is needed for a join, although it may allow rows that are not needed for the join. The Bloom filter will never jeopardize data integrity by preventing appropriate rows for joins, although it may not be as completely efficient as it might be (ideally) by letting some unnecessary rows be returned.

Prior to Exadata, Bloom filters were used for joins where the optimizer determined that they could contribute to the optimal execution path.

With Exadata, the use of Bloom filters has been pushed to the Exadata Storage Server, which means that this performance-enhancing technique no longer requires CPU utilization on the database server, and that the Bloom filter can cut down on the amount of data being returned from the Exadata Storage Server. The join itself is actually completed by the database instance.

NOTE
In the current release of the Exadata Storage Server Software, Bloom filters are also used for comparison with the maximum and minimum values in a storage index, which is described later in this chapter.

Join filtering further eliminates the amount of data returned to the database instance by removing rows that will not be needed for a join.

You can recognize a step in an execution plan that may use offloading by the use of a new keyword in the name of the operation, as shown in Figure 3-1. The word "storage" used in this section indicates that a predicate

```
PLAN_TABLE_OUTPUT
------------------------------------------------------------------------------------------------
Plan_hash value: 1503208043
```

Id	Operation	Name	Rows	Bytes	Cost (%CPU)	Time	Pstart	Pstop	TQ	IN-OUT	PQ Distrib
0	SELECT STATEMENT		950	37050	8 (25)	00:00:01					
1	PX COORDINATOR										
2	PX SEND QC (ORDER)	:TQ10005	950	37050	8 (25)	00:00:01			Q1,05	P->S	QC (ORDER)
3	VIEW		950	37050	8 (25)	00:00:01			Q1,05	PCWP	
4	SORT GROUP BY		950	100K	8 (25)	00:00:01			Q1,05	PCWP	
5	PX RECEIVE		950	100K	8 (25)	00:00:01			Q1,05	PCWP	
6	PX SEND RANGE	:TQ10004	950	100K	8 (25)	00:00:01			Q1,04	P->P	RANGE
7	HASH GROUP BY		950	100K	8 (25)	00:00:01			Q1,04	PCWP	
* 8	HASH JOIN		950	100K	7 (15)	00:00:01			Q1,04	PCWP	
9			950	53200	5 (20)	00:00:01			Q1,04	PCWP	
10	PX RECEIVE		950	53200	5 (20)	00:00:01			Q1,04	PCWP	
11	PX SEND HASH	:TQ10002	950	53200	5 (20)	00:00:01			Q1,02	P->P	HASH
* 12	HASH JOIN BUFFERED		950	53200	5 (20)	00:00:01			Q1,02	PCWP	
13	PX RECEIVE		139	3614	2 (0)	00:00:01			Q1,02	PCWP	
14	PX SEND HASH	:TQ10000	139	3614	2 (0)	00:00:01			Q1,00	P->P	HASH
15	PX BLOCK ITERATOR		139	3614	2 (0)	00:00:01			Q1,00	PCWP	
16	TABLE ACCESS STORAGE FULL	LOOKUP_CODE	139	3614	2 (0)	00:00:01			Q1,00	PCWP	
17	PX RECEIVE		950	28500	2 (0)	00:00:01			Q1,02	PCWP	
18	PX SEND HASH	:TQ10001	950	28500	2 (0)	00:00:01			Q1,01	P->P	HASH
19	PX BLOCK ITERATOR		950	28500	2 (0)	00:00:01	1	16	Q1,01	PCWP	
20	TABLE ACCESS STORAGE FULL	ORDER_HEADER	950	28500	2 (0)	00:00:01	1	256	Q1,01	PCWP	
21	PX RECEIVE		11887	603K	2 (0)	00:00:01			Q1,04	PCWP	
22	PX SEND HASH	:TQ10003	11887	603K	2 (0)	00:00:01			Q1,03	P->P	HASH
23			11887	603K	2 (0)	00:00:01			Q1,03	PCWP	
24	PX BLOCK ITERATOR		11887	603K	2 (0)	00:00:01	1	16	Q1,03	PCWP	
* 25	TABLE ACCESS STORAGE FULL	ORDER_DETAIL	11887	603K	2 (0)	00:00:01	17	32	Q1,03	PCWP	

```
Predicate Information (identified by operation id):

  8 – access("A"."ACCT_NUM"="C"."ACCT_NUM" AND "A"."CO_ID"="C"."CO_ID")
 12 – access("A"."PCODE"="B"."PCODE")
 25 – storage("C"."ASOF_YYYYMM"=200102 AND "C"."TRAN_AMT"<2000000000)
      filter("C"."ASOF_YYYYMM"=200102 AND "C"."TRAN_AMT"<2000000000
```

FIGURE 3-1. *Execution plan which uses Bloom filters*

is eligible to be offloaded to the Exadata Storage Server—in other words, if the predicate was used with a Smart Scan operation.

> **NOTE**
> *The presence of this keyword does not guarantee that the predicate was evaluated on the Exadata Storage Server, since there are other conditions that may prevent this from happening, as discussed in the following section.*

The use of Smart Scan can have a truly dramatic effect on the amount of data returned to the database instance. The storage system is no longer returning data blocks, which usually contain extraneous rows and columns, to the database instance for further evaluation as to whether they will actually be needed to satisfy a query. Instead, only the rows and columns needed to address the needs of the query are returned and, in the case of a join, the rows that may be used in the join (for the most part, as explained in the description of the operation of a Bloom filter). Less data returned means less bandwidth required, as well as potentially faster response times. Less data returned also saves on memory used by the database node. Smart Scan contributes mightily to the efficient use of I/O resources by dramatically reducing the amount of data returned from the storage system, as well as reducing the amount of data processed by the database instance itself.

Monitoring Savings from Smart Scan

Oracle provides some new measures in the standard V$ performance views that allow you to see how much I/O is being saved by the use of Smart Scan technology. The statistics are shown in Table 3-1.

The EXPLAIN PLAN, shown in Figure 3-2, gives an indication of the steps in an execution plan that will benefit from Smart Scan.

You can see that steps 12 and 14 have the word STORAGE in the name of their operation. There are two important things to understand about the use of these operation names. The first relevant fact is that you can control whether the EXPLAIN PLAN displays these types of operation names. The setting of the CELL_OFFLOAD_PLAN_DISPLAY parameter, set with

View column	Description
Cell physical IO bytes	The number of bytes returned to the database server from the Exadata Storage Server.
Cell physical read total bytes	The number of bytes read from physical disks. You can compare this with the cell physical I/O to see the overall savings implemented by Smart Scan.
Cell physical I/O bytes eligible for predicate offload	The number of bytes that could use the predicate offload feature of Smart Scan. By comparing this with the number of bytes returned to the database server, you can see the efficiency of the predicate offload process.

TABLE 3-1. *Monitoring Smart Scan Savings*

```
Execution Plan
-----------------------------------------------------
Plan hash value: 113084141
```

Id	Operation	Name	Rows	Bytes	Cost (%CPU)	Time	Pstart	Pstop	TQ	IN-OUT	PQ Distrib
0	SELECT STATEMENT		1	46	3129 (2)	00:00:57					
1	SORT GROUP BY		1	46							
2	PX COORDINATOR										
3	PX SEND QC (RANDOM)	:TQ10002	1	46					Q1,02	P -> S	QC (RAND)
4	SORT GROUP BY		1	46					Q1,02	PCWP	
5	PX RECEIVE		1	46					Q1,02	PCWP	
6	PX SEND HASH	:TQ10001	1	46					Q1,01	P -> P	HASH
7	SORT GROUP BY		1	46					Q1,01	PCWP	
* 8	HASH JOIN		21M	957M	3129 (2)	00:00:57			Q1,01	PCWP	
9	PX RECEIVE		8392	83920	5 (0)	00:00:01			Q1,01	PCWP	
10	PX SEND BROADCAST	:TQ10000	8392	83920	5 (0)	00:00:01			Q1,00	P -> P	BROADCAST
11	PX BLOCK ITERATOR		8392	83920	5 (0)	00:00:01			Q1,00	PCWC	
* 12	TABLE ACCESS STORAGE FULL	REGION	8392	83920	5 (0)	00:00:01			Q1,00	PCWP	
13	PX BLOCK ITERATOR		334M	11G	3116 (1)	00:00:57	50	52	Q1,01	PCWC	
* 14	TABLE ACCESS STORAGE FULL	TRANSACTION	334M	11G	3116 (1)	00:00:57	50	52	Q1,01	PCWP	

```
Predicate Information (identified by operation id):
---------------------------------------------------

   8 - access("T"."BSNS_UNIT_KEY"="S"."ORG_BSNS_UNIT_KEY")
  12 - storage("S"."STATE"='AZ' OR "S"."STATE"='CA' OR "S"."STATE"='NM' OR "S"."STATE"='TX')
       filter("S"."STATE"='AZ' OR "S"."STATE"='CA' OR "S"."STATE"='NM' OR "S"."STATE"='TX')
  14 - storage("T"."DAY_KEY"<=20080903)
       filter("T"."DAY_KEY"<=20080903 AND SYS_OP_BLOOM_FILTER(:BF0000,"T"."BSNS_UNIT_KEY"))
```

FIGURE 3-2. *An EXPLAIN PLAN for a query that may use Smart Scan*

an ALTER SYSTEM or ALTER SESSION command, controls the display with the following settings:

- AUTO, the default, will use these display names if an operation can be offloaded to the Exadata Storage Server, if there is a storage cell attached, and if the table in question is on an attached cell.

- ALWAYS shows these operation names if an operation could be offloaded, whether there is a cell attached or not.

- NEVER does not show these extended operation names.

You can understand the reason to use each of these—AUTO for a situation where an Exadata Storage Server is part of the environment, ALWAYS to see which portions of a query could benefit from the presence of an Exadata Storage Server, and NEVER to simply ignore this possibility.

The second important fact to understand is that the presence of the STORAGE keyword, either in the operation name or the predicate information at the bottom of the plan, does not guarantee that a step will be offloaded. Instead, think of this keyword as indicating eligibility for offloading. The actual decision to use offload processing or not is done by the Exadata Storage Server, and there are scenarios where the Exadata Storage Server will decide that using Smart Scan will not result in any performance gain, as described in the Exadata documentation.

The only foolproof way to see if a query used Smart Scan is to query the V$SQL or related tables for one of the categories listed previously.

Other Offloaded Processing

The term "Smart Scan" is sometimes used by Oracle to describe all the operations that are shifted from the database instances to the Exadata Storage Server. Although these other processes are executed on the Exadata Storage Server, the same place where the Smart Scan processing takes place, these other operations do not operate in the same way, so they will be described in this section on offloaded processing.

Fast File Creation

Whenever the Oracle database has to add to its internal storage, the disk blocks need to be initialized, which is a process that requires writing to each individual block in the extent.

The Exadata Storage Server Software can handle this initialization process with the CPUs that are part of the Storage Server. When data blocks need to be added and initialized, the database server sends the meta-data to the Exadata Storage Server and the Storage Server handles the actual write operations for the process. This feature means that file creation, as well as the addition of more storage space, is much cheaper than the standard method of using database CPU cycles.

Although fast file creation does not necessarily occur very often, the ability to essentially make delays previously caused by this process disappear provides a noticeable increase in response time in the scenarios that require this operation, including tasks such as migrating data to the Exadata platform.

You can see the I/O savings realized by this feature with the following statistic in the V$SYSSTATS, V$SQL, and related views:

```
cell physical IO bytes saved during optimized file creation
```

Incremental Backup

Backup is one of those tasks with a stealth profile, an absolute requirement for any professional IT operation, but one whose impact is unnoticed until it rears its ugly head and interferes with other operations seen as more crucial for day-to-day operations. These scenarios typically occur when backup operations start to intrude on the production use of an Oracle database.

Oracle has added a lot of features over the years to reduce the impact of essential backup operations, which is a good thing, as the volume of data has steadily grown. Most shops use an incremental backup, which only backs up data that has changed since the last incremental or full backup. Oracle Recovery Manager (RMAN), the primary backup and recovery for the Oracle database, uses block tracking to reduce the amount of data required in an incremental backup. Block tracking marks blocks that have changed since the last backup, and then backs up only groups of blocks that have been marked.

The Exadata Storage Server Software extends the savings produced by block tracking by allowing a smaller amount of data to be sent to the database node running the RMAN operation. The software will only send back the blocks that have been changed, reducing the amount of data sent to the database server and processed for backup, which improves the overall performance of the database backup.

Data Mining Scoring

In Chapter 2, you read about data mining, where the Oracle database could use sophisticated algorithms to look for trends and anomalies in historical data. Oracle Data Mining can produce results that can be extremely valuable in making strategic decisions, such as how to increase sales to your best existing customers or which trends indicate a profitable change in allocating production resources.

Data mining uses the value embedded in your historical data to direct and support your best business analysts, but the process of rating the data to produce results, known as *scoring,* can be CPU intensive.

Exadata Storage Server Software can push this scoring to the CPUs on the Storage Server, eliminating the need to use resources on the database server to perform this task. Internal comparisons have shown that offloading scoring can deliver responses that are up to ten times faster than using database server resources for this operation.

Although not all shops use Oracle Data Mining, where this valuable feature is used, the ability to eliminate the CPU processing required for data mining from the database servers reduces the load on these servers. This reduction not only results in faster performance for the queries that include data mining, but also in improved performance across the board, as the previously required CPU resources can be used for other operations.

Encryption

Encryption is a tool used by an increasing number of Oracle shops, as compliance requirements become more restrictive and universal. Oracle Advanced Security Option provides a capability known as Transparent Data Encryption. As its name implies, Transparent Data Encryption allows data to be encrypted without any change in the application code that accesses the encrypted data. This feature means that organizations can achieve compliance through encryption without the time-consuming and error-prone process of modifying their home-grown applications, as well as allowing packaged applications to benefit from encryption.

Most database operations can be performed on encrypted data without having to go through a decryption operation. The data is only decrypted before it is sent back to the user, which means that the database server does not have to waste CPU cycles decrypting data that is not actually required to satisfy the SQL request.

Exadata Storage Server Software takes these advantages even further. First of all, Exadata Smart Scan operations can be performed on encrypted data, allowing the benefits from these features to be used with encrypted data. Second, the actual decryption of data can be performed on the CPUs in the Storage Server, eliminating virtually all the overhead required for this process from the workload of the database server. Third, encryption works well with compression, which reduces the size of the data and correspondingly reduces the overhead of encrypting data. Finally, as mentioned in the previous chapter, the Exadata Storage Server and X2-2 database nodes can offload decryption operations to hardware-based instructions in the Westmere chip.

The interaction between Exadata Storage Server Software and Transparent Data Encryption is a great illustration of the power of the complete Oracle solution. A useful feature is not only supported by the advances of the Oracle Exadata Database Machine, but extended to allow the use of the feature with even better performance.

Exadata Hybrid Columnar Compression

Storage is one of the key resources used by any database. Storage volume continues to grow, not only because of requirements for new applications and data collection, but also due to the inevitable growth of data as it accumulates over time.

Compression is one of the key approaches used by Oracle and other databases to reduce the amount of storage required for data. Compression not only reduces the storage requirements for historical data, but also reduces the size of data used by the Oracle database, with corresponding reductions in memory usage and an increase in I/O bandwidth.

Oracle has had compression for many years, as discussed in Chapter 2. Oracle introduced compression with what is now referred to as basic table compression. This compression capability is included as a part of the standard Oracle database, but the compression only works on direct load operations. This restriction meant that any data added to the database or modified through update operations would not be compressed, which limited the benefit that could be gained through this type of compression.

Oracle Database 11*g* introduced Advanced Compression, which includes a compression option known as OLTP compression. This compression not only uses a better algorithm for compression and decompression, which increases the amount of data compression while reducing the overhead needed to decompress the data, but also compresses data added through database writes without the overhead of compression spawned by every database change.

NOTE
The OLTP designation in the name of this feature is somewhat misleading, as Advanced Compression is also used by many data warehouses, since compression is implemented for data added to the warehouse by many types of refresh operations that operate with smaller amounts of data.

Exadata Hybrid Columnar Compression is an Exadata feature that offers the benefits of compression in a slightly different way.

What Is Exadata Hybrid Columnar Compression?

Exadata Hybrid Columnar Compression (EHCC) is a type of compression that is only available on the Exadata Storage Server. As its name implies, one of the distinguishing features of Exadata Hybrid Columnar Compression is that data using this type of compression is organized for storage by columns. But there is much more to Exadata Hybrid Columnar Compression than simply a different type of storage.

The "hybrid" portion of the feature name refers to a difference in how Oracle stores columnar data, which allows better utilization across the complete spectrum of database operations, allowing for broader usage of Exadata Hybrid Columnar Compression. In addition, Exadata Hybrid Columnar Compression uses different types of compression algorithm.

How It Works

Columnar storage is not a brand-new concept in the database world. Other databases have offered columnar storage for a while, but universal columnar storage, even for a single table, can present problems.

Virtually no feature provides equal benefits for all types of operations, whether in a database or any other type of software. The sweet spot for columnar storage is those tables where only a few columns will be accessed in a typical query. In order for a database to satisfy a data request, the columns requested have to be accessed and assembled. A larger number of columns results in more work for a pure columnar storage database when many of these columns are requested by a query. And, unfortunately, queries that require a large number of columns coupled with a small number of rows are not that uncommon in the overall mix of a production database. These queries end up requiring pure columnar databases to perform a lot of work for a small result set, reducing the benefit produced by columnar storage in general.

Exadata Hybrid Columnar Compression takes a slightly different approach, as shown in Figure 3-3. Exadata Hybrid Columnar Compression uses the concept of a compression unit, which stores data by columns, but only for a set of rows.

A compression unit can be retrieved with a single I/O operation, which is more efficient than a purely columnar storage option, which requires one or more I/O operations per column. This advantage, in turn, means less unnecessary overhead for those queries that require a greater number of columns, which means you can use the advantages of Exadata Hybrid Columnar Compression for a broader set of tables, increasing the overall benefits you can gain from this feature.

Exadata Hybrid Columnar Compression creates compression units for data as the data is initially loaded into the database with direct load operations. You can use an ALTER TABLE statement to modify how new direct loaded data is compressed, but the only way to get uncompressed data to use EHCC is to use the DBMS_REDEFINITION package to change the compression on a partition or table. Data added to a table with Exadata Hybrid Columnar Compression with INSERT operations after this initial load is still compressed, but at a lower level of compression.

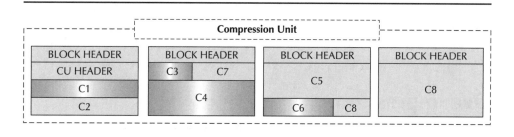

FIGURE 3-3. *Exadata Hybrid Columnar Compression compression unit*

The same conditions apply when data in a compression unit is updated—the new data is removed from the compression unit and compressed with an alternate compression method, and the entire compression unit is locked for the duration of the update, which means that you typically only want to use Exadata Hybrid Columnar Compression for data that is no longer being updated.

As you look at the diagram of a compression unit, you can see that the overall unit holds data from all the columns in the table. As data is loaded into a table or partition with Exadata Hybrid Columnar Compression enabled, the Exadata Storage Server Software estimates the number of rows that can fit into a compression unit, based on the size of the rows and the estimated compression of the data, using the Exadata Hybrid Columnar Compression compression algorithms.

Compression Options

Exadata Hybrid Columnar Compression allows you to choose between two different levels of compression, and each of these levels allows a further specification of high or low compression. Query compression can reduce storage requirements to a tenth of standard storage. Queries can sometimes run faster with this type of compression, as the decompression (described later in this chapter) does not impose a very large CPU impact and the number of I/O operations is reduced due to the compression.

Archive compression can provide even greater storage compression, with improvements from 15 times to 70 times, depending on the composition of the data. Query performance for tables or partitions with archive compression is frequently a bit slower, but archive compression can still accommodate schema changes, so you can add and drop columns to a table with the archive compression option for Exadata Hybrid Columnar Compression in use. The potentially dramatic difference in storage requirements for archive compression leads to the possibility of keeping historical data available online, which makes any query overhead insignificant when compared with the option of having to bring historical data back online.

Decompression

Compression saves storage and reduces I/O operations, but the data still needs to be decompressed before it can be used in result sets.

Although all compression is performed by the CPUs in the database nodes, EHCC data can be decompressed by the CPUs in the Exadata Storage

Server or those in the database nodes. The choice is made based on the type of query processing performed. A Smart Scan query returns result sets directly to the PGA, so the CPUs on the Exadata Storage Server perform the decompression. Queries that cannot use Smart Scan return standard data blocks to the database node—if these blocks are compressed with EHCC, the database server CPUs must decompress them, which requires cycles and memory space to store the decompressed data.

NOTE
This decompression only has to happen on the columns required by the query. Remember that the block headers in an EHCC block detail where the different columns are stored, so if a block does not contain requested columns, there is no need for decompression.

These different locations for decompression have some impact on resource utilization on the database nodes, which you should be aware of as you plan your compression approach.

Advantages

Of course, Exadata Hybrid Columnar Compression gives you the benefit of reduced storage, saving disk costs and allowing for the use of larger amounts of data in your Exadata-based databases. But the size reduction provided by Exadata Hybrid Columnar Compression also has implications for the use of other resources.

For instance, a reduced storage footprint leads to a corresponding reduction in memory requirements for active use of the compressed data. Reduced memory requirements not only provide for greater efficiency in the use of memory, but can also alter the way that queries are satisfied. A tenfold reduction in the size of data could mean that an entire table can now be cached in the Exadata Smart Flash Cache, which will be discussed later. Think of the benefits produced here—the complete elimination of traditional disk I/O for the table.

Keep in mind that Exadata Hybrid Columnar Compression will have the greatest impact on queries that are disk-bound, as opposed to queries where the limitation is the CPU. The source of benefits comes from reduced storage, which has an effect if the performance of a query is bounded by I/O speed.

ILM and Oracle Compression

As you have already read, Exadata Hybrid Columnar Compression is not the only compression option available for the Oracle database. Although Exadata Hybrid Columnar Compression will usually produce the greatest benefits with the highest levels of compression, you may not want to use it in all scenarios. For instance, if your database usage patterns call for a lot of INSERT and UPDATE activity, you may find that the ability of Advanced Compression to compress these types of data produces more benefits overall for those portions of data that experience this type of activity.

The practice of Information Lifecycle Management, or ILM, is designed to achieve maximum benefits for your data in terms of both performance and storage savings throughout its useful life. This lifecycle involves periods of a lot of write activity, when the data is relatively current, and a gradual reduction in changes as the data ages. Oracle's multiple compression options, coupled with the ability to apply the options to partitions as well as complete tables, are ideally suited to implementing an ILM strategy.

You can choose to use Advanced Compression for partitions that receive the bulk of write activity, getting a good level of compression savings while still having data actively compressed as it is added or modified, while possibly leaving the most active partitions uncompressed. As the data in a partition ages, you can convert the compression to query compression with Exadata Hybrid Columnar Compression, increasing the compression benefits while still allowing rapid access of the data in the partition. As the partition's data moves towards almost complete quiescence, you can modify the Exadata Hybrid Columnar Compression level to archive compression, providing even more benefits while still having the data available online.

Storage Indexes

Storage indexes, like Exadata Hybrid Columnar Compression, are a feature of the Exadata Storage Server Software that extends benefits already provided by the Oracle database. As reviewed in Chapter 2, partitioning provides a way to eliminate portions of a table that will not be relevant for a query through the means of partition pruning. Storage indexes provide a similar benefit, but work in a different and more flexible way.

A storage index tracks high and low values for columns in rows stored in 1MB storage regions on the Exadata Storage Server. The Exadata Storage Server Software can use the values in the storage index to eliminate storage regions from consideration for use in satisfying a query, the same way that partitions are used to eliminate data that will not contribute to query results. Although the benefit produced by storage indexes is basically the same as that produced by partitions, storage indexes are in-memory structures that are automatically collected for multiple columns in a region. The Exadata Storage Server Software can use values for any of the columns tracked in the storage index to perform storage region elimination based on the values in the index.

How Storage Indexes Work

Storage indexes are fairly simple in concept, as shown in Figure 3-4.

When a table is accessed as part of a Smart Scan query, the Exadata Storage Server Software tracks the data in 1MB storage regions. For each storage region, Exadata tracks the high and low values for many of the columns stored in the region. The storage index is an in-memory collection of these statistics for all storage regions.

When a Smart Scan query hits the Exadata Storage Server, the values in the storage index may be used to eliminate storage regions from consideration in the query, based on predicate evaluation or the use of a Bloom filter for joins, as with standard Smart Scan processing.

Storage indexes are not enabled for National Language Support (NLS) columns or columns containing large objects. If an operation writes to a storage region and changes values for a column being tracked in the storage

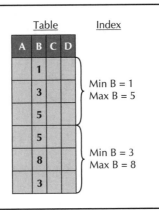

FIGURE 3-4. *Storage indexes*

index, the write could invalidate the column values if that new value falls outside the high and low boundaries for the column.

Storage indexes are memory structures that are built the first time a Smart Scan query hits the storage region. If a cell has to be rebooted, the storage index for that cell has to be rebuilt. Whether a column's storage index values have been invalidated or the entire storage index is gone, the new values are calculated whenever a Smart Scan query accesses data in the storage region. Successive Smart Scan queries also refine the values kept for a storage region by only tracking for those columns whose high and low values allow for effective selectivity for the storage region.

Because of the potential for invalidation or destruction, you should think of a storage index as an evolving entity. You don't have to do anything to aid in the periodic recovery of the storage index or its values—the natural operation of Smart Scans will take care of this for you.

You can see how much value a storage index is providing by looking for the

```
cell physical IO bytes saved by storage index
```

value in the V$SYSSTAT, V$SQL, and related views.

Storage Indexes at Work

The most important thing to know about storage indexes is the simple fact that storage indexes never have an adverse effect on performance. There are times when storage indexes can help to eliminate a significant amount of physical I/O, reducing demands on the Exadata Storage Server disks, as well as bandwidth required to move the data to the database server nodes, cases where storage indexes will provide faster response time and performance. Other cases will not benefit from storage indexes, but they will not suffer any performance degradation from this lack of usage.

The queries that can get the most benefits from storage indexes are those where the values for a column used as a selection criteria are closely bunched in storage. In other words, if a query does a selection based on a column like ORDER_NUMBER, if those numbers can be grouped so that a compact range occupies a 1MB storage region tracked by a storage index, the index will have maximum effect in eliminating regions where the values will not be selected.

Since data is placed in blocks as it is inserted into the database, you can maximize the effect of storage indexes if you sort data on columns that will benefit from storage indexes—columns whose similar values will make the storage index on 1MB of data more selective. This sorting will often result in effective storage indexes for columns where similar ranges of values are collocated in a record. Take the example of an order header, which includes a unique ORDER_NUMBER that increases with each new order; an ORDER_DATE, which should follow the same incremental pattern; and a SHIPPING_DATE, which will also typically increment along the same lines, although this value may have more variation. A query that used any number of these columns would probably benefit from storage indexes if the data was inserted into the table with sorting along the lines of any of these columns.

Storage indexes can also work in conjunction with partitioning in a similar manner. Using the same columns as the previous example, assume that you have a table partitioned on the ORDER_DATE column. If a query were to select based on this column, partition pruning would kick in to eliminate rows that did not match the selection criteria. But any query that selected on the ORDER_NUMBER or the SHIPPING_DATE would not benefit from this partitioning scheme. However, storage indexes would provide similar I/O elimination benefits based on the collocation of those values. The storage index would allow for elimination of storage regions based on these columns whose values closely track those of the partition key without any administrative work or overhead.

Storage indexes work to eliminate I/O from being performed, which saves cycles in the Exadata Storage Server as well as increasing effective use of bandwidth between the Exadata Storage Server and the database nodes of the Sun Oracle Database Machine by avoiding having to send that data to the database nodes.

Exadata Smart Flash Cache

The Exadata Storage Servers include some flash storage as a hardware component, as will be described in the next chapter on Exadata hardware. However, there is a significant amount of intelligence in the software that utilizes this hardware component, which is covered in this section on Exadata Smart Flash Cache.

What Is the Exadata Smart Flash Cache?

The hardware component of the Exadata Smart Flash Cache is a set of PCIe flash cards that come with each Exadata Storage Server cell. The PCIe designation refers to the Peripheral Component Interconnect Express, an interconnect that provides much greater bandwidth than older interfaces. Each PCIe card has 96GB of storage, and each cell has four cards, bringing the total flash storage to 384GB per cell. Although a detailed discussion of this hardware component is beyond the scope of this chapter, be aware that these flash cards have the capability of avoiding issues related to degradation through use, as well as providing stable storage capabilities.

The main benefit that the hardware component of Exadata Smart Flash Cache provides is much faster access than standard, disk-based access. The throughput and size of the flash cache provided by the Exadata Smart Flash Cache provides the foundation for enhanced performance, but the way that the Exadata Storage Server Software uses the Exadata Smart Flash Cache leverages these enhancements for maximum effect.

NOTE
Please do not confuse the Exadata Smart Flash Cache with the Database Flash Cache. Although both use flash technology, the Database Flash Cache is located in the database server node and essentially provides an extension to the standard operations of the SGA. The Exadata Smart Flash Cache, as you will see in the following pages, works in a different manner and is a part of the Exadata Storage Server. In addition, the Database Flash Cache is not supported in the Exadata environment.

How Can You Use the Exadata Smart Flash Cache?

The Exadata Smart Flash Cache can be used in two basic ways. The first, and most popular, way to use the cache is as a standard cache. The Exadata Storage Server Software caches data blocks into the Exadata Smart Flash Cache and ages blocks out of the Exadata Smart Flash Cache as required.

You can also use the Exadata Smart Flash Cache to create a flash disk. This disk is used just as you would use a standard cell disk—you can build grid disks from the flash disks. This approach would give you what appears to ASM as a standard Exadata grid disk, but with the performance of flash.

There are two basic reasons why this approach is not widely used. The first involves how disks are normally used by ASM—with redundancy for availability. Even if you use normal redundancy for your flash disks, you would lose half the capacity of the flash storage as the data is mirrored.

The second reason is because of the optimizations built into the Oracle database long ago. As you know, the Oracle database uses "lazy writes" to write to actual database blocks, allowing these potentially time-consuming writes to be taken out of the critical path for write performance. Instead, Oracle only requires a write to a sequential log file to complete a transaction while guaranteeing integrity. A write to a sequential log file is a fast operation—in fact, a write to a sequential file on disk is essentially as fast as the same write to a flash-based disk. This reality reduces the performance gains that can come from flash-based grid disks.

The Exadata Smart Flash Cache simply passes write operations through to disk, and so you would lose at least half the capacity of the cache by using it as a flash-based disk (depending on the level of redundancy) without a great increase in benefits, most customers decide to simply use the Exadata Smart Flash Cache as a cache.

How Does Exadata Smart Flash Cache Determine What Is Cached?

Exadata Storage Server Software makes intelligent decisions on what data to cache in the Exadata Smart Flash Cache. When data is read as part of a SQL operation, the Exadata Storage Server Software checks to see if the data is likely to be accessed again and if the data is not part of a large scan. The Exadata Smart Flash Cache does not cache the results of large I/O operations, since this would end up pushing a lot of data out of the cache as it added the scan results to it. If the data does not fit this profile and the data is not a large object, the data block is placed into the Exadata Smart Flash Cache.

The Exadata Storage Server Software will also cache data from some modify operations. Once the write to the log file is confirmed, allowing the write operation to complete, the block can be considered for addition to the Exadata Smart Flash Cache. The Exadata Storage Server Software is smart enough to know to eliminate some types of writes from consideration, such as writes for backups, mirroring operations, Data Pump operations, ASM rebalances, and the like.

The decision process described previously is the default process, used by data objects that have the CELL_FLASH_CACHE attribute set to DEFAULT. There are two other options for this attribute. If the attribute is set to NONE, the data object is not considered for storage in the Exadata Smart Flash Cache. If the attribute is set to KEEP, the data object is kept in the Exadata Smart Flash Cache, regardless of the type of operation that presented the data to the Exadata Storage Server Software. By using the KEEP attribute, you can ensure that data that would not normally be kept in the Exadata Smart Flash Cache, such as an LOB or data that is part of a full table scan, will be placed into the cache.

Data kept in the KEEP portion of the Exadata Smart Flash Cache cannot be forced out of the cache by the algorithm used for default objects. However, the KEEP cache does have an aging algorithm, but one that is much less aggressive than the algorithm used for default objects. In general, the KEEP cache algorithm will change the attribute of its data to DEFAULT after a certain period, at which point the data is subject to the default aging algorithm.

In addition, no more than 80 percent of the storage in the Exadata Smart Flash Cache on a cell can be used for the KEEP portion of the cache. As a best practice, you should typically not assign the KEEP attribute to data objects that cannot fit simultaneously into the Exadata Smart Flash Cache, which will mean the objects are never aged out of the cache. Since the whole purpose of the KEEP attribute is to ensure that a data object will be present in the Exadata Smart Flash Cache, assigning more data to this cache would undercut the essential aim of the attribute.

You can change the CELL_FLASH_CACHE attribute on an object at runtime, as you would other attributes on data objects. This would change the attribute on data from an object that is already in the cache, but will not actually affect the residency of those blocks. For instance, if you were to change the CELL_FLASH_CACHE attribute of a data object from KEEP to NONE, the data blocks for that object already in the cache would have their attribute set to DEFAULT, which would cause them to be affected by the default algorithm. The data blocks would not, however, be flushed out of the cache.

NOTE
You can flush the Exadata Smart Flash Cache by using the DROP FLASHCACHE command of CellCLI.

Exadata Smart Flash Cache Statistics

There are two places you can get statistics regarding the use of the Exadata Smart Flash Cache. The first is by using the LIST METTRICCURRENT command of CellCLI, which is discussed later in this chapter, as partially shown in the following code:

```
CellCLI> LIST METRICCURRENT WHERE -
            objectType='FLASHCACHE'
    FC_BY_USED              72119 MB
    FC_IO_RQ_R          55395828 IO requests
    FC_IO_RQ_R_MISS       123184 IO requests
```

More than 30 statistics relating to the use of the Exadata Smart Flash Cache are available.

You can also use the FLASHCACHECONTENT object with CellCLI commands, described later in this chapter, to determine whether an object is currently being kept in the Exadata Smart Flash Cache. The following code shows an example of the type of information you can get about an object. Please note that you have to get the objectNumber for an object by querying the DBA_OBJECTS view for the object_id of the object.

```
CellCLI> LIST FLASHCACHECONTENT
        WHERE objectNumber=57435 DETAIL
            cachedKeepSize:          0
            cachedSize:      495438874
            dbID:                70052
            hitCount:           415483
            missCount:            2059
            objectNumber:        57435
            tableSpaceNumber:        1
```

Using the same object_id, you can find out how many reads for a particular object were satisfied from the Exadata Smart Flash Cache:

```
SQL> SELECT statistic_name, value
  2      FROM V$SEGMENT_STATISTICS
  3      WHERE dataobj#= 57435 AND ts#=5 AND
  4      statistic_name='optimized physical reads';
STATISTIC_NAME                   VALUE
-----------------------          ------
optimized physical reads         743502
```

Keep in mind that another, similarly named statistic—physical read requests optimized—includes both those reads that were satisfied from the Exadata Smart Flash Cache and the number of disk I/Os eliminated by the use of a storage index.

You can also get cumulative statistics regarding the effectiveness of the Exadata Smart Flash Cache from the V$SYSSTAT view, as shown here:

```
SQL> SELECT name, value FROM V$SYSSTAT WHERE
2 NAME IN ('physical read total IO requests',
3          'cell flash cache read hits');
NAME                                          VALUE
physical read total IO requests               15673
cell flash cache read hits                    14664
```

By comparing the cell flash cache read hits with the physical read total I/O requests, you can determine the comparative effectiveness of the Exadata Smart Flash Cache.

Benefits from Exadata Smart Flash Cache

It may seem a bit reductionist to have to call out the advantages of a cache. The faster performance of the flash storage means that data is retrieved faster, improving response time, right? But keep in mind that Exadata Smart Flash Cache actually can do more than just improve performance by reducing retrieval time.

The Exadata Storage Server Software is aware of the amount of data that will need to be retrieved to satisfy a query. And although data is retrieved from the Exadata Smart Flash Cache much faster than from the disk in a storage cell, the retrieval does take some amount of time. When appropriate, the Exadata Storage Server Software will retrieve data from both the Exadata Smart Flash Cache and disk, delivering maximum data flow. In this way, the throughput produced by the Exadata Smart Flash Cache and standard disk retrieval are combined to give maximum throughput to satisfy a particular query and provide maximum efficiency.

I/O Resource Manager

I/O Resource Manager is different from the software features discussed previously in this chapter in two ways. First of all, I/O Resource Manager does not directly improve efficiency of operation by reducing the amount of resources required. Instead, I/O Resource Manager contributes to improved efficiency by ensuring that in a scenario where there is more demand for a resource than can be simultaneously supplied by the Exadata Storage Server, the most critical operations will deliver a consistent quality of service.

The second way that I/O Resource Manager is different from the previously discussed features is that I/O Resource Manager is essentially an extension of an existing feature of the Oracle Database—the Database Resource Manager.

But you should not let these differences deter you from an appreciation of the benefits that I/O Resource Manager can deliver, as these benefits can be substantial.

Benefits from I/O Resource Manager

I/O Resource Manager gives you the ability to provision the I/O bandwidth from the Exadata Storage Server to the database grid by consumer group, database, and category. In doing so, I/O Resource Manager, or IORM, delivers the most precious quality of performance—consistency.

Remember that there are really two definitions of performance. The definition used by IT personnel has to do with actual timings of discrete or aggregate operations. The more important definition comes from users, who have an expectation of performance that trumps the more mundane measurement. A SQL query that takes 5 seconds to return results could be seen either as slow if the query was expected to return in 2 seconds or blazingly fast if the expectation was for results in 20 seconds.

By dividing up the overall bandwidth for a database or cell, IORM lets you ensure that there will be sufficient resources to meet customer expectations. IORM, like other resource plan aspects, does not start to limit I/O resources until those resources are oversubscribed, which means that this feature will not "waste" bandwidth by limiting access when there is enough to spare. Instead, IORM guarantees that a particular group of sessions will always get at least a particular percentage of I/O bandwidth.

The actual implementation of IORM plans gives you a great deal of flexibility, as the next section details.

Architecture of an IORM Plan

You can use IORM to provision bandwidth in a number of ways. As mentioned previously, IORM is an extension of Database Resource Manager, so before describing these options, a brief review of key Database Resource Manager concepts is appropriate.

Database Resource Manager was described in detail in Chapter 2. The basic unit that Database Resource Manager uses to define resource limits is the consumer group, which can be identified in a wide variety of ways, from user names to applications to time of day, or any combination of these and other factors. Database Resource Manager creates a resource plan, which is used to allocate resources between different consumer groups. Individual sessions can switch consumer groups based on conditions, and the entire resource plan can be changed at runtime without any interruption in service.

A resource plan has multiple levels of priorities, with resources divided between different consumer groups at each level. A superior priority will take all the resources that are assigned to different consumer groups at that level—any remaining resources will be given to the next priority level, which assigns these resources based on its own directives. You will see the operation of levels and resource assignments in the next section, which details IORM at work.

You can assign allocation directives, which associate a consumer group with a percentage of resources, to three different entities, as shown in Figure 3-5.

You can divide I/O bandwidth between different workloads accessing a single database, which is referred to as *intradatabase* resource management.

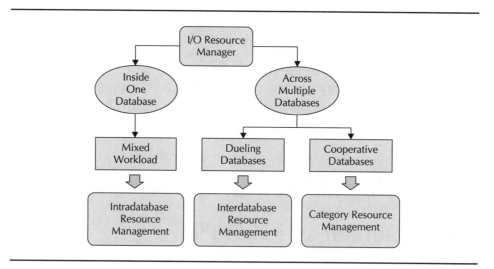

FIGURE 3-5. *IORM plans*

This type of division gives you the ability to allocate the overall percentage of I/O operations for a database between different consumer groups. For instance, if you had the same database being used by executives, people taking orders, and batch jobs running production reports, you could divide the resources between them to ensure an appropriate minimum level of service for each group. Intradatabase directives are part of an overall Database Resource Manager resource plan, defined in the Database Resource Manager framework.

You can also divide I/O bandwidth between different databases, which is referred to as *interdatabase* resource management. With interdatabase directives, you divide up the I/O for an entire cell between different databases that reside within that cell. Interdatabase directives are defined using the ALTER IORMPLAN CellCLI command. As this command implies, you can only have a single IORMPLAN defined for an Exadata Storage Server cell at a time. The interdatabase plan can have multiple levels in the same way that a plan defined by the Database Resource Manager can. Although an interdatabase resource plan is associated with a specific Exadata cell, the current plan persists through a cell reboot.

The last method of allocation of I/O resources is a category. Just as consumer groups allow you to collect groups of database resource consumers, a category is a collection of consumer groups. A consumer group is associated with a category when it is defined through the Database Resource Manager interface. A category plan divides resources between different categories, and can have multiple levels like the other types of plans.

The different levels of I/O plans are implemented in the following way. If a category plan exists, resources are first divided between the different categories, based on the directives in the plan. If a particular Exadata cell contains more than one database and an interdatabase plan exists, the allocated resources are again divided between the participants in the plan. Finally, the I/O resources allocated to the database are divided according to the intradatabase plan.

IORM at Work

With the previous brief description, you understand the basic architecture of how plans are defined for use by the I/O Resource Manager. The illustration shown in Figure 3-6 gives you some idea of how the various levels of the plan work together.

The plan is shown for a single Exadata cell, which is labeled Cell 1. For the sake of clarity, each section of the plan only has a single level.

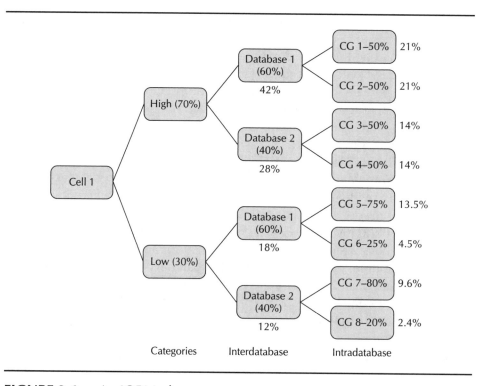

FIGURE 3-6. *An IORM plan*

However, please remember the way priority levels work—only the I/O resources not consumed by a superior level are made available to a lower level, where directives can further divide the allocation.

You can see that there are directives dividing I/O requests between two categories, simply named High and Low, with 70 percent and 30 percent allocation, respectively. Consumer groups 1, 2, 3, and 4 are part of the High category, with consumer groups 5, 6, 7, and 8 comprising the Low category.

There are interdatabase directives that divide the I/O bandwidth between Database 1, which gets 60 percent of the resources, and Database 2, which gets the remaining 40 percent. In practice, this means that I/O from Database 1 for the High category will get 42 percent of I/O bandwidth in times of oversubscription, since this is 60 percent of the 70 percent given to that category. Similarly, Database 1 for the Low category will get 18 percent of the I/O bandwidth, since this is 60 percent of the 30 percent allotted for that category.

There are also directives for intradatabase allocations, which further divide the I/O bandwidth. Consumer group 1 gets 50 percent of the I/O for Database 1, which works out to 21 percent of the overall I/O available—50 percent (the intradatabase percentage) of the 42 percent available for Database 1 in the High category. Consumer group 5, which gets 75 percent of the allocation for Database 1 in the Low category, ends up with 13.5 percent, 75 percent of the 18 percent for that category and database.

You can start to see how flexible I/O Resource Management can be, especially when you couple it with the fact that resource plans can be dynamically changed. But you may be wondering how the Exadata Storage Server Software is able to implement these potentially complex scenarios.

It really is not that hard, as you can see in Figure 3-7.

You can see that the end of the line is a simple queue used to grab I/O requests. The disk simply takes requests off the disk queue. Upstream from this queue are a number of separate queues, one for each consumer group. The percentage allocations assigned by the different directives in the plan are used to control which queue is used by IORM next. So if a queue for consumer group 1 calls for the group to get 80 percent of the requests for Database 1, IORM would go to that queue first 80 percent of the time. At the end of the line, the plan directs the I/O Resource Manager how to prioritize requests for each database.

IORM, like other aspects of the Exadata Storage Server Software stack, also makes sure that essential operations proceed without interruption. Write operations for the redo log, essential in completing write operations with integrity, and control file I/Os always take top priority, regardless of the resource plan. You can either assign DBWR (database writer) operations to a specific consumer group or leave them in a default group. You can also

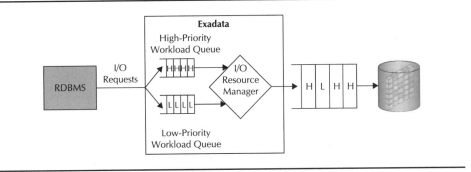

FIGURE 3-7.   *IORM queue management*

assign a priority for fast file creation operations, described earlier, as part of the overall plan.

The Exadata Storage Server provides a rich set of metrics, which can give you a great deal of information about the operation of IORM at the category, database, or consumer group level. For more details on these tracking options, please refer to the Exadata documentation.

Interacting with Exadata Storage Server Software

This chapter has described the special software features that come with the Exadata Storage Server. Most of these features just work and do not require extensive interaction from you. There is also software included with the Exadata Storage Server that is used to control and monitor the operation of the previously described features. You have seen a few mentions about this software earlier in this chapter, and will learn much more about the actual use of these programs and command interfaces in subsequent chapters, most notably Chapter 5 on management, as it relates to specific tasks. But before leaving this chapter, you should get a general introduction to the management software that comes with Exadata, as well as a general overview of the command interface to this software.

Management Software Components

Figure 3-8 illustrates the basic components of management software that control the Exadata Storage Server.

The key operational component is the CELLSRV process. This process handles incoming requests from the database grid and returns data to that grid. As the CELLSRV process handles all input and output operations to an Exadata Storage Server cell, this component is also responsible for implementing the directives imposed by the I/O Resource Manager.

The primary interface to the operations of the Exadata Storage Server for administrators is the Management Server, usually referred to as MS. Administrators talk to the MS through the CellCLI interface, which uses commands that will be described in more detail later. The Management Server runs on the Exadata Storage Server cell that it controls.

The Restart Server, or RS, monitors the status of the cell and the Management Server and, as the name implies, is used to restart either of these in the event of a failure.

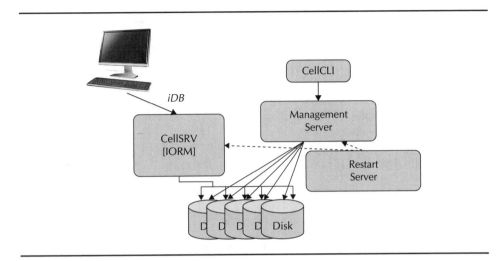

FIGURE 3-8. *Management components of the Exadata Storage Server*

Command Interfaces

Three command interfaces are used to interact with the Exadata Storage Server—the CellCLI, dcli, and ADRCI, which are described in the following sections.

CellCLI

The CellCLI is the command interface to the Management Server, which handles the configuration and monitoring of the Exadata Storage Server cells. The CellCLI operates on a set of *objects,* which are detailed in the CellCLI command overview section that follows. Each type of object has a set of attributes that affect the operation of a particular instance of the object. An administrator has five basic actions that can be performed on an object:

- LIST, which describes the object and its attributes, either at a summary level or with the modifier DETAIL for a more complete listing. You can use a WHERE clause with the LIST command to limit the object instances, which are displayed based on attribute values, as well as using this command for a single instance of an object.

- CREATE, which creates a new instance of the object.

- DROP, which removes a specific instance of an object.

- ALTER, which modifies the object and its attributes.
- DESCRIBE, which gives information about the object and its attributes.

The basic format of all CellCLI commands is

```
<verb> <object-type>   [ALL |object-name] [<options>]
```

You can use the LIST command on all objects, but some objects cannot be created, dropped or altered, as detailed in the object table (shown later; Table 3-3).

dcli

dcli is a way to issue commands on multiple cells from a single interface. You can use dcli to run either CellCLI commands or standard operating system commands on Exadata Storage Server cells. You cannot run dcli commands interactively—the commands are simply sent to a collection of cells and executed. You can specify the cells that should execute the commands with command options.

A dcli command returns a result that indicates if the command was completed successfully on all target cells, whether the command did not complete on some cells, or whether a local error prevented any of the commands from being executed. Keep in mind that if a local dcli process is terminated, the commands sent to the remote cells may still run.

ADRCI

ADRCI is the interface to the Automatic Diagnostic Repository (ADR), which is located on each Exadata Storage Server cell. This repository tracks information relating to any problems on the cell. ADRCI includes the Incident Packaging System, which places all relevant information into a package for communicating details of an incident to Oracle support.

CellCLI Command Overview

There are actually two types of commands used with CellCLI—the commands used to control the CellCLI process and those commands used on CellCLI objects. Tables 3-2 and 3-3 list the administrative commands and then the object types used by CellCLI.

Command	Description
HELP	Displays information about commands and options for CellCLI.
SET	Sets parameters that affect the operation of CellCLI, including DATEFORMAT, which controls how dates are displayed, and ECHO, which controls whether commands in a script file are shown on the screen.
SPOOL	Controls where the returned results from commands are sent with a variety of options, including those that allow results to be either sent to a new file or appended onto an existing file.
START or @	Runs a command file specified with the *filename* parameter following this command.
EXIT or QUIT	Leaves the CellCLI environment and returns to the operating system shell.
CREATE KEY	Generates a random hexadecimal string, which can be used as a client security key.
ASSIGN KEY	Used to assign a security key to a client or to remove a security key from a client.
CALIBRATE	Runs raw performance tests on a cell to validate cell performance.
EXPORT CELLDISK	Prepares cell disk(s) for movement to another cell.
IMPORT CELLDISK	Imports a cell disk to a new physical disk, used in conjunction with EXPORT CELLDISK when a cell is failing.

TABLE 3-2.   *CellCLI Administrative Commands*

Object Name	Description	LIST only?
CELL	The current or local cell, which holds disks and on which the CellCLI is running	N
CELLDISK	Associated with a particular physical disk or LUN	N
GRIDDISK	Logical portion of a cell disk, which is used to create an ASM disk group	N
IORMPLAN	The interdatabase and category portions of the I/O resource plan	N
KEY	A unique hexadecimal string used to identify a particular client	N
LUN	The address for a physical disk in a cell, automatically created for each cell disk	N
PHYSICALDISK	A physical disk in a cell	Y
ACTIVEREQUEST	A view of client I/O requests, based on a client or an application	Y
METRICCURRENT	Current value of a metric listed in METRICDEFINITION	Y
METRICDEFINITION	An object that describes a metric kept for a cell	Y
METRICHISTORY	Collection of past metric readings	Y
ALERTDEFINITION	Definition of alerts, which can be produced on a particular cell	Y
ALTERHISTORY	History of alerts that have been issued on the cell	N

TABLE 3-3. *CellCLI Objects (continued)*

Object Name	Description	LIST only?
THRESHOLD	Rules that define the level a metric must reach and how long it must maintain that level to generate an alert	N
FLASHCACHE	The part of the Exadata Smart Flash Cache allocated as a cache	N
FLASHCACHECONTENT	List of objects that are currently in the Exadata Smart Flash Cache	Y

TABLE 3-3. *CellCLI Objects*

Summary

This chapter covered the main features of Exadata software. Smart Scan and other types of offload processing from database nodes to the Exadata Storage Server provide a way for the performance of overall workloads to be significantly improved. This occurs by both reducing the amount of data sent to the database servers from storage and correspondingly reducing the amount of work required by those database servers.

Exadata Hybrid Columnar Compression is a completely new form of compression that can deliver a significant reduction in database storage for the tables or partitions that use this feature. Reduced data not only saves storage space, but also can improve query performance by requiring less I/O. EHCC has several compression options, and is appropriate for data that is not subject to much write activity.

Storage indexes work transparently to reduce the amount of I/O to satisfy query requirements for Smart Scan queries. The reduction means less work by the Exadata Storage Servers and improved performance where applicable.

The Exadata Smart Flash Cache uses flash-based storage to improve the retrieval performance for commonly used data, and Exadata software makes intelligent choices to determine what type of data can provide the biggest benefit from being stored in the flash cache.

I/O Resource Manager provides a way to provision I/O bandwidth among different groups of users. I/O Resource Manager can provision I/O operations within a single database, between databases, or between categories of databases.

This chapter closed with an overview of Exadata software used to interact with the Exadata Storage Servers for management as well as monitoring.

The next chapter will cover the hardware components of the Oracle Exadata Database Machine.

CHAPTER
4

Oracle Exadata Database Machine Platform Hardware Components

arlier in the book, we described how computer platforms evolved from systems consisting of tightly integrated servers, storage, and databases to systems assembled from components provided by multiple vendors. We also described how tightly integrated hardware and database solutions from single vendors are becoming popular again now that cost and complexity of integration of these components and the trade-offs in performance are realized. Now, we'll describe the pre-integrated system and prebalanced hardware platform that is the Oracle Exadata Database Machine product.

We'll begin by describing how system performance is optimized in hardware and how the components come together in the packaging of the Database Machine. We'll also take a look at how those components evolved in the Database Machine and how this evolution could affect your upgrade strategy. We'll then describe how the Oracle Exadata Database Machine is linked to the outside world for communications and how it is connected to other devices. Last, we'll cover high availability characteristics built into the hardware.

We do not intend to provide you with a recipe for building your own look-alike Database Machine from components in this chapter. The amount and complexity of the testing and integration of the Sun hardware and Oracle software required to deliver an Oracle Exadata Database Machine makes duplicating that effort a losing proposition. Whatever you might gain in cost savings by acquiring components separately is lost in the time and expense of testing and validating hardware and software components and in the time to delivery of a complete business solution. To make matters worse, Oracle is not able to support the Oracle Exadata Server Software for custom-built configurations. However, the information provided in this chapter should give you a fundamental understanding of how the Oracle Exadata Database Machine should be planned for, deployed, and upgraded within the technical architecture of your company or organization.

Finally, as you learned in the previous chapter, merely assembling hardware components leaves out the essential component of Exadata software, which provides unique advantages to the Database Machine.

Latency and Balance

Before we get into the specifics of the Oracle Exadata Database Machine, let's review some computer hardware basics to better understand the impact of server and storage components in enabling optimal performance.

Great performance occurs when a system is well balanced such that it can deliver the needed volume of data residing in storage to fully use the processing power of the CPUs which, in turn, return results to the business users in time for them to make decisions. Balancing large storage volumes, speedy and powerful processors, and adequate throughput is fundamental to the design of an optimal system. Of course, selection of all of these components by your platform vendor must also include having an eye on the pricing of the components and of the overall system that is assembled. Since the evolution of key system components proceeds at different rates over time, maintaining a balanced system over that system's lifetime presents its own set of challenges.

The Oracle Exadata Database Machine holds a reputation for delivering such a balanced system, dating from the platform's introduction through its subsequent iterations. We'll next explore how the components work together as an optimal system and will consider the roles of the Intel-based CPUs, memory, InfiniBand interconnect, and flash and disk storage technologies in the Database Machine.

Processor Speeds, Memory Capacity, and Storage

The concept of balanced computer systems has been well understood since the earliest computers were designed by hardware engineers. Early efforts by these engineers mandated specific custom processors, memory, and storage to form the systems. The invention of the microprocessor built upon the integrated circuit suddenly changed the speed of development and dynamics in the creation of new systems. As CPUs were supplied by a variety of competing vendors, the speed of change in this important component in a computer system escalated faster than some of the other key system components. Processors began to double in performance every 12 to 18 months, and memory capacities increased at a similar rate of change. But increases in speed of disk drives, relying on mechanical parts, occurred much more slowly. Disk capacities did increase at escalating rates, though, and so retrieving data became more problematic because of throughput limitations. To regain system balance, more disk spindles were needed to deliver data off of disk. More connections to storage over faster interconnects from the disks to memory were also needed.

So how does a system like the Oracle Exadata Database Machine deliver large data volumes from storage to the processors and eliminate time delays or latency in getting data to the CPUs? You will see in tables appearing later in this chapter that the Intel CPUs in the Oracle Exadata Database Machine have continued to advance in processing power and number of cores. Clearly, the closer data is to the CPUs in a system, the better the performance of queries and operations upon the data. Closest to the CPUs are small amounts of memory called cache. For example, Intel-based CPUs in the Oracle Exadata Database Machines contain multiple cache levels. The Level 1 cache is smaller than the Level 2 cache on a per-core basis. The smaller the cache size, the faster all of the information in the cache can be retrieved. Today's Level 1 and Level 2 caches generally contain tens to hundreds of KB per core. Since these cache sizes are so small, they typically contain data coherency objects and the like. Where Level 3 cache is present, it can scale into a few MB and might contain some data. Main memory in the database server nodes provides much more capacity. For example, each database server node contains 96GB of memory in X2-2 nodes and 1TB of memory in X2-8 nodes. The memory is linked to the CPUs via an on-die memory controller. However, the amount of memory in an individual node or even a cluster is not enough to hold the volume of data needed in large-scale transaction and data warehousing systems by itself.

Disk storage devices are sized to hold the remaining data in an uncompressed state, a compressed state, or a combination of the two options. Individual disks have grown in size to terabytes. But as we noted previously, they are limited in delivering needed throughput. To offset that, you'll observe that there are a large number of disks in the Database Machine. More recently, an additional storage solution delivering a higher level of performance entered the picture in the form of flash solid-state storage.

The Sun flash technology in the Oracle Exadata Database Machine that is the Exadata Smart Flash Cache scales to more than 5TB of storage in a Full Rack configuration and provides much faster throughput. It functions much like the cache in a conventional storage array, providing an important intermediate level of storage larger in capacity than memory but also providing more throughput than disk. To assure the flash will not wear out prematurely, the flash controller hardware features "wear leveling" to assure writes and erase cycles are rotated among all of the blocks in the device. (There are actually 32GB of pages on each Smart Flash Cache card for every 24GB of raw storage presented.) Even where 25TB per day are written to flash in an Exadata Storage Server cell, the design point of supporting 100,000 write and/or erase cycles will not be exceeded in a five-year period.

Given the introduction of faster components and the growing popularity of clustered databases and grid computing, another key consideration is the system interconnect throughput rate. The interconnect serves two purposes in an Oracle Exadata Database Machine. It links together database nodes forming a cluster, and it provides connections between the database server nodes and storage cells. Oracle actually began to deliver a low-level database communications protocol that supported InfiniBand prior to the delivery of the first Database Machine. A Zero-loss Zero-copy Datagram Protocol (ZDP) is used in communications between the database and the Exadata Storage Servers, and is based on the Reliable Datagram Sockets (RDS) OpenFabrics Enterprise Edition. The InfiniBand interconnect protocol uses Direct Memory Access (DMA).

Prior to the introduction of the first Database Machine, Oracle-based clusters were more commonly configured by hardware vendors and IT organizations with an Ethernet interconnect. Such Ethernet interconnects at that point in time delivered a bandwidth rate of 1 Gb per second. The InfiniBand interconnect introduced in the first Database Machine greatly improved bandwidth, supporting a rate of 20 Gb per second. The bandwidth rate was doubled to 40 Gb per second in the original Sun Oracle Database Machine with the inclusion of Sun's InfiniBand switch technology.

So, how do these components work together when processing a typical workload?

How Hardware Components Work Together

Figure 4-1 illustrates the relative latency and capacity of the components. When the goal is optimal performance, you will want to have the most recently updated or queried data where it can be accessed again the fastest—generally first in the Level 3 cache (if present), then in memory, flash, and finally in disk storage.

For online transaction processing systems, when an insert or update of a row occurs, it is critical that recovery of committed transactions takes place if the system fails for any reason. Most systems designers view physical disk as the one part of a system that is nonvolatile, in that once a row is physically written to disk, it can be recovered. That said, where large numbers of transactions are being updated, such systems are usually configured with as much memory as possible to speed access, since the most recently updated transactions can be found in memory.

A data warehouse workload is quite different and often requires retrieval of a large number of rows that will not fit into memory. For this reason, the

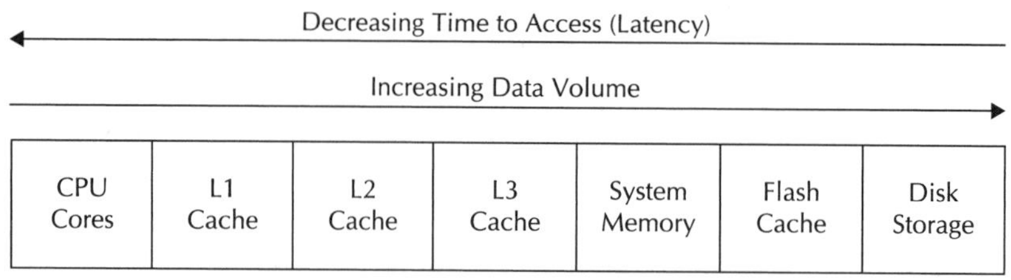

FIGURE 4-1. *Server data storage hierarchy*

configuration focus turns to speed of transfer of the rows from storage (or throughput). Of course, if the same data is held in cache, memory, or flash as a result of earlier similar queries, the need to go to disk disappears. The Exadata Storage Server Software also performs query offload processing in storage, returning projected columns from selected rows through Smart Scans to further speed this processing.

Let's explore a bit deeper what happens when a query occurs. Needed data typically would be looked for in the L3 cache, followed by main memory, followed by flash, and followed last by disk. The lowest level in the system where the data is found then passes it back in the other direction up the line.

Of course, all of this takes place transparently to a user of the database. A well-designed system has a database optimally "tuned" to the hardware and taking maximum advantage of these components. That is one reason why the Oracle database is able to perform optimally on the Oracle Exadata Database Machine. The ratios of the components and interconnects are well thought out and perform optimally for a variety of Oracle workloads. The database is deployed with preset initialization parameters that are aligned to the system resources available. The Exadata Storage Server Software further optimizes database performance by pushing some of the key database processing into the Exadata Storage Server cells, as described in Chapter 3.

Oracle Exadata Database Machine Packaging Basics

This brings us to the specifics of Oracle Exadata Database Machines and how the components are packaged. Let's begin with the building blocks of the systems that are built upon standard Sun servers, the database server nodes, and Exadata Storage Server cells. Today, each database server node in the X2-2 Database Machine contains two sockets (or eight sockets in each node in the X2-8 Database Machine) and memory, as well as enough disk storage for the operating system and the Oracle database software. Table 4-1 shows the evolution of the database server nodes through 2010.

Database Server Node	HP Oracle Database Machine	Sun Oracle Database Machine	Oracle Exadata Database Machine X2-2	Oracle Exadata Database Machine X2-8
Date of Introduction	September 2008	October 2009	September 2010	September 2010
Server Building Block	HP Proliant DL 360-G5	Sun Fire X4170	Sun Fire X4170 M2	Sun Fire X4800
CPUs	2 Quad Core Intel Xeon 5430 (2.66 GHz)	2 Quad Core Intel Xeon E5540 (2.53 GHz)	2 Six Core Intel Xeon X5670 (2.93 GHz)	8 Eight Core Intel Xeon X7560 (2.26 GHz)
Memory	32GB RAM	72GB RAM	96GB RAM	1TB RAM
Disk	4 146GB SAS 10K RPM disks	4 146GB SAS 10K RPM disks	4 300GB SAS 10K RPM disks	8 300GB SAS 10K RPM disks
Host Bus Adapter (HBA)	E200i with 128MB battery-backed cache	Controller with 512MB battery-backed write cache	Controller with 512MB battery-backed write cache	Controller with 512MB battery-backed write cache
Host Channel Adapter (HCA)	Dual-port (20 Gb/second) InfiniBand HCA	Dual-port QDR (40 Gb/second) InfiniBand HCA	Dual-port QDR (40 Gb/second) InfiniBand HCA	4 Dual-port QDR (40 Gb/second) InfiniBand HCA
Ethernet Ports	2 embedded Gb/second Ethernet ports and port for HP iLO2	4 embedded Gb/second Ethernet ports and port for Sun ILOM	2 X 10 GbE ports based on Intel 82599, 4 X 1 GbE ports, 1 ILOM port	8 X 10 GbE ports based on Intel 82599, 8 X 1 GbE ports, 1 ILOM port

TABLE 4-1. *Evolution of Database Server Nodes*

Each Exadata Storage Server Cell in these configurations contains two CPUs and memory, as well as 12 disk drives and four flash cards. The Exadata Storage Server cells include CPUs and memory, also running an operating system and Exadata Storage Server Software that provides "intelligent storage" database optimization that improves overall performance of the platform. Table 4-2 shows the evolution of the Exadata Storage Server cells through 2010.

Exadata Storage Server Cell	For HP Oracle Database Machine	For Sun Oracle Database Machine	For Oracle Exadata Database Machine X2-2 & X2-8
Date of Introduction	September 2008	October 2009	September 2010
Cell Building Block	HP Proliant DL 180-G5	Sun Fire X4275	Sun Fire X4270 M2
CPUs / cell	2 Quad Core Intel Xeon 5430 (2.66 GHz)	2 Quad Core Intel Xeon E5540 (2.53 GHz)	2 Six Core Intel Xeon L5640 (2.26 GHz)
Memory / cell	8GB RAM	24GB RAM	24GB RAM
Exadata Smart Flash Cache/cell	None	4 96GB Sun Flash F20 PCIe (384GB/ cell)	4 96GB Sun Flash F20 PCIe (384GB/ cell)
Flash Data Bandwidth/cell (maximum)	N/A	3.6 GB/second uncompressed data	3.6 GB/second uncompressed data
High Performance Disk Capacity/cell	12 × 450GB	12 × 600GB (7.2TB raw disk capacity; 2TB uncompressed user data capacity)	12 × 600GB (7.2TB raw disk capacity; 2TB uncompressed user data capacity)
High Performance Disk Bandwidth/ cell (maximum)	1 GB/second uncompressed data	1.5 GB/second uncompressed data	1.8 GB/second uncompressed data

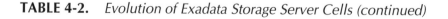

TABLE 4-2. *Evolution of Exadata Storage Server Cells (continued)*

Exadata Storage Server Cell	For HP Oracle Database Machine	For Sun Oracle Database Machine	For Oracle Exadata Database Machine X2-2 & X2-8
High Capacity Disk Capacity/cell	12 × 1TB (12TB raw disk capacity; 3.3TB uncompressed user data capacity)	12 × 2TB (24TB raw disk capacity; 7TB uncompressed user data capacity)	12 × 2TB (24TB raw disk capacity; 7TB uncompressed user data capacity)
High Capacity Disk Bandwidth/ cell (maximum)	0.75 GB/second uncompressed data	0.85 GB/second uncompressed data	1.0 GB/second uncompressed data
Host Bus Adapter (HBA)	P400 with 256MB battery-backed cache	Controller with 512MB battery-backed write cache	Controller with 512MB battery-backed write cache
Host Channel Adapter (HCA)	Dual-port (20 Gb/ second) InfiniBand HCA	Dual-port QDR (40 Gb/second) InfiniBand HCA	Dual-port QDR (40 Gb/second) InfiniBand HCA
Ethernet Ports	Embedded Gb/ second Ethernet port and port for HP iLO2	Embedded Gb/ second Ethernet port and port for Sun ILOM	Four 1 GbE ports and additional ILOM port

TABLE 4-2. *Evolution of Exadata Storage Server Cells*

A Rack contains database server nodes, Exadata Storage Server cells, InfiniBand switches, an Ethernet switch, and power. Racks come in Quarter, Half, and Full Rack configurations. Tables 4-3, 4-4, and 4-5 show the evolution of the Quarter Rack, Half Rack, and Full Rack standard configurations through 2010. Though the components within these configurations will continue to change over time (maybe by the time you read this book), there are some basics as to the packaging that should hold true for these configurations that you should understand, regardless of what version of the hardware you have.

Quarter Rack	HP Oracle Database Machine	Sun Oracle Database Machine	Oracle Exadata Database Machine X2-2
Date of Introduction	September 2008	October 2009	September 2010
Server Nodes	N/A	2	2
Storage Cells	N/A	3	3
Total Server Node CPUs and Cores	N/A	4 CPUs/16 cores	4 CPUs/ 24 cores
Total Memory	N/A	144GB	192GB
Total Flash	N/A	1.1TB	1.1TB
InfiniBand Switches	N/A	2	2
High Performance Disk Capacity	N/A	21TB	21TB
High Capacity Disk Capacity	N/A	72TB	72TB

TABLE 4-3. *Evolution of Database Machine Quarter Rack Configuration*

Not shown in the previous tables is the Ethernet switch provided in each Rack for administration of the Database Machine. A keyboard, video display unit, and mouse (KVM) are provided for local administration with X2-2 configurations. Also included is a spares kit that includes an extra disk and extra Smart Flash Cache card for the Quarter and Half Rack or two extra disks and two extra Smart Flash Cache cards for the Full Rack, and InfiniBand cables.

Oracle has tightly defined what optimal ratios of components (such as processor cores, memory, and throughput) in database server nodes and storage cells should be. Though it is possible to activate only part of a Rack configuration, in Oracle Exadata Database Machines, Oracle recommends that you maintain the ratio of four database server nodes for every seven storage cells in X2-2 configurations if you do. That is similar to the ratio that exists in the Half and Full Racks in X2-2 configurations. For X2-2 Rack configurations where you activate just a quarter of a Full Rack, use the ratio of two database server nodes and three storage cells. The only deviation to

Half Rack	HP Oracle Database Machine	Sun Oracle Database Machine	Oracle Exadata Database Machine X2-2
Date of Introduction	September 2008	October 2009	September 2010
Server Nodes	4	4	4
Storage Cells	7	7	7
Total Server Node CPUs and Cores	8 CPUs/ 32 cores	8 CPUs/ 32 cores	8 CPUs/ 48 cores
Total Memory	128GB	288GB	384GB
Total Flash	N/A	2.6TB	2.6TB
InfiniBand Switches	2	2	3
High Performance Disk Capacity	38TB	50TB	50TB
High Capacity Disk Capacity	84TB	168TB	168TB

TABLE 4-4.   *Evolution of Database Machine Half Rack Configuration*

these ratios might occur where additional storage is to be used as part of an Information Lifecycle Management (ILM) strategy for online backups and the storage is configured in a separate rack.

High-Performance disks (referenced as SAS disks in early configurations) are generally selected where the goal is optimal performance, while the High-Capacity disk (referenced as SATA disks in early configurations) is selected when the goal is to provide more storage capacity in a rack. High-Performance and High-Capacity storage cannot be intermingled in the same Database Machine Rack configuration. However, separate Database Machine Racks containing High-Performance and High-Capacity disks can be linked, provided the storage in each is configured in different disk groups.

In the previous tables, we indicated disk capacity but not the amount of user data that can be stored. This amount is highly variable. Since Oracle

Full Rack	HP Oracle Database Machine	Sun Oracle Database Machine	Oracle Exadata Database Machine X2-2	Oracle Exadata Database Machine X2-8
Date of Introduction	September 2008	October 2009	September 2010	September 2010
Server Nodes	8	8	8	2
Storage Cells	14	14	14	14
Total Server Node CPUs and Cores	16 CPUs/ 64 cores	16 CPUs/ 64 cores	16 CPUs/ 96 cores	16 CPUs/ 128 cores
Total Memory	256GB	576GB	768GB	2TB
Total Flash	N/A	5.3TB	5.3TB	5.3TB
InfiniBand Switches	4	3	3	3
High Performance Disk Capacity	76TB	100TB	100TB	100TB
High Capacity Disk Capacity	168TB	336TB	336TB	336TB

TABLE 4-5. *Evolution of Database Machine Full Rack Configuration*

fully mirrors the data in a standard database installation, the amount of data you can store on the available disk is immediately cut in half. You can also choose to mirror data twice for even higher levels of availability, which will result in only a third of the available disk being used for data. You should also consider that database logs, temp spaces, and other database structures will take up some space. However, the Advanced Compression Option and Hybrid Columnar Compression, described elsewhere in this book, might allow you to store far more data on this storage than the available space left after taking these factors into account.

When sizing the Database Machine, Oracle should be consulted. Disk capacity is but one sizing parameter used in selecting the size of the Rack and type of disk. Different workloads have different characteristics and demands. Oracle will sometimes use comparative sizing techniques to compare current platform characteristics to those of the Database Machine to establish a common baseline for expected performance. The fact that the Database Machine provides a balanced server, storage, and throughput configuration by design helps assure scalability for a variety of workloads.

Of course, workloads can become quite complex where the Database Machine is deployed supporting multiple Oracle databases for purposes of server and storage consolidation. Projected future workloads are often less understood. In such situations, Oracle uses predictive sizing techniques to compare the impact of potential workload variability on performance and recommend the right platform configuration.

Installation and Initial Deployment Considerations

The Oracle Exadata Database Machine is a large and heavy server. Tables 4-6, 4-7, and 4-8 outline the physical characteristics of the Database Machine Rack configurations.

Quarter Rack	HP Oracle Database Machine	Sun Oracle Database Machine	Oracle Exadata Database Machine X2-2
Date of Introduction	September 2008	October 2009	September 2010
Frame Dimensions	N/A	42U 78.66 inches (1988 mm) H × 23.62 inches (600 mm) W × 47.24 inches (1200 mm) D	42U 78.66 inches (1988 mm) H × 23.62 inches (600 mm) W × 47.24 inches (1200 mm) D
Weight	N/A	907 lbs. (411.4 kg)	902 lbs. (409.1 kg)
Maximum Power	N/A	3.6 kW (3.7 kVA)	3.6 kW (3.7 kVA)
Cooling Maximum	N/A	12,300 BTU/hour	12,300 BTU/hour

TABLE 4-6. *Database Machine Quarter Rack Physical Characteristics*

Half Rack	HP Oracle Database Machine	Sun Oracle Database Machine	Oracle Exadata Database Machine X2-2
Date of Introduction	September 2008	October 2009	September 2010
Frame Dimensions	43 inches (1,092 mm) H × 24 inches (610 mm) W × 39.7 inches (1,008 mm) D	42U 78.66 inches (1,988 mm) H × 23.62 inches (600 mm) W × 47.24 inches (1200 mm) D	42U 78.66 inches (1,988 mm) H × 23.62 inches (600 mm) W × 47.24 inches (1,200 mm) D
Weight	820 lbs. (373 kg)	1,307 lbs. (594.1 kg)	1,329 lbs. (602.8 kg)
Maximum Power	7.051 KW	7.2 kW (7.3 kVA)	7.2 kW (7.3kVA)
Cooling Maximum	22,491 BTU/hour	24,600 BTU/hour	24,600 BTU/hour

TABLE 4-7. *Database Machine Half Rack Physical Characteristics*

Prior to installation, Oracle works with you to assure that the Database Machine can be moved in a vertical fashion from your loading dock to the data center as part of the on-site planning process. Oracle's Advanced Customer Services (ACS) are often additionally priced into Exadata purchases and include pre-installation planning identification of available network addresses for the InfiniBand switch, the internal Ethernet switch used for administration, and other Ethernet connections that are required. After the Database Machine is installed, ACS then configures and networks all of the servers and creates a fully mirrored default Oracle database. Performance and functionality of the installed database is then validated.

The number of network addresses needed for installation will depend on the Rack configuration. For example, the Oracle Exadata Database Machine X2-2 Full Rack InfiniBand switches require 22 addresses (one for each of eight database server nodes and 14 Exadata Storage Server cells in the Full Rack). These can be on a private subnet if the InfiniBand network is not

Full Rack	HP Oracle Database Machine	Sun Oracle Database Machine	Oracle Exadata Database Machine X2-2	Oracle Exadata Database Machine X2-8
Date of Introduction	September 2008	October 2009	September 2010	September 2010
Frame Dimensions	42U 78.7 inches (2,000 mm) H × 24 inches (613 mm) W × 39.7 inches (1,015 mm) D	42U 78.66 inches (1988 mm) H × 23.62 inches (600 mm) W × 47.24 inches (1,200 mm) D	42U 78.66 inches (1,988 mm) H × 23.62 inches (600 mm) W × 47.24 inches (1,200 mm) D	42U 78.66 inches (1,988 mm) H × 23.62 inches (600 mm) W × 47.24 inches (1,200 mm) D
Weight	1,350 lbs. (614 kg)	2,119 lbs. (963.2 kg)	2,131 lbs (966.6 kg)	2,080 lbs (943.5 kg)
Maximum Power	13.7 kW	14.0 kW (14.3 kVA)	14.0 kW (14.3 kVA)	14.0 kW (14.3 kVA)
Cooling Maximum	48,000 BTU/ hour	47,800 BTU/ hour	47,800 BTU/ hour	48,600 BTU/ hour

TABLE 4-8. *Database Machine Full Rack Physical Characteristics*

going to be exposed outside of the Database Machine. Racks are also typically configured with two Ethernet subnets. For an Oracle Exadata Database Machine X2-2 Full Rack, 70 addresses are needed to support connections for Integrated Lights Out Management (ILOM), the KVM, other management, client/application access, and clustered servers. The ILOM connections enable monitoring of hardware generated alerts to Sun's Ops Center showing status and remote power management, as described in Chapter 5. The ILOM alerts can also be forwarded to Enterprise Manager Grid Control via an Ops Center connector. As of the release of Exadata Storage Server Software version 11.2.1.3.1, automatic service requests (ASRs) are generated and transmitted to Oracle by an ASR manager when faults occur in database server nodes and Exadata Storage Server cells.

When the Database Machine is installed, air cooling should flow from the front of a Database Machine Rack to its back, where the hotter air is then exhausted. Cool air inlets consisting of perforated tiles should be placed in front of each unit. Assuming each floor tile can deliver 400 cubic feet per minute (CFM), each Quarter Rack would require one perforated floor tile, each Half Rack would require three perforated floor tiles, and each Full Rack would require four perforated floor tiles to deliver the necessary cooling.

Each X2-2 Rack, regardless of configuration, comes with two 15 kVA Power Distribution Units (PDUs), while each X2-8 Rack comes with two 24 kVA PDUs. Two PDUs are provided for redundancy purposes. For X2-2 systems shipped to the Americas, Japan, or Taiwan, low-voltage, single- or three-phase PDUs are available in the packaging. For other locations in the world, high-voltage, single- or three-phase PDUs are available for X2-2 systems. Regardless of location, there are three plugs per PDU for X2-2 Racks where the PDUs are single phase (six plugs total), and just one plug per PDU where the PDUs are three phase (two plugs total). For X2-8 Full Racks, there are two plugs per low-voltage, three-phase PDU (four plugs total) in systems shipped to the Americas, Japan, or Taiwan and also two plugs per high-voltage, three-phase PDU (four plugs total) in systems shipped to other countries.

The hardware comes with a one-year parts and labor warranty with a four-hour response time for priority 1 problems. Where 24 × 7 support is needed, Premier Support should be selected and offers 24 hours/7 days per week coverage and a two-hour response time where priority 1 problems are reported. Oracle maintains a single support line for reporting hardware and software problems. A disk retention service is offered so that failed disks that are under warranty can be replaced without returning them to Oracle, and is especially useful where data of a very sensitive nature is stored on the drives.

Some organizations require more help in order to accelerate their readiness and early implementation. Oracle offers a variety of services ranging from "Blueprint" architecture services to migration, consolidation strategy, and managed services. Many of Oracle's partners also offer complementary and extended services, including applications and data warehousing data model implementations.

Upgrade Choices for Existing Systems

As workloads change and the business user community and data grow, you could face the need to upgrade your system. For organizations that want to grow an existing footprint, several choices exist. Within configurations that are partially full X2-2 Racks, Quarter Rack to Half Rack and Half Rack to

Full Rack field upgrades are available. These upgrades to the larger configurations include the additional components necessary to match the configurations noted in Tables 4-4 and 4-5. In addition to providing additional database server nodes and Exadata Storage Server cells (or Racks containing those), upgrades include additional InfiniBand and Ethernet cables to connect the components and a spares kit. When growing beyond a Full Rack, additional Full Racks can be added by connecting them through the third "spine" switch present in the Full Racks. Up to eight Full Racks can be connected through the spine switches without the need for additional external switches. (A Half Rack may also be connected to a Full Rack or another Half Rack where a third spine switch is present.) Note that Oracle does not allow re-racking of servers and switches since there is substantial testing by Oracle behind the predefined configurations to assure better support and maintainability. However, additional storage can be put into an external rack for purposes of Information Lifecycle Management.

Where organizations anticipate a future need to rapidly add database server nodes and Exadata Storage Server cells caused by changing business conditions and want to avoid the time associated with ordering additional components and awaiting delivery, an alternative is to buy a larger standard configuration and only activate the nodes and cells initially needed (licensing the Oracle software components accordingly). As noted previously, when taking this approach, the ratio of database server nodes to Exadata Storage Server cells activated should be the same as that in a similar Half Rack or Full Rack.

As hardware ages, additional choices enter the picture. Oracle has supported the ability to connect different versions of Racks together, as illustrated where the HP Oracle Database Machine can be connected to the Oracle Exadata Database Machine using Cx4-to-QSFP cables. Newer Oracle Exadata Database Machine X2-2 components can be added to partially filled Database Machines purchased earlier as Sun Oracle Database Machines. However, some organizations might choose to use such opportunities to deploy the completely new platform for the most performance-demanding applications and recycle the older configurations for other applications as separate self-contained complexes.

Connecting to the Database Machine

Business users can communicate directly with the Database Machine via Ethernet connections to the database server nodes that contain Ethernet ports. More commonly for modern applications, the business user connects to an application server that is networked to the Database Machine. An internal Ethernet switch is provided in the Database Machine, but that switch is intended for administration purposes. For higher-speed communications and support of other devices, gateway products and media servers can be connected to the Database Machine via InfiniBand, provided there is no change made to the Oracle InfiniBand software on the Database Machine. For example, Oracle Exalogic hardware running WebLogic can be connected to the Exadata Database Machine using InfiniBand and provide load balancing and failover integration from the middle tier through a GridLink for Exadata feature in the software.

Media servers are commonly used as intermediate servers in performing tape backups. For example, Sun Fire X4275s or similar servers might serve as Oracle Secure Backup Media Servers. Two or more servers are typically configured for high availability and performance and connect the Database Machine into a wider InfiniBand QDR network. Where performance requirements are lower, media servers might be connected directly into Ethernet ports. The TCP/IP protocol is used over the network connections by Oracle Secure Backup. The media servers are also connected to a Fibre Channel SAN that is then attached to a large-scale tape backup device. One RMAN channel is set up per tape drive.

Figure 4-2 illustrates how a typical configuration might look where media servers are provided to connect the Database Machine to a tape

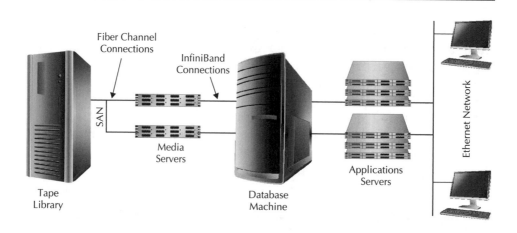

FIGURE 4-2.   *Typical deployment with media servers and applications servers*

library and applications servers are provided to link business users to the Database Machine and host the front ends of the applications. Where InfiniBand connections are shown, standard 4X QDR InfiniBand copper cables with QSFP connectors can provide connection lengths of up to five meters. InfiniBand 4X QDR optical cables can extend the distance limitation, since cables with lengths as long as up to 100 meters can be deployed.

Highly Available Hardware Considerations

In Chapter 6, we will describe Oracle's Maximum Availability Architecture (MAA) and strategies for deploying to it. Oracle's MAA strategy is a mixture of hardware and software components designed to minimize planned and unplanned downtime. In this section, we'll simply summarize some of the high-availability features included in the hardware.

Single points of hardware failure are eliminated in the standard Rack configurations. Redundant hot-swappable power supplies are built into the Database Machine database server nodes and Exadata Storage Server cells. All Racks are configured with at least two InfiniBand leaf switches, and connections are configured in a redundant fashion. Where multiple Racks are deployed with the additional spine switch, redundant connections are also provided between the spine switches. RAC assures that database server node failures are tolerated, and the Exadata Storage Server Software assures that Exadata Storage Server cell failures are tolerated. In standard installations, ASM is used to fully mirror data across storage. A minimum of three Exadata Storage Server cells are required to assure redundancy, since the Oracle Clusterware Oracle Cluster Registry (OCR) requires "voting" to manage recovery from a failure.

The storage supports bad block mapping and performance pipelining, and the disks in the database server nodes and Exadata Storage Server cells are hot-swappable. When a disk fails in an Exadata Storage Database Server cell, the database remains available and a replaced disk will rebuild itself automatically. As noted earlier, disk retention services enable Oracle to replace any failed disk without return of the failed disk to Oracle.

Database Machines can be configured in "stretch clusters" for purposes of high availability. The current distance limitation is 100 meters between

Database Machines due to the InfiniBand cable length limitations mentioned previously. ASM failure groups must be created at each separate site, and Exadata storage should be added to the local failure group. A third failure group to provide "voting" disk in a quorum is deployed on shared storage such as a Network File System (NFS) filer. In Chapter 6, we will also discuss disaster recovery scenarios where Database Machines are placed at physical locations much more widely separated.

It is possible to have multiple Database Machine environments with different patch levels on the same Database Machine Rack or complex. This might be particularly desirable for deploying production, test, and development environments. Such environments must be physically partitioned and not share database server nodes or Exadata Storage Server cells.

Summary

In this chapter, we covered the basics of balanced hardware and how the components in such platforms work together to achieve optimal performance. We then discussed how Oracle Exadata Database Machine components are configured in complete rack configurations. As you have seen, the overall system is built upon leading-edge CPUs, interconnect technology, and storage that evolves over time. Oracle is closely following the evolution curve of each of these components and continually reassessing how to incorporate these components in a balanced system.

Individuals in IT organizations will sometimes ask whether they can substitute their own components within the system or otherwise modify the standard configurations. Oracle does not generally allow such changes. For example, with the exception of possibly substituting your own Ethernet switch for the administrative switch that is provided, Oracle states that any other custom components and devices must reside outside of the Oracle Exadata Database Machine. However, such policy does assure the right balance, reliability, and support that most IT organizations seek from a complete Oracle platform.

Since the focus of this chapter was the hardware platform, we said very little about the software. We certainly covered that topic in Chapters 2 and 3, and refer to it throughout the rest of the book. But clearly, the differentiation for this platform is that it is a tightly integrated Oracle hardware and software solution. That makes it a unique offering compared to other Oracle database deployment options on other hardware platforms.

In a sense, what Oracle has created is a unique platform by assembling standard server, storage, interconnect, and database components. By building a system of standard components, Oracle should be able to take advantage of future breakthroughs in these components and continue to deliver the highest-performing complete and manageable platforms at competitive prices. In the end, you will be the true evaluator of that as you build and update your Oracle Exadata Database Machine footprint.

PART

II

Best Practices

CHAPTER
5

Managing the
Exadata Database
Machine

nce the Oracle Exadata Database Machine is deployed in your data center, you are required to perform ongoing administration tasks on its software and hardware components, as you would with any other system.

The initial setup and configuration of the Database Machine is typically priced into Exadata proposals by Oracle and performed by Oracle Advanced Customer Services (ACS) upon delivery and installation of the hardware. The setup process includes the installation and configuration of the operating system and the Oracle software, and the configuration of InfiniBand and Ethernet networks. At the end of the setup process, the Database Machine is ready and configured and includes a working Oracle database. You are then able to create additional new databases and start migrating databases from non-Exadata platforms, or start deploying your brand-new database applications. Since you might want to better understand the installation process or might want to configure additional databases on the Exadata Storage Servers on your own, we cover this process in this chapter.

The Exadata Storage Server Software components, including the Exadata Storage Server Software and the Oracle Linux operating system, need to be administered on an ongoing basis. The administration tasks include patching and upgrading of the operating system and the Exadata Storage Server Software, and monitoring of the software and hardware components. Apart from the regular administration activities, you may also perform tasks related to the setup of advanced Exadata Storage Server Software features, such as I/O Resource Manager and Exadata security.

This chapter will discuss the different processes and tools available for performing administration tasks on the Exadata Storage Server components. The topics covered in the remainder of this chapter are focused on the architecture, administration, and monitoring of the Exadata Storage Servers.

NOTE
This chapter does not focus on administration of the database servers in the Exadata Database Machine. The database servers are managed, maintained, and monitored similar to a regular Oracle Database 11g Release 2 utilizing Real Application Clusters (RAC) and Automatic Storage Management (ASM). When required, you would patch the Oracle database and the grid infrastructure software, perform administration tasks, monitor and tune the databases, back up the database and operating system, and perform database upgrades, just as you would on standard Oracle systems. Moreover, you need to manage the database server nodes operating system (Oracle Linux or Solaris) and the hardware as you would normally manage any other Intel-based servers in your data center. Please also refer to Chapter 2.

Exadata Storage Server Architecture

At a high level, the Exadata Database Machine is composed of a database grid, a storage grid, and the InfiniBand network that provides the unified fabric for storage and database interinstance communication. The Oracle Sun servers that comprise the database and the storage grids are built using open standards-based hardware, and are made of components that are normally found in enterprise-class servers such as CPUs, memory, PCIe slots, hard disks, Host Channel Adapters (HCA), and Ethernet interfaces. The operating system managing the Oracle Sun servers that are the Oracle Exadata Storage Server cells in the storage grid is Oracle Linux.

In the following section, we will discuss the architecture of the software components of Exadata Database Machine in detail.

Database Server Software Components

The database grid of the Database Machine utilizes Oracle ASM as the storage management layer. Oracle ASM acts as the cluster volume manager for the storage served by the Exadata Storage Servers, and is the only software that can be used to manage the storage grid of the Database Machine. Moreover, you are not allowed to directly attach or mount the storage served by the Exadata Storage Servers to any other server or storage volume manager.

Oracle ASM provides data placement and management services on the Exadata Storage Servers, stripes and mirrors the database extents into chunks called ASM allocation units (ASM AU, also called ASM extents), and spreads them across the disks served by the Exadata Storage Servers. Oracle ASM provides high availability of the extents and eliminates single points of failure by keeping a mirrored copy of the extent available at all times. The striping of data by ASM provides optimal I/O performance, as the I/O requests will be parallelized across all the available Exadata Storage Servers in the grid that houses the striped data.

Oracle ASM will be active during the initial placement of data, and also when performing ongoing management operations, such as rebalancing of data across the Exadata Storage Servers. The database server processes initiate I/O requests directly with the Exadata Storage Servers and bypass the Oracle ASM instance, thus reducing the unnecessary overhead of involving ASM for each database I/O operation. The direct communication of the database with the storage is possible because the database server stores the extent maps of ASM files in the SGA, which enables read/write I/O requests directly with the Exadata Storage Servers without requiring the Oracle ASM instance. This method of initiating I/O requests is the same when the ASM files reside on non-Exadata–based storage.

The database server process and the Oracle ASM instance communicate with Exadata Storage Servers using the *i*DB protocol. *i*DB is a data transfer protocol implemented in the Oracle kernel and provides intelligence that enables the database and ASM instances to utilize Exadata-specific features such as offload processing and I/O Resource Manager (IORM). *i*DB is built upon Reliable Datagram Sockets (RDS), which is the same protocol used by database RAC interinstance communication over the InfiniBand network. RDS incorporates optimizations such as Remote Direct Memory Access (RDMA) to minimize the network protocol overhead by allowing distributed applications to transfer data directly between their memory structures without involving the operating system memory, a feature that is more commonly referred to as Zero-copy Datagram Protocol (ZDP).

The RDS protocol also enables *i*DB to facilitate I/O bandwidth allocations for Exadata IORM, and provides bandwidth aggregation and failover of the InfiniBand network. The *i*DB communication is facilitated by

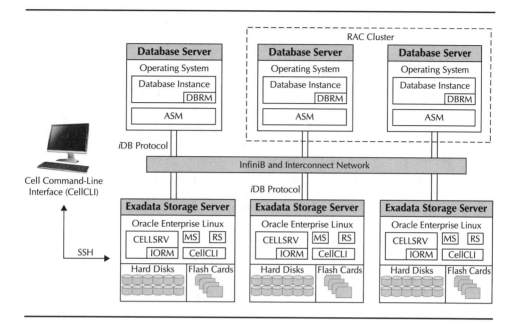

FIGURE 5-1. *Software components of the Oracle Exadata Database Machine*

software processes that reside on the database nodes and the Exadata Storage Servers, as shown in Figure 5-1.

The Database Resource Manager (DBRM) component of the Oracle database performs management of CPU and I/O resources. DBRM communicates with Exadata Storage Server processes for performing I/O Resource Management for intradatabase resource manager plans. IORM utilizes the DBRM intradatabase plans generated by administrators, and regulates the I/O utilization among different consumer groups within the database.

Exadata Storage Server Software Components

The storage grid in the Exadata Database Machine is composed of multiple Exadata Storage Servers, with each server providing a network-accessible storage device to be utilized by Oracle ASM. The operating system managing the Exadata Storage Servers is Oracle Linux, and the Oracle software providing the core features of the Exadata Storage Server is Oracle Exadata Storage Server Software.

The Exadata Storage Server Software consists of the following components:

- **Cell Server (CELLSRV)** The CELLSRV process is the main kernel of Exadata Storage Server Software and is responsible for serving *i*DB requests initiated by the database and ASM instances. The CELLSRV process handles simple block I/O requests along with offload processing requests. The CELLSRV process implements IORM plans and performs throttling of I/O bandwidth based on I/O priorities as defined by the plan. CELLSRV also interacts with DBRM for implementing intradatabase resource manager plans.

- **Management Server (MS)** The MS process provides management and monitoring functions for the Exadata Storage Server Software. The MS process is responsible for triggering alerts when exceptions are encountered by the Exadata Storage Server components. The MS process communicates with CELLSRV and the operating system utilities in order to check the health of the software and hardware components.

- **Restart Server (RS)** The RS process handles startup and shutdown requests of the Exadata Storage Server Software. The RS process monitors the CELLSRV and MS process, and restarts them when they die abruptly. There is also a backup RS process that takes care of restarting the primary RS process if the primary itself is not running.

- **CellCLI** The Cell Command Line Interface (CellCLI) is the utility that you use to perform management and administration functions on the Exadata Storage Server Software. More details on CellCLI are covered later in this chapter.

Exadata Storage Layout

The components of the Exadata Storage Servers that provide persistent storage services are the High Performance or High Capacity hard disks and the flash disks that are created on Sun Flash Accelerator F20 PCIe cards. In this section, we will discuss the best practices for provisioning these storage devices and presenting them to Oracle ASM. Once the storage is presented to Oracle ASM, you can create ASM diskgroups, and eventually create tablespaces in the Oracle database that utilizes the diskgroups to store database objects.

LUNs, Cell Disks, and Grid Disks   As shown in Figure 5-2, each hard disk gets presented to the Exadata Storage Server Software and the OS as a logical unit (LUN). A LUN is the representation of the hard disk to the OS. The Exadata Storage Server Software will take the LUN and format it to create a *cell disk*. There is a one-to-one relationship between a LUN and a cell disk.

When the cell disk is created, it reserves a small portion of the available storage on the LUN for a system area. The system area is used to store information about the LUNs, cell disks, and *grid disks* (discussed next) created on top of the cell disks. The system area on the first two drives is special since it stores the Oracle Linux operating system and the Linux file systems of the Exadata Storage Server.

Grid disks add another layer of logical abstraction on the physical storage and are created on top of cell disks. Grid disks are the entities that get presented to Oracle ASM as ASM disks, and ASM diskgroups get created across the available ASM disks (i.e., grid disks). You can create multiple grid disks per cell disk, and when a grid disk is created, it will carve out a chunk of space from the unused outer tracks of the physical disk. The first grid disk created on the cell disk will allocate space from the outer tracks and move towards the inner tracks, reserving the number of tracks that correspond to the size of the grid disk. This grid disk provides the fastest performance since the outer tracks of a hard disk provide the best read/write performance. The next grid disk you will create starts from the tracks where the first grid disk ends, and this process repeats until you exhaust all the space on the cell disk or you are done creating the grid disks.

Creating multiple grid disks per cell disk allows you to create multiple pools of storage on the same Exadata Storage Server. The multiple grid disks can be assigned to separate ASM diskgroups, which can be provisioned to different databases. Even within the same database, you can store your

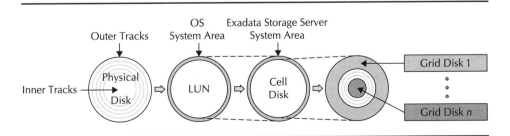

FIGURE 5-2.   *Relationship between LUNS, cell disks, and grid disks*

active data on the grid disks created on the outer tracks and the less active data on the grid disks created on the inner tracks. The best practice for creating grid disks is to create a minimum of two grid disks per cell disk. The first grid disk will be used to store user data since it provides the best performance. The second grid disk can be used to store the database Fast Recovery Area (FRA) for storing the database flashback logs, archive logs, and backups.

Interleaved Grid Disks   One drawback of creating multiple grid disks per cell disk as just described is that it does not provide the second grid disk the opportunity to be placed on the faster outer tracks. Moreover, the space utilization within a grid disk is such that only half of the space tends to be used for hot data, and the remaining half is used for mirrored blocks or colder data, which does not need the higher performance of the outer tracks. This situation can be mitigated by creating *interleaved grid disks* instead of regular grid disks, as shown in Figure 5-3.

With interleaved grid disks, you would provide the second grid disk the opportunity to be placed towards the faster-performing outer tracks. This mechanism is useful when you set up the Exadata Storage Server for multiple storage pools by creating multiple ASM diskgroups. All the ASM diskgroups will have the opportunity to utilize the faster-performing areas of the cell disk, and thus attempt to equalize the performance.

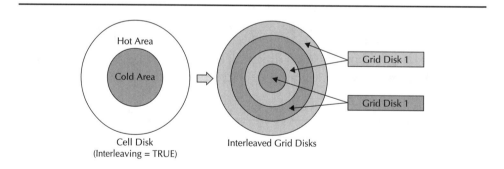

FIGURE 5-3.   *Interleaved grid disks*

Interleaving is enabled at the cell disk level by setting the INTERLEAVING attribute at the cell disk creation time. When you enable interleaving, it divides the cell disk into two equal parts; the first part is the faster-performing or the hot part, and is allocated towards the outer tracks; the second part is slower-performing or the cold part, and is allocated towards the inner tracks. When you create the interleaved grid disk on the cell disk, half of the interleaved grid disk is placed in the hot area and the remaining half is placed in the cold area. The process will be repeated when you create multiple interleaved grid disks until you exhaust the space on the cell disk or you no longer wish to create additional grid disks.

Flash Disks and Exadata Smart Flash Cache   Each Exadata Storage Server in the Exadata Database Machine comes preinstalled with Sun Flash Accelerator F20 PCIe cards. The PCIe-based flash storage technology is primarily used to speed up access to data, since I/Os against flash are much faster than I/Os against the hard disks. Each flash card is divided into multiple modules, and each module is exposed to the operating system as one LUN, and this LUN is categorized as a flash disk LUN, as shown in Figure 5-4.

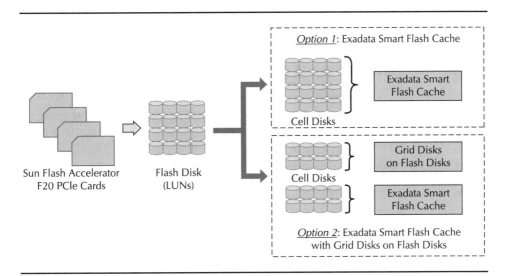

FIGURE 5-4.   *Relationship between flash disk, Exadata Smart Flash Cache, and flash-based grid disks*

The three main options for managing and utilizing the flash disks in the Exadata Storage Server are highlighted here:

■ **Exadata Smart Flash Cache** The first option is to let the Exadata Storage Server Software, described in detail in Chapter 3, manage the flash disks and configure them to be used by the Exadata Smart Flash Cache feature. The Exadata Smart Flash Cache will store the frequently accessed data (hot data) into the flash cards, leading to a substantial improvement in disk read performance on hot data, whereas the infrequently accessed data (cold data) resides on the cost-effective, hard disk–based storage. When the database server requests read or write operations from the Exadata Storage Server Software, it sends additional information about the request that indicates whether the blocks are candidates to be read again. Based upon this additional information, the Exadata Storage Server decides on caching the blocks in the Exadata Smart Flash Cache.

When the I/O requests sent to Exadata Storage Server are for random reads and index reads (db file sequential reads), the blocks are likely to be read again and hence will be cached by the Exadata Smart Flash Cache algorithm. In case of I/Os involving table scans, backups, redo log writes, and ASM mirrored writes, the blocks are most likely not read again and will bypass the Exadata Smart Flash Cache. However, there is an exception to this rule, and it applies to tables and partitions that are defined using the KEEP qualifier, as described in Chapter 3 and also next.

Exadata Smart Flash Cache is configured by default and is also the best practice for managing the flash disks, since the Exadata Storage Server Software will be responsible for managing the flash without requiring any user intervention or tuning.

■ **Pinning Objects in Exadata Smart Flash Cache** This option is an extension to the first one, and it allows the user to enable the database objects such as tables, indexes, partitions, and LOB columns, to be pinned in the Exadata Smart Flash Cache. The objects that are specified to be pinned are not exactly pinned in the cache 100 percent of the time, but rather given special treatment by the Exadata Smart Flash Cache algorithm, and the treatment is to keep the object in cache more aggressively and longer than the other objects. It is important to point out that the Flash Cache does not get preloaded with the pinned objects, but rather, the individual blocks of the object get loaded in an incremental manner upon being accessed by the users.

The database object-level setting of the CELL_FLASH_CACHE attribute determines whether the object is enabled to be pinned in the Flash Cache. The CELL_FLASH_CACHE storage attribute can be set to KEEP, DEFAULT, or NONE. When set to KEEP, the object will be enabled for pinning, and when set to NONE it will never be cached. The DEFAULT attribute invokes the default caching algorithm, which is what was discussed in the first option.

The default behavior of the caching algorithm when it encounters Exadata Smart Scans is to skip the Smart Scan blocks from being cached altogether. However, if you have the CELL_FLASH_CACHE set to KEEP on the table undergoing a Smart Scan operation, the table will be cached in the Flash Cache.

You can modify the caching behavior on the object with a simple ALTER statement. In this example, the *stocks* table is enabled to be pinned in the Flash Cache.

```
SQL> ALTER TABLE stocks STORAGE (CELL_FLASH_CACHE KEEP);
```

NOTE
Be aware that changing the CELL_FLASH_ CACHE from KEEP to NONE or DEFAULT will not remove the kept blocks from the Flash Cache—this change will simply subject the pinned blocks to the more aggressive aging algorithm used for the NONE or DEFAULT settings.

■ **User Managed Flash Disks**   The third option of managing the flash disks is to have them partially managed as Exadata Smart Flash Cache and partially managed by the user for manually placing database objects. When the user manages the flash disk, the grid disks are created on a portion of the flash-based cell disks and exposed to Oracle ASM. Oracle ASM creates ASM diskgroups that reside on the flash disks, and thus provide the extreme I/O performance of flash storage. This option allows you to place the hot or frequently accessed tables directly on a tablespace that is created on the flash-based ASM diskgroup.

One of the drawbacks of this method is that it requires the user to analyze and identify the tables that qualify as "frequently accessed", and also when the access pattern of the data changes, the user needs to perform ongoing management of the flash disk space by moving objects in and out of the flash-based ASM diskgroup.

Another drawback of this method is that you will be wasting at least half of the flash disk space by mirroring the data using NORMAL or HIGH redundancy settings on the ASM diskgroup. You cannot do away with mirroring since flash-based storage has higher failure rates when compared with the hard disks and mirroring will provide you a better level of protection.

ASM Disks and ASM Diskgroup   An ASM diskgroup is the primary storage entity of ASM that is exposed to the Oracle Database for storing database files. The ASM diskgroup is composed of one or more ASM disks, which are nothing but the grid disks exposed from each Exadata Storage Server to Oracle ASM. It is important to know that all ASM disks within an ASM diskgroup should reside in the Exadata Storage Servers in order for the database to utilize the Exadata-related features such as Exadata SQL offload processing.

With Oracle ASM, you can define *failure groups* in an ASM diskgroup. An ASM failure group is composed of ASM disks within the ASM diskgroup that have the tendency to fail together because they share the same hardware. The reason for creating failure groups is to identify the ASM disks that are candidates for storing mirrored copies of data. You do not want to store the mirror copy of an ASM extent in an ASM disk that belongs to the same failure group, because they both can fail together and you can end up losing your data. When you are creating ASM diskgroups in an Exadata environment, the failure groups are created automatically by the ASM instance since ASM knows to group the disks belonging to the same Exadata Storage Server in the same failure group.

An Exadata Grid redundant array of inexpensive disks (Grid RAID) uses ASM mirroring capabilities by specifying a redundancy level when creating the ASM diskgroup. In order for the ASM extents to be available during

Exadata Storage Server failures, it is a requirement to use ASM mirroring by using NORMAL or HIGH redundancy diskgroups. The NORMAL redundancy option will allocate one mirror copy of the ASM extent in a different failure group as the one allocated to the primary copy, whereas the HIGH redundancy option will allocate two mirrored copies of the extent in two separate failure groups.

The NORMAL redundancy tolerates a single Exadata Storage Server failure or multiple failures within the same Storage Server at a time, and the HIGH redundancy tolerates two Exadata Storage Server failures or multiple failures confined to two Storage Servers at a time in the storage grid. When you choose the redundancy level, ensure that the post-failure capacity and performance due to reduced number of Exadata Storage Servers in the Database Machine provide an acceptable level of service to the applications.

In the example shown in Figure 5-5, there are two Exadata Storage Servers—*Server A* and *Server B*. Two ASM diskgroups are created across *Server A* and *Server B* in the grid. The DATA diskgroup is defined on the faster-performing (or hot) grid disks, and the RECOV diskgroup is defined on the slower-performing (or cold) grid disks. The diskgroups are created with NORMAL redundancy, which implicitly creates two failure groups per each diskgroup, and the extents from *Server A*'s failure group will be mirrored to *Server B*'s failure group. If *Server A* fails, then Oracle ASM transparently fetches the mirrored extent from *Server B* and satisfies the I/O request without incurring any downtime.

The names of the ASM disks are the same as the Exadata Storage Server grid disks, and can be retrieved from the ASM instance by querying the *name* attribute of *v$asm_disk.* By looking at the ASM disk name, you can pinpoint the Exadata Storage Server and the cell disk to which the ASM disk belongs. This is possible because the ASM disk name contains the Exadata

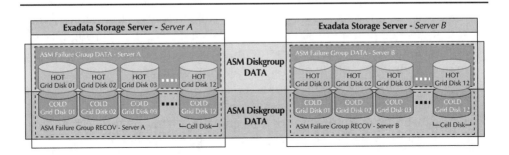

FIGURE 5-5. *ASM diskgroup architecture*

Storage Server name and the cell disk name as a prefix. The prefix is added by the system and works well to locate the cell disk to which the grid disk belongs. However, when you have multiple grid disks created per cell disk, in order to identify whether the grid disk was created on the *hot* or the *cold* areas of the hard disk, you need to add a user-defined prefix to the system-defined name. This is accomplished by using the PREFIX attribute of the CREATE GRIDDISK command. The PREFIX needs to be meaningful to the user and should be defined such that it will help you identify the location of the grid disk within the cell disk.

Exadata Storage Server Administration

To perform administration tasks on the Exadata Storage Servers, you first need to establish a communication path to the server's terminal console. One of the options for accessing the console is through KVM (keyboard, video and mouse) hardware that comes with X2-2 configurations of the Oracle Exadata Database Machine and its predecessors. But to access the KVM hardware, you need to be physically present alongside the Database Machine, and you have no choice but to use KVM when configuring the Database Machine for the first time. Once you perform the initial configuration steps that are outlined in the Exadata Storage Server *first boot sequence* section later in the chapter, the Exadata Storage Servers are made accessible over the Ethernet network and you can then use alternative methods that allow you to log in remotely.

Once the server is accessible over the network, you can use the Secure Shell (SSH) protocol to login remotely using an SSH-enabled client. The KVM console can also be redirected over the network to your desktop using the Sun Integrated Lights Out Management (ILOM) remote client. Another method to access the server console without the graphics is to redirect the console to a serial port and use ILOM to access the serial port through its web-based interface. No matter what remote method you use, the host you log in from should be able to access the Ethernet management network of the Exadata Database Machine.

Once you are at the OS login prompt, you need an OS user with privileges that are appropriate for performing administration tasks. The OS users and groups that exist on the Exadata Storage Servers are configured during the factory install process, and you will use only these preconfigured users to log in.

After logging in with the appropriate user, you have access to a variety of OS tools and the Cell Command-Line Interface (CellCLI). The CellCLI utility is available only on the Exadata Storage Servers, and if you need to access this utility from a remote host, you can use the Distributed Command Line Interface (dcli). The dcli utility has the ability to execute CellCLI commands, simultaneously and in parallel, against a set of Exadata Storage Servers, thereby eliminating the need to run the same command multiple times on each Exadata Storage Server. Dcli comes in quite handy when performing certain configuration and monitoring steps. The CellCLI and dcli utilities are discussed next.

Using CellCLI

Using CellCLI, you can configure the Exadata Storage Server Software components, perform administration tasks such as startup and shutdown of the Exadata Storage Server Software, and perform monitoring and maintenance activities. CellCLI is a command-line executable that comes preinstalled on the Exadata Storage Servers and allows you to administer only the Storage Server on which the utility resides. You can execute CellCLI either by directly logging on to the Storage Server or through a networked server that can access the Storage Server using SSH.

NOTE
The term "Cell" is sometimes used to reference the Exadata Storage Server. The Cell is also an object within the Exadata Storage Server that can be queried through CellCLI. The Cell object refers to the Exadata Storage Server itself and stores its attributes such as the name, status, and network settings.

The commands that can be executed at the CellCLI prompt follow syntactical rules as with any other command-line interface. The lexical syntax of CellCLI commands is

```
{admin-command | object-command object} [options] ;
```

The first part of the command indicates the type of the command, and this can be of type *admin-command* or the *object-command*. The detailed description on the lexical syntax is given here:

- *admin-command* dictates an administration action to CellCLI. These commands will perform operations that are directed to the CellCLI utility. Common admin commands are START, SPOOL, HELP, and QUIT.

- *object-command* will direct administrative actions to be performed on the *cell objects*. The object command is qualified by an *object* clause, which is the cell object upon which the command will be applied. Examples of cell objects are the *cell disks, grid disks, flash cache*, and the *cell*. Common object commands are CREATE, ALTER, and LIST.

- *options* provides the ability to specify additional parameters or options to the command.

CellCLI can be invoked in an interactive mode, which is the default mode and does not require any options to be specified at the command line. The interactive mode allows users to execute multiple commands in a single session until the user executes the QUIT or EXIT command.

The following example invokes the CellCLI utility and runs the LIST command to list the attributes of the *Cell* object. The *Cell* object is associated with the Exadata Storage Server and will store its attributes such as the cell name, online/offline status, and the IP addresses configured for the server. The LIST command is explained in detail in the monitoring section of this chapter.

```
$> cellcli
CellCLI> LIST CELL DETAIL
CellCLI> QUIT
```

You can also invoke CellCLI with the *–e* option and supply the CellCLI command directly at the OS command line as shown next. This command will display the same result as the previous example.

```
$> cellcli -e LIST CELL DETAIL
```

Exadata Storage Server OS Users and Privileges

The CellCLI utility does not have its own authentication mechanism and will rely on the operating system authentication of the Linux user. Based upon the user that invokes CellCLI, the users will be assigned appropriate privileges within the CellCLI domain. The pre-created OS users that you will use to log in to the Exadata Storage Server are *root, celladmin,* and *cellmonitor,* and these are the only users allowed on the Storage Servers. These users are authorized to perform tasks related to administration, monitoring, and maintenance of the Exadata Storage Server and the Exadata Storage Server Software. Since you will have super-user privileges on the server with the root user, remember that performing any modifications to the Exadata Storage Server or its components is prohibited by Oracle, and this includes installation and modification of both existing and new software and hardware components, except for the modifications done by applying ongoing Exadata Storage Server patches and upgrades.

The Exadata Storage Server OS users have the following characteristics and privileges associated with them:

- **cellmonitor**   The cellmonitor user can perform monitoring functions on the Exadata Storage Server using the CellCLI interface. The user is authorized only to execute the CellCLI LIST command, and all other commands that modify the configuration of the Exadata Storage Server, such as CREATE and ALTER commands, are blocked for cellmonitor.

- **celladmin**   The celladmin user has the authority to perform administration tasks from the CellCLI interface. The administration tasks include creating, altering, and deleting of cell objects, such as grid disks and cell disks. The only CellCLI command that the celladmin user is not authorized to run is the CALIBRATE command, which is the command to capture I/O performance metrics of hard disks and Exadata Smart Flash Cache by exercising an I/O load against these devices.

  At the OS level, the celladmin user can access the Automatic Diagnostics Repository Command Interface (adrci) utility to package incidents for sending to Oracle support.

■ **root**   The root user has super-user privileges at the OS and the CellCLI levels. The root user can execute OS utilities for performing maintenance and setup of Exadata Storage Server hardware and software components. Root can modify the OS parameter files, which is required for certain configuration steps, such as modifying the Exadata Storage Server IP addresses and setting up Exadata security.

Root is also a super-user on the CellCLI interface and has the authority to run all CellCLI commands, including CALIBRATE.

Using dcli

The dcli utility provides a centralized command-line interface for managing multiple Exadata Storage Servers from a single location. The dcli utility allows you to execute an OS command, in parallel, against a set of Exadata Storage Servers. When the command completes, the output of the command from each of the Exadata Storage Servers is combined into one and displayed as a unified result.

By using dcli, you can execute a CellCLI command against a set of Exadata Storage Servers in parallel, and you can observe the output returned by the command from all the Storage Servers from one central location. The dcli utility comes in extremely handy when you want to execute the same command against multiple servers without having to type them individually, in contrast to the CellCLI utility that will only allow you to run commands on a single Storage Server at a time.

The dcli utility can be set up on any host, provided the following requirements are met:

■ The dcli executable residing on the Exadata Storage Server needs to be copied to the host that will execute dcli commands. The Exadata Storage Servers have dcli preinstalled with the factory image.

■ dcli is a Python script and requires Python to be installed and accessible by the user invoking dcli. Python is preinstalled and configured on the database servers and the Exadata Storage Servers, and if you plan on using a server residing outside of the Database Machine, ensure that it can support Python 2.3 or later.

■ SSH equivalence of the user executing the dcli commands on the remote host needs to be set with the Exadata Storage Server user that will be used to execute the commands. This configuration needs to be done on all Exadata Storage Servers that you will be managing from dcli. You can use the dcli utility itself to set up SSH equivalence. Refer to the *Exadata Storage Server Software Users Guide—Using the dcli* for more details.

The dcli utility is invoked from the OS command line and has the usage syntax specified here:

```
$> dcli [options] [command]
```

The two parameters that the dcli takes as input are *options* and *command.* The *command* is the OS command that you will execute on the Exadata Storage Server. The CellCLI command is our focus for this chapter, but essentially, you can execute any OS commands (for example, OS-level monitoring commands such as *vmstat*) from dcli as long as the user that was used for the SSH equivalence has the authority to run the command on the Exadata Storage Server. A point to be noted is that dcli executes one command at a time and does not allow executing multiple commands in a single invocation.

Some frequently used *options* of dcli are listed here:

■ –c *cells*   Allows you to specify the Exadata Storage Server(s) that you want to execute the command on. Multiple servers are separated by a comma.

■ –g *group_file*   You can add the list of Exadata Storage Servers to *group_file* and use the file instead of a long, comma-separated list.

■ –l *user*   This option will log in to the Exadata Storage Server using the *user* specified. The *user* needs to be set up for SSH equivalence, with the remote OS user invoking dcli.

■ –k   This option is used to set up SSH equivalence. It will also need the –c or the –g option to specify the Exadata Storage Servers to set up SSH equivalence.

■ –x *script*   If the command is too long to be specified on the command line, you can save the command in a *script* file and use the –x option to execute the script file.

■ –h   This will display the help on dcli.

When executing CellCLI through dcli, you should use the *–e* option of CellCLI at the dcli command line.

dcli Examples

To set up SSH user equivalence using dcli, create a text file (named *group_ file* for this example) that contains all Exadata Storage Server hostnames or IP addresses, and execute the dcli command with the *–k* option, as shown next. The command prompts you to enter the password for the user that will have the SSH equivalence set. The password is required to set up the SSH equivalence key files.

```
$> dcli -k -g group_file
```

If you want to display the name and status of the grid disks on each Exadata Storage Server, execute the following dcli command. The command will execute the LIST GRIDDISK command on all the Exadata Storage Servers that are specified in the *group_file.*

```
$> dcli -g group_file "cellcli -e LIST GRIDDISK ATTRIBUTES name, status"
```

Exadata Storage Server Setup

The initial setup and configuration of the Exadata Storage Servers will be performed when the Exadata Database Machine gets installed at the customer site. We will touch upon the initial configuration setup steps briefly in this section.

At a high level, the setup process of the Exadata Storage Servers can be divided into two phases. The first phase deals with configuring the Exadata Storage Server and the operating system to make them accessible via the management network by listening on the appropriate Ethernet IP addresses. This phase will also configure the Fully Qualified Domain Name (FQDN), Domain Name Server (DNS), and a few other steps that we will discuss in the next section.

The steps involved in the second phase configure the Exadata Storage Server Software and carve out storage devices to make the Exadata Storage Server presentable to Oracle ASM as ASM disks. The ASM disks will be used to configure ASM diskgroups, and eventually used to create tablespaces in the Oracle Database.

The next section will first discuss the steps required for configuring the Exadata Storage Server and the OS.

Phase 1: Exadata Storage Server and OS Configuration

The Database Machine gets delivered to the customer site with a preinstalled factory image of the OS and the Exadata Storage Server Software. The OS and the software are not fully configured upon delivery, since the configuration steps require IP addresses of InfiniBand and Ethernet networks to be set up and routable (among other requirements, which we will see later), and this is only possible when the machine is at the customer site and not at the factory.

Exadata Storage Server First Boot Sequence   When the server is booted for the first time using the factory image, it will undergo a *first boot* sequence. The sequence is a series of prompts requesting your input, and, based on the information you provide, the Exadata Storage Server will be configured to listen on the network using the IP addresses provided at the prompt.

It will be necessary to have the following information ready prior to going through the first boot sequence:

- DNS Servers: It is not a requirement to register the Ethernet IP addresses of the Exadata Storage Server in the DNS, but if you are doing so, the Primary and Secondary DNS Server information needs to be provided.

- Time zone and location of the Exadata Storage Servers.

- Network Time Protocol (NTP) Servers are needed for network time synchronization.

- Ethernet and InfiniBand IP addresses: You will require one InfiniBand IP address during the first boot sequence. Even though you have two InfiniBand ports in each Exadata Storage Server, the ports are bonded for high availability on each server and will be presented to the OS as one port requiring one IP address. You also need one Ethernet IP address for the management network that connects the Ethernet ports of the Exadata Storage Server to the Exadata Database Machine's Ethernet admin switch.

- Fully qualified domain name (FQDN) for the server.

■ Oracle ILOM setup: The Oracle ILOM interface will be set up during the first boot sequence, and its configuration requires one IP address upon which its built-in web server will listen upon. Once ILOM is configured, you will be able to use a web browser to connect to ILOM and perform server-level management functions, such as startup and shutdown of the server, monitor the hardware, and many more tasks. More details on ILOM are discussed later in this chapter.

After the first boot configuration is complete, the Exadata Storage Server will be booted to the Linux prompt and you are ready to log in with the built-in users. Once you log in, the Exadata Storage Server Software processes are started, but still will not be fully functional and require additional configuration, which will be discussed in the next phase.

Perform Sanity Checks on the Exadata Storage Server Using CALIBRATE

In order to make sure that the Exadata Storage Server hardware is performing as advertised, you should execute the CellCLI CALIBRATE command. The CALIBRATE command will exercise the storage devices of the server with a prebuilt I/O load profile, and will monitor the raw I/O performance at the block level. You should compare the metrics you get from the result of CALIBRATE and compare it with the advertised values. An example of running the CALIBRATE command is shown next. The use of the FORCE parameter will be mandatory if you have already created the Exadata Cell object (the Exadata Cell object is discussed in the next section).

```
[root@cell01 ~]# cellcli
CellCLI: Release 11.2.1.2.0 - Production on Mon Nov 02 16:42:06 PST 2009
Copyright (c) 2007, 2009, Oracle. All rights reserved.
Cell Efficiency ratio: 1.0
CellCLI> CALIBRATE FORCE
Calibration will take a few minutes...
Aggregate random read throughput across all hard disk luns: 1601 MBPS
Aggregate random read throughput across all flash disk luns: 4194.49 MBPS
Aggregate random read IOs per second (IOPS) across all hard disk luns: 4838
Aggregate random read IOs per second (IOPS) across all flash disk luns: 137588
Controller read throughput: 1615.85 MBPS
Calibrating hard disks (read only) ...
Lun 0_0 on drive [20:0] random read throughput: 152.81 MBPS, and 417 IOPS
Lun 0_1 on drive [20:1] random read throughput: 154.72 MBPS, and 406 IOPS
...
```

```
Lun 0_10 on drive [20:10] random read throughput: 156.84 MBPS, and 421 IOPS
Lun 0_11 on drive [20:11] random read throughput: 151.58 MBPS, and 424 IOPS
Calibrating flash disks (read only, note that writes will be significantly
slower).
Lun 1_0 on drive [[10:0:0:0]] random read throughput: 269.06 MBPS, and 19680
IOPS
Lun 1_1 on drive [[10:0:1:0]] random read throughput: 269.18 MBPS, and 19667
IOPS
...
Lun 5_2 on drive [[11:0:2:0]] random read throughput: 269.15 MBPS, and 19603
IOPS
Lun 5_3 on drive [[11:0:3:0]] random read throughput: 268.91 MBPS, and 19637
IOPS
CALIBRATE results are within an acceptable range.
```

NOTE
The CALIBRATE command will exhaust all the available I/O resources on the Exadata Storage Server. Take caution when running this command, especially if you have databases that are actively utilizing the storage.

Phase 2: Exadata Storage Server Software Configuration

Before you start configuring the Exadata Storage Server Software, you need to decide on the provisioning model of the grid disks and the flash disks. The points to be considered are the number of grid disks to be created per cell disk, use of interleaved grid disks, and whether to utilize the flash disks as Exadata Smart Flash Cache or as grid disks, or a mix of the two. The best practice is to create at least two grid disks per cell disk, and to configure all the flash disks as Exadata Smart Flash Cache. For more details, refer to the earlier section in this chapter about architecting the storage on the Exadata Storage Servers.

The first step in configuring the Exadata Storage Server Software is to configure the Cell object. The Cell object refers to the Exadata Storage Server Software instance as a whole, and some of the parameters that you will set up in this step are the interconnect network that the Exadata Storage Server uses to serve the data traffic to the database nodes and the SNMP settings for monitoring of and forwarding of alerts. The steps that will follow the Cell creation step deal with configuring Exadata cell disks, grid disks, and Exadata Flash Cache.

Create the Exadata Cell Object   When configuring the Cell object, ensure that the interconnect network that the Exadata Storage Server uses to route data to the database nodes is the InfiniBand network. You can do this by verifying the name of the InfiniBand network interface using the Linux *ifconfig* utility. The dual ports of the InfiniBand network interface are configured during the initial setup process in a bonded mode and given a logical name of *bond0*.

Some of the other optional settings that you can perform during the Cell creation are to set up the Simple Mail Transfer Protocol (SMTP) server information for forwarding of alerts via e-mails and to set up the Simple Network Management Protocol (SNMP) to forward SNMP traps to a management and monitoring software infrastructure. You can also assign the logical *realm* name to the Exadata Storage Server. Realms are a logical grouping of Exadata Storage Servers for security purposes, and are discussed later in this chapter.

To create the Cell object, invoke the CellCLI utility and execute the CREATE CELL command.

```
CellCLI> CREATE CELL cell01 interconnect1=bond0, realmname=prod_cells
Cell cell01 successfully altered
```

Create the Cell Disks and Grid Disks   The LUNs (logical units) presented to the Exadata Storage Server Software are used to create cell disks and grid disks. Use the CREATE CELLDISK command shown next to create cell disks on the LUNs for which the cell disks have not yet been created, using default values. The cell disk is created on the entire LUN, and you are only allowed to create one cell disk per LUN, since there is a one-to-one mapping between a cell disk and a LUN. The CREATE CELLDISK command can be run repeatedly without affecting the LUNs or cell disks that were created earlier. This step should be repeated on all Exadata Storage Servers available in the Database Machine.

```
CellCLI> CREATE CELLDISK ALL
CellDisk CD_00_cell01 successfully created
...
CellDisk CD_10_cell01 successfully created
CellDisk CD_11_cell01 successfully created
```

After creating the cell disks, the next step is to create the grid disks. You can create one or more grid disks on a cell disk, and the first grid disk you create will be placed on the outermost tracks of the cell disks, unless you use interleaved grid disks, as described previously. The outer tracks are faster performing than the inner tracks, so the data that gets placed on grid disks residing on the outer tracks of the hard disk can be fetched much quicker than the data placed on the grid disk created on inner tracks. The best practice is to create a minimum of two grid disks on each cell disk and use the first (and the faster) grid disk for storing user data, and the second (and the slower) grid disk will be assigned to the ASM diskgroup that will house the FRA of the Oracle database.

The commands listed next will create two grid disks, allocating 300GB to the first disk and the remaining to the second. The PREFIX clause will prefix a text string to the name of the grid disk, which is useful for identifying the grid disks from ASM as mentioned earlier.

```
CellCLI> CREATE GRIDDISK ALL PREFIX=data, size=300G
GridDisk data_CD_1_cell01 successfully created
...
GridDisk data_CD_12_cell01 successfully created

CellCLI> CREATE GRIDDISK ALL PREFIX=recov
GridDisk recov_CD_1_cell01 successfully created
...
GridDisk recov_CD_12_cell01 successfully created
```

Create the Exadata Smart Flash Cache   Each Exadata Storage Server has flash disks created on the Sun Flash Accelerator F20 PCIe card modules, with each module exposed as one flash disk. As described earlier, you have a choice of creating Exadata Smart Flash Cache using the flash disks, or a combination of Flash Cache and grid disks. The default and the best practice configuration of flash disks is to create Exadata Smart Flash Cache on all the available flash disks, using the command shown here:

```
CellCLI> CREATE FLASHCACHE ALL
Flash cache cell01_FLASHCACHE successfully created
```

ASM and Database Configuration   The Oracle ASM cluster on the database nodes needs to be configured to use the grid disks created by the previous steps. Oracle ASM will be creating ASM diskgroups across the grid disks that are exposed by the Exadata Storage Servers. The database server also needs to be configured to communicate with the Exadata Storage Servers. The list of steps provided here configures the database and ASM nodes.

1. **Set up the configuration files on the database and ASM host.** The database and ASM nodes need the *cellip.ora* and *cellinit.ora* files that will be used by the database and the ASM cluster for routing the storage traffic to the Exadata Storage Servers via the InfiniBand network. The cellip.ora file stores the IP addresses of the Exadata Storage Server that will be accessed by the database and ASM clusters. The cellinit.ora file stores the IP address of the local database host InfiniBand network interface. These files are located in the /etc/oracle/network-config/ directory on the database and ASM hosts. The sample contents of these files are as shown:

   ```
   $> cat /etc/oracle/cell/network-config/cellip.ora
   $> cat /etc/oracle/cell/network-config/cellinit.ora
   ```

2. **Configure the database instance.** The database cluster initialization parameter file needs to have the COMPATIBLE parameter set to 11.2.0.1.0 in order to ensure communication with the Exadata Storage Server Software. The ASM and database binaries require the COMPATIBLE parameter to be set to the version of the Exadata Storage Server Software. The parameter cannot be dynamically modified and will require a restart of the database. Use this command to set COMPATIBLE:

   ```
   SQL Plus> ALTER SYSTEM SET COMPATIBLE='11.2.0.1.0' SCOPE=SPFILE;
   ```

3. **Configure the ASM instance.** In order for the ASM instance to be able to discover the grid disks on the Exadata Storage Servers, the ASM instance parameter file needs to be updated with the appropriate ASM_DISKSTRING parameter. The ASM_DISKSTRING parameter will determine the discovery path of the storage devices exposed by the Exadata Storage Servers to ASM. For the grid disks created on the Exadata Storage Servers, the storage path is *o/*/*. You can update the ASM_DISKSTRING parameter dynamically with the following *alter system* command:

   ```
   SQL Plus> ALTER SYSTEM SET ASM_DISKSTRING='o/*/*' SCOPE=BOTH;
   ```

4. **Create ASM diskgroups.** The Exadata Storage Server grid disks available to Oracle ASM are used to create ASM diskgroups. The grid disks can be queried from the ASM instance using the following SQL against the *v$asm_disk* view:

```
SQL> SELECT PATH, header_status STATUS FROM V$ASM_DISK
       WHERE path LIKE 'o/%';
```

Once you have the list of the available ASM disks, you can use the CREATE DISKGROUP command shown next to create ASM diskgroups. This example will create two ASM diskgroups—DATA and RECOV. Note that you do not require the FAILGROUP clause, since ASM will define a failure group for each Exadata Storage Server. You are required to set the COMPATIBLE.RDBMS and COMPATIBLE.ASM attributes to 11.2.0.1.0, and the CELL.SMART_SCAN_CAPABLE attribute to *true*. This attribute enables the SQL offload processing on the objects that are placed in this ASM diskgroup.

```
SQL> CREATE DISKGROUP data NORMAL REDUNDANCY DISK 'o/*/DATA*'
ATTRIBUTE 'AU_SIZE' = '4M',
'cell.smart_scan_capable'='TRUE',
'compatible.rdbms'='11.2.0.1.0',
'compatible.asm'='11.2.0.1.0';
SQL> CREATE DISKGROUP recov NORMAL REDUNDANCY DISK 'o/*/RECOV*'
ATTRIBUTE 'AU_SIZE' = '4M',
'cell.smart_scan_capable'='TRUE',
'compatible.rdbms'='11.2.0.1.0',
'compatible.asm'='11.2.0.1.0';
```

Exadata Storage Server Security Configuration

The grid disks on the Exadata Storage Servers are the logical entities that will be used by ASM and the database to store database objects. Using the security features that are built into the Exadata Storage Server, you can configure permissions and set access controls on a grid disk and thereby authorize it to be accessed by a specific database or ASM cluster. This feature is useful in a consolidation environment with multiple databases deployed on the Exadata Database Machine, requiring you to control access to grid disks to a database or set of databases.

Exadata Security can be configured using one of the following modes:

- **Open security**   In open security (or no security) mode, no access controls are set on the grid disks. Open security is useful when you are running development or test databases on the Exadata Database Machine and do not require stringent security requirements, or when you are running a production database and have secured access to the Database Machine by securing the network and the operating system. This is the default security mode, and out of the box, this is the mode that gets configured during the default setup of the Database Machine.

- **ASM-scoped security**   Using the ASM-scoped security mode, you can set access controls on a grid disk and make it available to a specific ASM cluster, and to all databases that are accessing the ASM cluster. ASM-scoped security can be used when all databases that utilize an ASM cluster need the same level of access controls on the grid disks.

- **Database-scoped security**   The database-scoped security mode allows you to set access controls on a grid disk such that it is made available to a specific database cluster. ASM-scoped security is a pre-requisite for setting up database-scoped security. This mode of security is appropriate when you want to control the access to grid disks at the individual database cluster level.

Exadata Storage Server Realms

Exadata Storage Server *realms* are logical groups of Exadata Storage Servers that are associated with a specific database or ASM cluster. Realms are optionally defined at the Storage Server level, with each server being associated with at most one realm, and the grid disks that belong to the server all reside in the same realm. Exadata Storage Servers belonging to a realm will have the same level of security and access controls set for the database and the ASM clusters. Figure 5-6 shows a typical use of realms.

There are multiple reasons for implementing Exadata Storage Server realms. One reason is to create multiple pools of storage in the storage grid. Storage pools are useful when you are consolidating multiple database environments on the Database Machine and you require dedicated storage

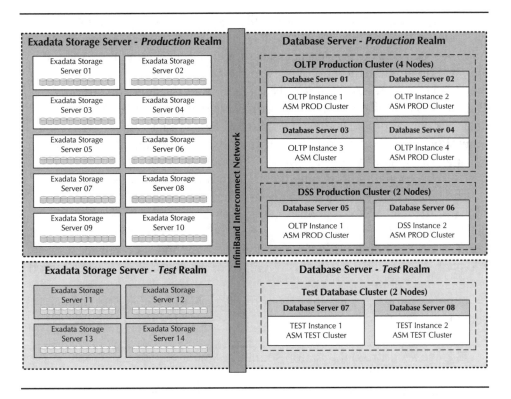

FIGURE 5-6.   *Exadata Storage Server realms*

pools for a particular database or ASM cluster. Another reason to use realms is to group Exadata Storage Servers together based upon similar security and access policy requirements of the database and ASM instances.

You can associate an Exadata Storage Server with a realm when you execute the CREATE CELL command using CellCLI. Or, you can use the ALTER CELL command to associate a realm with an existing Exadata Storage Server on which the Exadata *Cell* object was already created, as shown here:

```
CellCLI> ALTER CELL realmname=my_production_realmn
```

Implementing Exadata Security
The mechanism used for authenticating and authorizing grid disks to ASM and database clusters is based on security keys. The Exadata Storage Server

assigns keys to grid disks, and the entities requesting access to the grid disk will need to provide this key during the security handshake phase. In case of ASM-scoped security, the ASM cluster provides the key, and the Exadata Storage Server will match up the key to the assigned keys of the grid disk. If they match, then the ASM cluster is authenticated to access the grid disk. The process is similar for the database-scoped security, except that the database cluster provides the key to the Exadata Storage Servers when requesting access to the grid disks. This authentication mechanism is transparent to the end user and happens underneath the covers, and only needs to be configured one time when performing the initial setup.

The keys for the grid disks are created and assigned using the CREATE KEY and ASSIGN KEY commands at the CellCLI prompt. The keys for the database-scoped and ASM-scoped security will be stored in the cellkey.ora file. The cellkey.ora file is located on the database and ASM cluster nodes, and each ASM and database cluster will have its own cellkey.ora file stored in different locations on the server.

Use the following guidelines as best practices for configuring Exadata Security:

- The security configuration should be implemented on all database servers that belong to the same realm. You cannot just configure a few nodes within a realm and not all of them. Ensure that the cellkey.ora file is the same for all the nodes within the realm in order to avoid a mismatch in the configuration, which could result in errors.

- ASM-scoped security and database-scoped security should not be mixed in the same realms; you will configure the realm to use one or the other, but not both.

- When you configure the security on the grid disks, you can use the dcli utility to avoid mismatch of access control configuration for grid disks that belong to the same ASM diskgroup. Dcli will ensure that you run the same command across multiple grid disks and will ensure consistency across the grid disks access control definitions to minimize errors.

Exadata Storage Server Monitoring

The need for monitoring the hardware and software components comprising the Exadata Database Machine is unquestionable. Sometimes, a malfunctioning hardware component or an erratic behavior of a software component can cause failures that can adversely affect performance, or even the availability of the Exadata Database Machine. Being able to proactively detect and fix hardware and software issues will ensure optimal performance and healthy functioning of the Database Machine components.

This section will discuss the different tools and utilities available to monitor the Exadata Storage Servers. The monitoring methods will ensure that the different software and hardware components of the Exadata Storage Servers are operating as advertised and, more importantly, performing to their full potential without incurring undue bottlenecks. Any anomalies in the behavior of these components will be captured by the monitoring infrastructure, and the administrators will be alerted so that the corrective actions can be immediately implemented.

The tools available for monitoring the Exadata Storage Servers are the command-line utilities such as CellCLI and SQLPlus, and the web-based Oracle Enterprise Manager. The following options for monitoring the Exadata Storage Servers are discussed in this section:

- Monitoring with metrics and alerts

- Monitoring of active requests on the Exadata Storage Server

- Monitoring using the Oracle Database v$views

- Using Oracle Enterprise Manager for monitoring

- Using Oracle Integrated Lights Out Manager

Monitoring with Metrics and Alerts

The Exadata Storage Server Software has a built-in infrastructure to monitor the overall health of the server and the health of its individual hardware and software components. The monitoring infrastructure periodically collects information about certain parameters that are deemed critical for the normal functioning of the Exadata Storage Server. When these parameters cross predefined threshold boundaries, the monitoring infrastructure will automatically trigger alerts to the concerned administrators. The alerts will assist administrators to take corrective actions in a timely manner and help ensure a speedy resolution to the problem. These types of problems, if left unresolved, can hamper the availability of the Exadata Storage Servers and the Exadata Database Machine.

Metrics and alerts form the core infrastructure behind the monitoring of Exadata Storage Servers. These topics are discussed in this section.

Metrics

The software and hardware components that comprise the Exadata Storage Server are characterized into entities called *objects*. Examples of objects are cell disks, grid disks, Exadata Smart Flash Cache, host interconnect network, and the Exadata Storage Server itself. Each object is associated with certain properties that measure its performance or state, and these properties are characterized as *metrics*. An example of a metric associated with the cell disk object is the property that measures the total MBs read from the cell disk due to large I/O requests (the metric *MBytes read from disk for large I/Os*).

The metrics are categorized into the following types based on their values:

- *Instantaneous metrics* always capture the current value of the property of the object being measured.

- *Cumulative metrics* measure the property of the object whose values have accumulated since the metric was created.

- *Rate metrics* record the rate of change of the metric value measured over a given period.

- *Transition metrics* capture a change in the state of the object when the object transitions to a different state.

The metric values are categorized into different domains called *thresholds*. The different types of thresholds that are predefined by the system are *normal, warning,* and *critical*. When the object associated with the metric is working as expected, the metric value will fall in the *normal* range, below the warning threshold. A metric that falls over the *critical* threshold indicates that the Exadata Storage Server has encountered a critical issue with the object or the metric and the object may not be functioning as expected. The metric value that falls between the warning and critical thresholds is considered to be in the *warning* range.

Metrics are measured in units that correlate to the type of metric. For example, the CPU utilization metric will be measured as a percentage, and the CPU temperature will be measured in degrees Celsius.

Multiple metrics will be associated with an object, and all the possible metrics that have an effect on the overall functioning and behavior of the Exadata Storage Server have been predefined by the Exadata Storage Server Software. Users are not allowed to modify or add to the system-defined metrics; however, they are allowed to modify the preset thresholds or create new thresholds on the built-in metrics.

The metric collection process in the Exadata Storage Server is similar to the Automatic Workload Repository (AWR) metrics collection of the Oracle database. The CELLSRV process periodically records the metric values in the main process memory. The Management Server (MS) process will periodically flush the metrics accumulated by CELLSRV from the main memory and persist it to the hard disk. The metrics are then kept on disk for a default period of seven days. This default period can be modified, if needed, by altering the *metricHistoryDays* attribute using CellCLI. This example will modify the *metricHistoryDays* attribute to store 12 days' worth of metric history:

```
CellCLI> alter cell set metricHistoryDays=12
```

NOTE
The complete list of system-defined metrics, objects, alerts, and thresholds are described in the Oracle Exadata Storage Server Software Users Guide.

Alerts

Alerts are notices of important events occurring in the Exadata Storage Server. The events leading to an alert will generally indicate that the server has encountered an issue that can hamper its normal function. The Exadata Storage Server Software has predefined alerts on critical events that are known to interfere with the normal functioning of the Exadata Storage Server.

The MS process is responsible for triggering alerts. MS will trigger alerts when it encounters the following issues:

- **Hardware issues**   Errors due to the failure of a hardware component such as the flash card.

- **Software issues**   Internal errors raised by the CELLSRV process or errors due to a misconfiguration of the Exadata Storage Server Software.

- **Metrics having critical or warning values**   When metric values cross into the warning or critical threshold range, alerts can be triggered. These alerts will be triggered once the users define thresholds on the metric values.

Alerts can be *stateful* or *stateless*. Stateful alerts indicate a condition that can be tested again to see if the issue still exists. Alerts that are raised due to a cumulative metric exceeding a threshold value is an example of a stateful alert. Stateless alerts are events that have occurred at a point in time and the condition that triggered the alert no longer exists. An example of a stateless alert is the ORA-00600 errors raised by the CELLSRV process in the Automatic Diagnostics Repository (ADR) due to internal software issues that were encountered in the past.

Alerts are associated with a severity level of critical, warning, clear, or informational. The level of severity determines the degree of the fault that occurred in the system.

- *Critical* alerts indicate a condition that can interfere with the normal functioning of the Exadata Storage Server. Critical alerts will require immediate attention from the administrators to take corrective actions. If the alert definition is based on a metric (not hardware or internal alerts), the critical alert is raised when the metric value crosses over to the critical threshold. For hardware and internal alerts, the critical alerts are raised based on predefined conditions.

- *Warning* alerts indicate an issue that is categorized as a warning condition, or a condition that has the tendency to become critical if it is not immediately taken care of. If the alert definition is based on a metric, the warning alert is raised when the metric value crosses into the warning threshold.

- A *clear* alert is signaled by the system when the previously raised warning or critical alert gets cleared because the condition no longer exists. If the alert definition is based on a metric, the clear alert indicates that the metric value is now within the normal threshold.

- *Informational* alerts are merely messages that do not require administrative actions. These alerts are neither notified by e-mail nor propagated through the SNMP agents, but can be viewed through the CellCLI interface.

The health of the Exadata Storage Server can be monitored either by querying metrics and alerts using the CellCLI interface or by configuring automated mechanisms for propagating alerts to the administrator responsible for managing and maintaining the Exadata Database Machine. The alerts can be notified using e-mails, or can be propagated to external SNMP agents, or can be monitored using the Oracle Enterprise Manager Exadata plug-in. The next few topics talk about the monitoring of metrics and alerts using the CellCLI interface.

Monitoring Metrics Using CellCLI

The CellCLI interface allows you to query internal system objects that are used by Exadata Storage Server Software to persist data collected by the monitoring and alerting infrastructure. The metric definitions and their values are internally stored in the *metricdefinition, metriccurrent,* and the *metrichistory* objects. The *metricdefinition* object stores the definitions of the metrics and their configuration; the *metriccurrent* object stores the current values of the metrics; and the *metrichistory* object stores the historical values of the metrics.

To get a detailed list of all the attributes of these objects, use the DESCRIBE command from the CellCLI interface.

```
CellCLI> DESCRIBE METRICDEFINITION;
```

To query the metrics and their values from these objects, you will use the LIST command. You can filter the results of the LIST command by using a WHERE clause. You can display either specific columns of interest using the ATTRIBUTES clause or all columns using the DETAIL clause. For a detailed usage of the LIST command, refer to the *Oracle Exadata Storage Server Software Users Guide.*

Example 5-1

If you would like to get a list of all metrics that have been defined in the system, use the LIST METRICDEFINITION command. The command in the next example will display the metrics associated with the *cell* object, along with their descriptions and units. The cell object is associated with the Exadata Storage Server hardware.

```
CellCLI> LIST METRICDEFINITION WHERE objectType='CELL' -
         ATTRIBUTES name, description, unit
```

Monitoring Current Metrics   When interested in monitoring the current state of the system, you would start with the *metriccurrent* object. The LIST METRICCURRENT command is used to display the current value of a metric. Depending on the type of metric, the current value can indicate an instantaneous value, cumulative value, rate of change, or a transition in the state of the metric.

Here are a few examples of monitoring using *metriccurrent* object.

Example 5-2

The LIST command shown next displays the current value of *cl_fans* metric. The *cl_fans* metric is an *instantaneous* metric that displays the number of working fans in the Exadata Storage Server, and is a metric associated with the *Cell* object.

```
CellCLI> LIST METRICCURRENT CL_FANS DETAIL;
```

Example 5-3

The next example displays the current value of the *cd_io_by_r_lg* metric for the *celldisk* object. The *cd_io_by_r_lg* metric is the cumulative MBs read for large I/Os from a cell disk. The *celldisk* object is associated with the cell disks of the Exadata Storage Server.

```
CellCLI> LIST METRICCURRENT CD_IO_BY_R_LG WHERE objectType='CELLDISK'
```

Monitoring Metric History   Monitoring historical values of metrics helps you to correlate current issues with the ones that occurred previously and to predict potential issues that could arise based on a historical pattern discovery, and thereby empowers you to prevent future problems. The LIST METRICHISTORY command will display the historical values associated with the metric. As discussed earlier, the number of days of metric history that is stored in the system is determined by the *metricHistoryDays* setting on the Exadata Storage Server.

Example 5-4

At times, you might be interested in getting a list of historical values of a metric that raised an alert because the value of the metric was in an abnormal range. The following example will display the historical values of *fc_io_rq_r* for which a critical or warning alert was triggered. The *fc_io_rq_r* metric stores the cumulative value of the read I/O requests that were satisfied from the Exadata Smart Flash Cache.

```
CellCLI> LIST METRICHISTORY FC_IO_RQ_R WHERE alertState!='normal' -
         ATTRIBUTES name, alertState, metricValue
```

Example 5-5

Similar to the previous example, the next example displays the historical values of the cumulative metric *n_mb_sent* for the cases when the accumulated value of the metric exceeded 100MB. The *n_mb_sent* metric is the cumulative number of MBs transmitted from the Exadata Storage Server to the database server.

```
CellCLI> LIST METRICHISTORY N_MB_SENT WHERE metricValueMax > 100
```

Monitoring IORM Metrics   I/O Resource Manager (IORM), described in detail in Chapter 3, is the key engine behind the scheduling of I/O resources in the Exadata Storage Server. The metric collection process will capture metrics related to the utilization of I/O resources for each IORM plan configured on the server. It is possible to monitor the I/O resource consumption of the different plans and, more importantly, to identify if the I/O requests are waiting to be scheduled because they have exceeded their I/O allocations as defined by the plan. Once the IORM waits are identified, they can be tuned by altering the plan's I/O allocations or by adding resources to satisfy the I/O requests.

Each of the three types of IORM plans (intradatabase, category, and interdatabase plans) have a set of metrics that are captured by the Exadata Storage Server Software. For each plan, the metrics will capture:

- Total I/O requests generated

- I/O requests per second issued in the last minute

- Total number of seconds the I/O requests waited due to scheduling by IORM

- The average number of seconds the requests waited to be scheduled in the last minute

These metrics are captured separately for small I/Os and large I/Os. Large I/Os are full scans typically generated by data warehousing workloads and the I/O size is larger than 128K. Small I/Os are typically generated by OLTP workloads where the I/O size is smaller than or equal to 128K. Refer to the *Oracle Exadata Storage Server Software Users Guide* for the complete list of system-defined IORM metrics.

The IORM metrics are queried from the *metriccurrent* and *metrichistory* objects by using the *objectType* attribute as the filter. The IORM-related *objectType* has the values of IORM_CATEGORY, IORM_DATABASE, and IORM_CONSUMER_GROUP for the category, interdatabase, and intradatabase IORM plans, respectively. The *metricObjectName* attribute identifies the different resources within the IORM plan, and the *metricValue* stores the current I/O utilization rate. In an interdatabase plan, the *metricObjectName* attribute will display the database instance that is part of the IORM plan.

Certain system-defined IORM categories exist in the Exadata Storage Server that are associated with system-generated I/O requests, such as ASM rebalance I/O operations, I/O requests generated by database background processes, and backup I/O. The I/O priorities of these requests are predefined by the system, and some I/O requests, such as redo and control file I/O, will have higher priority over the user-generated I/O. Other requests such as ASM rebalance and backup I/O will have a lower priority than the user I/O.

Here are some examples of monitoring IORM metrics.

Example 5-6

This example will list the current IORM metrics related to interdatabase, category, and intradatabase plans. The attributes displayed will be the *name, metricObjectName, metricValue,* and the *collectionTime.* The *collectionTime* will store the timestamp of the metric collection.

```
CellCLI> LIST METRICCURRENT WHERE objectType = 'IORM_DATABASE' -
          ATTRIBUTES name, metricObjectName, metricValue, collectionTime
CellCLI> LIST METRICCURRENT WHERE objectType = 'IORM_CATEGORY' -
          ATTRIBUTES name, metricObjectName, metricValue, collectionTime
CellCLI> LIST METRICCURRENT WHERE objectType = 'IORM_CONSUMER_GROUP' -
          ATTRIBUTES name, metricObjectName, metricValue, collectionTime
```

Example 5-7

Monitoring historical values is important to understand the trend in I/O utilization rates by the consumers so you can tune your IORM plan allocations. The next example lists the historical values of interdatabase plan metrics that measure waits incurred due to scheduling of I/O requests by IORM. These metrics have the _io_wt_ string in the *name* attribute.

```
CellCLI> LIST METRICHISTORY WHERE objectType = 'IORM_DATABASE' -
         AND name like '.*_IO_WT_.*' AND metricValue > 0 -
         ATTRIBUTES name, metricObjectName, metricValue, collectionTime
```

Example 5-8

The metrics with _io_rq_ string in the name display the I/O requests issued by each IORM plan to the Exadata Storage Server. The following command will list the historical values of these metrics for the category IORM plan, the result of which you can use to find the category plan that initiated the most I/O requests and modify the I/O resource allocations for the plan as appropriate.

```
CellCLI> LIST METRICHISTORY WHERE objectType = 'IORM_CATEGORY' -
         AND name like '.*_IO_RQ_.*' AND metricValue > 0 -
         ATTRIBUTES name, metricObjectName, metricValue, collectionTime
```

Monitoring Alerts Using CellCLI

The possible alerts that can be raised by the system are queried from the *alertdefinition* object using the LIST command. The alerts raised due to hardware and software issues are predefined and cannot be altered or deleted by the users. However, the users can create their own alerts based on the predefined metrics and thresholds. A few examples of monitoring alerts using CellCLI are provided next.

Example 5-9

This example executes the LIST command to display all alerts that are defined in the system (the results are truncated). As you can see, the metric-based alerts have the *metricName* attribute populated. The system-defined alerts, such as *ADRAlert* and *HardwareAlert,* are not based on a metric and hence do not have a *metricName.* The alert *StatefulAlert_CD_IO_ERRS_MIN* is based on the *cd_io_errs_min* metric, which is the metric that captures the rate of I/O errors on a cell disk per minute.

```
CellCLI> LIST ALERTDEFINITION ATTRIBUTES name, metricName, alertType,
description
        ADRAlert                             Stateless "Incident Alert"
        HardwareAlert                        Stateless "Hardware Alert"
        StatefulAlert_CD_IO_ERRS_MIN CD_IO_ERRS_MIN Stateful  "Threshold Alert"
```

Example 5-10

This LIST command displays the definition of the *HardwareAlert* in detail.

```
CellCLI> LIST AERTDEFINITION HardwareAlert DETAIL
        name:                    HardwareAlert
        alertShortName:          Hardware
        alertSource:             Hardware
        alertType:               Stateless
        description:             "Hardware Alert"
        metricName:
```

Alert History   Alerts are captured in the *alerthistory* object. The *alerthistory* object can be manually queried to display a detailed history on the alerts triggered in the system since the last *metricHistoryDays*. The *alerthistory* object has the *examinedBy* attribute, which gets updated when the alert is acknowledged by an administrator.

This example will list all alerts that are of *critical* severity and the ones that have not been acknowledged:

```
CellCLI> LIST ALERTHISTORY WHERE severity = 'critical' -
        AND examinedBy = '' DETAIL
```

Acknowledging Alerts   To acknowledge an alert, use the ALTER command and update the *examinedBy* attribute. This action will notify other administrators that the alert has been acknowledged and worked upon. The ALTER ALERTHISTORY command allows you to modify either individual alerts (by providing the alert identifier) or all alerts in the system. These examples illustrate the use of this command:

```
CellCLI> ALTER ALERTHISTORY 123456633 examinedBy='JohnSmith'
CellCLI> ALTER ALERTHISTORY ALL examinedBy='JohnSmith'
```

Propagating Alerts via SNMP and SMTP   When alerts are triggered by the system, they can be optionally configured to be propagated through e-mails or SNMP agents to the outside world. The e-mails are sent to predefined addresses using SMTP, and the SNMP messages will be propagated to external SNMP agents. The Exadata Storage Server Software needs to be configured in order to enable this propagation.

The cell object attributes associated with SMTP and SNMP settings are

- *smtpToAddr*   The e-mail address where the SMTP notifications are delivered

- *snmpSubscriber*   The SNMP subscriber hosts receiving the SNMP alerts

- *notificationPolicy*   The policy dictating the types of alerts that will be forwarded

- *notificationMethod*   Indicates the notification methods that are active

This example configures the SMTP and SNMP settings. The other attributes used in the example should be self-explanatory.

```
CellCLI> ALTER CELL smtpServer='smtp.example.com', -
         smtpFromAddr='exadataV2@example.com', -
         smtpFrom='John Smith', -
         smtpToAddr='john.smith@example.com', -
         snmpSubscriber=((host=host1),(host=host2)), -
         notificationPolicy='critical,warning,clear', -
         notificationMethod='mail,snmp'
```

The SMTP and SNMP settings can be validated by using these ALTER CELL VALIDATE commands:

```
CellCLI> ALTER CELL VALIDATE MAIL
CellCLI> ALTER CELL VALIDATE SNMP
```

Creating Threshold Alerts
To configure alerts based on metrics, you need to create thresholds on the metric values using the CREATE THRESHOLD command. Thresholds can be created on metrics that are defined in the *alertdefinition* object and have

the *description* attribute set to *'Threshold Alert.'* Based on the thresholds, an alert will be triggered when the metric value transitions to the warning or a critical range.

Use this LIST command to display the metrics upon which you can define thresholds:

```
CellCLI> LIST ALERTDEFINITION WHERE description = 'Threshold Alert' DETAIL
```

Example 5-11

The example shown next creates a threshold that triggers alerts based on the *gd_io_errs_min* metric. The *gd_io_errs_min* metric measures the rate of I/O errors on a grid disk per minute. The threshold created will raise a warning alert when the *gd_io_errs_min* metric value crosses over 100, and will raise a critical alert when the value crosses 200.

```
CellCLI> CREATE THRESHOLD gd_io_errs_min.gd_threshold warning=100, critical=200, -
         comparison='='
```

Monitoring Flash Cache Statistics

The *flashcachecontent* object stores information about the objects stored in the Exadata Smart Flash Cache. You can query the size occupied by the objects and the utilization statistics such as the cache hit-and-miss ratios by querying the *flashcachecontent* object. To view all the attributes of the *flashcachecontent* object, use the DESCRIBE command, as shown here:

```
CellCLI> DESCRIBE FLASHCACHECONTENT
         cachedKeepSize
         cachedSize
         dbID
         hitCount
         hoursToExpiration
         missCount
         objectNumber
         tableSpaceNumber
```

Monitoring an Object's Placement in Exadata Smart Flash Cache   If you would like to verify that a specific object has been placed in the Exadata Smart Flash Cache, you should first look up the *object_id* of the object from the *dba_objects* dictionary view and then match the *object_id* against the *objectNumber* attribute of the *flashcachecontent* object, as shown in this example:

```
SQL> SELECT object_id FROM DBA_OBJECTS WHERE object_name='SALES';
    OBJECT_ID
    ---------
        12354
CellCLI> LIST FLASHCACHECONTENT WHERE objectNumber=12354 DETAIL
            cachedSize:         192244484
            dbID:                   34211
            hitCount:              215241
            missCount:               1014
            objectNumber:           12354
            tableSpaceNumber:           1
```

Monitoring Exadata Flash Cache Status   The details on the Exadata Smart Flash Cache and its status can be monitored using the *flashcache* object. When the object is queried, it will display the cell disks that comprise the Flash Cache, along with the total size of the cache and its overall status.

```
CellCLI> LIST FLASHCACHE DETAIL
            name:           cell1_FLASHCACHE
            cellDisk:       FD_00_cell1,FD_01_cell1,FD_02_cell1,FD_03_cell1
            creationTime:   2009-11-05T06:55:16-08:00
            id:             a86a91ba-73e4-422a-bc83-7a9dbe715a0f
            size:           1.5625G
            status:         normal
```

Monitoring Active Requests

The I/O requests that are actively processed by the Exadata Storage Servers can be monitored using the *activerequest* object. Use the DESCRIBE ACTIVEREQUEST command to get the complete list of attributes monitored by this object. A few relevant attributes of this object are listed here:

- *ioGridDisk*   The grid disk serving the I/O request.

- *ioReason*   The reason why the I/O is generated.

- *ioType*   The type of the I/O activity.

- *requestState* Determines the state of the active request. Some values of this attribute are accessing from disk, sending or receiving from the network, and waiting in the queue for predicate pushing (Exadata Smart Scans).

- *objectNumber* The database *object_id* associated with the request.

The following command displays all active requests of type *predicate pushing,* which indicates that the request is performing a Smart Scan operation on the Exadata Storage Server:

```
LIST ACTIVEREQUEST WHERE ioType = 'predicate pushing' DETAIL
```

Monitor Using the Oracle Database

Using the database dictionary views from the database instance, you can monitor the efficiency of the Exadata Storage Server Software and the individual SQLs utilizing the Exadata Storage Server features such as Smart Scans, storage indexes, and Exadata Smart Flash Cache.

The following topics are discussed in this section:

- Monitoring SQL offload processing execution plans

- Using SQL to monitor the Exadata Storage Server features

Monitoring SQL Offload Processing Execution Plans

The Smart Scan feature of the Exadata Storage Server Software will offload processing of certain SQL operations to the Exadata Storage Servers, thereby allowing the data to be processed closer to where it resides. SQL offload processing is enabled by default at the database instance level by the initialization parameter CELL_OFFLOAD_PROCESSING.

When CELL_OFFLOAD_PROCESSING is TRUE, the database will attempt to offload the SQL to be processed by the Exadata Storage Servers. The decision to offload the SQL is a runtime decision and depends on several factors, which are detailed in the *Exadata Storage Server Software Users Guide.* When CELL_OFFLOAD_PROCESSING is set to FALSE, the database processes the SQL in the database servers and the Exadata Storage Servers will merely serve regular blocks to the database nodes.

CELL_OFFLOAD_PROCESSING can be set at the system and the session level by using the ALTER SYSTEM or the ALTER SESSION commands. This command enables SQL offload processing for the session executing the command:

```
SQL> ALTER SESSION SET CELL_OFFLOAD_PROCESSING = TRUE;
```

You can also enable (or disable) the CELL_OFFLOAD_PROCESSING for a SQL by using the OPT_PARAM hint. The SQL-level setting overrides the session-level settings, which in turn overrides the system-level settings. This example will enable offload processing only for the SQL using the OPT_PARAM hint:

```
SQL> SELECT /*+ OPT_PARAM('cell_offload_processing', 'true') */ COUNT(*)
        FROM SALES;
```

Whether the SQL query is offloaded to the Exadata Storage Server for processing or not, you can always look at the execution plan of the SQL with the EXPLAIN PLAN command and determine the predicate or portion of the SQL that will be a candidate for offload processing. The EXPLAIN PLAN command has been enhanced to display the offloaded predicates in the *storage* section of its output. This feature of EXPLAIN PLAN exists even when you do not have the Exadata Storage Servers as the storage grid serving the database.

The database parameter CELL_OFFLOAD_PLAN_DISPLAY must be set to AUTO or ALWAYS in order for the EXPLAIN PLAN to display the predicate offload information. You can modify the parameter by using the ALTER SESSION or ALTER SYSTEM command, as shown in this example:

```
SQL> ALTER SESSION SET CELL_OFFLOAD_PLAN_DISPLAY = ALWAYS;
```

The possible values for CELL_OFFLOAD_PLAN_DISPLAY are

- **AUTO**   This is the default value. AUTO will instruct EXPLAIN PLAN to display the *storage* section when the Exadata Storage Servers are configured as the storage layer.

- **ALWAYS**   This setting will display the *storage* section, regardless of whether the database storage layer resides on Exadata Storage Servers or not.

- **NEVER**   The *storage* section will never be displayed.

The output shown here is an example of EXPLAIN PLAN with the *storage* section (highlighted in bold):

```
SQL> select count(*) from SALES where CUSTOMER_ID>2000;
Execution Plan
----------------------------------------------------------------
Plan hash value: 2189604569
----------------------------------------------------------------
|Id| Operation                | Name| Rows | Bytes| Cost (%CPU)| Time    |
----------------------------------------------------------------
| 0| SELECT STATEMENT         |     |    1 |   13 | 5815    (1)| 00:01:10 |
| 1|  SORT AGGREGATE          |     |    1 |   13 |         |         |
|*2|   TABLE ACCESS STORAGE FULL| SALE|1347K|  16M| 5815    (1)| 00:01:10 |
----------------------------------------------------------------
Predicate Information (identified by operation id):
----------------------------------------------------------------
   2 - storage("CUSTOMER_ID">(2000))
       filter("CUSTOMER_ID">(2000))
```

Using SQL to Monitor the Exadata Storage Server

In this section, we will discuss the frequently used monitoring commands that you can execute from the database nodes using SQL for calculating efficiencies of various Exadata Storage Server features.

Calculating the Exadata Smart Scan Efficiency   The efficiency of Exadata Smart Scans is defined as the ratio of bytes fetched by the hard disks on the Exadata Storage Server to the bytes forwarded to the database servers for further processing. The higher values of this ratio indicate that the Storage Servers are filtering more results and are forwarding only the relevant information to the database servers, thereby indicating a higher efficiency of Smart Scans. When there are no Smart Scan operations occurring, the offload efficiency will be 1.

The Smart Scan efficiency can be computed for individual SQL statements, and also for the Exadata Storage Server. The formula for computing the efficiency at the Exadata Storage Server level using the *v$sysstat* statistics is given here:

(cell IO uncompressed bytes + cell physical IO bytes saved by storage index)/(cell physical IO interconnect bytes returned by smart scan)

The v$sysstat statistics referenced in this calculation are defined here:

- *Cell IO uncompressed bytes* is the statistic that represents the total size of uncompressed data processed on the Exadata Storage Server. When the data is compressed and needs to be decompressed on the Exadata Storage Server for evaluating Smart Scan predicates, the size of data after decompression is added to this statistic instead of the compressed size.

- *Cell physical IO bytes saved by storage index* represents the total I/O bytes saved by the storage index, which otherwise would lead to a physical I/O if the index didn't exist. In the equation for calculating Smart Scan efficiency, this statistic is added to the *cell IO uncompressed bytes,* and this is done in order to separate the benefits obtained by the storage indexes from that of the Smart Scans.

- *Cell physical IO interconnect bytes returned by Smart Scan* is the total I/O bytes returned by the Exadata Storage Server to the database server for Smart Scan operations only. Other I/Os that are not related to Smart Scans are excluded from this statistic.

Use the following SQL to calculate the Smart Scan efficiency for the Exadata Storage Server:

```
SELECT (a.value+b.value)/c.value as efficiency
  FROM v$sysstat a, v$sysstat b, v$sysstat c
 WHERE a.name = 'cell IO uncompressed bytes'
   AND b.name = 'cell physical IO bytes saved by storage index'
   AND c.name = 'cell physical IO interconnect bytes returned by smart scan';
EFFICIENCY
----------
45.9
```

Monitoring Storage Index Utilization   The statistic that you will use to measure the benefit of Exadata storage indexes is the *cell physical I/O bytes saved by storage index.* This statistic will display the I/O bytes saved by the storage indexes that otherwise would have led to a physical I/O. The statistic is available in the *v$sysstat, v$sesstat,* and *v$mystat* tables, and also the corresponding *gv$* tables for the Oracle RAC cluster.

```
SELECT name, value
  FROM v$sysstat
 WHERE name = 'cell physical IO bytes saved by storage index';
```

Monitoring Exadata Smart Flash Cache Efficiency   The relevant statistic to measure the hits against Exadata Smart Flash Cache is *cell flash cache read hits.* The statistic will display the cumulative number of I/O requests that were satisfied by Exadata Smart Flash Cache. The statistic is available in the *v$sysstat, v$sesstat,* and *v$mystat* tables, and also the corresponding *gv$* tables for the RAC cluster.

```
SELECT name, value
  FROM v$sysstat
 WHERE name = 'cell flash cache read hits';
NAME                            VALUE
------------------------        -----
cell flash cache read hits      19876
```

Monitoring with Oracle Enterprise Manager

Oracle Enterprise Manager provides a broad set of system management functions for managing the entire stack of Oracle and non-Oracle products deployed in the enterprise-wide data center. With Enterprise Manager, you have a centralized mechanism for managing, monitoring, and administering the complete Oracle ecosystem, all the way from business processes and applications to the disk subsystem that houses the critical enterprise data. Enterprise Manager has a single web-based management console providing a unified interface that integrates seamlessly with other Enterprise Manager add-on components.

Enterprise Manager reduces the cost and complexity of managing grid-based applications by providing a rich service-level management functionality that enables top-down service-level monitoring that is focused on end-user performance. This capability will accelerate the diagnosis and resolution of critical performance issues that spawn multiple components of the enterprise grid by allowing the user to correlate issues across the components of the grid, and all this is available through a single unified interface.

Enterprise Manager can manage non-Oracle technologies through the use of System Monitoring Plug-ins. The System Monitoring Plug-in is a piece of software that has the core technology to interface with third-party targets and sometimes even Oracle targets such as the Exadata Storage Server. This functionality provides an integrated solution for managing the entire technology stack, both Oracle and non-Oracle, using the single unified Enterprise Manager console.

Enterprise Manager provides Management Connectors through which you can integrate third-party management software by using SNMP trap notifications. This capability allows the reuse of existing management tools that the company has already invested in, through a bidirectional event exchange mechanism of critical messages and events between the third-party tool and the Oracle Enterprise Manager. With this integration, you can create further actions to be taken by the third-party management tool from the alerts generated by Oracle Enterprise Manager, and vice versa. For example, by using the Management Connectors, it is possible to propagate an alert triggered by a target managed in Oracle Enterprise Manager to third-party incident management software that could automatically generate trouble tickets upon receiving the alert.

The System Monitoring Plug-ins and Management Connectors can also be created by third-party software vendors by following the guidelines that are set by Oracle. This allows you to extend and customize Oracle Enterprise Manager to monitor any component, including custom applications and network infrastructure, and enable you to integrate Enterprise Manager with other management tools that are able to monitor these components at a more granular level.

The components listed next comprise the Enterprise Manager architecture, as illustrated in Figure 5-7.

- **Oracle Management Service (OMS)**   OMS is the heart of the Oracle Enterprise Manager architecture and is responsible for providing the management interface and the means for communicating between an Oracle Management Agent and the Oracle Management Repository.

- **Oracle Management Agent (Management Agent)**   The Management Agent collects information from the monitored targets and feeds into the Oracle Management Repository through OMS.

- **Oracle Management Repository (Management Repository)** Management Repository stores the information collected by the target systems through the Management Agents. The Management Repository resides in an Oracle Database.

- **Oracle Enterprise Manager Grid Control Console (Grid Control Console)**   The web-based front end to the Management Service. Grid Control Console can be accessed through the network, and allows the user to monitor and manage all the targets from a single location.

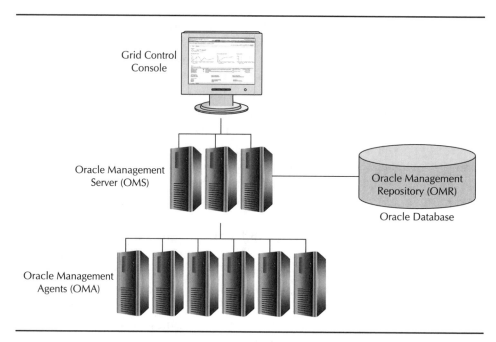

FIGURE 5-7. *Enterprise Manager architecture*

Oracle Enterprise Manager can monitor the Exadata Storage Servers through the System Monitoring Plug-in for Exadata and the Enterprise Manager Ops Center connector. These topics are discussed next.

Oracle Enterprise Manager System Monitoring Plug-In for Exadata

The System Monitoring Plug-in for the Oracle Exadata Storage Server enables you to manage and monitor Exadata Storage Server targets using Oracle Enterprise Manager. The plug-in allows you to gather storage configuration and performance information about the Exadata Storage Server components such as cell disks, grid disks, and the Exadata Smart Flash Cache.

The plug-in also allows you to utilize the notification and alerts infrastructure of Enterprise Manager to propagate alerts originally triggered by the Exadata Storage Servers, made possible by setting thresholds on the Exadata Storage Server metrics within Enterprise Manager. Moreover, the rich graphical user interface of the Grid Control Console and the comprehensive reporting capability of the tool will allow you to have a point-and-click administration interface to the Exadata Storage Server.

The System Monitoring Plug-in uses the Management Server and utilizes the Management Agent to manage the Exadata Storage Server targets. The Management Agent can be installed on any host (including the OMS host) that can communicate with the Exadata Storage Servers through the Secure Shell (SSH) protocol, connecting to the Exadata Storage Servers using the management Ethernet IP addresses. However, you should not install the agent on the Exadata Storage Server targets, because such an installation is not supported by Oracle. The setup and configuration of the System Monitoring Plug-in is documented in the *System Monitoring Plug-in Installation Guide for the Oracle Exadata Storage Server.*

You can start monitoring the Exadata Storage Server targets once the plug-in is installed and configured. The *target* section of the Grid Control Console will show the Exadata Storage Server targets. You will land at the home page of the Exadata Storage Server when you click one of the Exadata Storage Server targets.

The home page for an Exadata Storage Server is composed of the General, Alerts, Configuration, and the Related Actions sections, as shown in Figure 5-8. The *General* section shows the current status of the Exadata Storage Server, and the uptime during the last 24 hours is displayed as a percentage. You can also configure a *Black Out* schedule from this section by clicking the Black Out link. A Black Out schedule is used to suspend monitoring activities such as the triggering of alerts on the server, and is normally used for planned maintenance operations.

The *Alerts* section displays a list of alerts that are triggered by the Exadata Storage Servers. The attributes of the alerts that are displayed are the metric name, metric value, and the time of the alert. The *Configuration* section has links that allow you to view the saved configurations and settings of the Exadata Storage Servers, compare configuration settings, and view configuration history. The *Related Links* section navigates you to screens that help accomplish other monitoring tasks.

Configuring Enterprise Manager Alerts   The Exadata Storage Server metrics will determine the health of the Storage Servers. When these metrics reach critical levels, the administrators need to be notified immediately so that the situation can be rectified in order to ensure the stability and availability of the Exadata Database Machine. You can monitor the metrics

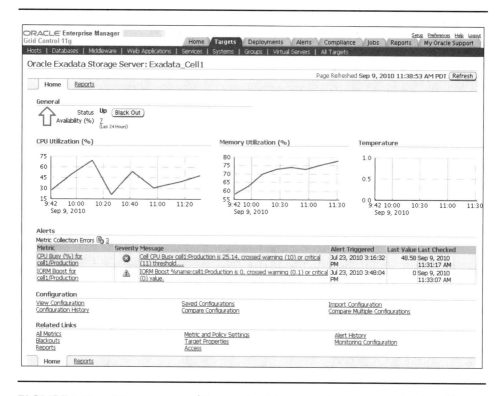

FIGURE 5-8. *Home page of Enterprise Manager System Monitoring Plug-in for Exadata*

and alerts by executing CellCLI commands on the Storage Servers, or you can configure the Storage Servers to forward alerts and metrics to Enterprise Manager. Once the metrics are propagated to Enterprise Manager, you can configure alerts to be triggered, run reports on metrics, and modify thresholds, and all this is possible using the point-and-click interface of Grid Control Console.

In order for the Exadata Storage Server alerts to be propagated to Enterprise Manager, you would configure SNMP settings on the Storage Servers to forward alerts to the Management Agent. The Management Agent will store the alerts in the Management Repository, which enables the Enterprise Manager to further forward the alerts to administrators using the notifications and alerts policies defined in the Management Repository. This empowers the administrators to take corrective actions.

You can use the following commands to configure the Exadata Storage Servers for SNMP:

```
CellCLI> ALTER CELL notificationPolicy='critical,warning,clear', -
         notificationMethod=SNMP -
         snmpSubscriber=((host='abc.server.com',port=1234))
```

The *snmpSubscriber* attribute will specify the *host* and *port* number of the Oracle Management Agent that is monitoring the Exadata Storage Servers. The Exadata Storage Server will forward the alerts whose severity matches the one defined by the *notificationPolicy.* Once you are done with the SNMP setup, you can validate the setup by using the *alter cell validate snmp* command.

```
CellCLI> ALTER CELL VALIDATE SNMP
```

The configuration and settings of the alerts in Enterprise Manager are done in the *Metric and Policy Settings* page, shown in Figure 5-9. On this

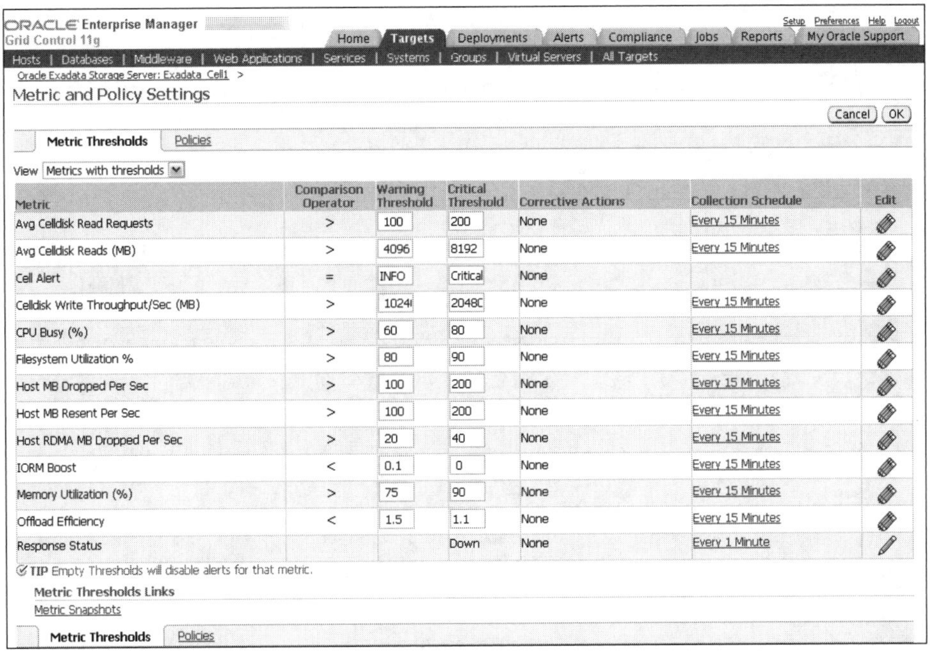
ORACLE Enterprise Manager
Grid Control 11g
Setup Preferences Help Logout
Home Targets Deployments Alerts Compliance Jobs Reports My Oracle Support
Hosts | Databases | Middleware | Web Applications | Services | Systems | Groups | Virtual Servers | All Targets
Oracle Exadata Storage Server: Exadata_Cell1 >
Metric and Policy Settings
Cancel OK
Metric Thresholds Policies
View Metrics with thresholds
Metric | Comparison Operator | Warning Threshold | Critical Threshold | Corrective Actions | Collection Schedule | Edit
Avg Celldisk Read Requests | > | 100 | 200 | None | Every 15 Minutes
Avg Celldisk Reads (MB) | > | 4096 | 8192 | None | Every 15 Minutes
Cell Alert | = | INFO | Critical | None
Celldisk Write Throughput/Sec (MB) | > | 1024 | 2048 | None | Every 15 Minutes
CPU Busy (%) | > | 60 | 80 | None | Every 15 Minutes
Filesystem Utilization % | > | 80 | 90 | None | Every 15 Minutes
Host MB Dropped Per Sec | > | 100 | 200 | None | Every 15 Minutes
Host MB Resent Per Sec | > | 100 | 200 | None | Every 15 Minutes
Host RDMA MB Dropped Per Sec | > | 20 | 40 | None | Every 15 Minutes
IORM Boost | < | 0.1 | 0 | None | Every 15 Minutes
Memory Utilization (%) | > | 75 | 90 | None | Every 15 Minutes
Offload Efficiency | < | 1.5 | 1.1 | None | Every 15 Minutes
Response Status | | | Down | None | Every 1 Minute
TIP Empty Thresholds will disable alerts for that metric.
Metric Thresholds Links
Metric Snapshots
Metric Thresholds Policies

FIGURE 5-9. *Configuring metric and policy settings using Enterprise Manager*

page, you can modify metric threshold values, edit monitoring settings for specific metrics, change metric collection schedules, and disable collection of a metric. For more information on the fields displayed in this page and how the thresholds can be modified, click *Help* from the top-right corner of this page.

Viewing Metrics and Reports   Enterprise Manager offers a comprehensive set of screens that allow you to view, modify, and report on metrics. You can view the list of the available metrics by clicking the *All Metrics* page. The All Metrics page of the Exadata plug-in is shown in Figure 5-10.

To access the built-in reports, click the *Reports* tab. The built-in reports will display the data related to the Exadata Storage Server performance and configuration, based on the data collected in the Management Repository. The reports have a *Refresh* icon, and clicking this icon will refresh the

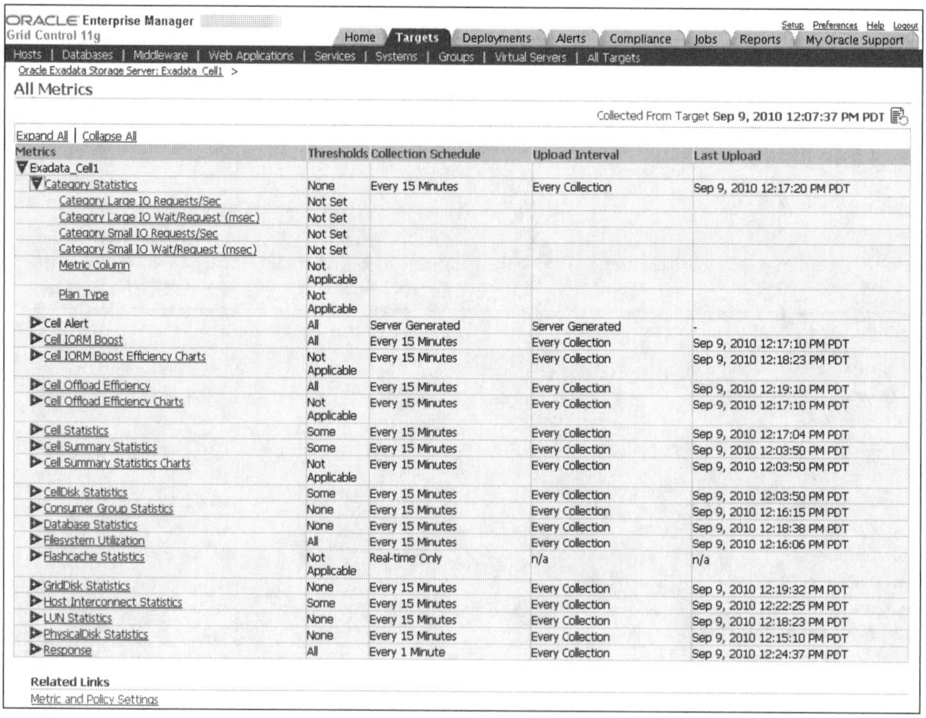

FIGURE 5-10.   *Enterprise Manager Plug-In for Exadata All Metrics page*

reports based on the data from the Management Repository, and does not get real-time data from the Exadata Storage Servers. Some of the built-in reports available in Enterprise Manager are performance reports of Exadata Storage Server components such as cell disks, grid disks, and I/O Resource Manager, as well as configuration reports of the Exadata Storage Server and the cell disks. Figure 5-11 shows a sample report.

Oracle Enterprise Manager Ops Center

Oracle Enterprise Manager Ops Center is a comprehensive, end-to-end, data center automation solution for managing Oracle Sun hardware, Solaris- and Linux-based operating systems, and Oracle virtualization technologies. Ops Center provides rich lifecycle management capabilities, starting from the discovery of bare-metal hardware to the provisioning and patching of operating systems and applications. Ops Center has a centralized management console that is integrated with hardware management infrastructure, such as Oracle Integrated Lights Out Manager (ILOM),

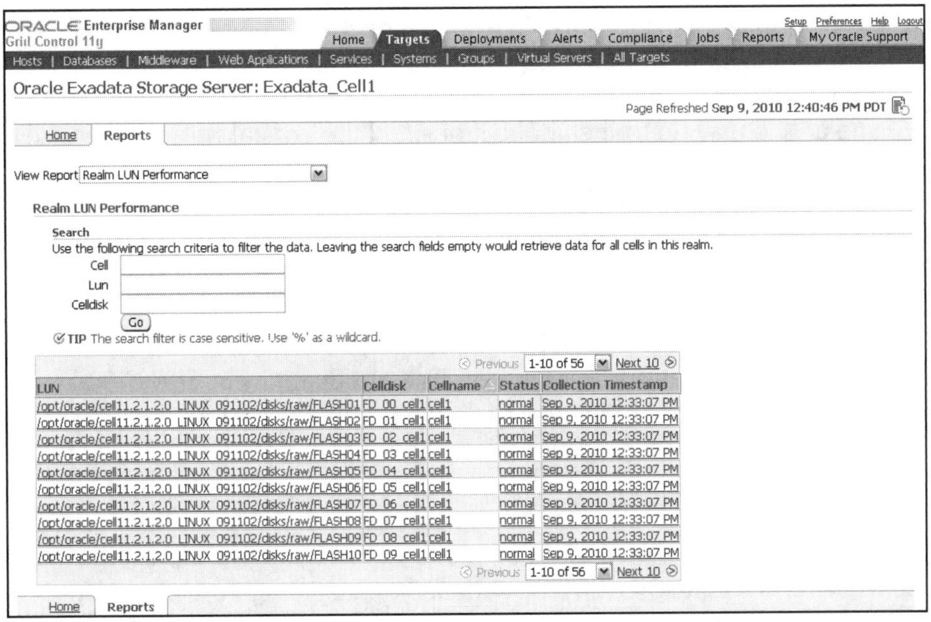

FIGURE 5-11. *Sample cell performance report*

for monitoring and management of hardware resources, virtualized environments, and applications.

Ops Center monitors the health of the operating system and the hardware resources for a variety of systems, including the Exadata Database Machine. Some of the hardware monitoring and management features of Ops Center are monitoring of hardware health status, power management and monitoring, ability to turn systems on and off, and monitoring the hardware connectivity. Ops Center also enables you to monitor the health of your Solaris, Linux, and Windows operating systems, including network connectivity, file system status, CPU usage, memory usage, and network bandwidth utilization.

Ops Center monitors certain parameters of the hardware and OS components that are of interest, and when these parameters cross predefined thresholds, notifications can be triggered. You can edit the thresholds that control how OS monitoring takes place. You can use notification profiles that trigger alerts to specific users. Refer to the Oracle Enterprise Manager Ops Center documentation for further details on managing and monitoring with Ops Center.

Oracle Enterprise Manager Ops Center Connector   If you utilize the monitoring capabilities of Ops Center within the Enterprise Manager Grid Control Console, you get the benefit of monitoring the storage, hardware, OS, and all the way up to the applications and the critical business services by using a centralized management console. This integration of Ops Center with Enterprise Manager is possible through the Oracle Management Connector for Ops Center. Using the connector, you can view consolidated information of the Exadata Database Machine servers, the network, and operating systems, within a single unified Grid Control Console.

The connector also enables the integration of alert notifications of Ops Center with Oracle Enterprise Manager. The notifications in Ops Center triggered due to Exadata Database Machine hardware component failures, or due to issues with operating system performance, or failures related to software components, will now become alerts in the Oracle Enterprise Manager. When combined with the System Monitoring Plug-in for Exadata, this capability provides a centralized platform for managing alerts, allowing you to better correlate alerts from Exadata Storage Servers with the alerts from Ops Center and accelerate the root-cause analysis when investigating issues.

Some of the other benefits of this integration are

- Consolidated event management of applications, database, and hardware

- Better visualization of critical issues across the technology stack for a faster resolution

The notification events occurring in the Ops Center will be forwarded by the Ops Center Management Console to the Oracle Enterprise Manager through the web services interface. Once the notifications are propagated to Oracle Enterprise Manager, they are treated as native Oracle Enterprise Manager alerts, and will utilize the built-in notifications framework and the policies that are set up in Enterprise Manager for notifying administrators of critical events occurring in the system.

The key features of the Ops Center Connector are

- The notifications forwarded by Ops Center to Enterprise Manager will be associated with the appropriate targets they originated from, depending on the mapping option that you select. The connector tracks the alerts forwarded from Ops Center and automatically updates the information in Enterprise Manager.

- The alerts will be cleared from Enterprise Manager based on the properties set for notification options in the Grid Control Console.

- The Ops Center notification severities of *low* and *medium* are mapped to the Enterprise Manager alert severity of *warning,* whereas the Ops Center severity of *high* is mapped to the Enterprise Manager alert severity of *critical.*

- From Ops Center, you can choose the alerts that should propagate to Enterprise Manager by configuring the monitoring parameters and the user notification profile.

Oracle Integrated Lights Out Manager

Oracle Integrated Lights Out Manager (ILOM) is a systems management and monitoring tool that can remotely manage Oracle Sun servers, including the Exadata Storage Servers and the database servers of the Exadata Database Machine. ILOM provides a true lights-out management of the system, and can manage and monitor the system hardware independently of the state of the operating system.

The key abilities provided by ILOM are

- Remotely manage the power state of the systems.

- Display the hardware configuration of the system.

- Monitor the hardware for faults and receive alerts about system events as they occur.

- Remotely access the command line and the GUI consoles of the host, and perform management functions as if you were using a locally attached keyboard, video, and mouse.

- Observe the status of various system sensors and indicators.

The architecture of ILOM consists of service processor hardware, which resides on the system board, and the management software that runs within the service processor hardware. The ILOM software and hardware comes preinstalled and preconfigured on a variety of Oracle Sun server platforms. ILOM can be integrated with other management and monitoring tools that are already installed in your data center using the SNMP interface, such as the integration with Oracle Enterprise Manager Ops Center discussed earlier. This integration will allow you to combine the provisioning and patching features of Ops Center, and extending that, to manage the system BIOS and to perform firmware updates of hardware components.

The service processor hardware of ILOM has a dedicated Ethernet port that you will use to connect with the management network of your data center. The users will access ILOM by connecting to the Ethernet IP address using the interfaces provided here:

- **Web-based interface** You can use the industry-standard web browser to log in to the web interface of ILOM and perform management and monitoring functions. The service processor hardware runs an embedded web server that is able to service requests coming from the web browser. With this capability, you can redirect the server KVM to the web browser running on a remote system. You can also share the remote system's disk drive or CD-ROM with the server as if it was locally connected to the server that is being managed by ILOM.

■ **Command-line interface (CLI)**   Using the CLI, you can interface with ILOM to perform operations that otherwise would be accomplished using the web browser interface. The CLI will allow you to script out your actions, which you can schedule to run without user intervention. The CLI is based on industry-standard Distributed Management Task Force Specification.

■ **Intelligent Platform Management Interface (IPMI)**   IPMI is an industry-standard interface that will allow you to manage server hardware. Using IPMI, you can perform management and reporting of the servers, perform system monitoring, trigger alerts on exceptions, and recover systems by performing power resets. You can use the IPMITool utility to interface with ILOM and retrieve information about the server platform from the service processor hardware. The IPMITool is available on the host operating system of the server platform, or you can install it on a remote system and access the ILOM remotely.

■ **SNMP interface**   SNMP is an industry-standard systems management protocol that is used to manage systems and devices connected over a network. SNMP consists of managed devices that will send SNMP messages via the network to the central management station. ILOM acts like a managed device and will forward SNMP messages to central management stations such as the Oracle Enterprise Manager Ops Center, and also to third-party monitoring software.

Summary

The initial configuration of the Oracle Exadata Database Machine is typically performed by Oracle ACS upon delivery and installation. You will only need to perform routine ongoing management of its hardware and software components. The Oracle database and the Oracle Grid infrastructure components of the Database Machine are treated like any other Oracle install on a Linux or a Solaris platform, and are maintained and monitored just like you would maintain and monitor any other Oracle RAC system using ASM. The Exadata Storage Servers require minimal management since the bulk of administration tasks are performed during the initial setup phase.

The best practices of architecting the storage served by the Exadata Storage Servers are highlighted in this chapter. It is important that you understand the different ways of carving out the storage and the recommended best practices, especially when you deploy a consolidation environment and have a need to configure a shared storage grid among all workloads or a storage grid with dedicated storage pools for each workload.

The Exadata Storage Servers can be monitored using the command-line utilities such as the CellCLI and dcli, and the GUI-based Enterprise Manager Grid Control Console. You should use Enterprise Manager and utilize its unified management and reporting capabilities for managing and monitoring the Database Machine hardware, operating systems, Oracle database software, and the Exadata Storage Server Software, all in one centralized location. However, if you choose to utilize third-party monitoring software, you can integrate with the Database Machine through the SNMP interface and propagate alerts generated by the Exadata Storage Server Software, the Database Machine hardware, and even the Oracle Enterprise Manager system to the monitoring infrastructure of your choice.

CHAPTER
6

High Availability and
Backup Strategies

he continuous availability of business-critical information is a key requirement for enterprises to survive in today's information-based economy. Enterprise database systems managing critical data such as financial and customer information, and operational data such as orders, need to be available at all times. Making important business decisions based on these systems requires the databases storing this data to provide high-service uptime with enhanced reliability.

When the loss of data or the database service occurs due to planned events such as software patching and upgrading, or due to unforeseen events such as media failures, data corruption, or disasters, the data and the database service need to be recovered quickly and accurately. If recovery cannot be performed in the optimal timeframe as dictated by the business Service Level Agreements (SLA), the business can incur loss of revenues and customers. Choosing the right high-availability architecture of the Exadata Database Machine will enable the enterprises to safeguard critical data and provide the highest level of service, availability, and reliability.

The basic premise of high-availability architectures is based on redundancies across the hardware and software components in the deployment architecture. Redundant systems provide high availability when remaining active at the same time. High availability can also be built into the software layer by incorporating features that provide continuous availability of data. A few examples are the features that help repair data corruption, perform online maintenance operations, and help you recover from user errors while the database remains available.

Oracle provides a myriad of high-availability technologies for implementing highly available database systems. This chapter highlights such technologies and the recommended practices and guidelines for implementing them. We will also discuss the best-practice methods of performing backup and recovery on the Oracle Exadata Database Machine.

Exadata Maximum Availability Architecture (MAA)

Oracle Maximum Availability Architecture (MAA) is the Oracle-recommended best-practice architecture for achieving the highest availability of service with Oracle products, using Oracle's proven high-availability technologies.

MAA best practices are published as a series of technical whitepapers and blue prints, and assist in deploying highly available Oracle-based applications and platforms that are capable of meeting and exceeding the business service-level requirements. The MAA architecture covers all components of the technology stack, includes the hardware and the software, and addresses planned and unplanned downtime.

MAA provides a framework for high availability by incorporating redundancies into the components of the technology stack, and also by utilizing certain built-in high-availability features of the Oracle software. For example, the Database Flashback feature enables you to recover from user errors such as an involuntary DROP TABLE statement by using a simple FLASHBACK TABLE command. This cuts down the recovery time drastically, which otherwise would be needed for performing a point-in-time recovery using backups.

Figure 6-1 represents the MAA architecture using the Exadata Database Machine. The Database Machine MAA architecture has identically sized Database Machines on the primary and standby sites. The primary site contains a production database configured with Oracle Real Application Clusters (RAC). Oracle RAC provides protection from database server and

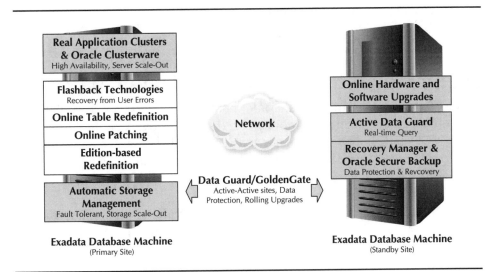

FIGURE 6-1.   *Exadata Database Machine MAA architecture*

instance failures. The standby site contains a physical standby database that is synchronized with the primary database by using Oracle Data Guard. The Active Data Guard option enables the physical standby database to be open in a read-only state while the database is kept in sync with the primary database. Active Data Guard enables you to offload read-only queries to the standby site and enhances the overall availability of the database by utilizing an otherwise idle standby site for reporting purposes. The figure also depicts the use of Oracle database technologies such as Flashback, RMAN, and ASM for providing high availability during planned and unplanned downtime.

We'll next cover the Oracle high-availability features that address planned and unplanned downtime. The intent is not to cover the complete set of MAA technologies, but only the topics that relate to the Exadata Database Machine and the common tasks that will be performed on the Machine. The topics discussed in this section are listed here:

- High availability with Oracle Data Guard

- Using Oracle GoldenGate with Database Machine

- Database Machine patches and upgrades

- Exadata Storage Server high availability

- Preventing data corruption

High Availability with Oracle Data Guard

Oracle Data Guard is an integral component of MAA and the best-practice solution for ensuring high availability and disaster recovery of the Oracle database. Data Guard provides an extensive set of features that enable you to recover from planned and unplanned downtime scenarios, such as recovering from data corruption, performing near-zero database upgrades, and conducting database migrations.

Data Guard provides the software to manage and maintain one or more standby databases that are configured as a replica of the primary database, and protects from data loss by building and maintaining redundant copies of the database. When a data loss or a complete disaster occurs on the primary database, the copy of the data stored on the standby database can be used to repair the primary database. Data Guard also provides protection from data corruptions by detecting and repairing corruptions automatically as they happen, using the uncorrupted copy on the standby database.

The Data Guard architecture consists of processes that capture and transport transactions occurring on the primary database and applying them on the standby databases. Oracle redo generated on the primary site is used to transmit changes captured from the primary to the standby site(s), using a synchronous or asynchronous mechanism. Once the redo is received by the standby site, it is applied on the standby databases using one of two possible methods: Redo Apply or SQL Apply.

The *Redo Apply* process uses the database media recovery process to apply the transactions to the standby databases. Redo Apply maintains a block-for-block replica of the primary database, ensuring that the standby database is physically identical to the primary one in all respects. The standby database that uses Redo Apply to sync up with the primary is called a *physical standby*. The physical standby database can be open and made accessible for running read-only queries while the redo is being applied; this arrangement of the physical standby is called *Active Data Guard.*

The *SQL Apply* process mines the redo logs once they are received on the standby host, re-creates the SQL transactions as they occurred on the primary database, and then executes the SQL on the standby database. The standby in this case is open for read-write activity, and contains the same logical information as the primary database. However, the database has its own identity with possibly different physical structures. The standby database that uses the SQL Apply as the synchronization method is called a *logical standby.*

NOTE
The SQL Apply has some restrictions on the data types, objects, and SQL operations that it supports. Refer to the Oracle Data Guard manuals for further details.

The MAA best practices dictate the use of Data Guard Redo Apply as the synchronization method for achieving the highest availability with the Database Machine. MAA also proposes the use of Active Data Guard to enhance the overall availability of the database machine by utilizing the standby database for reporting and queries.

Data Guard is tightly integrated with the Oracle database and supports high-transaction volumes that are demanded by the Exadata Database Machine deployments. When you follow the best practices for configuring Data Guard, the typical apply rates that you can achieve with Redo Apply can be over 2 TB/hr. Keep in mind that this means 2 TB/hr of database changes, which is a high transaction rate.

Although the primary purpose of Data Guard is to provide high availability and disaster recovery, it can also be utilized for a variety of other business scenarios that address planned and unplanned downtime requirements. A few such scenarios are discussed next:

- **Database rolling upgrades** The Data Guard standby database can be used to perform rolling database upgrades with near-zero downtime. The standby database is upgraded while the primary is still servicing production loads, and the primary database is switched over to the standby, with minimal interruption.

- **Migrate to the Database Machine** Data Guard can be used to migrate Oracle databases to the Database Machine with minimal downtime, using the physical or the logical standby database. The standby database will be instantiated on the Exadata Database Machine and then switched over to the primary role, allowing the migration to happen with the flip of a switch. Refer to Chapter 10 for further details.

- **Data corruption detection and prevention** The Data Guard Apply process can detect corruptions, and also provide mechanisms to automatically recover from corruptions. This topic is discussed in detail later in the chapter.

- **User error protection** You can induce a delay in the Redo Apply process to queue the transactions for a specified period (delay) before they are applied on the standby database. The delay provides you with the ability to recover from user or application errors on the primary database, since the corruption does not immediately get propagated and can be repaired by using a pristine copy from the standby.

- **Offload queries and backups**   Active Data Guard can be used to offload read-only queries and backups to the active standby database. Offloading the queries from the primary database will improve performance and accelerate the return on investment on the standby, which otherwise would be sitting idle. Backups created on the standby can be used to recover the primary database, since the standby will be a block-for-block copy of the primary.

- **Primary-primary configuration**   Instead of having a traditional Data Guard setup of a primary site and a standby site, with all primary databases configured on the primary site, you can configure both sites to be primary sites and spread the primary roles across the available machines on both sites. For example, if you have a traditional Data Guard setup of OLTP and DSS / data warehouse databases in the primary roles on *site A* and *site B* housing their standbys, you can configure *site A* with the primary OLTP database and the standby DSS database, and *site B* with standby OLTP and primary DSS. The primary-primary setup allows you to utilize all the systems in the configuration and spread the production load over to the standby, which leads to an overall increase in performance and at the same time, decreases the impact of individual site failures.

When configuring Data Guard with the Exadata Database Machine, special consideration needs to be given for Exadata Hybrid Columnar Compression (EHCC) and for transporting the redo traffic over the network. These considerations are discussed next.

Data Guard and Exadata Hybrid Columnar Compression

The Exadata Hybrid Columnar Compression (EHCC) feature is the Oracle compression technology available only to the databases residing on the Exadata Storage Servers. If you plan on using EHCC compression with the Database Machine in a Data Guard configuration, the best practice is to have the primary and the standby databases both reside on the Exadata Storage Servers. Such a Data Guard configuration will provide the best performance and the highest availability of your critical data in the event of failures.

If you intend to configure a standby database on traditional storage (non-Exadata–based) for a primary database residing on Exadata Storage Servers, you need to consider the limitations mentioned next. The limitations arise mainly because EHCC compression is not supported on databases residing on non-Exadata storage.

- When performing a switchover operation to the standby on the traditional storage, the EHCC-compressed tables need to be uncompressed on the standby before they can be accessed by the applications. The time to uncompress EHCC tables can significantly affect the availability of the database and add to the total recovery time needed for the switchover. Since EHCC is normally used for less frequently updated or historical data, the inability to access this data momentarily may not be a serious problem for the business.

- If you need to uncompress the EHCC tables on the standby database, you should factor in the additional space needed on the standby to accommodate the uncompressed data. The additional space is dependent on the compression ratios provided by EHCC, and could range from 10 to 50 times the original compressed space.

- If the standby database is going to be utilized for production loads after the switchover, it needs to be able to sustain the throughput and load characteristics of the primary database. The reality is that it probably cannot match the Database Machine performance, in which case, the standby will be running in a reduced performance mode.

- Active Data Guard is not supported on the standby if you plan on using EHCC on the primary database.

NOTE
A simple way to move an EHCC-compressed table to non-EHCC is by using the ALTER TABLE MOVE command.

Data Guard Network Best Practices

The network utilized to push the Data Guard traffic (redo) from the primary database to the standby should be able to handle the redo rates generated by the primary. Otherwise, you will encounter apply lags, which can add delays to the switchover process and hamper the recoverability of data.

Before deciding on the best method of routing the redo between the primary and the standby, calculate the bandwidth required by the redo generated by the primary database. This can be easily done from the Automatic Workload Repository (AWR) report by looking at the *redo size per second* metric. The metric should be captured during peak loads on the primary and accumulated from all the instances generating redo in the RAC cluster. You should also add the overhead of the TCP network (~30 percent due to TCP headers) to come up with the final bandwidth requirement.

Once you calculate the bandwidth required, consider the following options for deciding the best method applicable for routing the redo:

- **Public network**   Investigate the bandwidth available on the public network to push redo. If the standby is in a remote location, this might be the only option available to you, unless the primary and the standby data centers are networked using dedicated lines. Since the public network is shared with other traffic, consider using quality of service (QoS) features to guarantee the bandwidth allocation required for Data Guard.

- **Dedicated network**   If the public network is unable to handle the required bandwidth, consider isolating the traffic through a dedicated gigabit network. Each database server in the Database Machine has a set of 1 GigE and 10 GigE ports that you can use to route redo. You should be able to get an effective transfer rate of 120 MB/s through a 1 GigE port and 1 GB/s through a 10 GigE port. If you require more bandwidth than what is available from a single port, consider bonding multiple ports together or shipping the redo from multiple servers. For example, using two 1 GigE ports can give you a combined aggregated throughput of 240 MB/s, and two 10 GigE ports can give you a throughput of 2 GB/s.

- **InfiniBand network**   Use the InfiniBand network to route redo when the redo rates cannot be accommodated using the 1 GigE or the 10 GigE ports. InfiniBand cables have a distance limitation (typically 100 m), so the distance between the primary and the standby Database Machines will be one of the deciding factors to determine if InfiniBand can be used. Using the InfiniBand network with TCP communication (IPoIB), you should be able to get a throughput of about 2 GB/s by using one port.

- **Data Guard redo compression**   Consider transmitting the redo in a compressed format by using the Oracle Advanced Compression option. This is useful if none of the options are available to satisfy your bandwidth requirements.

Using Oracle GoldenGate with Database Machine

Oracle GoldenGate is a real-time, log-based, change data capture and replication tool that supports Oracle and non-Oracle sources and targets. Oracle GoldenGate replicates committed transactions from the source database in real time while preserving transactional integrity. GoldenGate has the intelligence to interface with the proprietary log formats of different database vendors, and using this intelligence, it can re-create the SQL statement of the transaction as it is executed on the source system and apply the re-created SQL on the destination system. GoldenGate performs these steps in real time and with minimal overhead on the source and thus, provides a solution that enables high-speed and real-time transactional data replication.

Oracle GoldenGate supports a variety of use cases, including real-time business intelligence, query offloading, zero-downtime upgrades and migrations, disaster recovery, and active-active databases with bidirectional replication, data synchronization, and high availability. A few use cases of GoldenGate focused on providing high availability for the Database Machine deployments are discussed here:

- GoldenGate can perform migrations of Oracle and non-Oracle databases to the Exadata Database Machine with minimal to zero downtime. The migration process starts by instantiating the source database on the Database Machine, replicating transactions from the source database to the Database Machine, keeping the two systems in sync for a time, and eventually switching the production system to the Oracle database. This method will allow you to perform comprehensive testing of your applications on the Exadata Database Machine, using production data volumes, tune them if necessary, and more importantly, allow you to attain a comfort level with the migration process before performing the actual switchover. Refer to Chapter 10 for further details on performing migrations to the Database Machine using GoldenGate.

■ GoldenGate supports active-passive replication configurations with which it can replicate data from an active primary database on the Exadata Database Machine to the inactive standby database. GoldenGate can keep the two systems in sync by applying changes in real time. The standby database can be used to provide high availability during planned and unplanned outages, perform upgrades, and accelerate the recovery process on the primary.

NOTE
The term standby database *in this context is used to refer to a standby database replicated by GoldenGate, and should not be confused with the Data Guard standby database.*

■ GoldenGate supports active-active replication configurations, which offer bidirectional replication between primary and standby databases. The benefit of active-active is that the standby database (which is also another primary) can be used to offload processing from the primary. The standby database would otherwise be idle and will be utilized only during outages. This setup will allow you to distribute load across the primary and the standby databases based on application types and geographic location. Utilizing an idle database, which is usually considered a "dead" investment by the IT departments, will help you to justify the cost of purchasing a standby Database Machine.

■ The Database Machine can be used as a real-time data warehouse in which other Oracle and non-Oracle databases can feed real-time transactions using GoldenGate. Real-time data warehouses are used by the enterprises in today's competitive landscape for performing real-time analytics and business intelligence.

■ GoldenGate can be used in situations that require the Exadata Database Machine to feed other database systems or data warehouses that require changed data to be captured from the Database Machine and propagated to the destination systems in real time. These types of deployments allow coexistence and integration of the Database Machine with other databases that you may have deployed in the data center.

Oracle GoldenGate Architecture

The primary components of the Oracle GoldenGate software are shown in Figure 6-2. Each component is designed so that it can perform its task independently of the other. This design ensures minimal dependencies and at the same time preserves data integrity by eliminating undue interference.

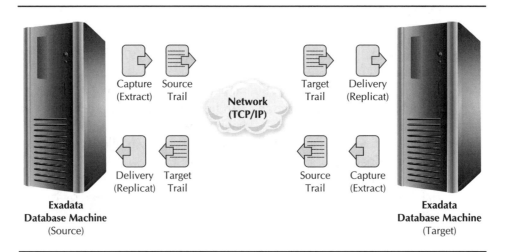

FIGURE 6-2. *Oracle GoldenGate architecture*

The main components comprising the GoldenGate software architecture are the following:

■ **Extract process** The *extract* process captures new transactions as they occur on the source system. The extract process interfaces with the native transaction logs of the source database and reads the result of insert, update, and delete operations in real time. The extract can push captured changes directly to the *replicat* process, or generate *trail files.*

■ **Trail files** Trail files are generated by the extract process. They contain database transactions captured from the source system in a transportable and platform-independent format. Trail files reside outside the database to ensure platform independence, and to enhance the reliability and availability of transactions. This architecture minimizes the impact on the source system because additional tables or queries are not required on the source for supporting the data capture process.

■ **Replicat process** The *replicat* process takes the changed data from the latest trail file and applies it to the target using the native SQL for the appropriate target database system. The replicat process preserves the original sequence of the transactions as they were captured on the source system, and thereby preserves transactional and referential integrity at the target.

■ **Manager process** The manager process runs on the target and the source systems, and is responsible for starting, monitoring, and restarting other GoldenGate processes, and also for allocating data storage, reporting errors, and logging events.

■ **Checkpoint files** Checkpoint files contain the current read and write positions of the extract and replicat processes. Checkpoints provide fault tolerance by preventing the data loss when the system, the network, or the GoldenGate processes need to be restarted.

■ **Discard files** Discard files are used by GoldenGate to record failed operations either by the extract or the replicat process. For example, invalid column mappings are logged into the discard file by the replicat process so that they can be further investigated.

Oracle GoldenGate and Database Machine Best Practices

As discussed previously, GoldenGate requires a set of key files to accomplish its tasks. The best practice for storing these files on the Database Machine is to store them in the Oracle Database File System (DBFS). DBFS is discussed in Chapter 2; in a nutshell, it provides a distributed, NFS-like file system interface that can be mounted on the database servers. DBFS and NFS are the only methods currently available in the Database Machine to allow sharing of files among the database servers. The advantage of DBFS over NFS-like file systems is that DBFS inherits the high availability, reliability, and disaster recovery capabilities of the Oracle database since the files placed in DBFS are stored inside the database as a SecureFiles object.

NOTE
NFS file systems can be mounted on the database servers using the InfiniBand network or the 1 GigE or 10 GigE ports. The underlying transport protocol supported for NFS is TCP (IPoIB for InfiniBand).

The best-practice considerations for implementing GoldenGate with the Exadata Database Machine are as follows:

- Use DBFS to store GoldenGate trail files and checkpoint files. If a database server in the Database Machine fails, the GoldenGate extract and replicat processes will continue to function, since the trail and checkpoint files will still be accessible from the other database servers.

- Ensure that the extract and the replicat processes run only on a single database node. This requirement guarantees that multiple extract/replicat processes do not work on the same set of transactions at the same time. One way to prevent them from starting up concurrently from other database nodes is to mount the DBFS file system only on one node and use this node to run these processes. Other nodes cannot accidentally start them, since DBFS will not be mounted on them.

This check is built in when using a regular file system to store the checkpoint and trail files instead of DBFS. Using file locking mechanisms, the first extract/replicat process will exclusively lock the files and ensure that the second process cannot start. DBFS currently does not support such methods and hence, the manual checks are required.

■   The best practice for storing checkpoint files on DBFS is to create a symbolic link from the GoldenGate home directory to a directory on DBFS, as shown in the following example. Use the same mount point names on all the nodes to ensure consistency and seamless failover.

```
# DBFS is mounted on /mnt/dbfs
# GoldenGate is installed on /OGG/v10_4
% mkdir /mnt/dbfs/OGG/dirchk
% cd /OGG/v10_4
% rm -rf dirchk
% ln -s /mnt/dbfs/OGG/dirchk dirchk
```

■   The DBFS database should be configured as a separate RAC database on the same nodes that house the databases accessed by GoldenGate. Perform checks to ensure that the DBFS file system is mountable on all database nodes. However as a best practice stated earlier, only one node will mount the DBFS at a time.

■   Install the GoldenGate software in the same location on all the nodes that are required to run GoldenGate upon a failure of the original node. Also ensure that the manager, extract, and replicat parameter files are up to date on all nodes.

■   Configure the extract and replicat processes to start up automatically upon the startup of the manager process.

■   Configure Oracle Clusterware to perform startup, shutdown, and failover of GoldenGate components. This practice provides high availability of the GoldenGate processes by automating steps required to initiate a failover operation.

■   The *page* and *discard* files should be set up on the local file system and within the GoldenGate installation directory structure. The page file is a special memory-mapped file and currently not supported by DBFS.

Database Machine Patches and Upgrades

Applying patches and performing upgrades are normal events in the lifecycle of software, and the Exadata Database Machine software components are no exception. The software installed on the database servers, the Exadata Storage Servers, and the InfiniBand switches are candidates for being patched or upgraded when Oracle releases their newer versions.

Oracle Enterprise Manager (OEM) has the capability to patch the Oracle software stack. You can use OEM to simplify the patching experience on the Exadata Database Machine. OEM's integration with My Oracle Support enables you to identify recommended patches for your system by searching Knowledge Base articles, validating them for any conflicts, finding or requesting merge patches, and lastly but not least, automating the patch deployment process by using OEM Provisioning and Patch Automation features.

We will next describe the Database Machine patching process using methods that provide zero downtimes. Database high-availability features such as RAC and Data Guard, and the built-in high-availability features of Exadata Storage Server, make zero downtime patching achievable.

We will also discuss the methods available for upgrading the database, ASM and Clusterware, with minimal downtime using Data Guard.

NOTE
The patches for the Database Machine are categorized into database software patches, database system patches (which include the OS, firmware, database, and OFED patches), and the Exadata Storage Server patches. A separate system-level patch for the Exadata Storage Server does not exist, since this is bundled into the Exadata Storage Server patch.

Exadata Storage Server Patching

The Exadata Storage Server patches encompass patches to the Exadata Storage Server Software, Oracle Linux OS, firmware updates, and patches to Open Fabrics Enterprise Distribution (OFED) packages. Under no circumstances should users apply OS, firmware, or OFED patches directly on the Exadata Storage Servers. These patches will be supplied by Oracle and will be bundled into an Exadata Storage Server patch. The patch will be applied to all the servers in a rolling fashion and one at a time, without incurring any downtime.

Exadata Storage Server patches are one of two types: *overlay* and *staged.* Overlay patches require a restart of the Exadata Storage Server Software processes (CELLSRV, RS, and MS). Upon the restart of the Exadata Storage Server Software, ASM issues an automatic reconnect and the service resumes normal operation. This process does not incur any downtime.

Staged patches require the Exadata Storage Server to be rebooted upon application. The Exadata Storage Server will be taken offline and if any interim updates to the data residing in the offline Exadata Storage Servers occur during this period, they will be tracked by ASM. The updates will be synced when the Exadata Storage Server becomes available, using the ASM fast mirror re-sync feature. Staged patches do not incur any service downtime.

Database Patching with Minimal Downtime

Oracle database patches are broadly categorized into two types—patches and patch sets. A *patch* is a change to the Oracle software that happens between *patch sets* or upgrades, whereas a patch set is a mechanism for delivering a set of patches that are combined, integrated, and tested together, and delivered on a regular basis. Patches may be applied to an Oracle database with zero or near-zero downtime, using one of two techniques: the online patching feature introduced in Oracle Database 11*g* and rolling patching with Oracle RAC. We will describe both features in this section. The process of applying patch sets is treated similar to an upgrade, and you should use the methods outlined in the "Database Rolling Upgrades" section of this chapter to perform minimal downtime upgrades from patch sets.

NOTE
Oracle database patches can be Interim, Merge, Bundle, or Critical Patch Update (CPU) patches.

Rolling Patching with RAC   Oracle provides the ability to apply patches to the individual nodes of a RAC cluster in a rolling fashion, to one RAC node at a time, while the other nodes are still servicing user requests. The process of applying a rolling patch starts with taking one of the RAC nodes out of service, applying the patch to the node, and putting the node back in service. These steps are repeated until all instances in the cluster are patched.

Patches need to be labeled as "rolling" before they can be applied using this method. Usually, patches that modify the database and the shared structures between the RAC instances do not qualify as rolling. Moreover, only patches, and not patch sets, can be labeled as rolling capable.

Rolling patching using RAC guarantees the availability of the database service during the patching process. However, you will be running with one less node in the cluster until the process is completed, so the impact to the business due to reduced capacity should be considered prior to proceeding with this method.

Online Patching   Online patching is the process of applying patches to the Oracle instance while the database instance is up. A patch is capable of being applied online when the scope of changes introduced by the patch is small and the patch does not modify the database or the shared structures, which are also the requirements for rolling patches.

The criteria for qualifying a patch as online is more restrictive than the criteria for the rolling patch. If the patch is not qualified as rolling, then it definitely cannot be qualified as online. Examples of patches that usually get qualified as online are the interim and debug patches.

When applying an online patch, you specify the ORACLE_HOME of the binaries that you like to patch, along with the database instance. The online patch will patch the binaries residing in the Oracle home as with a regular database patch. The online patch will also patch the database instance processes. Each database process periodically checks for patched code and copies the new code into its execution space. This means that the processes might not pick up the new patched code at the exact time the patch is applied and there might be some delay.

You will see an increase in the overall memory utilization of the patched database processes due to the extra space needed in the Program Global Area (PGA) for running patched code. The extra memory is released once the database instance is restarted. You need to consider the total free memory available on the database host before applying the patch so you can investigate the impact of the memory increase to other resources.

Typically, each patched process requires about 3 to 5 percent more memory, but the actual memory will depend on the number of changes introduced in the patch. The best way to measure it would be to test the patch on a test system before applying it to the production system.

Apart from using Enterprise Manager, you can also use the opatch utility to apply online patches. Use this opatch command to query whether the patch is qualified as online. If it is, the output from the command will be "Patch is an online patch: true".

```
$ opatch query <path to patch directory> -is_online_patch
```

Oracle Clusterware and Oracle ASM Rolling Upgrades

Oracle Database 11*g* Release 2 is capable of performing rolling upgrades of Oracle ASM and Oracle Clusterware when configured in a cluster environment, thereby making the cluster available to the database and the applications during the upgrade process.

Starting with Database 11*g* Release 2, Oracle ASM and Clusterware are both executed from one Oracle home installation called the grid infrastructure. Upgrading the grid infrastructure binaries to the next release takes care of upgrading Oracle ASM and Clusterware software.

With the rolling upgrade feature, you will take one node in the cluster down, upgrade the Oracle grid infrastructure, start up ASM and Clusterware, and put the node back in the cluster. You will repeat this process on all the nodes, one at a time, in a rolling fashion. The cluster is available during this process, and no downtime is incurred to the database.

Oracle ASM and Clusterware can run at different versions of the software until all nodes in the cluster are upgraded. It should be noted that any new features introduced by the new versions of ASM or Clusterware are not enabled until all nodes in the cluster are upgraded.

Database Rolling Upgrades

Using Oracle Data Guard, it is possible for you to upgrade from older versions of the database and apply patch sets, in a rolling fashion and with near-zero downtime, to the end users and applications. Data Guard rolling upgrades were introduced with Oracle Database 10*g* Release 1 using the SQL Apply process of the logical standby database. Oracle Database 11*g* enhances this capability by using a transient logical standby method that utilizes a physical standby database.

Rolling upgrades using the transient logical standby method start by using an existing physical standby database and temporarily converting it to a logical standby for the purpose of the upgrade, followed by the upgrade of the logical standby to the latest release. The logical standby database is then made the new primary by a simple Data Guard switchover process. Keep in mind that there are restrictions, based on data types and other factors, that impact the use of logical standby databases; please refer to the documentation for more details.

> **NOTE**
> *During rolling upgrades, when converting the physical standby database to the logical standby, you need to keep the identity of the original physical standby database intact by using the KEEP IDENTITY clause of the ALTER DATABASE RECOVER TO LOGICAL STANDBY statement. This clause ensures that the logical standby has the same DBID and DB_NAME as the original physical standby.*

During the rolling upgrade process, the synchronization of the redo is paused before the upgrade process is started on the logical standby; the redo from the primary is queued to be applied and resumes after the upgrade completes. The SQL Apply process is capable of synchronizing the redo generated by a lower release of the primary database with a higher release of the upgraded logical standby database, and this ensures that all the transactions are propagated to the standby and there is no data loss. This capability of the SQL Apply process forms the basis of performing rolling upgrades. The primary and the standby databases can remain at different versions until you perform sanity checks on the upgraded logical standby and confirm that the upgrade process has completed successfully.

At this point, you can perform a Data Guard switchover to the standby database, resulting in changing the role of the upgraded logical standby to primary. You can upgrade the old primary database by following a similar process as the one followed for the standby, and initiate a second switchover to the original production system.

There are several benefits of using the transient logical standby method for upgrades. In fact, this method is the Oracle MAA recommended best practice, because the method is simple, reliable, and robust, and requires minimal downtime. Some of the benefits of transient logical standby are highlighted here:

- The transient logical standby method utilizes an existing physical standby database for performing the upgrade and does not require the extra space for creating a new logical standby database solely for the purpose of performing the upgrade.

- The rolling upgrade process provides the added benefit of testing the upgraded environment prior to performing the switchover. The tests are performed using the new version of the Oracle software, with production data and production-like workloads.

- This method greatly reduces the downtime required by running the pre-upgrade, upgrade, and post-upgrade tasks on the standby while the production system is still online and accessible to the users. The downtime incurred by this method is essentially the time it takes for the database to perform a switchover operation to the standby database.

Online Application Upgrades Using Edition-Based Redefinition

Switching gears a bit, this section focuses on providing high availability during database application upgrades, and not Oracle software upgrades as we were discussing earlier.

Upgrading user applications and database objects with zero downtime is possible by using the edition-based redefinition feature of Oracle Database 11*g* Release 2. Edition-based redefinition allows you to upgrade the application and its associated database objects to a newer edition (or version), while the old edition of the application and the database objects coexist and are still accessible by the users. Once the upgrade process is complete, the new connections from the upgraded application will be accessing the new edition of the objects, and the users that were still connected to the old edition will continue to be serviced until they disconnect the session.

The database concepts that enable edition-based redefinitions are

- **Editions** An edition associates the versions of the database objects that together form a semantically intact code release. The release can include all the objects, which is the case when the code is installed for the first time, or a subset of objects—if the objects are modified using a patched release. Database sessions execute in the context of an edition and a user is associated with an edition upon connect time.

- **Editioning views** An editioning view of a database object is the definition of the object as it existed in a particular edition. Editioning views expose different definitions of the database object and allow the users to see the definition that applies to its edition.

- **Cross-edition triggers** Cross-edition triggers are responsible for synchronizing data changes between old and new editions of tables. For example, if a table has new columns added in its latest edition, the users connected to the old edition can still perform updates using the old definition, and the cross-edition trigger will take care of populating the new columns behind the scenes.

Exadata Storage Server High Availability

Ensuring the high availability of the database storage grid is important for enhancing the overall availability of the Database Machine. Oracle ASM provides built-in high-availability features by incorporating Grid RAID, as outlined in Chapter 5. With Grid RAID, when an underlying disk on the Exadata Storage Server fails, the data is still available from the mirrored copy placed on a different Exadata Storage Server. ASM also incorporates built-in protection from data corruption, through which it will transparently access a mirrored copy when the primary copy is found to be corrupt.

Although the ASM redundancy level of NORMAL provides protection from multiple, simultaneous, failures and corruptions occurring in a single Exadata Storage Server, it may not protect you when the failures are spread across multiple Exadata Storage Servers. In such situations, your option for recovery is to perform a restore from a backup or to fail over to the Data Guard standby database (if it is configured).

The best practices outlined next guarantee higher availability and recoverability of the storage grid upon simultaneous, multiple failures that spread across multiple Exadata Storage Servers.

Storage Configuration Best Practices

The recommended ASM diskgroup best-practice configuration as discussed in Chapter 5 is to create a minimum of two diskgroups in the Database Machine. The first diskgroup will store the user and system tablespaces, and the second will store the database Fast Recovery Area (FRA). The database FRA is used for storing archived logs, flashback logs, redo logs, and control files. For the purpose of this discussion, let us assume the diskgroup that stores user data is named DATA and the diskgroup that stores the FRA is named RECOV.

> **NOTE**
> *A third ASM diskgroup is created by Oracle when configuring the Database Machine. This diskgroup is typically used to store OCR and voting disks required by Oracle Clusterware, and is created on the grid disks residing on the outermost tracks.*

The DATA diskgroup should be created on grid disks that reside on the hot or outer tracks of the cell disk, whereas the RECOV diskgroup should reside on the cold or inner tracks of the cell disk. This ensures higher performance for the applications by ensuring faster access to the data blocks from the hot areas of the cell disk.

Storage Configuration with Data Guard   The Data Guard setup ensures that you can tolerate all types of failures on the primary site, up to and including a total disaster of the primary. Also, for failures that are limited to a single Exadata Storage Server, the Grid RAID features will make the data available at all times without requiring the need to fail over to the standby site.

The MAA best practices for configuring DATA and RECOV diskgroups with Data Guard are

- Create DATA and RECOV diskgroups using ASM NORMAL redundancy.

- The DATA and RECOV diskgroups should be created across all available Exadata Storage Servers in the Database Machine.

- This setup guarantees maximum protection due to failures, and at the same time provides the best performance by utilizing all available Exadata Storage Servers in the storage grid.

Storage Configuration Without Data Guard   When you do not have Data Guard configured, as stated earlier, you are only protected from single failures or multiple failures confined to one Exadata Storage Server when you use ASM NORMAL redundancy. The MAA best practices for configuring DATA and RECOV diskgroups without Data Guard are

- Create the DATA diskgroup using ASM NORMAL redundancy.

- Create the RECOV diskgroup using HIGH redundancy. The HIGH redundancy ensures protection from double failures occurring across the Exadata Storage Servers and guarantees full recovery with zero data loss.

NOTE
If you are using ASM NORMAL redundancy without a Data Guard setup, there is a chance of data loss when multiple failures occur across a set of Exadata Storage Servers. For example, if you lose both copies of a redo log due to multiple failures, and if the redo was marked "active" by the database indicating that it was an essential component for performing a full recovery, you have essentially lost your data that was in the redo.

Preventing Data Corruption

Data corruption can occur anytime and in any layer of the hardware and the software stack that deals with storing and retrieving data. Data can get corrupted when it is in the storage, during its transmission over the network, in the memory structures, or when the storage layer performs an I/O operation. If data corruption is not prevented or repaired in a timely manner, the database will lose its integrity and can result in irreparable data loss, which can be catastrophic for the business.

In this section, we will discuss the best practices for preventing and detecting corruption, and the methods available for automatically repairing corruption when it occurs. Although the best practices can help you prevent almost all types of corruption, you might still end up with some, as corruption cannot always be completely prevented. If you have discovered corruption, you can use database recovery methods such as block-level recovery, automated backup and recovery, tablespace point-in-time recovery, remote standby databases, and transactional recovery. Keep in mind that the recovery process can be time consuming, so every effort should be taken to minimize the occurrence of corruption.

Detecting Corruption with Database Parameters

The Oracle database has internal checks which help detect corruption occurring in the database block. The checks involve calculating a checksum on the block contents, and storing it along with the block number and a few other fields in the block header. The checksum is used later to validate the integrity of the block, based on the settings of a few database parameters, that we will define shortly.

The database can also help detect *lost writes*. A lost write is an I/O operation that gets successfully acknowledged by the storage subsystem as being "persisted," but for some reason the I/O was not saved to the disk. Upon a subsequent read of the block that encountered a lost write, the I/O subsystem returns the stale version of the block, which might be used by the database for performing other updates and thereby instigate the propagation of corruption to other coherent blocks.

Corruption detection is built into Oracle ASM when the ASM diskgroups are configured with NORMAL or HIGH redundancy. ASM is able to detect block corruption by validating the block checksum upon a read, and if it detects a corruption, it transparently reads the block again from the mirrored copy. If the mirrored block is intact, then ASM will return the good block to the database, and also try to write the good block over the bad block to fix the corruption. This process is transparent to the database and does not require any setup or tweaks.

When block corruption is detected by RMAN and database processes, it is recorded in the database dictionary view V$DATABASE_BLOCK_CORRUPTION. The view is continuously updated when corrupted blocks are repaired, thus allowing you to detect and report upon the status of corruption much sooner than was ever possible.

The parameters that you use to configure automatic corruption detection in the database and to prevent lost writes are

- **DB_BLOCK_CHECKSUM**   This parameter determines whether the database will calculate a checksum for the block and store it in the header each time it is written to disk. DB_BLOCK_CHECKSUM can have the following values:

  - **FALSE** or **OFF**   Checksums are only enabled and verified for the SYSTEM tablespace.

  - **TYPICAL**   Checksums are enabled on data blocks and computed only upon initial inserts into the block. This is the default setting.

  - **TRUE** or **FULL**   Checksums are enabled on redo and data blocks upon initial inserts and recomputed upon updates/deletes only on data blocks.

- **DB_BLOCK_CHECKING**   This parameter enables the block integrity checks to be performed by Oracle using checksums computed by the DB_BLOCK_CHECKSUM parameter. DB_BLOCK_CHECKING can have the following values:

  - **FALSE** or **OFF**   Semantic checks are performed on the objects residing in SYSTEM tablespace only. This is the default setting.

  - **LOW**   Basic block header checks are performed when blocks change in memory. This includes block changes due to RAC interinstance communication, reads from disk, and updates to data blocks.

  - **MEDIUM**   All LOW-level checks plus full semantic checks are performed on all objects except indexes.

  - **TRUE** or **FULL**   All MEDIUM-level checks plus full semantic checks are performed on index blocks.

- **DB_LOST_WRITE_PROTECT**   This parameter enables (or disables) logging of buffer cache block reads in the redo log. When set to TYPICAL or FULL, the system change number (SCN) of the block being read from the buffer cache is recorded in the redo. When the redo is used by Data Guard to apply transactions from the primary to the standby database, the redo SCN can be compared to the data block SCN on the standby database and evaluated to detect lost writes.

Lost write detection works best when used in conjunction with Data Guard (this topic is covered in the next section). When you do not use Data Guard, RMAN can detect lost writes when it performs recovery.

DB_LOST_WRITE_PROTECT can have the following values:

- **NONE** This is the default setting and disables buffer cache reads from being recorded in the redo.

- **TYPICAL** Buffer cache reads involving read-write tablespaces are recorded in the redo.

- **FULL** All buffer cache reads are recorded in the redo, including reads on read-write and read-only tablespaces.

As of Oracle Database 11g Release 1, you are not required to individually set each of the three parameters discussed earlier. You can set one single parameter, DB_ULTRA_SAFE, and that takes care of implementing the appropriate level of protection by setting DB_BLOCK_CHECKING, DB_BLOCK_CHECKSUM, and DB_LOST_WRITE_PROTECT. The DB_ULTRA_SAFE can have the following values:

- **DATA_AND_INDEX** This value turns on the following settings for data and index blocks:

  - DB_BLOCK_CHECKSUM to FULL

  - DB_BLOCK_CHECKING to FULL

  - DB_LOST_WRITE_PROTECT to TYPICAL

- **DATA_ONLY** This value turns on the following settings only for data blocks:

  - DB_BLOCK_CHECKSUM to FULL

  - DB_BLOCK_CHECKING to MEDIUM

  - DB_LOST_WRITE_PROTECT to TYPICAL

■ **OFF** This is the default setting. OFF will default to the individual settings of DB_BLOCK_CHECKSUM, DB_BLOCK_CHECKING, and DB_LOST_WRITE_PROTECT.

Turning on these parameters at various levels will incur additional overhead on the system. The overhead will typically vary between 1 and 10 percent, depending on the application and the available system resources. It is a best practice to perform sample tests to calculate the overhead as it applies to your system. The overhead should be compared to the benefits of automatically detecting and preventing corruption, especially when dealing with systems requiring high availability.

Using Data Guard to Prevent Corruptions

Oracle Data Guard provides protection from data corruption by keeping an identical copy of the primary database on the standby site. The database on the standby site can be utilized to repair the corruption encountered on the primary database, and vice versa. Moreover, the Data Guard redo apply process performs data block integrity checks while applying the redo, and ensures that the corruption on the primary database does not get propagated to the standby.

Data Guard also helps recover from logical corruption initiated by the user or the application on the primary database by delaying the application of redo to the standby site. With the delay in place, if you notice the corruption before it is propagated to the standby, you can stop the apply process and recover the data from the intact copy on the standby. You can also use the database Flashback features on the primary or the standby to recover from logical corruption.

To enable corruption protection with Data Guard, the best practice is to set the database parameter DB_ULTRA_SAFE to DATA_AND_INDEX on the primary and the standby database. As stated earlier, setting DB_ULTRA_SAFE to DATA_AND_INDEX will incur a slight performance overhead on the system, but the benefits of protecting the critical data from corruptions will surely outweigh the impact.

If performance impact on the primary database becomes an issue, at a minimum, you should enable this parameter on the standby database.

Enhanced Lost Write Protection   The *lost write* detection feature discussed earlier is most effective when used in conjunction with Data Guard Redo Apply. When this feature is enabled, the apply process on the standby database reads the transaction system change number (SCN) from the redo log shipped from the primary database and compares it with the SCN of the corresponding data block on the standby. If the redo SCN is lower than the data block SCN, it indicates a lost write occurred on the primary. If the redo SCN is higher than the data block SCN, it indicates a lost write occurred on the standby. In both situations, the apply process raises an error, alerting the database administrator to take steps to repair the corruption.

To repair lost writes on the primary database, you must initiate failover to the standby database and restore or recover the corrupt block on the primary. To repair a lost write on a standby database, you must re-create the standby database or restore a backup of the affected files.

Enhanced lost write protection is enabled by the setting DB_LOST_WRITE_PROTECT to TYPICAL as discussed earlier.

Automatic Block Repair Using Physical Standby   The automatic block repair feature enables automatic repairs of corrupt data blocks as soon as the database detects a block corruption, thereby improving the availability of data by fixing corruptions promptly. Without this feature, the corrupt data is unavailable until a block recovery is performed from database backups or Flashback logs. The automatic block repair feature is available when you use Oracle Data Guard physical standby operating in real-time query mode.

When the Data Guard setup is configured with automatic block repair and the primary database encounters a corrupt data block, the block automatically is replaced with an uncorrupt copy from the physical standby. Likewise, when a corrupt block is accessed by the physical standby database, the block is replaced with an uncorrupt copy from the primary database. If, for any reason, the automatic block feature is unable to fix the corruption, it raises ORA-1578 errors.

Automatic block repair is enabled by setting LOG_ARCHIVE_CONFIG or FAL_SERVER parameters. For detailed instructions on setting these parameters, refer to the Oracle Data Guard manuals.

Exadata Storage Server and HARD

The Hardware Assisted Resilient Data (HARD) is an initiative by Oracle to help prevent data corruptions occurring at the storage management layer when writing Oracle data blocks to the hard disk. With the HARD program, the storage vendors implement internal checks to validate the integrity of the Oracle block right before (or after) the block gets written to (or read from) disk. If the integrity of the block is violated, the storage management layer raises I/O errors to the database so it can retry the I/O. This feature is implemented underneath the covers in the storage layer, and is transparent to the end users and the database administrators.

Exadata Storage Server is fully compliant with HARD and provides the most comprehensive protection to prevent corruptions from being propagated to the hard disk. The HARD checks implemented by the Exadata Storage Server are more thorough and provide higher protection than the checks implemented by third-party storage vendors. For example, Exadata HARD performs extensive validation of block locations, magic numbers, head and tail checks, and alignment errors that are not typically performed by non-Exadata HARD implementations.

In order to enable HARD checks on the Exadata Storage Server, you need to set the DB_BLOCK_CHECKSUM to TYPICAL or FULL. Alternatively, you can set DB_ULTRA_SAFE to DATA_AND_INDEX as discussed earlier.

Exadata Database Machine Backup and Recovery Best Practices

A comprehensive and reliable backup and recovery strategy is the most important piece of a database high-availability strategy. Regardless of the type and size of databases, an effective strategy is focused on the methods and procedures for backing up critical data, and more importantly, for recovering the data successfully when required. While recoverability is the ultimate goal, the potential downtime incurred to recover should also be considered. The downtime includes the time to identify the problem, formulate the recovery steps, and perform recovery.

NOTE
Recovering a database using backups is generally used to recover from media failures within a single site. For recovering from a complete disaster of the site, or to recover with minimal downtime, the recommended strategy is to use Oracle Data Guard as discussed earlier in this chapter.

An effective backup and recovery strategy of the Exadata Database Machine should include all of the components that are housed within the Database Machine for which there are no built-in recovery mechanisms. The components that need to be a part of the strategy are the Oracle databases, the operating system (OS) and file systems of the database servers, the InfiniBand switch configuration, and the ILOM configuration.

The OS on the Exadata Storage Server has built-in recovery mechanisms and does not need separate backups. When OS recovery is needed on these servers, they will be restored by using the supplied CELLBOOT USB flash drive. The CELLBOOT USB drive stores the last successful OS boot image of the server. Since Oracle does not allow any deviations from the default OS install and setup of the Exadata Storage Servers, restoring using the CELLBOOT USB will be sufficient to perform OS-level recovery. Moreover, the OS resides on a file system that is configured on the first two disks of the Exadata Storage Server and uses software RAID-1 protection. If one of the first two disks fails, the server will still be available.

NOTE
You should back up the database server OS and the local file systems separately. The local storage on the database server is configured with RAID-5 protection, which can tolerate single drive failures. When two or more drives fail, the OS and the file systems need to be recovered from the backup. You should also back up the ILOM and InfiniBand switch configuration files using the native tools and methods provided for them.

This section of the chapter is focused on the backup and recovery best practices for Oracle databases residing on the Database Machine. You will see that the procedures you use for the Database Machine are no different from what you would use for Oracle Database 11*g* Release 2 on other hardware platforms.

We will start this section by discussing the tools available to perform backups and their best-practice considerations. Next, we will discuss the backup strategy and architecture for performing tape and disk-based backups. Last, we will touch upon the high-level best practices for performing recovery.

Backup Tools Best Practices

Oracle RMAN and Oracle Secure Backup are the two tools you will use to perform backups. This section provides an overview of the capabilities of these tools and the best practices of configuring them for performing backups on the Exadata Database Machine.

Oracle Recovery Manager (RMAN)

Backup and recovery of Oracle databases using *user-managed* mechanisms are not possible for the databases utilizing Exadata Storage Servers as the storage. You can only perform backups that are managed by Oracle RMAN.

RMAN is the Oracle-supplied tool that can back up, restore, and recover Oracle databases. RMAN is a client/server application that uses database server processes to perform the backup I/O operations. When performing backups of databases in the Database Machine, you can parallelize the backup task across the available database servers and the Exadata Storage Servers, and leverage the CPU, network, and disks of the entire grid to provide optimal performance.

RMAN does not back up directly to tape. However, it will integrate with media management software such as Oracle Secure Backup and utilize their capabilities to manage tape libraries.

NOTE
If you are considering third-party tools for performing backup and recovery of databases in the Database Machine, the tools should be able to interface with Oracle RMAN, and RMAN will initiate the backup and restore operations.

RMAN provides the ability to administer and manage backups by keeping a record of the backup metadata in a repository. When RMAN formulates restore procedures, it uses the repository to identify files needed for recovery. You can also generate reports of backup activity using the information available in the repository.

Oracle Enterprise Manager (OEM) provides a GUI-based interface to the RMAN client by using a comprehensive set of wizard-driven screens. The screens provide similar functionality as the RMAN client and allow you to create and schedule backup tasks, set up backup policies and procedures, formulate recovery steps based on the recovery objectives, and perform recovery.

The RMAN features that help to set the context for our discussion on backup and recovery practices on the Database Machine are discussed next.

RMAN Backup Formats   RMAN backups can be created as *image copies* or *backup sets.* An image copy is a bit-for-bit copy of a database file, whereas a backup set is an RMAN-specific format that consists of one or more database files known as backup pieces. Backup sets are the default format used by RMAN and is the only format supported when storing backups to tape. The advantage of backup sets over image copies is that they allow the use of RMAN compression features (discussed shortly).

Image copy backups, on the other hand, are only possible for disk backups. They utilize the same space as the database files since they are an exact copy. Image copies have the advantage of being restored faster than backup sets, since the database blocks do not need to be re-created during the restore process, which is the case when restoring backup sets.

Although it is not possible to use RMAN compression features with image copies, you can use compression mechanisms provided by the storage systems, such as the built-in compression features of the Sun ZFS Storage appliance. In this case, the compression performed by the storage will be totally transparent to RMAN.

RMAN Backup Types   At a high level, RMAN backups can be one of two types—*full* or *incremental.* Full backups, as the name suggests, are the backups of the complete database, whereas incremental backups only store modified blocks since the last full or incremental backup. Incremental backups can only be stored as backup sets and not image copies.

NOTE
You can apply an incremental backup to an existing image copy, which will update the image copy to reflect the changes in the incremental backup. This feature is described in more detail later in the chapter.

Incremental backups are subcategorized into two types, *differential* and *cumulative*. Differential backups contain changed data since the last full or incremental, and is the default type when no other type is specified. Cumulative backups contain changed data since the last full backup. If you have a cumulative backup, you can recover by applying just two backups, the last full and the cumulative incremental. This reduces the recovery time since fewer backups are applied during recovery. Cumulative backups are preferred when shorter recovery time is a priority over disk space.

During media recovery, RMAN prefers incremental backups over archived logs and will use one if present. This is because the incremental backups also capture changes made by NOLOGGING transactions, which by their definition are not logged into the archived logs. Such transactions are lost if recovering using archived logs.

RMAN and Compression   RMAN has several features that enable you to store backups in compressed format. Compressing the backup will provide you storage savings and also give you better performance because the backup I/O will involve fewer blocks.

NOTE
The RMAN compression features are applicable only when you create backups in the backup set format and not with image copy.

A compression feature that is inherent with RMAN and cannot be disabled is the *unused block compression*. With this feature, RMAN skips blocks from the database files that are not allocated to any database objects or, if allocated, have never been used to store any data (also known as null blocks). The unused block compression can also skip blocks that once had data but are now empty (blocks under the high watermark). The empty block compression feature is available when performing backups to disk, and also to tape but only when Oracle Secure Backup (OSB) is the media manager.

RMAN is also capable of performing *binary compression* of backup sets using industry-standard compression algorithms. Binary compression will compress the backup sets before they are written to disk. The compression can be performed using different algorithms (BZIP2, LZO, and ZLIB) and the appropriate algorithm is selected when you set the compression level (BASIC, LOW, MEDIUM, or HIGH) before initiating the backups. Based upon the compression-level settings, you get different compression ratios and backup performance.

> **NOTE**
> *Compression levels of LOW, MEDIUM, and HIGH requires you to be licensed for the Advanced Compression Option for the Oracle database. The BASIC level is included with the Oracle database license.*

If you are using database compression features such as OLTP compression and Exadata Hybrid Columnar Compression, you are already reducing the overall disk footprint of database files. The best practice in such a case is not to compress the data again using RMAN. Compressing the same data twice does not provide any measurable savings, and in fact in some cases, might even be an overhead.

RMAN Best Practices   Follow the RMAN best practices specified here to get higher performance and availability with the Database Machine.

- **Use block change tracking**   Enhance the performance of RMAN incremental backups by using the block change tracking (BCT) feature. When BCT is enabled, the database keeps track of the blocks that get modified using a block change tracking file. The BCT file gets one entry when one or all blocks in a chunk (32K) gets modified. When RMAN starts an incremental backup, it uses the block change tracking file to identify the changed blocks since the last incremental backup, and reads only the changed blocks from the disk. Otherwise, without BCT, all blocks are read and the SCN on each block is checked to identify if the block was modified.

The incremental backup offloading feature of the Exadata Storage Server is able to filter unchanged blocks directly in the storage layer, which further improves the incremental backup performance by only sending changed blocks to RMAN for backup. The Exadata Storage Servers are capable of identifying the changed blocks at a finer granularity than the BCT feature. As you can see, the BCT and the incremental backup offload features are complementary to one another.

Best practices indicate that block change tracking provides the most benefit when 20 percent or fewer blocks get modified since the last incremental or full backup. When changes are greater than 20 percent, you might still benefit, but you need to evaluate it against the data in your environment.

- **Configure DB_RECOVERY_FILE_DEST_SIZE** The database FRA is used to store database archived logs and other recovery files including backups, and can get filled quickly if the space is not managed properly. Use DB_RECOVERY_FILE_DEST_SIZE to bind the space for each database in the FRA. If there are multiple databases on the Database Machine, the total combined FRA from all databases should be less than the free space on the ASM diskgroup allocated for FRA. In fact, you should leave enough space on the diskgroup to account for disk failures, and preferably for one complete Exadata Storage Server failure.

- **Configure RAC Services for backup/restore** The best practice is to execute the RMAN backup task across multiple database nodes in the RAC cluster by defining Oracle RAC Services. By using Services, you can allocate specific RAC nodes that you would like to take part in servicing the backup load.

  When the RMAN clients connect to the database using Services, they get load balanced and the backup task gets distributed across the nodes defined in the service. This ensures even distribution of the CPU load across the database servers and prevents overloading of the resources on just one node.

■ **Use Recovery Catalog for RMAN repository**   Always use a separate
database to store the RMAN catalog. The database should reside
outside of the Database Machine to guarantee recoverability from
local failures. You can use the servers set aside for management
tools such as OEM Management Repository or the Oracle Secure
Backup Administrative server.

Oracle Secure Backup (OSB)

Oracle Secure Backup (OSB) is a centralized tape backup management
software providing solutions to back up and restore file systems and Oracle
databases. OSB is tightly integrated with RMAN features such as unused
block compression and UNDO optimizations, and with this integration, it is
able to deliver extremely efficient backup and restore operations.

OSB interfaces with the *tape library* for storing backups to tape. A tape
library is a device that contains two or more tape drives for reading and
writing backup data, along with a collection of tape cartridges. It is designed
for continuous, unattended operations using robotic hardware that has
mechanisms to scan, mount, and dismount the tape cartridges.

The OSB software that manages the tape library resides on a *media
server*. The media server facilitates communication with the tape devices,
and is used by RMAN to perform tape backups. The media servers connect
to the Database Machine using the InfiniBand, the 1 Gigabit, or the 10
Gigabit Ethernet interfaces. Using the InfiniBand interface gives you the best
performance for backups and restores; however, this option requires the
media servers to support the InfiniBand connectivity through a suitable Host
Channel Adapter (HCA) that is compatible with the Database Machine.

An OSB *backup domain* is a network of backup clients, media servers,
and the tape libraries. The backup domain contains an *administrative server*
that serves the backup clients, and also stores the OSB *backup catalog*. The
OSB catalog is the black box of the backup domain and contains information
about the backups.

An architecture diagram of Oracle Secure Backup for performing backups
of the Database Machine is provided later in this chapter in Figure 6-3.

OSB Best Practices   Consider the following best practices when configuring
Oracle Secure Backup with the Database Machine:

■ **Configure persistent bindings**   Each tape device is assigned a logical
unit number (LUN) on the media server based on the order of its

discovery. To ensure the LUNs are consistent when they are accessed from multiple media servers, you need to configure persistent bindings. Persistent bindings are configured at the operating system or the Host Bus Adapter (HBA) level. Consult the documentation specific to your media server operating system for further details.

- **Back up the OSB catalog** The Oracle Secure Backup catalog maintains the backup metadata that includes configuration and scheduling information for the backup domain. It is important to protect the catalog by taking regular backups using the OSB-supplied methods.

- **Configure the preferred network interface (PNI) for InfiniBand** When using the InfiniBand network to communicate with the media servers from the Database Machine, configure Oracle Secure Backup to favor the InfiniBand network to route backup traffic. This is done by setting the preferred network interface configuration in Oracle Secure Backup.

Oracle Database Backup Strategy

The business continuity plan (BCP) forms the basis for architecting an effective backup and recovery strategy. The BCP is the plan to ensure the continuity of business operations when a disaster or failure strikes. The elements of BCP that will influence the backup and recovery strategy are the recovery point objective (RPO) and the recovery time objective (RTO).

The RPO is the number of hours of data loss that can be tolerated by the business. When determining the RPO, you should take into account the cost incurred due to the loss of data for the timeframe specified in the RPO and compare it with the cost of the infrastructure needed to minimize the data loss. Assessing the impact of data loss up front will help justify the appropriate hardware, storage, and software costs needed to meet the RPO set by the business. Lower RPO will require more frequent backups and additional hardware that can support the recovery within short timeframes.

The RTO defines the acceptable timeframe that is allowed to recover to the recovery point. Note that the total recovery time includes the time to identify the problem, plan the appropriate recovery steps, restore the backups, perform database media recovery, and restore the hardware, storage, operating system, and the Oracle software.

Apart from the RPO and RTO requirements, you also need to capture the backup retention requirements and devise a backup retention policy that ensures sufficient backups are available to meet the RPO and RTO requirements. The longer the retention policy, the larger the space required to retain backups.

Based on the business RPO and RTO requirements, the appropriate backup and recovery strategy can be formulated. If you have databases of size 50TB or more with short RTO requirements and zero-data-loss RPO requirements, relying only on tape backups might not suffice. Disk backups and other high-availability solutions such as Data Guard should be considered.

A backup strategy documents the method and infrastructure needed to perform backups, along with the retention policies. Essentially, you have the option to back up to disk, tape, or a combination disk/tape called a *hybrid* approach. Our focus in this chapter is to discuss tape and disk backups. The hybrid methods can be concocted from the two.

NOTE
The intention of this book is not to debate which backup method is the best, but rather to equip you with the options available, along with the appropriate architectures, and to enable you to select the best strategy for your environment.

Backups to Tape

Tape backups are considered to be the most cost-effective solution for backups, especially when you already have a tape-based backup infrastructure in the data center. However, the performance of backups and restores needs to be evaluated against the recovery time objective to ensure that you are able to perform the backup and recovery tasks within the allowable timeframes. Generally speaking, tapes are slower than disk with respect to read and write performance and are usually less reliable over time.

NOTE
Backups to virtual tape library (VTL) are treated similar as backups to tape. VTL emulates a standard tape interface on disk-based storage arrays, thereby exposing the arrays as tape and making the VTL invisible to the media management software.

Figure 6-3 depicts a typical architecture for performing backups to tape using the Database Machine, media servers, and the tape library. The architecture should be used as a typical building block when you are architecting a tape backup solution. The components comprising this architecture are discussed next.

■ **Tape library** The tape library holds the tape drives. The speed of the tape backup is based on the number of tape drives that can be used in parallel to accomplish the backup. The backup speed can be

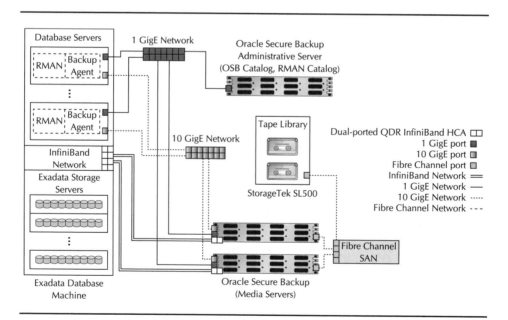

FIGURE 6-3. *Architecture of the Database Machine for performing backups to tape*

increased almost linearly by adding more drives, provided no other bottlenecks exist.

- **Media servers** The media servers are connected to the tape library either directly as a Network Attached Storage (NAS) device or through a Fibre Channel (FC) Storage Area Network (SAN) switch. Media servers house the Oracle Secure Backup media manager. A minimum of two media servers is preferred for high availability. Performance can scale when you add more, provided other bottlenecks do not exist.

- **Backup network** The backup network is the route of the data from where it currently resides (i.e., the Exadata Database Machine) to the backup device (i.e., the tape library). The performance of the backup and restore operations depends on the throughput of the backup network and the throughput of the processes consuming/generating the backup traffic at the network end-points. The slowest link in the network path limits the overall throughput.

  The Database Machine connects to the media servers using the InfiniBand ports available on the InfiniBand switch or through the 1 GigE and 10 GigE ports available on the database servers. Connecting through the InfiniBand ports will give you the best network throughput. When the 1 GigE option is used, rest assured, the bottleneck for backup performance in most cases will be the 1 GigE network.

  The network protocol used is TCP/IP for both, InfiniBand as well as Gigabit Ethernet.

- **Exadata Database Machine** The Database Machine contains the databases that need to be backed up. As mentioned earlier, Oracle RMAN is the only mechanism to back up the databases that utilize Exadata Storage Servers as the storage. RMAN processes run on the database servers and interact with the Oracle Secure Backup (OSB) agent, which further interacts with the media management software and enables RMAN to communicate with the tape library.

Oracle RMAN can run from one database server and up to all the available database servers in the Database Machine RAC cluster. The number of nodes that you allocate to run RMAN depends on whether adding more RMAN clients will increase the total throughput of the backup. You can also tune the throughput by increasing the number of channels allocated to each RMAN process.

■ **OSB administrative server** The OSB administrative server stores the OSB catalog. You can designate any server as the administrative server, and the best practice is to have it separate from the servers in the backup domain for ensuring high availability. You can use the administrative server to house the RMAN catalog database and the Oracle Enterprise Manager repository, and increase the utilization rate of the server.

Now that you have seen how the tape backup infrastructure fits together, we will look at the process involved in sizing and tuning the individual components. The goal is to have an architecture that achieves the best throughput possible while meeting the constraints set by recovery time objective and, of course, the cost.

Tape Infrastructure Sizing Best Practices   Before you start sizing and configuring the backup infrastructure, capture the performance characteristics of each component that is involved with the transfer/processing of the backup data (tape library, network, media servers, and database servers).

The next step is to start with one component of the architecture and add more instances of it until you get the scalability benefits and an effective increase in throughput. You should repeat this process for all the components, namely, the tape library, network, media servers, and the database servers. The trick here is to make sure you do not induce bottlenecks while you perform the scaling exercise and stay focused on making the overall configuration balanced.

An example of a typical tape backup infrastructure with throughput rates of each component is depicted in Figure 6-4. For illustrating the sizing process, we assume the media servers connect to a full-rack Exadata Database Machine X2-2 using the 40 Gb/s InfiniBand network, and to the tape library using 8 Gb/s SAN links. The tape library used is the Oracle

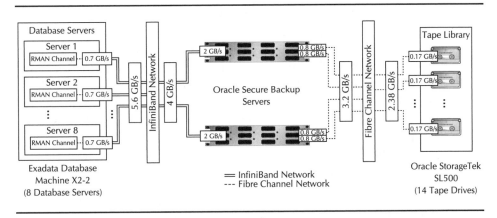

FIGURE 6-4. *Tape infrastructure sizing for maximum throughput*

StorageTek SL500. The throughput for each of the components is measured in GB/s, which is the size of data in GB (gigabytes) processed in one second. The throughput numbers used in this exercise are specific to this environment. The numbers will vary based on your environment-specific hardware and its configuration.

- As a best practice, you need to start with a minimum of two media servers and add more once you have exhausted their capacity. Each media server needs one dual-ported InfiniBand HCA card. Although each card has two ports, the ports are bonded and configured for high availability, which effectively gives you the performance of one port.

- The connectivity between the media server to tape library is through 8 Gb/s SAN links, with each link providing an effective throughput of 0.8 GB/s. Having a total of four SAN links will provide you with a combined throughput of 3.2 GB/s, which is sufficient to handle the throughput needed to saturate up to 16 tape drives.

- The connectivity from the Database Machine to the media servers is through the dual-ported InfiniBand HCA card. Each link of InfiniBand from the media server to the Database Machine will give you an effective data transfer rate of 2 GB/s, using the TCP/IP protocol with InfiniBand (IPoIB). With two media servers, this configuration provides a combined theoretical throughput of 4 GB/s (two media servers × one InfiniBand card × 2 GB/s throughput per card).

- A single RMAN channel in the Exadata Database Machine is capable of streaming data at the rate of about 0.7 GB/sec to the media server. When you use RMAN for tape backups, the best practice is to configure the same number of channels as the number of available tape drives. Each tape performs serial writes, and it does not help to add more parallelism on the RMAN side by adding more channels than the number of tapes. Since we are using full-rack Exadata Database Machine X2-2, the effective RMAN throughput using eight RMAN channels will be about 5.6 GB/s (0.7 per RMAN channel × eight channels).

- For the tape-based backups, the slowest component is the tape library. The Oracle StorageTek SL500 tape library used in the example has 14 tape drives, and each drive within the library is capable of providing 0.17 GB/s. No matter how you scale the other components, the tape library limits you to a maximum theoretical throughput of 2.38 GB/s (14 drives × 0.17 GB/s).

In Figure 6-4, we used two media servers, eight database servers with eight RMAN channels, 8 Gb/s SAN links, and 14 tape drives to achieve an effective backup throughput of 2.38 GB/s, which translates to 8.6 TB/hr.

NOTE
If you are using Gigabit Ethernet (1 GigE) network between the media server and Exadata Database Machine, your bottleneck will shift to the 1 GigE network instead of the tape library. In a full-rack Exadata Database Machine X2-2, you can achieve a maximum theoretical throughput of 960 MB/s (120 MB/s × 8) with one 1 GigE port per database node. If you bond two 1 GigE ports per each database server, you should be able to achieve a combined theoretical throughput of up to 1,920 MB/s.

The recommended Oracle tape backup strategy with the Exadata Database Machine is discussed next.

Recommended Tape Backup Strategy   For performing database backups to tape, follow the Oracle MAA recommended strategy specified here:

- Perform database archive log backup to FRA. Use backup retention policies; otherwise, files may get deleted in FRA when it gets full and needs to make additional space.

- Perform weekly full backups (RMAN level 0) of the database to tape.

- Perform daily, cumulative incremental backups (RMAN level 1) of the database. This will ensure that you only need to recover one full and one incremental backup during a recovery, along with the archived logs.

- Perform daily backups of the Oracle Secure Backup catalog.

Backups to Disk

Disk backups dramatically improve the speed and accuracy of the recovery process, and are an attractive option for the business that needs short recovery times. They are also able to meet aggressive backup windows, which is a key requirement for databases requiring high availability. Nowadays, with the declining cost of hard disks, the gap between the disk and tape is closing rapidly, and disk backups are increasingly becoming affordable and being implemented even by small to mid-sized businesses.

NOTE
Recovery time with disk backups can be reduced further by using the RMAN incremental backup merge feature. With this feature, the previous full database backup created using image copies can roll forward and be made current by applying incremental backups. When you need to recover, you will restore only the full image copy backup and not the incremental (plus any archived logs as necessary).

Disk backups can coexist with tape backups, and it is a best practice to use both when the disk backup systems reside in the same data center as the system being backed up. In such a situation, when a site failure occurs, the data and also its backup would be lost. A hybrid strategy with a combination of disk and tape backups should be pursued. With this strategy, the backup on disk can saved to tape in an offline fashion, which can be sent offsite for disaster proofing.

If you are considering implementing disk backups for the Database Machine, you have the option to either store backups on the FRA of the Database Machine or to attach additional networked storage in an external cabinet solely for the purpose of housing backups. These options are discussed next.

Backup to Fast Recovery Area (FRA)   The purpose of the database FRA is to store recovery files. You can use it to store backups, provided you have enough space allocated. This option provides the best backup/restore performance, as the I/O operations are performed in parallel against a set of Exadata Storage Servers using the high-speed InfiniBand network. Moreover, backups are protected from media failures because the FRA resides in the diskgroup that is mirrored using ASM redundancy settings.

The drawback of this method is that a chunk of your investment in the Database Machine will be allocated for backups, which considerably increases the disk cost per GB. Moreover, you still need to disaster-proof the backups by having a hybrid strategy as just discussed.

The best practices of sizing the Database Machine FRA when storing backups is to allocate 60 percent of the total capacity to FRA and the remaining 40 percent for user data. Not only are you losing 60 percent of the storage capacity of the Database Machine in this case, you may also lose 60 percent of bandwidth and I/O operations per second (IOPS) performance, especially when you configure a *dedicated* FRA. A dedicated FRA is the MAA best-practice configuration to guarantee availability from multiple Exadata Storage Server failures when a Data Guard standby site is not configured. This best practice is discussed in the "Exadata Storage Server High Availability" section of this chapter.

An option that might make backups to FRA a bit more attractive is when you use an Exadata Expansion Cabinet. The Exadata Expansion Cabinet is a set of Exadata Storage Servers in a rack, connected to the Database Machine rack using the InfiniBand switch. You can configure the database FRA to reside completely in the Expansion Cabinet and dedicate all the Exadata Storage Servers in the Cabinet for the sole purpose of performing backups. Even though the Storage Servers reside external to the Database Machine, they are just an extension of the Database Machine storage grid.

The Expansion Cabinet can be configured with High Capacity drives even if your Database Machine uses High Performance drives. This reduces the total disk cost per GB and makes the backup-to-disk proposition using Exadata Storage Servers even more attractive.

This setup utilizing the Expansion Cabinet guarantees the best performance for backup/restore operations and at the same time provides best performance to the application since all Exadata Storage Servers inside the Database Machine rack will be dedicated 100 percent to user traffic.

Backup to NAS   If the earlier option to back up to FRA is not feasible, consider performing backups to a Network Attached Storage (NAS) device. You can attach an NAS device to the Database Machine and use it for the purpose of backups. This option is the most cost effective, since most data centers already use some sort of NAS storage.

The best practice for attaching the NAS device is through the InfiniBand network. NAS devices such as the Sun ZFS Storage appliance depicted in Figure 6-5 have built-in support for InfiniBand, 10 Gigabit, and 1 Gigabit Ethernet networks. If your NAS appliance does not provide InfiniBand connectivity, or if the NAS InfiniBand HCA card or the protocol is not supported by the Database Machine, use the Gigabit Ethernet interfaces.

NAS devices also offer real-time compression and deduplication features. By using these features, you can significantly reduce the disk footprint of backups. Of course, there could be an overhead, and as with any feature that has an impact, a good strategy would be to test it out in your environment and with your data.

NOTE
If you have an external NAS attached to the Database Machine, you can also utilize it for a variety of other purposes. You can use NAS to stage files when performing migrations and data loads, or use it as a springboard to push data into DBFS from servers residing outside of the Database Machine.

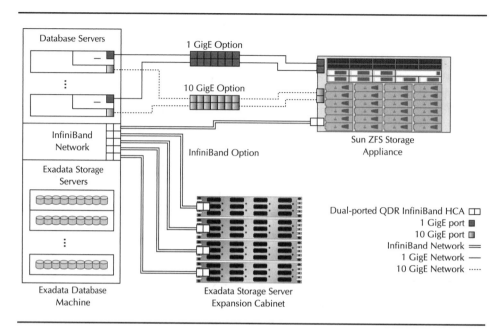

FIGURE 6-5. *Disk backup options for the Database Machine using externally attached storage*

Disk Backup Configuration Best Practices　Use the following guidelines as best practices for configuring the number of instances running RMAN and the number of RMAN channels per instance:

■ Always start with one database instance running RMAN with two channels. In most cases, two RMAN channels per instance will give you the required throughput gains, although you might gain some improvements with four channels. Each RMAN channel is capable of processing about 0.7 GB/s, and two channels translate to 1.4 GB/s, which is close to the 2 GB/s throughput limitation of one database server.

■ Add instances to run RMAN as required, each with two channels. Measure throughput gains, and if you are not getting any additional gains, you stop.

- As a RMAN best practice mentioned earlier, configure RAC services to dictate the database servers that will run RMAN.

- Set DB_RECOVER_FILE_DEST_SIZE to bind space in the FRA for backups. This was discussed in the section on RMAN earlier.

NOTE
Typical backup throughput was achieved using a full-rack Exadata Database Machine X2-2 with two instances configured to run RMAN, and each instance with four RMAN channels, with RMAN using image copies, was 7.1 TB/ Hr. The backup was stored on FRA residing inside the Database Machine.

Recommended Disk Backup Strategy   The Oracle MAA strategy for performing backups to disk is the following:

- Use the FRA to store archived logs and database backups. If using NAS as the backup destination, use a file system on NAS instead of FRA.

- Perform an initial full backup using image copies (RMAN level 0).

- Perform daily incremental backups (RMAN level 1).

- With a delay of 24 hours, roll the incremental backups into the full backup using the RMAN incremental merge feature. The delay is to ensure the user-initiated data corruptions do not propagate into the backups.

- Consider a hybrid backup strategy to disaster-proof your backups, and copy the backups made on disk and persist them by performing another backup to tape.

Database Recovery Best Practices

Earlier in this chapter, we discussed using Oracle Data Guard as the best practice to achieve high availability and protection from planned and unplanned failures. If media failures occur on the Database Machine and you do not have a Data Guard configuration, you have no choice but to recover the database using backups.

Oracle RMAN is the only tool that can recover databases residing on the Exadata Storage Servers. RMAN makes the recovery process simple by using just two commands, *restore database* and *recover database.* When you run these commands, RMAN will search its catalog and retrieve the list of backups needed to perform recovery, along with their respective locations. RMAN will then restore all the required backups and perform further media recovery that might be required to complete the recovery process.

The throughput of the restore operation depends on whether you are restoring in place and the original file already exists (but is now corrupt) or to a new location. In the case where the original file exists, higher restore rates are possible. This is because the initial allocation of a file incurs an overhead, especially when the files are large, and restore timings will improve if the initial allocation can be avoided. The throughput also depends on a number of other factors such as the number of RMAN channels, the backup network capacity, the number of tape drives (if restoring from tape), and the disk subsystem throughput (if restoring from disk).

The restore process is a write-intensive operation. If you use InfiniBand to connect the Database Machine to the backup infrastructure, the chances are that the restore operation will be the bottleneck and not the InfiniBand network or the tape drives.

Use these best practices to speed up recovery performance:

- If you are restoring into preexisting files, use all database instances for RMAN and configure two RMAN channels per each instance. If restoring from tape, the number of RMAN channels you use will be restricted by the number of tape drives.

- If the files are not preexisting, use two database instances for RMAN and two to four RMAN channels per each instance. Again, if restoring from tape, do not use more channels than the number of tape drives.

- When you are restoring using the 1 GigE network of the database servers, use all available 1 GigE ports for achieving the highest throughput. Each database server has four 1 GigE ports, which can be bonded in groups of two to get 240 MB/s to 480 MB/s throughput on each database server.

NOTE
Typical restore rates achieved by a full-rack Exadata Database Machine X2-2 utilizing the InfiniBand network is about 23 TB/hr, and this was possible when restoring into preexisting files.

Summary

For a business to succeed, it needs to have access to highly available systems. When the service becomes unavailable due to unplanned or planned reasons, the business can lose revenue, credibility, and customers. Solutions that are designed to enhance availability help minimize the impact of hardware and software failures and enhance the availability of applications by shortening the service downtimes.

There are multiple approaches to achieving high availability with Oracle products. These approaches complement one another, and can be used alone or in combination. They range from the basic strategy of using highly reliable and redundant hardware and software to the more advanced process for detecting and repairing corruption, as well as performing zero downtime upgrades and active-active databases.

The chapter highlights the various high-availability features and technologies available on the Database Machine and guides you in choosing a solution that meets the need for stringent business continuity requirements. For more detailed information on each topic, refer to the Exadata section on the Oracle Technology Network and the Oracle database documentation.

CHAPTER
7

Deploying Data Warehouses on the Oracle Exadata Database Machine

 hen Oracle first launched the Oracle Exadata Database Machine, it was aimed only at the broad solution area defined as data warehousing. The reason why the initial focus was on data warehousing was simple. Predesigned hardware configurations are well accepted in the data warehousing market and were available from many of Oracle's competitors. Over the past decade, they have evolved from providing merely balanced server and storage configurations containing fast interconnects to delivering hardware-specific optimizations for typical data warehousing workloads.

Although Oracle's entry into this arena of providing integrated hardware and software solutions is relatively recent, Oracle is not new to providing data warehousing solutions. In fact, information technology analysts generally agree that Oracle has provided the leading database for data warehousing for many years. Oracle began to introduce key optimization techniques for data warehousing in its database more than 20 years ago. For many organizations, these database optimization techniques provided solutions to their business needs while delivering the solutions on a familiar database engine that was also deployed elsewhere in their organization for transaction-processing applications. However, growing data volumes and workload demands would sometimes tax the capabilities of Oracle-based data warehousing solutions designed around optimization provided by just the database software. Even more challenging, many data warehouses were deployed without careful consideration of the impact of storage throughput needed to deliver the required query response time at the server(s).

In this chapter, we'll give you a complete view of data warehousing considerations when deploying the Oracle Exadata Database Machine. We'll start with a basic definition of data warehousing and a description of common topologies. We'll then review some of the key features in the Oracle database that enable better reporting and ad hoc query performance, some of which were covered in more detail in Chapter 2. Since another desired capability of data warehousing is analytics, including trending and forecasting and predictive analysis through data mining, we'll also cover how the Oracle database supports those workloads.

After covering generic Oracle data warehousing topics, we'll discuss specific capabilities that are unique to the Oracle Exadata Database Machine and Exadata Storage Servers. We'll cover unique optimization techniques and the role of Hybrid Columnar Compression. We'll then describe how the generic features and special features for this platform work together to provide great performance in solving a query. We'll also point out some of the best practices for data loading, partitioning, and backing up data specific to data warehousing. Finally, we'll cover surrounding business intelligence tools, data models, security considerations, and how to justify purchase of the Oracle Exadata Database Machine for your data warehousing project.

Data Warehousing Basics

A data warehouse can be defined as providing a repository of trusted historical data in a form especially useful and optimized for reporting and performing ad hoc queries and analyses. Examples of analyses include trending, forecasting, and mathematical modeling where outcomes are influenced by a complex set of variables. A data warehousing system differs from an online transaction processing (OLTP) system, in that the data held in the data warehouse is nonvolatile and generally retained for long periods. The data is cleansed of errors and duplication during an extraction, transformation, and loading (ETL) process. The data warehouse sometimes incorporates sources of data outside of the company or organization to augment internal data sources.

Data warehousing has its roots in what were once called decision support systems that gained popularity in the late 1970s. While OLTP systems predate this concept, the initial design point of transaction processing systems is to provide a repository for current and frequently updated data. As a result, the primary focus of OLTP systems is to report on the current business situation. But as organizations gather more and more data, business strategists envision new usages of such data to better understand historical business trends and predict future trends and business results. Thus was born the need for a separate repository flexible enough to handle this rather different workload with the ability to grow and support extremely large amounts of data.

Initially, the schema (the collection of tables, views, indexes, and synonyms) was most often deployed with third normal form design for a data warehouse, the same type of schema design used for OLTP databases. In such a schema, tables contain only detailed data, stored only once, and nonprimary attributes are linked among tables using foreign keys. Figure 7-1 illustrates such a schema containing customer, order, product, and shipping information. The third normal form schema is ideal where the goal is to provide fast and

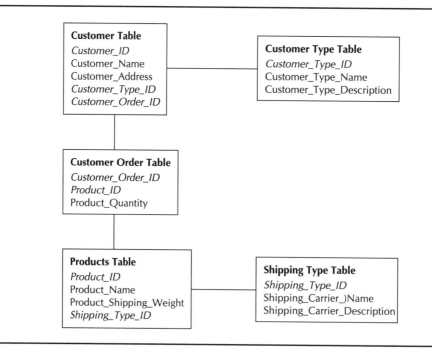

FIGURE 7-1. *Third normal form schema*

frequent updates. For enterprise data warehouses that provide a gathering point for data from many sources, such a schema can align with business needs when the IT organization is prepared to build business intelligence reports (since IT is most adept at understanding such an irregular data model). Bill Inmon is most associated with this approach and has long described the benefits of the enterprise data warehouse. However, if the goal is to have a schema that enables more of a self-service reporting and query experience for business analysts and users, then either the IT organization must build views to help the analysts navigate the schema or another schema choice must be made.

Ralph Kimball is largely credited with introducing a compelling alternative, the star schema. The schema might best be described as a large transaction or fact table that is surrounded by multiple dimension or look-up tables, where time is almost always one of the dimensions. The schema often evolves into a variation of a star, where dimension tables are further normalized and broken into multiple tables. That variation is called a snowflake schema. Figure 7-2 illustrates a snowflake schema as the customer dimension has been further normalized.

Dimension tables consist of multiple levels in the form of a hierarchy. So a time dimension might include fiscal years, months, and days, for example. Though the list is endless, a few examples of other commonly seen dimension hierarchies include products, geographic regions, channels, promotions, shipments, and human resources organizational structures.

The consistent form and support of this schema by business intelligence ad hoc query tools enables self-service queries and reporting. Using our schema illustrated in Figure 7-2, a typical query might be, "Show me how many overnight shipments I made of a certain product in the northeast region over the past six months." Another query could be, "What discount levels are associated with deals for products that were shipped overnight over the past six months?"

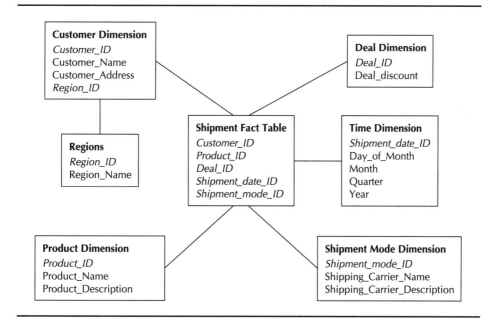

FIGURE 7-2. *Snowflake variation of star schema*

As star schemas became popular, they were most often deployed outside of the enterprise data warehouse as data marts. Data marts might be deployed in lines of business to address the business needs specific to those portions of the business. Where efforts are well coordinated among lines of business and IT, the data marts remain "dependent" on data definitions established in the enterprise data warehouse. When established separately instead as "independent" data marts where data definitions vary, organizations often face dealing with multiple versions of the truth (e.g., the same query in different departments using different data marts would generate different results). Figure 7-3 illustrates a classical topology, including source systems, data warehouses and data marts, and business intelligence tools.

The difficulty and expense in keeping data marts and enterprise data warehouses aligned and maintaining them as separate entities led many data warehouse architects to consider a "hybrid" approach. Data marts consisting of a star schema are embedded in the enterprise data warehouse in a hybrid. As database optimizers such as Oracle's became more sophisticated, such hybrids became more practical. Oracle further expanded

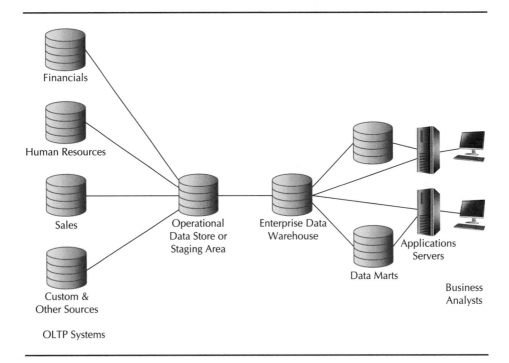

FIGURE 7-3. *Classic data warehouse topology*

the hybrid model by introducing the ability to embed Oracle OLAP multidimensional cubes in the relational database.

The Oracle Exadata Database Machine is often considered when organizations evaluate a platform to serve as an enterprise data warehouse (typically where a platform such as Teradata might also be under consideration) or where the platform serves as a high-performance data mart (typically where platforms such as those provided by IBM / Netezza or Microsoft might also be under consideration). Given the sophistication of the platform, many Oracle data warehousing implementations on the Oracle Exadata Database Machine contain consolidated data marts and warehouses. Consolidation can take several forms, including the hosting of multiple data warehouses and data marts in separate databases or merging data marts and the enterprise data warehouse into a single hybrid data warehouse database. Figure 7-4 serves to illustrate such possibilities, where the Oracle Exadata Database Machine is represented by the gray shading in the figure. In addition

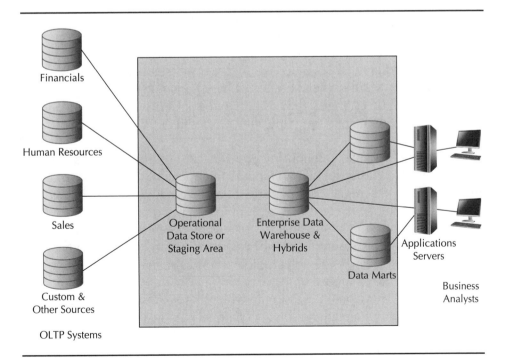

FIGURE 7-4. *Oracle Exadata Database Machine roles in data warehouse topology*

to providing a more manageable and cost-effective deployment model, consolidation efforts are sometimes put in place to eliminate the need for federated queries that attempt to assemble very large result sets returned across relatively slow network connections. We cover consolidation considerations in a separate chapter in this book.

Before we get into the specifics of the Oracle Exadata Database Machine, we will next look at some of the key Oracle database data warehousing features that are available anywhere that the Oracle database runs. These features will play an important part in your Oracle Exadata Database Machine deployment strategy as well.

Generic Oracle Query Optimization

Oracle first began to put special emphasis on the support of data warehousing workloads with the introduction of Oracle7 in the early 1990s. At that time, most Oracle databases were deployed with a database optimizer that was rules-based. Essentially, the database administrators (DBAs) influenced the rules that would be applied when SQL was submitted. Of course, the most interesting queries submitted to a data warehouse by business analysts are usually of an ad hoc nature. Recognizing the manpower, expertise, and planning needed in the rules-based approach, Oracle embarked on evolving the database that would instead use a cost-based optimizer to solve queries, where the database estimated the costs, in terms of CPU and I/O, of different potential execution paths. Over time, the cost-based optimizer replaced any need for rules-based techniques.

One of the first data warehousing–specific features introduced to the Oracle database was static bitmap indexes in Oracle7. Static bitmap indexes are useful to represent data of low cardinality (e.g., having relatively few variations in comparison to the number of rows). The data is stored in bitmaps, with a "1" indicating that a value is present and a "0" indicating that the value is not present. In cost-based optimization, bit-wise operations take place that provide extremely fast joins. A side benefit is the reduced storage required for bitmaps.

Oracle7 also was the first version in which the optimizer recognized a star schema and optimized the solving of a query against such a schema. Initially, the optimizer used only Cartesian product joins to solve the query, first generating Cartesian products for the dimension tables, then doing a single join back to the fact table to speed performance. In Oracle8, the optimizer added more advanced techniques to be used where the number of dimensions was quite large or data within such tables was found to be sparse. Star query optimization typically occurs today on such schemas where a bitmap index is created on the foreign key column in the fact table and the Oracle database initialization parameter STAR_TRANSFORMATION_ ENABLED is set to TRUE.

Of course, many queries are submitted by business analysts that return answer sets containing subtotals or summaries of detailed data. For example, a query might be issued to return results of shipments by region over the past six months against the schema illustrated earlier in Figure 7-2. For those sorts of queries that can rely on summary data (such as regions in our example schema), Oracle introduced materialized views in Oracle8i. Essentially, materialized views are physical tables in the Oracle database containing the aggregated or summary-level data, so regions might be deployed in materialized views. A faster answer to the query occurs because the query is transparently redirected to the aggregated data table and detailed data does not need to be scanned to provide the answer. Over subsequent releases of the Oracle database, the optimizer made better use of materialized views so that today, they can be joined even where they don't align at exactly the same levels of detail. The creation of materialized views also became much more automated since Oracle's Automatic Database Diagnostics Monitor can make recommendations as to where materialized views are useful, the materialized views advisor in Oracle Enterprise Manager can recommend their creation, and DBAs can simply respond positively to the recommendation to create them.

An additional database feature, the Oracle database Partitioning Option, is more often associated with effective Oracle data warehouse management. We will describe its importance in enabling an effective loading and backup strategy in a few sections. But the Oracle Partitioning Option also has important implications for query optimization.

The Oracle Partitioning Option is used simply to separate the database into smaller sets of data, using ranges, hashes, or other means of distributing the data. The most popular strategies for using the Partitioning Option are to manage the database based on a range of dates, or a range of values, or a composite mix of the two. However, since many queries also often map to specific date ranges or values when determining results, the Oracle optimizer is smart enough to direct queries to only the partitions that contain results. Thus, the Partitioning Option is often used as part of a performance optimization approach for large-scale data warehousing where hundreds of such partitions might exist. Query results are much faster, since large numbers of partitions that are outside the bounds of ranges that contain data needed to answer the query are avoided. A Partition Advisor in the SQL Access Advisor can recommend table, index, and materialized views partitioning strategies for optimal query performance.

Let's look again at our schema example in Figure 7-2, assuming that the shipment fact table has been partitioned by shipment dates. If we query the database and seek shipments between specific date ranges, the query optimizer will only explore the relevant partitions that can contain query answers when assembling the results set. Figure 7-5 illustrates this concept for a query that seeks the products shipped to the northeast region from October 1 through November 30, 2010. Only the October 2010 and November 2010 partitions are explored.

Query performance can be improved even more by enabling the usage of partition-wise joins. This optimization technique minimizes the data exchanged among parallel execution servers when joins execute in parallel. If both tables are equally partitioned on their join keys, a full partition-wise join will occur. If only one table is partitioned on the join key, the Oracle database optimizer can choose to dynamically repartition the second table based on the first and perform what is called a partial partition-wise join.

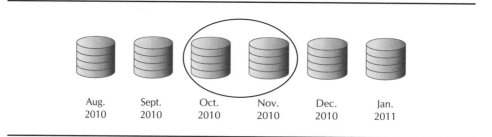

| Aug. 2010 | Sept. 2010 | Oct. 2010 | Nov. 2010 | Dec. 2010 | Jan. 2011 |

FIGURE 7-5.   *Partition elimination optimization based on dates in a query*

Embedded Analytics in Oracle

Advanced optimization techniques in the database optimizer can speed query results. But data warehousing is about more than simple ad hoc queries. More advanced statistics, trending and forecasting, and modeling through data mining can be useful when fully trying to understand what is happening in the business and what will happen in the future. These types of analyses often deal with large quantities of data. To speed performance, you can execute these analyses in the database where the data lives.

Embedded analytics in the Oracle database provide everything from basic statistics to OLAP to data mining. In this section, we'll cover these three topics. As with many of Oracle's advanced features, these were introduced and improved over a series of Oracle database releases.

SQL Aggregation and Analytics Extensions

Basic statistical and analytic functions are provided as extensions to Oracle database SQL, including extensions that follow the International Standards Organization (ISO) 1999 standards. Other extensions are also present that provide functionality beyond what the standards addressed. Oracle first started to extend SQL for analytics by adding basic CUBE and ROLLUP extensions to GROUP BY functions in Oracle8i. Such aggregation extensions are used to improve the performance of the data warehouse. Today, the SQL aggregation extensions also include GROUPING functions and the GROUP SETs expression, as well as pivoting operations.

The database also provides a host of SQL analytics covering analysis, reporting, and other types of calculations and clauses. Examples of these extensions include ranking functions, windowing functions, reporting functions, LAG/LEAD functions, FIRST/LAST functions, linear regression functions, inverse percentiles, hypothetical rank and distribution, and a useful MODEL clause for multidimensional data. Table 7-1 briefly describes what each is used for.

OLAP

When trying to better understand the future of the business by analyzing trends and preparing forecasts, OLAP solutions often enter the picture to provide faster resolution of queries and provide additional advanced

Type of SQL Analytic Function	Usage
Ranking	Calculate value rank, percentile, and n-tiles in a set of data
Windowing	Calculate cumulative and moving aggregates working with a variety of statistical functions (SUM, AVG, MIN, MAX, COUNT, VARIANCE, STDDEV, FIRST_VALUE, LAST_VALUE, and others)
Reporting	Calculate share such as market share working with a variety of the statistical functions (SUM, AVG, MIN, MAX, COUNT, VARIANCE, STDDEV, RATIO_TO_REPORT, and others)
LAG/LEAD	Find a value in a row a specified number of rows from the current row
FIRST/LAST	Find the first or last value in an ordered group
Linear regression	Calculate linear regression line-value statistics, coefficient, slope, and intercept
Inverse percentile	Determine the value in a data set that corresponds to a specified percentile
Hypothetical rank and distribution	Determine the rank or percentile that a row would have if inserted into a data set
MODEL clause	Create multidimensional arrays from query results and apply specified rules to calculate new values

TABLE 7-1. *Oracle SQL Analytic Functions*

analysis techniques. Oracle offers two different multidimensional OLAP (MOLAP) engines most applicable for different situations and used for storing "cubes." The cube terminology is somewhat a misnomer, as multidimensional objects frequently contain more than three dimensions, but long ago gained popularity for describing these objects.

One of the engines Oracle offers is Essbase, a MOLAP database engine that is external to the Oracle relational database (and therefore is deployed outside of the Oracle Exadata Database Machine). Essbase is especially useful where business analysts want to extract data from Oracle and other data sources for custom analyses of their own design. But in some situations, data volumes can be so large that moving data out of an Oracle database across a network link and into Essbase is not desirable. In these scenarios, deploying in-database OLAP can make sense as an alternative approach.

Oracle provides in-database OLAP via the Oracle OLAP Option. OLAP cubes are stored as embedded objects called analytic workspaces within the relational structure of the Oracle database. The cubes are created by defining dimensions, levels, and hierarchies within dimensions, attributes, and mappings from relational source schema to the OLAP cube dimensions. Cubes and other dimensional objects appear in the Oracle database data dictionary. Oracle's Analytic Workspace Manager (AWM) is commonly used as the tool for creating and managing this process as an alternative to using SQL commands. AWM can also be used to set up and populate allocations of data down a hierarchy.

Access to the OLAP Option analytic workspace data structures is most commonly via SQL, though a Java OLAP application programming interface (API) is also supported for applications development. A variety of functions are available within the OLAP Option, including analytic functions, arithmetic functions, aggregations, statistical time-series, and allocations. Forecasts can be generated for short periods using a time-series approach and for longer periods by doing causal analysis using statistical regression.

As of Oracle Database 11g, cube-based materialized views provide views over the cubes that have already been created, populated, and aggregated. As a result, SQL queries to an Oracle relational database will be transparently redirected to the proper level in the OLAP Option cube to answer a query, much the same as would occur where any materialized view is present. Cube-based materialized views also enable OLAP Option cube data refreshes to be handled like those of any materialized views. The OLAP Option can provide a highly desirable and simpler alternative database structure in comparison to maintaining large quantities of materialized views across many dimensions in an Oracle relational database.

Data Mining

Data mining addresses the problem of how to analyze the likelihood of observed outcomes when there are too many variables to easily understand the driving factors. Typically, organizations build and deploy mathematical models based on the algorithm that best predicts when such very good or very bad outcomes are likely to occur. Example applications might include fraud detection, churn analysis, cross-sell effectiveness, threat detection, and a host of others. The designers of the models are usually among the most advanced statisticians and analysts within an organization. One emerging trend is the embedding of such data mining models into applications to make the sophistication of them transparent and available to a much wider group of business analysts.

A variety of data mining algorithms are provided in the Oracle Data Mining Option to address different business problems, since predicting their outcomes will likely align with a specific algorithm. For example, clustering algorithms are ideal when segmenting groups; classification algorithms are commonly used to predict response; regression is used when estimating values; feature extraction is used to create new but fewer attributes that represent the same information; attribute importance identifies key predictors of outcomes; associations are used to find groups of items with affinity to each other; and anomaly detection identifies rare situations and events. Table 7-2 indicates the specific data mining algorithms available in the Oracle database and when these data mining techniques are required.

Data Mining Technique	Oracle Data Mining Algorithms
Clustering	Enhanced K-Means, Orthogonal Planning
Classification	Decision Tree, Logistical Regression, Naïve Bayes, Support Vector Machine
Regression	Multiple Regression, Support Vector Machine
Feature Extraction	Non-negative Matrix Factorization (NMF)
Attribute Importance	Minimum Description Length
Association	Apriori
Anomaly Detection	One-Class Support Vector Machine

TABLE 7-2. *Data Mining Techniques and Oracle Data Mining Algorithms*

When developing a data mining analysis workflow, Oracle's Data Miner tool is used for data exploration, data preparation, determining the appropriate Oracle Data Mining model, and model scoring. Data mining steps are outlined using Data Miner's graphical interface, and PL/SQL can then be generated to create data mining applications. For analysts that instead would prefer to use the R language (an open-source offering that is part of the GNU project and also features a runtime environment with graphics and a debugger), there is an Oracle Data Mining Option interface.

Unique Exadata Features for Optimal Query Response

Thus far, we described Oracle data warehousing features that are available for any server and storage platform that Oracle supports. The Oracle Exadata Database Machine with Exadata storage provides additional optimization techniques that are unique to this platform. Exadata consists of a storage hardware solution, previously described in this book, and Oracle Exadata Storage Server Software, whose features were covered in Chapter 3. Though the Oracle Exadata Storage Server Software enables storage-specific optimization, the optimization is handled under the covers of the Oracle database so it is transparent to SQL queries.

Much of the early focus of the Oracle Exadata Storage Server Software was to provide optimization for data warehousing. Oracle continues to roll out additional data warehousing optimizations with each release of the Oracle Database and Exadata Storage Server Software. For example, with the Oracle Database 11g Release 1 (version 11.1.0.7), the corresponding Oracle Exadata Storage Server Software introduced Smart Scans, row filtering based on a "where" predicate, join filtering, and incremental backup filtering. The Oracle Exadata Storage Server Software introduced with Oracle Database 11g Release 2 added storage indexing, support for scans on encrypted data, data mining model scoring, support for the Smart Flash Cache, and Hybrid Columnar Compression. Oracle Database 11g Release 2 introduced the Database File System (DBFS).

To give you an appreciation of Smart Scans, let's first look at a simplified version of how Oracle handles SQL queries on a non-Exadata system. Where Oracle is deployed on non-Exadata systems, when a SQL query is executed, the database server will identify table extents and issue I/Os to storage.

If there is not a match of indexes that identify query results, a full table scan occurs. When dealing with large data warehouse tables, a large volume of data could be sent to the database server, where subsequent determination of the query results occurs prior to returning the results to the business analyst. Return of such large data volumes from storage to database server nodes through limited bandwidth is the reason that many poorly performing Oracle data warehouses are said to be throughput-bound.

In comparison, where Exadata storage is present and Smart Scans are used, the database server kernel is "Exadata aware." In reality, there is constant modulation between database processes and the Exadata Storage Server cells, but to provide you with a simplified explanation and diagram, we show an iDB command sent to the Exadata Storage Server cells in Figure 7-6. A CELLSRV process in the Oracle Exadata Storage Server Software scans data blocks in each cell into memory and identifies only the rows and columns that provide valid results for the query. These results are returned from the Exadata Storage Server cells to the database server nodes in a constant flow of data that matches the predicates. There, the database consolidates the results and returns them to the client. This technique has

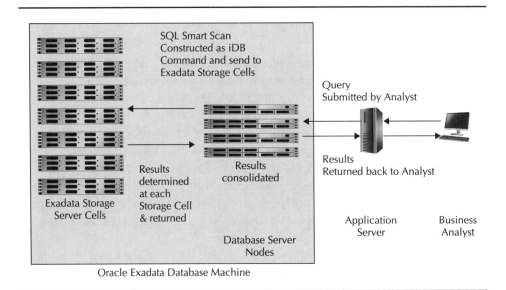

FIGURE 7-6. *Smart scans*

been described by some as a hybrid approach to solving queries, using a shared nothing technique in the Exadata Storage Server cells in combination with the Oracle database server's shared disk approach.

The presence of Smart Scans and the usage of these techniques enabled by the Exadata Storage Server Software can be observed in Explain Plans. Smart Scans are designed to provide predicate filtering and column projection. Bloom filters are constructed to provide join filtering in storage between large tables and small lookup tables (common in star schemas where fact tables are surrounded by dimension tables). Smart Scans also deal transparently with other Oracle database internal mechanisms and optimization techniques, as we'll describe in a subsequent section.

A couple of key management tasks for large-scale data warehouses are also much faster because of the Oracle Exadata Storage Server Software. Incremental database backups are much faster because changes are tracked at the individual Oracle block level. The CREATE TABLESPACE command can appear to be nearly instantaneous, as an InfiniBand *i*DB protocol command is sent directly to the Exadata Storage Server cells to create a tablespace and format blocks, instead of using the database CPUs for the formatting of these blocks before being written to storage.

Transparent creation and maintenance of storage indexes by the Oracle Exadata Storage Server Software was released with the introduction of Oracle Database 11*g* Release 2. Maintained in the Exadata Storage Server cell's memory, the storage index tracks minimum and maximum values for eight columns within each MB storage region in the cell. For queries that include a WHERE clause, the Oracle Exadata Storage Server Software will determine whether there are any appropriate rows contained between the minimum and maximum values in-memory, eliminating I/Os if there are not.

The Oracle Exadata Storage Server Software in this release also added offload processing to Exadata Storage Servers in Smart Scans against encrypted tablespaces and columns and offloading of data model scoring. Of course, such offloading provides significant performance gains. For mathematical and data mining functions that tend to be CPU-intensive, it is noteworthy that there are actually more CPUs and processing power in the Exadata Storage Server cells than in the Oracle database server nodes in a Oracle Exadata Database Machine configuration. More than 300 of the mathematical and analytic functions supported in the Oracle database are processed within Exadata storage.

Support of the Exadata Smart Flash Cache was also introduced with this release of the Oracle Exadata Storage Server Software and the Sun Oracle Database Machine. The Oracle Exadata Storage Server Software will cache frequently accessed data by default. However, the data returned by the full table scans common in data warehouses are not, by default, placed in the Flash Cache. In these scenarios, you can override the default by specifying the attribute "CELL_FLASH_CACHE KEEP" in the object definition or an ALTER statement for such an object. In fact, data could be read from both the cache and disk at the same time, achieving higher aggregate throughput.

Data Warehousing Compression Techniques

We discussed compression techniques available in the Oracle database in Chapters 2 and 3. Here, we'll focus on the role of compression when deploying a data warehouse, primarily used for reducing required storage and improving performance (since I/O is reduced when retrieving data). The types of compression often used for data warehousing are the basic compression included with the Oracle database; the Advanced Compression Option, used where there are frequent updates; and Hybrid Columnar Compression.

The basic compression and Advanced Compression Option provide row-based compression techniques. Typically providing compression ratios of two to four times, the Advanced Compression Option is often more associated with OLTP since it can also handle frequent updates of data. But use cases for data warehouses in some business processes are known to require updates to data on a frequent basis, even data that might reside in very old partitions. In such situations, Advanced Compression can be the optimal choice.

Hybrid Columnar Compression is included as part of the Oracle Exadata Storage Server Software and so is available only for Oracle Exadata Database Machines. It is designed to be used where the data is read-only and can deliver compression ratios that reach ten times or more. Hybrid Columnar Compression combines the benefits of compressing repeating columnar values (and other techniques) within the row-based Oracle database.

Where Hybrid Columnar Compression is used, data is loaded using bulk loading techniques (e.g., INSERT statements with the APPEND hint, parallel DML, SQL*Loader, and Create Table as Select). When the data is loaded, column values are stored separately from the rows as compression units. When a Smart Scan occurs, column projection, filtering, and decompression occurs in the Exadata Storage Server cells, as is normally the case when Smart Scans of compressed data occur. Data required to satisfy query predicates is not decompressed. Only the columns and rows to be returned to the client are decompressed in memory.

As Hybrid Columnar Compression provides choices in query and archival compression algorithms, you can balance your compression needs versus performance requirements. For example, query compression is designed for optimal I/O scan performance and has two settings: HIGH compression (by default) and LOW compression. HIGH compression typically provides about ten times the compression, whereas LOW compression typically provides only about six times the compression but with better load times. Archive compression is designed for optimal storage of infrequently accessed data with typical compression ratios of up to 15 times. But the tradeoff of using archive compression is diminished query performance when compared to warehouse compression.

The type of compression you will choose (basic, Advanced, or Hybrid Columnar) will depend on the frequency of updates and whether you want to optimize for query performance or storage savings. A common technique used in large-scale data warehousing is to apply Oracle's compression techniques most appropriate for read-only data only on older database partitions that are less likely to be updated and apply an Information Lifecycle Management (ILM) strategy. Hybrid Columnar Compression is often deployed on such older partitions where HIGH compression is used.

The Typical Life of a Query

When the Oracle database executes a query on the Oracle Exadata Database Machine, it will use a combination of optimizations traditionally provided by the Oracle database and optimizations that are specific to the Oracle Exadata Database Machine and Oracle Exadata Storage Server Software. So, as we illustrate the typical life of a query, we take into account several of the optimizations that we have already covered in this chapter.

In our example, the Oracle data warehouse contains seven years of customer data and requires 50TB of storage space to contain the data. The data in the database columns contains a significant number of repeating values. The data is partitioned in composite partitions by geographic region and date. A business analyst submits a query to obtain results that will show sales to customers who purchased over $100,000 in products during the first quarter of the year over the past three years in the northeast region.

Using Hybrid Columnar Compression for warehouse compression, the amount of storage required for user data in the entire data warehouse is reduced from 50TB to 10TB in our example. Since the data is partitioned, when the query is executed, only partitions containing data from the first quarter during the past three years is touched. This reduces the volume of data that is considered to about 2TB. In this stage of solving the query, the Exadata Smart Flash Cache might come into play if any of the partitions were pinned into cache.

Next, a Smart Scan occurs and storage indexes reduce the volume of data to just that where customers have purchased over $100,000. In this example, only about a few dozen rows of results data is obtained from the Exadata Storage Server cells. If some of the data was encrypted, before the Smart Scan is executed, the Oracle Exadata Storage Server Software will first decrypt that data and then it will be expanded as this constant data flow matches the predicates.

Taken together, the amount of query performance speed-up can greatly exceed ten times or more what might be possible on a non-Exadata system. Your performance speed-up will vary due to the number of factors that can come into play, and also will be dependent on how balanced (or unbalanced) the current server and storage platform you are comparing the Oracle Exadata Database Machine to is.

Best Practices for Data Loading

The approach you should take for data loading will depend on a number of factors, including the cleanliness of the source data, the volume of data to be loaded, and how quickly the data must be available in the data warehouse to business analysts. The Oracle database supports loading of data from external tables and via SQL*Loader, using transportable tablespaces to move data from one Oracle database to another, import and export mechanisms such as Oracle Data Pump, and insertion of individual records using database links to other Oracle databases or connectivity to other sources using gateways, ODBC connections, or Java Database Connectivity (JDBC) connections.

Oracle has tools that can aid in this process, including the ETL tools in the Oracle Data Integrator (ODI) Suite—Oracle Data Integrator and Oracle Warehouse Builder. Both of these tools push transformation and load processing into the target Oracle database for better performance. Where source data is clean and does not need extensive transformations, Oracle's GoldenGate can provide lighter-weight, near-real-time, simple data extraction and loading to the target Oracle database as data in the sources change.

Where large data volumes are going to be moved, as is typical in database loads where complex data transformations are necessary, a staging area is commonly established to store flat files prior to loading the database. The Oracle database features a DBFS that can be used for this purpose and enables the Oracle database to be used as an IEEE POSIX-standards compatible file system. Consisting of a PL/SQL package on the server and a Linux DBFS client, the combination enables files to be accessed easily by database applications and file-based tools to access the files stored in the database. DBFS is a distributed file system where files are stored as SecureFiles LOBs. The DBFS client is used to mount the file system with "direct_io" set where moving raw files. DBFS should reside in its own database, not in the data warehouse database.

If complex transformations are to occur in the target data warehouse database, an additional staging layer is sometimes set up to avoid impact on business analysts as these transformations are in progress. The speed of loading is, of course, directly affected by the number and speed of the CPUs used during the loading process. To do this effectively, Oracle must be able to look inside raw data files and determine where rows of data begin and end. For that reason, where performance is a key consideration, data is typically loaded as uncompressed, and partitions might later be compressed as they age.

The use of external tables is now recommended where you are loading from flat files. External tables allow transparent parallelization within the Oracle database, applying transformations via SQL and PL/SQL, precluding the need for a staging layer, and providing more efficient space management (especially with partitioned tables) when parallelizing loads. External tables are described using the CREATE TABLE syntax. Loading data from an external table is via a CREATE TABLE AS SELECT (CTAS) or INSERT AS SELECT (IAS) statement.

By default, a CTAS statement will use direct path loading, key to good loading performance, since database blocks are created and written directly to the target database during direct path loading and the loads can be run in parallel server processes. The IAS statement will also use direct path loading where you provide an APPEND hint. A direct path load parses the input data according to the description given in the external table definition, converts the data for each input field to its corresponding Oracle data type, and then builds a column array structure for the data. These column array structures are used to format Oracle data blocks and build index keys. The newly formatted database blocks are then written directly to the database, bypassing the standard SQL processing engine and the database buffer cache.

Since large-scale data warehouses are usually partitioned based on ranges or discrete values, another complementary technique often used during this loading process is the EXCHANGE PARTITION command. The EXCHANGE PARTITION command allows you to swap the data in a nonpartitioned table into a particular partition in your partitioned table. The command does not physically move data. Instead, it updates the data dictionary to exchange a pointer from the partition to the table and vice versa. Because there is no physical movement of data, an exchange does not generate redo and undo, making it a subsecond operation and far less likely to affect performance than any traditional data-movement approaches such as INSERT.

Partitioning, Backups, and High Availability in Data Warehouses

Backup and high availability strategies are important in large-scale data warehousing where the warehouses are used for tactical business decisions, as they are in other enterprise databases. A sound backup strategy for data in the data warehouse is critical to making such a warehouse recoverable in a reasonable amount of time. Reloads from source systems and re-creating complex data transformations that occurred over time are an impractical approach to recovery. However, even where backups are efficiently taken, the reload process might be too lengthy to meet business service-level requirements. In such scenarios, providing high availability by deploying and maintaining both primary and secondary data warehouses can be justified.

While we cover high availability strategies in Chapter 2, some considerations are especially relevant where a large-scale data warehouse is deployed. Part of a sound backup strategy for a data warehouse includes careful consideration of how data changes over time. Where the data warehouse contains very large data volumes, older data might not be undergoing updates. Where this situation exists, the Partitioning Option of the Oracle database can fulfill an important role in creating a more manageable backup scenario. As mentioned earlier in this chapter, data warehouses are often partitioned based on date ranges. A common backup strategy for any database is to provide ongoing backups frequently enough to capture critical updates that might have occurred that can affect business decisions. In a data warehouse, partitioning can separate data that is being updated from stagnant data. Older data that is nonchanging (read only) can be terabytes or tens of terabytes in size in such large-scale data warehouses and would not need to be backed up going forward if that data is held in separate partitions. For example, in Figure 7-5, if the August and September 2010 partitions contain nonchanging data, once they are backed up, no further backups are needed.

In some organizations, old data might be restated on an ongoing basis because of how business occurs. In others, tactical near-real-time business management using the data warehouse means that nonavailability of the system will not be tolerated during a system failure and subsequent reload process. Such scenarios will force you to create a highly available backup system containing a duplicate copy of the data. Oracle Data Guard can be used to maintain consistency between a primary and secondary site. Reporting can take place from the secondary site even while updates are occurring. An alternative to the Data Guard approach used in some organizations is to fork ETL processes from source systems simultaneously to primary and secondary locations. Generally where either method is used, the standby or backup system is configured identically to the primary (e.g., the same Oracle Exadata Database Machine configuration is used for both sites) to assure the same levels of performance in solving queries if the primary system fails.

Data Models, Business Intelligence Tools, and Security

An effective data warehouse deployment includes more than just the Oracle database and Oracle Exadata Database Machine. Also key to overall success are the quality of the data models, business intelligence tools, and the security mechanisms that are put into place.

Data models provide definitions and schemas that contain the data elements aligned to key performance indicators tracked by business analysts. Logical data models provide the data definitions and entity relationships among objects. The logical models are then translated into deployable physical data models designed to take advantage of the Oracle database's capabilities. Logical entities are generally mapped into tables in the physical data models; relationships are mapped into foreign key constraints; attributes are mapped into columns; primary unique identifiers are mapped into primary key constraints; and unique identifiers are mapped into unique key constraints. The schemas for the physical data models are of the types described earlier in this chapter.

Business intelligence tools provide a means for business analysts to access data residing in the data warehouse. Reporting, ad hoc query, and advanced analytics are delivered to the analysts through these dashboards and tools. The dashboards and tools are designed to be of a self-service nature when underlying data models in the data warehouse are properly aligned with business needs.

Security considerations come into play because of the value of the data and information available in the data warehouse and the broad user communities that can have access to it. Security features are used to restrict access to data on a need-to-know basis. They can be used to track who had access to data during specific periods.

We'll next go into a bit more detail regarding data models, business intelligence tools, and security and describe how each would fit in an Oracle Exadata Database Machine data warehousing deployment strategy.

Data Models

Until the past decade, developing physical data models for large-scale Oracle data warehouses was largely undertaken from the ground up by IT organizations or consulting services companies. Today, Oracle and a number of Oracle's partners have physical data models that are extremely useful in solving problems and serve as starting points in deployment. While many businesses and organizations start with such standard data models, most will customize them to reflect their own unique needs and strategies. Of course, these models can be deployed as schema in the database or databases on the Oracle Exadata Database Machine.

Examples of Oracle's physical data models for industries include data models in communications, finance, healthcare, retail, and utilities. The models range in schema type from completely third normal form for enterprise data warehouse solutions to "analytics" models that resemble star schemas more aligned for business intelligence self-discovery. In some industries, Oracle offers complementary models that address both sets of needs.

Oracle also has horizontal Oracle Business Intelligence Applications that address areas such as sales, marketing, service and contact centers, pricing, loyalty, financials, procurement and spend, supply chain and order management, projects, and human resources. The horizontal models are star schemas with conformed (common) dimensions that enable queries across the various models. The Business Intelligence Applications also come with prebuilt ETL available for sources such as Oracle's own suite of enterprise resource planning (ERP) applications and Siebel CRM.

Business Intelligence Tools

Business intelligence tools commonly generate SQL statements to the data warehouse database when queries are submitted and reports are to be populated with results. Given the transparency provided in Exadata optimizations, all of the major business intelligence tools vendors and open-source providers that support the current version of the Oracle database can support the Oracle Exadata Database Machine.

Oracle Business Intelligence Enterprise Edition (OBIEE) is one such set of business analyst tools, providing dashboards, reporting capabilities, ad hoc query capabilities, and action frameworks for automating business processes. These tools are deployed using applications server platforms that are configured to support Business Intelligence (BI) Server workloads. So this part of the infrastructure does not reside on the Oracle Exadata Database Machine, but instead resides on separate servers deployed around it. Figure 7-7 illustrates the ability of OBIEE 11*g* to drill into hierarchies as defined in the subject areas in the figure. These hierarchies could be stored as relational OLAP in the Oracle database or as MOLAP cubes.

In addition to standard relational data types, the Oracle database is capable of storing other data types, including spatial. Spatial data can be useful when determining and displaying query results that include geographic information. OBIEE 11*g* supports map views that are used to display data containing longitude and latitude information (geocodes) on maps.

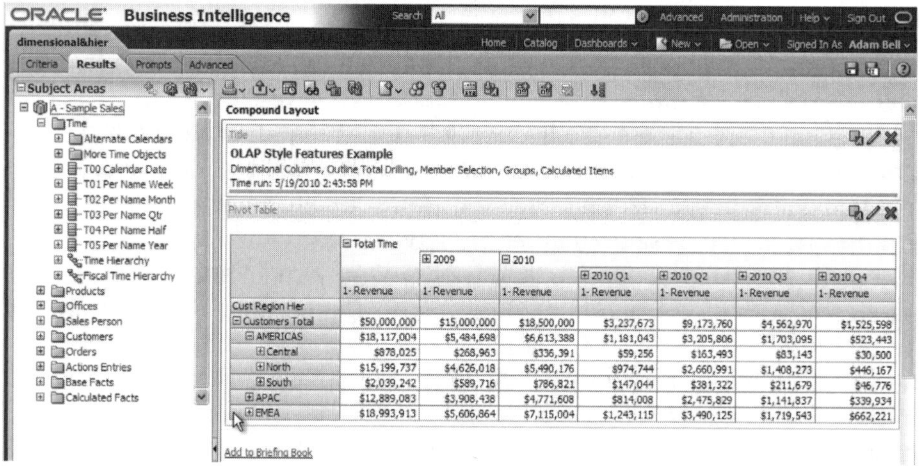

FIGURE 7-7. *OBIEE 11g ad hoc query interface*

The Oracle database contains a unique schema (named MDSYS) that denotes storage, syntax, and semantics of supported geometric data types; spatial indexing functions; and operators, functions, and procedures for "area of interest" queries. The Oracle Exadata Database Machine has demonstrated excellent performance speed-up in handling queries of spatial data, given the mathematical nature of resolving such queries and the number of mathematical functions handled in Exadata storage.

Oracle's industry vertical and horizontal business intelligence analytics development teams are continuing to build reporting engines and dashboards using OBIEE for use with their data models. Within the OBIEE BI Server, Oracle has what is called a "Common Enterprise Information Model." This model consists of a presentation layer, semantic object layer, and physical layer. The presentation layer defines the interface; the semantic object layer defines dimensions, hierarchies, measures, and calculations; and the physical layer provides a mapping and connections back into the physical data models residing in the Oracle database. For Oracle's analytics solutions, all of these layers are predefined and mapped to the data models.

Security Considerations

As business analyst communities grow and become more diverse, with members sometimes accessing data from outside the bounds of the organization that deploys the data warehouse, additional security considerations come into play. Given the usefulness of data residing in the very large data warehouses that are common on the Oracle Exadata Database Machine, the demand for such access and need for advanced security is common. For example, an organization might want to share access to data unique to a supplier or distributor with that supplier or distributor. They might want all of their suppliers and distributors to have similar access to the common data warehouse but only be able to see and work with their own detailed data. To protect who sees what, a virtual private database can be defined using a combination of the Oracle database and OBIEE. Different user communities are restricted to seeing only relevant data based on security profiles defined in the database.

Similarly, business analysts using OBIEE can be restricted from seeing certain records by deploying data masking in the database. Specific database fields might also be encrypted through database encryption to restrict access. In addition, the database might be more securely managed through the use of Database Vault (limiting DBA access to data residing in tables) and Audit Vault (to track who saw what data and when they saw it).

Sizing the Platform for Data Warehousing and Justifying Purchase

Sizing the Oracle Exadata Database Machine properly for a data warehouse implementation requires that the person performing the sizing have in-depth knowledge of current workload characteristics and future requirements, raw data storage requirements (both for current data size and planned data growth), compression techniques that might be used and their impact, and availability considerations. The last three of the aforementioned are typically well understood within an IT organization. But the current workload characteristics and future requirements are likely to be less well understood. Having knowledge of these is critical when developing a business case for purchase of the Oracle Exadata Database Machine and sizing it properly.

Data warehouses and enterprise-class platforms such as the Oracle Exadata Database Machine are usually deployed for one of two reasons—to better determine where to reduce bottom-line business costs or to increase top-line business growth. While IT management might initially want to focus on the ability to meet business Service Level Agreements or reduced IT costs by deploying this platform, this may not provide enough justification to get funding. Discussing the business analysis needs with lines-of-business communities might be thought of as difficult by some in IT. To help you along, the following questions might serve as a starting point in uncovering key business initiatives that could fund a data warehouse project on this platform:

- How is the data warehouse being used by the lines of business today?

- How accessible is the current data? Is it trusted and is it available in time to make key business decisions?

- What business key performance indicators (KPIs) and data will be needed in the future? What would be the potential business value in delivery of these additional KPIs and data?

- What is the mix of reporting, ad hoc query, analysis, and modeling today? How might that mix change in the future?

- How might data loading characteristics change in the future?

Table 7-3 lists some of the key data warehousing initiatives currently under way in selected industries that are driven by real business needs and, when linked to performance and availability criteria, can lead to an understanding of how to properly size the platform. The initiatives change over time based on changing business conditions. In shrinking economies or market segments, organizations most often focus on cost savings. In growing economies or market segments, the focus is more often on business growth. For government agencies that are typically much less influenced by economic conditions, the data warehousing initiatives tend to be about better delivery of information to sponsors and constituents to provide proof points as to the value that the agency provides.

Industry Segment	Key Data Warehousing Initiatives
Communications	Network optimization, targeted cross-selling
Financial	Customer cross-selling and risk analysis
Healthcare/Health and Human Services	Electronic medical records/quality of care
Manufacturing	Customer warranty analysis
Media and Online Services	Effectiveness of advertising and promotions
Public Safety and Environmental	Statistical mapping for reporting and analysis
Retail	Supply chain optimization, cross-selling
Taxation	Tax form candidates for audit
Transportation/Military Logistics	Equipment and manpower planning and analysis
Utilities (Smart Meter deployment)	Optimal pricing and tighter grid management

TABLE 7-3. *Key Data Warehousing Initiatives in Various Industries*

As an example, let's take a look at how the purchase of an Oracle Exadata Database Machine might be justified in solving a transportation or logistics problem. In our theoretical organization, if transported items do not arrive within 24 hours of their scheduled delivery time, the value of the contents is significantly diminished due to increased risk of spoilage. Lines of business in this organization track metrics that reflect the declining value of these items. They have measured the impact of delays as reducing the price of delivered goods by $88,000 per day. Analysis used in optimizing routing of the items currently occurs only once a day and prior to shipment since queries and analyses are so complex that they take hours to run.

The manager of logistics knows that if they could run queries and analyses every hour and see results within an hour (e.g., the results will come back five to eight times faster than currently possible), they'd run their business differently. They would be able to adjust routes and schedules and to changes in demand that appear during the day. By making these adjustments, they could reduce the revaluation of these items by 75 percent and save $66,000 per day through more on-time deliveries.

Given these business metrics, the IT organization can now size the Oracle Exadata Database Machine. They will need a configuration large enough to return query results submitted by the logistics analysts in about an hour to deliver the anticipated business cost savings. Upon sizing of the Oracle Exadata Database Machine configuration, the costs for the hardware and software required, implementation, and ongoing support can be calculated. The business sponsor, CFO, and CIO can then do a simple benefit-cost analysis and determine how long it will take to achieve a return on investment. In this example, the Oracle Exadata Database Machine likely will pay for itself within months.

At this point, you might have expected to read about best practices for executing data warehousing benchmarks. The fact is, unless you have identified business drivers similar to those covered in this example, it probably doesn't make any difference how much faster the Oracle Exadata Database Machine turns out to be in such a test. If you do decide you want to run performance tests on the platform before you make a final commitment to buying it, the criteria for a successful test should be driven by providing performance needed to deliver query and analysis results in time to make appropriate business decisions that deliver business value. Of course, you should also satisfy yourself that future deployment conditions are being simulated with the right mix of workload concurrency and database data volume that will give you confidence that your data warehouse will perform.

Summary

In this chapter, we quickly journeyed through the history of Oracle in data warehousing and provided descriptions of how the Oracle Exadata Database Machine and Oracle Exadata Storage Server Software combine to deliver functionality and performance that only a tightly integrated hardware and software solution can deliver. The flexibility of the Oracle database enables deployment of schemas appropriate for enterprise data warehouses, data marts, or hybrid combinations of these types. The Oracle Exadata Database Machine and Oracle Exadata Storage Server Software enable successful deployment of the largest and most complex configurations supporting all of these deployment models.

Given new classes of business problems that can be solved using this platform, data warehousing workloads will continue to grow more complex. Queries and analyses will be performed against ever-growing data volumes. Data loads will move toward near real-time in response to the need for faster tactical business decisions based on current information. As these loads become trickle feeds, the platform must not only perform traditional data warehousing workloads efficiently, but also exhibit excellence in performance and loading characteristics that can appear more akin to transaction processing workloads.

The Oracle Exadata Database Machine is designed to handle workloads that cross this entire spectrum of workload demands. Since the platform is balanced out-of-the box and incrementally grows in a balanced fashion, the CPUs, memory, flash, storage, and interconnect scale as workload demands grow, enabling consistent query response times to be delivered. Automatic Storage Management (ASM) provides a critical role in distributing data in a striped fashion across the disk. The Oracle Exadata Storage Server Software further speeds obtaining results to queries by processing more of the data in storage, where the data lives.

As you plan your data warehouse deployment, traditional Oracle and data warehousing best practices do apply to the Oracle Exadata Database Machine. But you will also find this platform to be a lot more forgiving and easier to manage than traditional Oracle database platforms. Of course, the business justification exercise will likely be similar to other data warehousing initiatives, but with new potential areas to explore due to new levels of performance delivered. The end result for you should be faster deployment of a platform that delivers the query response and analytics needed by your business analysts and delivers measurable business value.

CHAPTER
8

Exadata and OLTP

hen the first Oracle Exadata Database Machine, the HP Oracle Database Machine, was introduced, it represented the first version of the power of the Database Machine. This version was aimed at delivering extreme performance for data warehousing, performance many times faster than was previously achievable with standard database systems.

Version 2 of the Database Machine, the Sun Oracle Database Machine, was released about a year later, with additional capabilities. This version of the Database Machine not only further improved performance for data warehouse workloads, but also provided a solution that delivered extraordinary performance for OLTP workloads. The X2 versions of the Oracle Exadata Database Machine provided even more flexibility in deployment choices for OLTP workloads.

This chapter will explore the use of the Database Machine for OLTP workloads. As with data warehouse workloads, the power of the Oracle Exadata Database Machine stems from a combination of state-of-the-art hardware and software, which includes features that are standard in the Oracle Database 11*g* environment and features that are exclusive to the Exadata platform.

OLTP Workloads and Exadata Features

Before jumping into an examination of the features and functionality of the Exadata Database Machine as it relates to OLTP, we should start by reviewing some of the key aspects of both OLTP and Exadata software.

The first thing to discuss is the nature of OLTP workloads themselves. OLTP stands for Online Transaction Processing, a description that refers to the core nature of OLTP systems. OLTP systems are used to handle the tactical operations of an organization, that is transactions where data is written to and updated in the database on an ongoing basis. Although data is also written to data warehouses, that data input is traditionally in the form of some type of batch activity, while the write activity in an OLTP system comes in a large number of smaller transactions. Because of this, OLTP workloads typically have a higher number of database operations with a smaller data payload, and the performance emphasis is on the responsiveness of the database in handling these smaller transactions.

But OLTP workloads consist of more than just small write transactions. An OLTP workload inevitably includes read activity of a type more typical of OLTP than data warehousing (e.g., single row lookups) and activities like production reporting where the characteristics of the workload are similar to those of data warehouse workloads. Some of these portions of an OLTP workload will benefit from the features of a Database Machine in the same way that data warehouse workloads will benefit—from the dramatic reduction in data returned to the database nodes through predicate filtering in the Exadata Storage Server, the use of storage indexes to reduce the amount of I/O from storage disks, and join filtering to further reduce the amount of data returned from storage.

The second point to make is that Exadata features either improve the performance of database operations or remain transparent. Remember that, for instance, the Exadata Storage Server can return a greatly reduced set of data when using Smart Scan techniques, or that the Server can simply return data blocks, just like a standard storage for an Oracle database. Similarly, a storage index can help to eliminate storage regions from being read by the storage server, or simply remain in Exadata Storage Server memory until it can be used effectively—neither case negatively affects an operation that does not use the storage index.

This transparency works in two ways. Exadata features will not intrude on operations where they cannot help improve performance, and all the standard features of the Oracle 11g Database are available to all operations on a Database Machine. The Oracle Database has long been the leading OLTP database in the world, and nothing in the Exadata environment degrades any of that industry-leading functionality.

Another key aspect of the Exadata Database Machine is the imposition of best practices in hardware design through the use of a balanced configuration. The Database Machine is specifically architected to avoid bottlenecks due to oversubscription for resources, an all-too-common problem that can affect database servers supporting any type of workload. Remember that a resource shortage in one area is typically relieved by compensating with excess resource consumption in another area. By avoiding bottlenecks caused by read-intensive query operations, the robust configuration of a Database Machine helps to avoid unbalanced configurations for all systems, both data warehouse and OLTP.

Finally, remember the focal point of discussion in Chapter 3 on Exadata software. The overall direction of Exadata software is to improve the efficiency of database operations. Improved efficiency, once again, means better use of database resources across the board. In the following discussions, you continually see how the improved efficiency of the Exadata Database Machine leads to better resource utilization, resulting in improvement in all types of workloads and database operations.

Exadata Hardware and OLTP

Although, as should be abundantly clear at this point, Exadata is about much more than hardware, any discussion of OLTP and Exadata should include some mention of the hardware configuration and how this hardware is used by the Exadata Database Machine.

General Hardware and Infrastructure Considerations

Version 2 of the Exadata Database Machine used Xeon 5500 Nehalem CPUs with four cores per CPU—extremely fast, state-of-the-art processors. Version X2 of the Exadata Database machine uses six core processors in the X2-2 models and the Exadata Storage Server, and eight core processors in the X2-8 model. The X2-8 model also has 2TBs of DRAM. Given this history, you can expect future versions of the Database Machine to benefit from further increased capabilities in the core hardware components—and some of these improvements might have already happened by the time you are reading this sentence.

The Exadata Storage Server features a large number of disks—up to 168 disks in a full rack—so the overall system benefits from the ability to seek data across many disks through parallel operations. Automatic Storage Management (ASM) optimizes the use of large numbers of disks and, in so doing, gives you the benefits of distributed data and parallel retrieval without a large amount of overhead to manage the data placement.

The Exadata Database Machine is also built as a balanced configuration, which means that data flow does not encounter bottlenecks between the storage system and the database nodes. Although this type of configuration primarily benefits more I/O-intensive applications, such as data warehousing, the minimization of bottlenecks for all types of I/O ensures that OLTP workload components, like production reporting, will not limit the availability of bandwidth in a way that could compromise other OLTP workload components.

Finally, there is one internal change in the way that the Oracle database accesses data from the Exadata Storage Server. In a non-Exadata environment, the Oracle kernel queues and dequeues I/O requests using C libraries. In the world of Exadata, the Oracle kernel can request data directly from the processes on the Exadata Storage Server using Remote Direct Memory Access, or RDMA. When you think about OLTP workloads, you think about very large numbers of individual transactions and I/O requests. With Exadata, the queueing and dequeuing requests do not dive into the kernel, meaning less CPU overhead to perform all of these small I/Os.

This last point again illustrates that the Exadata Database Machine is much more than simply a bunch of hot hardware components strung together. The Exadata Smart Flash Cache combines a fast hardware component and flexible software intelligence in a similar way.

Exadata Smart Flash Cache

The Exadata Smart Flash Cache uses a fast hardware component, delivering data many times faster than retrieval from disk, coupled with smart software to optimize its benefits, as described in Chapter 3.

Each Exadata Storage Cell contains 384GBs of Flash Cache, located on 4 flash PCIe cards. This hardware means that a full rack contains around 5.4TBs of flash-based storage, a figure we will return to in our discussion of working sets later. In all scenarios, satisfying an I/O request from the Exadata Smart Flash Cache means that this request will not have to be satisfied from disk, resulting in greater available bandwidth for the requests that do go to disk. In addition, remember that I/O bandwidth is consumed by both reads and writes, so satisfying reads from the Exadata Smart Flash Cache removes those requests from the disk workload, increasing the number of operations available for writes to disk.

You can use the Exadata Smart Flash Cache in three different ways to support OLTP operations.

Default Usage

The Exadata Storage Server Software, by default, places the results of small I/O operations into the cache, for the same reasons that the data cache does not use the results of large I/O operations to avoid flushing the cache unnecessarily. These smaller I/O operations are the type that are typically performed by OLTP workloads, so, over time, the I/O operations performed by OLTP workloads end up populating the available Flash Cache. Since the default operation of the Flash Cache includes caching the results of write operations, reuse of these data blocks can also benefit from the speed of this cache.

The concept of a *working set* is one way to describe the way that OLTP workloads interact with storage. The term working set refers to the portion of data that is used by an application workload at any particular time. If a working set can be kept entirely available in high-speed access areas, such as the SGA or the Exadata Smart Flash Cache, the workload will not be subjected to any performance bottlenecks based on data used in read operations.

Exadata Smart Flash Cache can hold a little over 18 percent of the data stored on disks in the cell with High Performance storage, given normal redundancy and reserves for system space. This percentage is close to the commonly accepted size of an OLTP working set in relation to the overall store of data. Because of this and the way that the Exadata Smart Flash Cache operates, the Flash Cache can conceivably hold the entire working set providing improved OLTP workload performance.

Keep in mind that the default operation of the Exadata Smart Flash Cache allows for the composition of the cached data to evolve over time. As data moves into the "hot spots" of usage, the Exadata Smart Flash Cache software will automatically end up storing this heavily requested data into the cache. The dynamic nature of this population means that you can benefit from the speed improvements of Flash Cache without excessive management overhead.

KEEP Option

You can also use the STORAGE (CELL_FLASH_CACHE KEEP) option when defining or altering tables, partitions, and indexes. With this clause, all data blocks for the specified object are automatically placed into the Exadata Smart Flash Cache after they are initially read. You can use up to 80 percent of the capacity of the Exadata Smart Flash Cache for storing objects with the KEEP clause.

Bear in mind that the KEEP clause, as explained in Chapter 3, does not guarantee that all data blocks for an object will be in the Exadata Smart Flash Cache at any one time. The clause does specify that the KEEP objects will be aged out of the cache with a less aggressive algorithm and that data blocks being added to the cache with the algorithm used, by default, will not force out an object with the KEEP clause.

In general, you should not assign more data as KEEP objects than can be held simultaneously in that portion of the Exadata Smart Flash Cache. The reason you would use this clause is to ensure that this data is "pinned" in the cache, and if there is more data than can be held at one time, other KEEP data blocks could force blocks out of the cache. Remember this guideline if you are considering assigning an object this status, as database objects tend to increase in size over time. What may be less than 80 percent of the Exadata Smart Flash Cache today could end up being larger in the future, requiring management overhead to track and adjust.

Of course, the KEEP attribute is manually assigned, so the contents of the Exadata Smart Flash Cache will not evolve as usage conditions change, as they would with the default use of the cache. You can use this attribute to improve performance by keeping specific data in the Flash Cache, but you will obviously have to be familiar with usage patterns of your workload in order to best assign tables and partitions to the KEEP portion of the Exadata Smart Flash Cache.

Flash-Based Grid Disks

There is another way you can use the Exadata Smart Flash Cache with OLTP workloads. As described in Chapter 3, the flash storage can be provisioned as grid disks, just as you would use cell disks based on physical disks. These grid disks are used by ASM just as any other group of grid disks would operate.

When you use flash storage in this way, you can write directly to the flash drives, which is quite fast. However, this use of flash storage comes with a significant downside. You would lose either half the capacity of the Flash Cache, with ASM normal redundancy, or two-thirds of the capacity, with ASM high redundancy. Although the PCIe flash cards used in the Exadata Storage Server are highly reliable, the memory-based nature of flash grid disks would call for high redundancy, resulting in less flash to use.

This scenario could result in higher performance for extremely high levels of concurrent writes. However, keep in mind that the Oracle database already has implemented ways to process high levels of write operations, with the DBWR process performing "lazy" writes and the option to have multiple DBWR processes handling the workload. Before jumping immediately to an architecture that uses flash-based grid disks for high-write environments, you should test to see if the performance enhancement you are looking for actually materializes with this implementation.

NOTE
Are you thinking that you could realize performance gains by putting redo logs onto flash-based grid disks? Flash storage provides significant performance improvements over physical disks for random I/O writes, but not much of an improvement over physical disks for sequential writes. This approach will not really get you much in the way of improved performance. In addition, wear leveling in flash storage could result in unpredictable performance changes as data is reorganized in the storage - performance changes that result in writes being two orders of magnitude slower.

Exadata Smart Flash Cache and Data Integrity

The Oracle database has been supporting enterprise-class applications for decades, and the development team at Oracle knows that supporting the integrity of data is an absolute pre-requisite for their database. Flash Cache is memory-based, and memory is inherently less stable than disk. Does this difference cause any potential issues with data integrity, since data stored on flash-based storage could potentially disappear?

First of all, you should be aware that the particular flash cards used in the Exadata Storage Server have a number of features to compensate for potentially instability, including only using a portion of the available storage to allow for automatic detection and swapping out of bad blocks in memory, as well as an integrated super capacitor to supply power to the card in the event of a power failure. In addition to these hardware-based protections, if you choose to use the Exadata Flash as flash-based grid disks, you can use high-redundancy mirroring with ASM.

Second, one of the most crucial aspects of data integrity that could be affected by a loss of data in the cache would be if a user wrote data to the cache and the values were lost before they could be written to disk. The Oracle Database can handle data loss as long as the write activity has been written to the log file. The redo logs hold the primary responsibility for avoiding data loss in the event of a failure, and these logs are not stored in the Flash Cache.

Finally, remember that the Exadata Smart Flash Cache is normally used as a cache. If any portion of the cache goes away, all that happens is the Exadata Storage Server gets the requested data from disk. You would lose the performance advantages of the Flash Cache for the duration of the time that this portion of the cache was not available, but the failure would not have any other impact on the operating environment.

Oracle 11*g* and OLTP

The Oracle Database has long been the leading database for OLTP workloads. As the authors have updated some of their other books over the past few releases, we have found that not many features have been added to the Oracle Database to improve OLTP operations, for the simple reason that the product is fairly complete already in this area.

The Exadata Database Machine benefits from all of these features for OLTP, and, since Oracle on Exadata works transparently for all applications, these features can provide the same benefits on this new platform as on the classic Oracle Database.

Classic Oracle Features

There are a number of features and best practices that you should use for OLTP workloads on an Exadata Database Machine, which have been used with the Oracle Database for many years.

- **MVRC**   Multiversion read consistency was first introduced to the Oracle Database more than 20 years ago and still provides one of the key advantages for OLTP workloads. Just as Exadata technology improves the overall performance of a workload by removing bottlenecks, such as I/O bandwidth, MVRC performs a similar function by removing delays caused by contention for resources, primarily in OLTP environments. With MVRC, writers don't block readers, and readers don't block writers. MVRC provides additional benefits, as described in Chapter 2, but the core capability of removing delays caused by locks used to protect data integrity remains one of the most powerful features of the Oracle Database.

■ **Shared servers** Normally, each user process connecting to Oracle from a client has a shadow process, or dedicated server, on the server machine. Oracle allows you to use a shared server which, as the name implies, can share a server process among more than one user. Shared servers work by assigning clients to a dispatcher rather than a dedicated server process. The dispatcher places requests into queues, which are processed by a pool of shared server processes, as shown in Figure 8-1.

Since each server process consumes resources, reducing the number of servers required reduces resource demand and improves the scalability of an Oracle environment, especially in situations that support a large number of users, such as OLTP environments. Shared or dedicated servers are determined by configuration parameters, so applications can take advantage of this feature without any change in code.

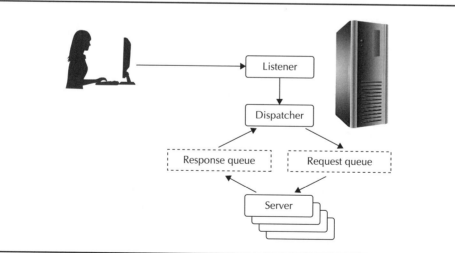

FIGURE 8-1. *Shared server architecture*

- **Connection pooling**   Just as server processes consume resources on the database server, connections from clients to those servers consume network resources as well as server resources. Connection pooling allows client connects to multiplex over a single connection, analogous to the way shared servers save resources. Once again, in a high-transaction OLTP environment, connection pooling can provide greater scalability with the same amount of resources.

- **RAC scalability**   Real Application Clusters, like MVRC, is both a key Oracle differentiator and a feature that provides benefits in several areas, including availability and scalability. For OLTP workloads, the scalability aspect of RAC is particularly important. OLTP workloads are typically CPU-bound, and with RAC, you can add more CPU power to an existing cluster by simply adding a node to an existing cluster. Without any changes in applications or client configuration, you can relieve any CPU stress on your RAC database. You can even accomplish this without bringing the database down. As you add more nodes to your RAC cluster, you are also spreading the pool of connections over more CPUs and servers, giving you greater scalability in this resource area as well. Although the number of nodes in a specific configuration of an Exadata database machine is fixed, you can upgrade the machine by filling out a partially full rack or add more racks, and you can have multiple RAC databases on a single Database Machine, shifting nodes between them as appropriate.

- **Bind variables**   The Oracle optimizer is used to generate an execution plan for all SQL statements—a task that requires some CPU resources. In an Oracle Database, the execution plan for a SQL statement is placed into the shared SQL area of the SGA. If the database receives another SQL statement that is identical to one stored in the SGA, Oracle retrieves and uses the existing execution plan, replacing a relatively resource-intensive operation with a simple retrieval from memory. This approach can save loads of resources in a high-volume transaction environment like OLTP.

An OLTP workload is characterized by a high number of short transactions, and many of these transactions use almost identical SQL statements, differing only by the use of different values for some clauses, such as WHERE clauses. For instance, a SQL statement could make a comparison with the same column and the same relational operator, with the only difference being the values that these are compared with.

As an example, the following two SQL statements

```
SELECT count(*) FROM customers WHERE last_name = 'SMITH'
```

and

```
SELECT count(*) FROM customers WHERE last_name = 'JONES'
```

could both be represented with this SQL statement, which uses bn as a bind variable:

```
SELECT count(*) FROM customers WHERE last_name = :bn
```

The first two statements would not be recognized as the same statement, while the bind variable version would reuse the version in the shared SQL area.

One of the key best practices for writing SQL statements as part of an OLTP-style application is to use bind variables instead of literal values wherever possible to allow for the reuse of execution plans. This approach does require some planning when creating applications, but can offer significant rewards. Remember, OLTP transactions are typically fairly small, so recompiling and creating a plan, and the corresponding impact of latching for shared pool resources, can be comparatively large.

This capability of the Oracle Database is not unique to Exadata, but still represents an important way that OLTP workloads can perform well in the Oracle environment.

- **Database Resource Manager** Database Resource Manager, as discussed in Chapter 2, is a key tool for dividing oversubscribed resources between competing applications or tasks. OLTP workloads tend to be CPU-bound, so the CPU allocation capabilities of Database Resource Manager can be used to ensure that response-critical components of the overall workload continue to receive adequate CPU, even in times of great demand.

   An OLTP workload usually has some response-sensitive portions, such as write requests, and some components that have less critical response requirements, such as production reporting or batch jobs.

For these types of workload mixes, the ability to divide resources at different priority levels is the key. With Database Resource Manager, you can specify that the response-critical components are in the top priority group, receiving either all resources or some percentage of overall CPU. All other groups will only receive the CPU cycles that are left over from this top priority group, ensuring that any CPU-bound delays affect all noncritical tasks before they touch the high priority group—just the type of allocation that an OLTP workload would benefit from.

One other standard Oracle feature requires some discussion as it applies to the Exadata platform and OLTP workloads. The Oracle Database supports a number of types of indexes, and these indexes are used for a variety of purposes, from implementing constraints, such as uniqueness and foreign constraints, to use as a way to improve the performance of specific data access operations. For non-Exadata environments, the use of a full table or full index scan could result in poor performance, since these operations incur a high I/O cost.

As you have seen, though, through the use of features such as offloading certain types of query processing, full table scans on an Exadata Database Machine can really fly—one published example showed that a full table scan of 2 million rows took approximately the same time as retrieving 10 to 15 single data blocks. This type of performance with full table and full index scans can eliminate the need for some indexes whose purpose is strictly to improve retrieval performance. Because of the elimination of this need, you can frequently eliminate a portion of existing indexes on your data, which can cut down correspondingly on the cost of database writes, since the eliminated indexes will not have to be updated. You can use the option of making an index invisible to the optimizer to quickly compare query performance with and without the use of one or more indexes.

Oracle and Linux

The Oracle Exadata Database Machine uses Oracle Enterprise Linux (OEL) as the operating system on both the database server nodes and the Exadata Storage Server. In 2011, Oracle also began supporting Solaris as an alternative operating system you might deploy on the database server nodes. Although you cannot modify the software or configuration of OEL on the Exadata

Storage Server, there is a useful configuration change you should make for Oracle Enterprise Linux on the database server nodes.

The effect of the configuration change will be to instruct applications, in this case, the Oracle database instance, to use *hugepages.* When Linux uses hugepages, there are two important effects. First of all, the page size for shared memory is increased from the default of 4KB to a much larger size, such as 2MB, meaning the management of those pages will be greatly reduced. Second, memory used by hugepages is locked, so it cannot be swapped out. These two effects mean that the Linux-based overhead of managing shared database memory, the SGA, is significantly reduced in a heavily loaded environment.

You should set the overall size for hugepages to a size greater than the memory requirements of all the SGAs you will have for all the instances the server will be supporting. This setting will avoid having to swap out the SGA, especially when you have a large number of client processes, as is typical with an OLTP workload.

You can find information on setting up hugepages for the OEL environment in a number of places in the Oracle Database documentation, including the *Administrator's Reference for Linux and UNIX-based Operating Systems.*

In the most current release of the Oracle Database software, you can set a parameter that will check to see if hugepages are properly configured before starting an instance and that will fail if hugepages are not properly configured.

Quality of Service Management

Oracle 11*g* Release 2 introduced one feature that can have a significant impact on using the Oracle Database for OLTP workloads. The feature is an expansion of the capabilities of Real Application Clusters to allow for dynamic reprovisioning of CPU resources in order to meet service levels— a method that will help you to guarantee quality of service (QoS) for a RAC-based database.

Server Pools

QoS is based on a few core concepts used for managing servers in a RAC environment. The first concept is that of a server pool. A server pool is a group of servers that are, in effect, partitioned to separate them from other server pools. A RAC installation has a default server pool, the free pool, and a generic pool, as well as any number of additional pools, which you can define.

Each server pool has a minimum number of servers, a maximum number of servers, and an importance. RAC allocates servers to the server pools until all pools have the minimum number of servers. Once this level is reached, RAC allocates any additional servers for a pool, up to the maximum number, based on the importance of the pool. Any servers left once these levels are reached remain in the free pool.

In the event of a server failure, QoS first determines if the failure results in the number of servers in a server pool dipping below the minimum specified. If the failure does not have this effect, no action is taken. If the number of servers in a pool does go below the specified minimum, QoS first looks to the free pool for a replacement server. If no servers are available in the free pool, QoS looks to server pools with a lower importance for replacement servers.

Performance Classes

The concept of a RAC-based service was described in Chapter 2. QoS management adds the concept of a performance class. A performance class consists of one or more services that share a performance objective. These performance objectives are used to evaluate the quality of service being provided by the managed RAC environment.

For instance, you could group a variety of sales applications as one performance class, with maintenance and batch operations grouped together in another performance class.

Policies

Performance classes and server pools come together in a policy. A policy associates the available server pools with performance classes, as shown in Figure 8-2.

Figure 8-2 shows more than one policy, based on the time of day and within a quarter. You can have multiple policies, but only one policy can be in place at any one time on any one server. A collection of policies is known as a *policy set*.

A policy also includes a performance metric associated with a particular performance class. In Figure 8-2, you could require that an application in the online server pool deliver an average response time of two seconds

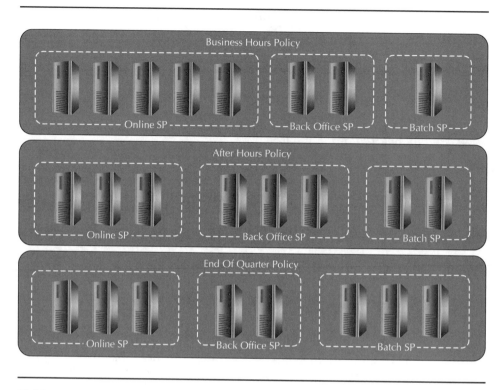

FIGURE 8-2. *Policies*

during normal business operations, but that this requirement is relaxed to four seconds in the after-hours policy or three seconds during the crunch in the end-of-the-quarter server policy.

A policy also contains server pool directive overrides. These overrides prescribe the action that should be taken in the event that a performance objective is not met. For instance, you could specify that the minimum number of servers be increased if a performance objective was not being achieved.

A policy can contain more than one performance class, so the performance classes can be ranked in importance. The ranking is used to determine which performance objectives should be satisfied in the event that the RAC database does not have sufficient resources available to meet all performance objectives. In this scenario, the higher-ranking performance class receives resources ahead of lower-ranking performance classes.

QoS at Work

Quality of service management works in the runtime environment by collecting performance metrics from the cluster every five seconds. Those metrics are evaluated every minute to determine if performance objectives are being met.

If an objective is not being met, there are two potential courses of action. One course is to allocate additional servers to the performance class. If servers in the free pool are available, they are added to the server pool for the performance class. If there are no servers in the free pool, QoS management looks to performance classes with a lower importance that have servers in excess of their minimum number. As a final choice, QoS looks to server pools with the same importance as the stressed pool where giving up a server node would not result in that node falling below the minimum number of servers.

Another course of action is for QoS to look at the consumer groups defined in Database Resource Manager to find a consumer group with a larger percentage of resources assigned. If this option is available, QoS migrates the underperforming services to this higher-priority consumer group to allocate more resources for the performance class.

QoS evaluates these options and more before it makes a recommendation to modify allocation of resources. In addition to looking at simply addressing the need to provide service to an underperforming performance class, QoS determines the impact that the recommended changes may have on the performance class that will lose resources. The recommendation, and the projected effect on all performance classes, is delivered to Enterprise Manager. With this recommendation, you can see the estimated impact on performance time for all performance classes defined for the policy currently in place.

In Chapter 2, you learned how you can use Database Resource Manager to design and implement highly flexible schemes for allocating resources to different groups of consumers. QoS management provides a similar level of flexibility in defining the use of resources and couples this design capability with real-time monitoring of service levels to ensure the optimal level of service for all types of work on an Oracle database.

At this time, QoS is all about OLTP workloads, since one measurement criterion is CPU response time, one of the key service levels used to evaluate performance for these workloads. When you use the Exadata Database Machine as an OLTP platform, or as a consolidation platform that includes

OLTP operations, you can use the monitoring and management capabilities provided by QoS management to ensure that the resources of the Database Machine are used to provide optimal performance across the spectrum of service levels required.

NOTE
Quality of Service does more than simply monitor CPU utilization. QoS also tracks memory use on individual nodes, preventing additional sessions from being directed towards nodes that do not have enough free memory to support more connections. In addition, QoS evaluates the negative impact of reallocating servers versus the positive impact of this action. If the negatives outweigh the positives, QoS may not recommend changing resource allocations. For more details on QoS and its implementation, please refer to the Oracle documentation.

Exadata Software and OLTP

As mentioned earlier in this chapter, the Exadata feature with the biggest impact on OLTP workloads is the Exadata Smart Flash Cache. The default operation of the Flash Cache is designed to provide high-speed access to the type of smaller I/Os that are characteristic of OLTP operations. With the KEEP option and the ability to define flash-based grid disks, the Exadata Smart Flash Cache gives you additional options for using this high-speed device for OLTP workloads. The other software features of Exadata play a smaller role in an OLTP environment.

Partitions have been a part of OLTP database design for many years, as they can eliminate the amount of data required to satisfy a query. Storage indexes, as described in Chapter 3, provide a similar benefit, but to an even more granular level of 1MB storage regions. Storage indexes will have their greatest effect when used with data that is loaded in sorted order, but even data added to the database through the small insert operations typical of OLTP workloads could potentially benefit from the use of storage indexes, as this data can share a fairly small set of values for some time-sensitive columns. And storage indexes, like other Exadata software features, do not harm performance, so any incremental gains produced with this technology will not be offset by any performance degradation caused by their implementation.

I/O Resource Management (IORM) is used to ensure that the I/O resources of the Exadata Storage Server are properly allocated across different consumer groups. The primary focus of IORM is I/O-intensive workloads, which describe data warehouse operations more than traditional OLTP. But, as stated previously, OLTP workloads include tasks that can generate a fair amount of I/O activity, such as production reporting. You can use IORM to ensure that OLTP operations receive adequate resources to avoid any potential bottlenecks. In addition, you can use IORM to avoid the potential for I/O-intensive workloads to require too much of the database CPUs by saturating them with requests to receive data from the Exadata Storage Server.

This last point comes around to the key reason why the Exadata Database Machine works for OLTP workloads as well as data warehouse workloads. With Exadata software and a balanced configuration, the Database Machine implements best configuration practices for any Oracle Database. In doing so, the Database Machine provides performance and throughput benefits for all types of workloads.

Exadata Nodes and OLTP

At Oracle OpenWorld in 2010, Oracle announced new configurations of the Exadata Database Machine, as described in Chapter 4. One of the biggest configuration changes was the introduction of a new type of database node, with eight CPUs, each of which has eight cores, and 1TB of memory.

Many highly utilized OLTP systems run on enormous SMP systems, where a single machine has a large number of CPUs as well as a large amount of memory. The new "heavyweight" database nodes in the X2-8 configuration have 64 database cores per server node, as well as 1TB of memory on each node. This configuration comes closer to matching the type of machine used for high-volume OLTP systems than the database nodes in the X2-2 series, which have 12 cores and 96GBs per server, although these systems can use eight of these nodes, rather than the two nodes used in an X2-8 system.

OLTP systems are designed to support many users running many short transactions, and the demands of this environment may be better met with a smaller number of large nodes, rather than a larger number of smaller nodes. Of course, the X2-8 models, with only two nodes, could be affected more seriously by a node failure, but some OLTP scenarios might find that the benefits of increased scalability outweigh this potential risk.

Exadata as a Complete System

There is one more aspect of the Database Machine that helps to improve OLTP workloads. OLTP systems are frequently stand-alone systems, where the database servers are completely dedicated to these systems. But these systems are also frequently tied into some type of shared storage arrangement, such as SAN disk arrays. Because of this, the owners of the system have to negotiate to ensure that the needs and priorities of the systems are properly handled by the shared resources, whether storage resources or network resources.

Unfortunately, these negotiations are not always totally successful. OLTP systems may not be able to get enough of these crucial resources, so their operations can suffer as the resources become inadequate under particular workloads.

The Oracle Exadata Database Machine is a self-contained unit, with all computing resources included. This ownership means that developers and administrators can allocate resources to best address the needs of their workloads.

Of course, the allocation tools available for Oracle and the Database Machine, including Database Resource Manager and the I/O Resource Manager, mean that you have a tremendous amount of flexibility in assigning resources dynamically. Without the need to compromise allocations based on reasons outside the immediate database environment, you will have the freedom to give your systems what they need to deliver optimal performance.

In this way, the self-contained implementation of the Database Machine means that you can avoid some of the external political issues that can interfere with your attempts to provide the highest levels of service for your customers.

Summary

The Exadata Database Machine can support both data warehouse and OLTP workloads. The features of the Database Machine that support data warehousing are also useful for the reporting aspects of OLTP systems, while a number of features, such as Exadata Smart Flash Cache, contribute directly to improved performance for OLTP workloads. In addition, the introduction of new nodes for the X2-8 configuration, with 64 cores and 1TB of memory per node, provide the type of heavyweight processing power needed by high volume OLTP systems.

The context for this chapter has been the assumption that you will be using an Oracle Exadata Database Machine for an OLTP application. The discussion of the features and the techniques used with the Database Machine have not really focused on some of the unique issues that arise when you have more than one application running on an Exadata system.

Of course, you likely will have more than one application on your Database Machine eventually, if not at the initial deployment, whether the multiple applications are all OLTP or a mixture of OLTP and more read-intensive applications, such as a data warehouse.

Certainly, many of the features discussed in this chapter have relevance to this type of consolidated platform, such as Database Resource Manager and I/O Resource Manager. And the overall benefit derived from a Database Machine could very well consist of some advantages for data warehouse workloads and others oriented towards OLTP applications.

The entire subject of consolidation is, in fact, the topic of the next chapter.

CHAPTER
9

Consolidating Databases
with the Oracle Exadata
Database Machine

egardless of economic conditions, IT is constantly feeling the
pressure to optimize resources that they provide to the
business. The senior management of your organization or
company expects IT to be able to deploy and run new
applications with agility, scale these applications while
meeting or exceeding Service Level Agreements (SLAs), and do it all
efficiently. The CIO is asked to significantly reduce IT costs but still remain
receptive to new business functionality without disrupting users or their
current applications.

That's quite a tall order. One way that many companies reduce costs,
improve return on investment, and meet future business needs is to standardize
and simplify IT costs through consolidation of computer servers, storage,
other hardware infrastructure, and software platforms. In this chapter, our
primary focus is how you can use the Oracle Exadata Database Machine to
deliver such solutions.

Why Consolidate?

Taking the consolidation path is not always simple. However, many IT
analysts today call attention to production server utilization rates that are
barely 10 percent where individual applications are dedicated to their own
specific legacy hardware. Therein lies a golden opportunity for IT departments
to support line-of-business objectives and transform their environment to
drive out costs while improving utilization and performance and reducing
management.

One example of a consolidation effort is the one that Oracle Corporation
itself went through between 2002 and 2004 that resulted in tremendous costs
savings and improved operating margins. During this time, Oracle consolidated
40 data centers down to 3 and moved from 52 applications to a single global
E-Business Suite. In many respects, what Oracle did is one of the most
difficult consolidation efforts to undertake, since it requires rationalization
of applications, databases, hardware platforms, and strong top-down
leadership that can overcome the political implications of such an effort.

Far more common is the consolidation of multiple overlapping databases
to single databases or simply using the Oracle Exadata Database Machine as
a single platform to host multiple Oracle databases. Since the Oracle
Exadata Database Machine also contains storage and its own high-speed
network, it also provides other forms of infrastructure consolidation.

The most obvious benefits to IT are usually associated with lower costs from reduced power consumption and a smaller data center footprint. But there are frequently other compelling benefits that should be explored as well. For example, speed of change management can greatly accelerate. A critical mass of IT skills is often easier to attain with fewer people since they focus on fewer technologies. Cost and complexity of integration should be dramatically reduced. Business benefits and time to value for deployment of new solutions can be achieved much faster.

Many organizations use such initiatives to transition IT into providing software and hardware infrastructure as a service. When deployed on corporate intranets behind firewalls to deliver high efficiency, high availability, and resources on demand (sometimes called elasticity), these are popularly described as "private clouds." When deployed to the Internet, these deployment models are known as "public clouds."

The Oracle Exadata Database Machine can help in a variety of ways to consolidate database deployment.

How the Oracle Exadata Database Machine Helps Consolidation

As described in earlier chapters, the Oracle Exadata Database Machine is a complete and integrated solution that provides database servers, storage servers, networking, and Oracle Database software and storage software. This optimal combination of Sun hardware coupled with software provides the performance and high-availability characteristics needed for consolidating Oracle Databases. Given the power and flexibility of the platform, it can enable consolidation of databases to a single machine that address workload types ranging from transaction processing to data warehouses.

The complexity you might introduce by moving such a wide variation in the types of databases to a single Oracle Exadata Database Machine depends on many factors. These factors can include the types and nature of any packaged applications, schema naming conventions and possible conflicts, and SLA and high availability requirements that could vary widely. Certainly, if you are considering moving both transaction processing and data warehousing databases to the same Oracle Exadata Database Machine, you should consider the consistency of their SLAs, whether you have an understanding of clear workload priorities across the databases, and whether you'll have excess capacity that might address some unplanned demands.

Consolidation of mixed workloads to a single Oracle Exadata Database Machine is possible. But where there is wide variation in workloads and other requirements, some organizations may choose to standardize on the Oracle Exadata Database Machine but deploy different racks of the platform in different ways that can best address unique workload and availability demands.

Database Server Consolidation

As in sizing any database server platform, when consolidating database servers, you must plan around a specific set of current needs on a specific platform footprint. This section covers how you might define that footprint. We'll examine the CPU and memory sizing considerations, I/O or throughput sizing, and overall system sizing considerations. We'll also examine storage and network consolidation aspects of the platform.

CPU Sizing Considerations

Although the Oracle Exadata Database Machine contains the latest generation of Intel CPU chips and high-performance memory, you still need to be careful when sizing legacy databases that are CPU-constrained on another platform. This is especially true for applications deployed on a single monolithic SMP (symmetric multiprocessor) platform. The Oracle Exadata Database Machine X2-8 configurations that provide large SMP nodes and memory can be especially relevant for handling such workloads. The architecture of SMP is often described as scale-up because the only options for this type of architecture, when constrained by CPU limits, are

- **Tuning the application(s)** Attempting to reduce CPU consumption by tuning Oracle SQL access paths through analysis of data structures and usage patterns by the application(s). This process involves investigation of SQL statements that may be causing excessive CPU usage, as well as selective denormalization, partitioning, compression, index reviews, and other schema adjustments that are typically used to improve access paths. Once these alterations have been made, the execution plan is frozen using a SQL Plan Baseline or a SQL Profile.

- **Upgrading existing CPUs**   Scaling up the platform by working with the hardware vendor to upgrade current system boards or adding/ activating more CPUs where the machine has spare capacity.

- **Buying a bigger machine**   The newer machine is likely to be relatively more expensive than adding CPUs to a current platform. These "fork-lift upgrades" can be expensive, especially as the new machines are normally sized for growth, and hence there can be a lot of initial capacity that is not used.

The Oracle Exadata Database Machine can provide scale-up within a single database server node, but also provides the capability for a scale-out approach. With a scale-out architecture, you can increase capacity by simply adding more database server nodes using Real Application Clusters (RAC) configurations to support the databases and their applications. This capability is consistent with Oracle's grid computing architectural vision.

When considering scale-up implications, you should take into consideration the CPU differences between the existing CPU power of the database servers and those of the suggested Oracle Exadata Database Machine. Standardized CPU benchmarks are used in the industry to compare the relative CPU performance of different servers. Although not an ideal measure of system performance, they are still a useful gauge. For instance, a SPECint rate indicates a CPU's integer processing power. Existing benchmarks that are published or unpublished, comparative system sizes, and proof of concept results can also be used to help system sizing.

In reality, Oracle looks at these performance results when sizing the system to support the required database servers while also including capacity to handle available application growth projections. The most reliable indicators are often comparative systems sizes and hence, it's useful when the following metrics have already been discovered for the current production system:

- **Database version**   Different versions of the Oracle Database have different capabilities, and databases from other vendors can have even larger functionality gaps that can affect hardware sizing.

- **Database options used**   Options such as compression can greatly influence storage required and partitioning can influence backup strategies.

- **Operating system** Variations among Linux, Unix, Windows, Z/OS, etc., should be taken into account when sizing the new platform.

- **Server hardware** Model number and make, as well as differences in the previous platform generation, also affect go-forward sizing.

- **Server CPUs** Differences in the number of cores available to support the database and the processor speed are a consideration.

- **Clustering method** Sizing considerations can be influenced by previous clustering types, federated approaches used, and how the processors were leveraged.

- **Growth predictions** The speed that the applications' workloads are growing and the projected future growth and utilization rates.

Based on these metrics, it is possible to determine how many raw database servers and Oracle Exadata Database Machine racks are needed to provide equivalent CPU horsepower. When you gauge the effect of the CPU speeds provided by the Oracle Exadata Database Machine, keep in mind that CPUs on your legacy systems are almost always slower than current server CPUs in your Database Machine. The CPU sizing process is especially critical where the applications to be consolidated are CPU-bound.

Keep in mind, though, that CPU sizing will give you an idea of the Exadata configuration that can handle the workload, but the performance gains provided by the Exadata software, described in Chapter 3, will allow CPUs to perform more work, since some of their normal operations will be offloaded to the CPUs in the Exadata Storage Server.

Memory Sizing

Legacy databases and earlier versions of Oracle use varying amounts of database server main memory, as they were optimized for the hardware platforms' memory capacities of the time. It is important to ensure that a new single consolidated database or all of the databases consolidated to the single Oracle Exadata Database Machine have access to at least the same amount of "usable" memory as before. As some legacy systems could be oversized on memory, it is also important to review the database usage reports to see the actual "peak" memory that is used by each database.

When migrating from another database where structures such as the Oracle PGA do not exist, memory should be carefully sized to ensure that the applications can take best advantage of the new Oracle environment.

Concurrency rates also need to be examined to determine what the peak memory is for both dedicated and shared user database connections. Buffer sizes for programs that attach directly to the database server should be considered (e.g., for backup servers or application-dedicated server attached processes). Finally, database option memory usage, such as for RAC, should be factored in.

Although it sounds complicated, memory sizing is relatively straightforward, as many of the important numbers are often stated in vendor installation manuals (especially the Oracle Database installation manuals) and retrievable from monitoring tools and database reports. It might be noted that when collecting the average number of Oracle-connected users to determine concurrency, the memory usage for this task is trivial since these statistics are easily viewable from the Oracle AWR or Statspack reports, as well as being accessible from internal database V$ and X$ views. In terms of consolidation, you will have to figure memory usage that is an aggregation from the different servers where the soon-to-be consolidated application databases are running.

Most importantly, though, the Oracle Exadata Database Machine comes in a limited number of configurations, each with its own allocation of memory. The memory included in each configuration is designed to support the model in a balanced configuration. Since adding or subtracting memory from a configuration is not an option, checking on the memory sizing is a way to double check the sizing provided by a comparison of CPU horsepower.

I/O Sizing

Oracle's best practices for Exadata Database Machine sizing is not to take into consideration possible I/O improvement from Smart Scan and to size the system for the maximum I/Os in terms of IOPS and throughput (GB/s). However, as an exercise, let's examine what would need to be considered if this wasn't the case. When looking at random I/O rates that need to be supported for physical reads, you should take into account the Exadata Smart Flash Cache I/Os provided by the Oracle Exadata Database Machine. For large sequential I/Os, you could also consider the impact of the use of Oracle Smart Scan Exadata software optimization and other I/O performance features such as storage indexes. In almost all cases, large sequential physical I/Os (table scans) can be offloaded to Smart Scans that take advantage of the memory and CPU power of the Oracle Exadata Database Machine storage server cells.

These offloaded operations have several effects—reducing the CPU requirements for the database servers, reducing the bandwidth requirements to send data to the database servers, and, in cases where storage indexes are used, actually reducing the I/O operations necessary to retrieve data from disks.

When you are considering database consolidation and I/O rates, you need to consider the following data points:

- Database version and server hardware version, as discussed earlier.

- How the data is stored (e.g., NAS, SAN, DAS, or hybrids).

- Storage array   Make, model, capacity, performance, connection architecture to database servers.

- HBAs and HCAs   The ability of the plumbing, that is, the ability of the storage networking and related database servers to transfer data. If you are going to consolidate many storage arrays and database servers on the Oracle Exadata Database Machine, you need a target that has lots of CPUs, wide pipes, and very fast server-to-storage connection points. The Oracle Exadata Database Machine has been designed with these in mind.

- I/O system metrics   MBPS, IOPS, peak rates, peak transfers, waits and queue lengths, and utilization rates. These metrics are all measures of disk and controller performance. IOPS refers to I/Os per second and is a useful measure of disk saturation. MBPS is short for megabytes per second and is a useful measure of the size of the disk transfer rate and the amount of data the disk can move. Peak rates and peak transfers are useful measures of maximum burst performance. These measurements can be useful where response times are critical because the system must also be able to handle peak rates without disrupting response times. Waits and queue lengths can be used to determine if the current I/O design is keeping up with its current usage. As disk waits and queue lengths increase, response times can suffer and the system can degrade. Utilization rates are useful to determine over and under capacity.

■ Cache sizes, utilization, and real performance rates.

■ Database I/O performance metrics   I/Os per partition, tablespace, I/O skewing, layout, I/Os per transaction, SQL, etc.

Normally, the current storage model and make and current utilization provide a good yardstick to understand how many equivalent storage cells are needed to exceed the current I/O performance. An offloaded Smart Scan utilizes the Exadata Storage Server CPUs in parallel, and as more and more unique Smart Scans and other offloaded activities such as encryption handling are being performed in parallel, it might be possible for the CPUs on the Exadata Storage Server to become saturated. If this happens, the system will automatically start to queue requests just like a normal server. If this type of condition could arise in a production environment, it is prudent to leverage I/O Resource Manager (IORM) or Database Resource Manager (DBRM) plans to control the prioritization of the applications and users.

System Sizing

When considering consolidation, all of the sizing guidelines for CPU, network, I/O, and memory are combined to form a comprehensive sizing methodology needed to determine the proper platform for your migration and consolidation of databases. Where packaged applications are being migrated, Oracle also bases sizing considerations on performance testing performed within the Oracle Solution Centers.

That said, complete system sizing can be more of an art than a science when all these pieces are combined. When consolidating databases and applications on the Oracle Exadata Database Machine, database performance might far exceed expectations to such a degree that the real limitation might be the number of middle-tier application servers. This can especially be true for large packaged applications. In such cases, you will be able to determine from the AWR reports that the database server is not waiting for anything the CPU utilization is very low. Increasing the number of transactions in the database server layer by increasing the number of connections from new middle tiers (or adjusting existing connection pools if the current middle tiers are not strained) will be needed to take full advantage of the processing power of the database server. In other cases, consolidating more applications that can access the Oracle database on the Oracle Exadata Database Machine can help ensure that the entire system is more equitably utilized.

Storage Consolidation

An Oracle Database deployed on legacy storage typically utilizes many different types of storage architectures, including NAS (Network Attached Storage), SAN (Storage Area Network), and DAS (Direct Attached Storage). You may have all these storage types deployed or hybrids of them. You might also have many different database versions within the infrastructure. Because of this, you might consider reviewing all existing deployed Oracle databases and consolidating all storage by deploying the Oracle Exadata Database Machine.

Storage consolidation is the result of a number of factors in the Exadata Database Machine. The Oracle Exadata Database Machine offers a choice of high-performance and high-capacity disk types. Combined with the various types of compression that the Oracle Database and Exadata Storage Server Software support, it is possible to store dozens of terabytes of data in a single rack and more where multiple racks are configured. Compression varies depending on such things as repetition of values in data sets, so capacity can vary. Most organizations size storage by first considering disk requirements when data is uncompressed and then use more conservative estimates of compression than might appear in the marketing literature.

The Oracle Exadata Database Machine's IORM feature allows the I/O from many different databases to be prioritized efficiently when those I/O resources are oversubscribed, and assists in meeting or exceeding SLAs when performing storage consolidation.

Network Consolidation

An InfiniBand network within the Oracle Exadata Database Machine runs a low-latency, database-specific protocol between the database servers and storage servers called *i*DB. Two InfiniBand switches within the racks are provided for redundancy. This lightweight, high-performance network is used in transfers of data between the database servers and the storage servers and also handles database interconnect communications, including RAC interconnect traffic for extremely fast database server-to-database server communications. A third switch is provided in Half Racks and Full Racks to enable connections to additional like configurations of the Database Machine.

This high-performance network architecture also allows the Oracle Exadata Database Machine to connect to InfiniBand-based clients for backup, restore, and archive activities. Architecturally, this opens up some interesting options and allows flexibility to connect to other Oracle-integrated hardware and software platforms. For example, the InfiniBand is used as a high-speed connection from the Oracle Exadata Database Machine to Oracle Exalogic.

An Ethernet GbE switch is also provided in the Oracle Exadata Database Machine for administrative purposes. External user connections are generally into 10 GbE ports that reside in the database server nodes.

Workload Consolidation and Isolation

As mentioned earlier in the chapter, the Oracle Exadata Database Machine enables database consolidation and can scale database(s) across database servers using RAC. When you need more steam (CPU or memory) from your database server platform, RAC can support a growing shared database cluster by simply adding more database server nodes into the cluster. Adjusting the number of nodes in a RAC cluster is a dynamic online process, such as when upgrading from a Half Rack to a Full Rack of the Database Machine. This flexibility in configurations allows more wiggle room for consolidation sizing and capacity planning. You could consolidate databases onto a RAC One single database server node until you start to saturate the available resources, and then you can decide to spread RAC-enabled databases across a single or many Oracle Exadata Database Machine racks. This provides flexibility and power to business owners and IT departments that want to save money and gain performance through consolidation. Within RAC, the concepts of workload management (services, server pools, and instance caging) can be used to assist in database consolidation. The actual implementation of RAC on an Exadata Database Machine used for consolidation is discussed later in this chapter.

Services

Oracle first introduced the concept of database services in Oracle Database 10g. This facility creates a virtual target to which database applications can connect. You can target a single application to a single service, multiple applications, or a functional subset of an application. A service can be to an instance so that it resides on a single database server, or it can run simultaneously across multiple database servers or even multiple Database Machines.

The service provides a high-availability target and simplified construct that hides cluster complexities from the connecting database application. The application connects to a service that runs on the database servers and is automatically directed to a suitable database server to handle the transaction. When SQL executes in parallel, services limit which database servers can be involved in the parallel execution. For instance, any session connection to a service can only start parallel server processes on database servers that are associated with that service.

Once you define a service, a resource profile is automatically created that describes how Oracle's Clusterware will manage that service, which instance the service will use as a failover target, and service dependencies between the instance and the database so that instances and services are started and stopped in the correct order.

The Oracle Database Resource Manager allows you to restrict resources that are used by the users who connect with that service to an instance. This is done by mapping a consumer group to a service so that the service users are members of the consumer group.

From a consolidation perspective, similar application transaction signatures can be mapped to the same service. For instance, you could create an order-taking service that could be used to receive orders from the database application. At the simplest level, you could create batch and data warehousing services and run these services on different database servers from the order-taking OLTP service.

Database Server Pools

When considering database consolidation, DBAs will typically have to understand which application databases require their own physical database servers and which can be consolidated onto single database servers. To assist in this process, Oracle Database server pools can be created, which logically divide up a cluster of database servers into database server pools, which were described as part of the implementation of Quality of Service in Chapter 8. Each pool can be defined by four attributes:

- **Server Pool Name**

- **Min** Specifies the minimum required number of database servers that should be run in the database server pool.

- **Max** Specifies the maximum number of database servers that can be run in the database server pool.

- **Imp** Specifies the "importance" of each pool. The relative value of importance or priority can be used to determine database server assignment when resources are short, for instance, after database server failure.

With a database server pool, the database server can only be allocated to a single pool at any one time. Database server pools can be automatically created by Database Configuration Assistant (DBCA) and managed by the Server Control Utility (SRVCTL) or Oracle Enterprise Manager. There are two main ways of doing a database server consolidation:

- **Administrator managed** Specify where the database should run with a list of database server names. Then define which services will run on each database instance. You can define PREFERRED instances, which are the instances that normally run that service, and also can define other instances to support a service if the service's preferred instance is not available. These instances are known as AVAILABLE instances.

- **Policy managed** Specify initial resource requirements based on the expected workload. Oracle will automatically start the required instances to support the workload. No direct association between a service and an instance is required. You can define this service as either UNIFORM so that it automatically runs on all instances in the database server pool or as SINGLETON so that it only runs on one instance in the database server pool. Oracle Clusterware will automatically start the service on a suitable database server within the database server pool.

Workload Management

Once database servers have been consolidated onto the Oracle Exadata Database Machine, the manner of client connection needs to be considered. A Single Client Access Name (SCAN) provides a single, consistent name for client access to a RAC database cluster.

The advantage of SCAN is that additions or removals of servers from the cluster require no application client connect changes and it also allows the use of the EZConnect client and the simple Java Database Connectivity (JDBC) thin URL to access any database instance in the cluster, regardless of which database server it is currently running on. Previously, each node in the cluster required a separate entry in the TNSNAMES.ora file, but now, only one entry is required that utilizes the SCAN syntax and the correct DNS or GNS entries. For the orders cluster shown here, you can connect to any node in the cluster by using the orders-scan entry:

```
Sqlplus system/manager@orders-scan:1521/oe
Jdbc:oracle:thin:@orders-scan:1521/oe
```

It is recommended that clients connecting to the Oracle Exadata Database Machine leverage the Universal Connection Pool (UCP). The UCP is a Java-based connection pool that supports JDBC, the Lightweight Directory Access Protocol (LDAP), and Java EE Connector Architecture (JCA) connection types from any middle tier. The UCP has integration with database-side functionality such as fast connection failover, runtime connection load balancing, and RAC connection affinity.

The UCP connection affinity feature allows two types of affinity: web session and XA. With the UCP and the Database Machine, the first connection request from the middle tier is load balanced using hints from the Load Balancing Advisory (e.g., least used node). Additional requests for the duration of a web session or XA transaction are directed to the same instance on the same database server as the initial request. This can improve performance by ensuring that interinstance RAC communication is significantly reduced for transactions that access the same segments from the database.

Meeting and Exceeding SLAs

Once the calculations have been made on how many databases can be consolidated onto a Oracle Exadata Database Machine, the next step is to ensure that for each database, SLAs are met or exceeded. A single database on a single Oracle Exadata Database Machine doesn't need to share anything except potentially the same InfiniBand network for the RAC interconnect and I/O traffic. However, as more databases are consolidated onto the same Oracle Exadata Database Machine, then I/O, memory, and CPU need to be shared if applications access these databases concurrently. Any resource-intensive database can significantly degrade the performance of the other databases unless steps are taken to enable resource management and isolation.

A number of techniques can be used to ensure SLAs are met or exceeded, and they can be used individually or they can be combined.

Instance Caging

Instance caging is the process by which a DBA can limit the physical cores that can be allocated to a database instance that runs on a particular database server. This is achieved by using the CPU_COUNT database parameter and the Oracle Database Resource Manager, which limits the amount of CPU that a particular database instance consumes. This technique is important from a consolidation perspective, because you do not want any particular database instance bringing a database server to its knees by using most of the CPU resources and affecting other database instances that might be running on that particular database server. The upper limit of CPU_COUNT can be adjusted to ensure that each instance cannot expend database server CPU cores that it is not authorized to access.

Enabling instance caging is a two-step process.

1. **Set the value of CPU_COUNT.** This dynamic parameter should be set to the maximum number of CPU cores (or logical hyperthread cores) that the database instance can utilize at any one time. For example, to set the parameter to 32, you would use the following syntax:

```
Alter system set cpu_count=32;
```

2. **Enable the Oracle Resource Manager plan.** The next step is to enable the Oracle Database Resource Manager plan that manages CPU. Any resource plan such as "DEFAULT_PLAN" or "DEFAULT_MAINTENANCE_PLAN" that uses CPU directives can be used. Alternatively, you can create your own resource plan, as shown in an example later in this chapter. The resource plan then needs to be enabled.

```
Alter system set resource_manager_plan = 'DEFAULT_
MAINENANCE_PLAN';
```

Instance caging is now enabled.

How do you make sure that you are running correctly? The following query can determine if the CPU_COUNT has been set correctly:

```
Select value from v$parameter where name='cpu_count' and
(isdefault='FALSE' or ismodified != 'FALSE');
```

This query should return the current value of CPU_COUNT if you have modified it; if you have not, it will return no rows.

Next, you need to determine if the right plan is active within the Database Resource Manager.

```
Select name from v$rsrc_plan where cpu_managed='ON' and is_top_
plan='TRUE';
```

If a row is returned, then the plan is active. Otherwise, either the Database Resource Manager is off or the Database Resource Manager is on but not managing the CPU.

Instance caging works by throttling database instance processes that require more CPUs than the instance is entitled to. The wait event "resmgr:cpu quantum" may appear in the AWR reports if this throttling becomes significant, after which point it may become necessary to increase CPU_COUNT or add another database server node via RAC dynamic cluster expansion. The v$rsrcmgrmetric_history view shows the amount of throttling and CPU consumption for each minute of the past hour.

From a consolidation perspective, there are two main methods of leveraging instance caging.

Highest SLA Database Instances

Highest SLA database instances are critical to a business and need to run without any adverse CPU effects from any other database instances that might be running on the same physical database server. The easiest option would be to consolidate each database instance onto its own physical database server, but this is likely to waste CPUs and result in low utilization, as the Oracle Exadata Database Machine CPUs are relatively powerful. In order to avoid low utilization rates on the database servers, it is possible to partition up a physical database server so that a single database instance on one physical database server will not affect the CPU of another database instance running on the same physical database server.

In Figure 9-1, we have partitioned up a single database server into four different CPU zones. Each zone runs a consolidated database instance. Each separate database instance has set its own CPU_COUNT, and the total CPU_COUNTs add up to the number of cores in the database server. This guarantees and limits the CPU consumption of each consolidated database instance and yet still meets any SLA goals related to dedicated CPUs. Later, we will see how to perform the same process for I/O.

Less Critical Database Instances

Less critical database instances are lower-priority database instances or test and development database instances that are used at different times and only need some processing power to be operational. Instance caging can be

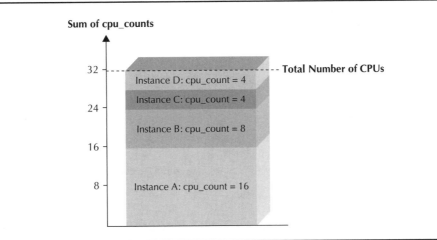

FIGURE 9-1. *Highest SLA example for a 32-way database server*

used to assure that any one database instance cannot spike and take resources from all the other running database instances.

This is best explained with an example. Assume we have four database instances that have been consolidated onto a single database server. If any one of these database instances should spike its CPU resource usage, we don't want it to consume the entire CPU on the database server. If we set CPU_COUNT = 3 for each of these four database instances, then each of them can never consume the entire database server CPU, but the Database Resource Manager can share the available CPU resources between them, as they are running concurrently.

Figure 9-2 helps show how this would work in practice. Here, the database server has only four physical cores to keep things simple. We have assigned CPU_COUNT = 3 for each database instance and have effectively overprovisioned the database server. The maximum percentage of CPU that a single database instance can consume at any point in time is its own limit divided by the sum of the limits for all active database instances.

In this example, if all four database instances are active and CPU bound, then one instance will only be able to consume 25 percent of the CPU, since all instances are allocated three CPU cores and all instances are requesting the maximum amount of CPU. The percentage is determined by adding up the cores requested by a single instance (3) and then dividing by the number of all the requested cores [3/(3 + 3 + 3 + 3) = 3/12 = ¼], as a

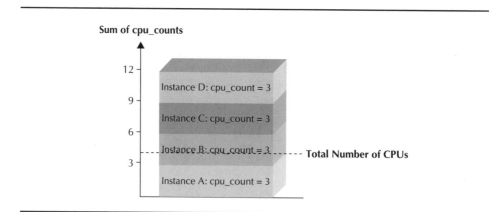

FIGURE 9-2. *Less critical database instances consolidated onto a single database server*

percentage (25 percent). If only two instances are active and CPU bound, then a third instance (not instance caged) will be able to consume 50 percent of the CPU ((3 + 3)/12 = 6/12 = 1/2 = 50%). Overprovisioning, or stacking and packing as many database instances as possible onto a single database server, will definitely reduce the idle CPU and wasted CPU, but instance caging will ensure that in the worse case possible, an instance can still acquire a predictable amount of CPU resources.

I/O Resource Manager (IORM)

Many traditional storage devices are unable to effectively isolate I/O requests and therefore distribute I/O loads between high-priority and low-priority workloads. In Figure 9-3, a low-priority workload can overwhelm a storage device that is also supporting a high-priority workload. The scheduling algorithms within the storage array are hard to influence unless they can somehow be integrated with the application that is making the initial I/O request. Although the storage scheduling algorithm may be able to reorder requests on the disk queue, this is not the best solution for I/O load isolation.

The Oracle Exadata Database Machine has a more advanced form of I/O scheduling, called the I/O Resource Manager or IORM (see Figure 9-4). This advanced scheduling, also described in Chapter 3, is possible because the storage layer understands that it is servicing one or more Oracle databases. This facility then allows a request to be queued if a higher-priority request needs to be serviced. This stops low-priority I/O requests from flooding the disk queue when both high- and low-priority requests are active. IORM can prioritize I/O requests from multiple consumer groups with multiple priority queues.

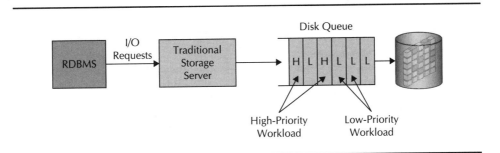

FIGURE 9-3. *Traditional storage I/O scheduling*

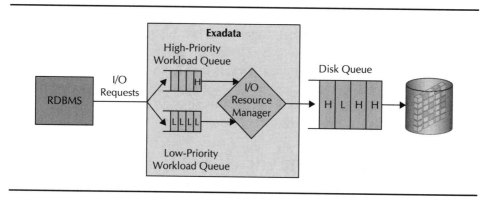

FIGURE 9-4. *Database Machine I/O scheduling*

You may be wondering if such disk scheduling intervention is expensive in terms of performance. Optimizations have been made to improve performance. If there is only one active workload or if the disks are not heavily utilized, then IORM does not manage the workload. IORM and the Oracle Database also ensure that Oracle background-process I/Os are scheduled appropriately. For instance, redo writes and control file accesses are always prioritized above other types of Oracle database I/Os.

The first step in setting up IORM is to group user sessions that have similar performance objectives into a consumer group, as illustrated in Figure 9-5. A resource plan is then created that defines how I/O requests should be prioritized. Then, session attribute rules are created that dynamically map

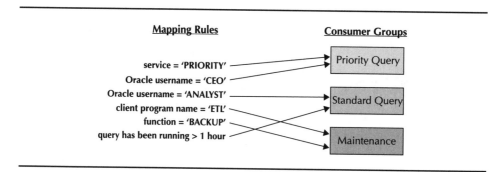

FIGURE 9-5. *IORM mapping*

sessions to consumer groups. Consumer groups and resource plans are created using the Database Resource Manager.

A resource plan is added that specifies how CPU and I/O resources are allocated among consumer groups for a specific database. We have already outlined how CPU can be limited using instance caging and the Database Resource Manager. Each consumer group in a resource plan contains a resource allocation directive, which consists of a percentage and a level (up to 8). Consumer groups at level 2 get resources that were available after all groups at level 1 received allocations up to their designated amounts. A level 3 consumer group would get resources that were not allocated or consumed at level 1 or level 2. This prioritization process continues until level 8. Resource plans can use percentages, priorities, or a combination of the two.

A resource plan can allocate I/O resources between different consumer groups in an individual database with an intradatabase plan, which was described in Chapter 3.

You might want to physically dedicate both CPU and I/O resources to a specific database instance or RAC clustered instances. This allocation can be achieved by using a single instance for a single database server and also allocating specific Oracle Exadata Database Machine storage server cells for a particular database ASM diskgroup. Each database would leverage its own ASM diskgroups and the diskgroups would never be on the same physical storage cells. Although an interesting physical isolation technique, it can lead to wasted resources and an inability for other databases to leverage resources like I/O that another database is not even using. In addition, each database would lose the ability to use the full bandwidth delivered by all Storage Server cells. A more efficient alternative method is to consider interdatabase I/O Resource Management.

Interdatabase I/O Resource Management allows the management of multiple databases that will be accessing the same Oracle Exadata Database Machine storage server cell. When you consolidate many database instances to a single database server or clustered database servers, you will have multiple databases that are accessing the same physical storage server cell. This means that the same principle of managing and prioritizing I/O requests to the Oracle Exadata Database Machine storage cells from different databases is needed to ensure that the I/O subsystem can be as efficient as possible without slowing down due to contention from conflicting I/O.

Interdatabase I/O management is configured using an interdatabase plan. This plan allocates how resources are shared among the database instances that are sharing cells. Only one interdatabase plan can be active on any server storage cell at any one time and it may only contain I/O resource directives. If an interdatabase plan is not specified, then all databases receive the same equal allocation of I/O from the storage cells.

If you are consolidating three separate database instances onto a single database server and you have already configured instance caging to lock down the CPU resources, you then will create an interdatabase plan to perform similar prioritization and isolation for the storage server cells. The Oracle Database Resource Manager has been enhanced to understand resources at the storage cell level and where user sessions can be mapped to particular consumer groups across a number of cells. Alternatively, interdatabase plans can be directed to individual database storage cells. Let's examine these two methods and how they can be used for consolidation.

You can allocate I/O to specific database instances by leveraging a strict percentage share. For instance, if your database applications are OrderEntry, Reporting, and Marketing, each using its own database, you might want to allocate I/O resources for the cells containing those databases as 65 percent I/O to OrderEntry, 15 percent I/O to Reporting, and 10 percent to Marketing. The remaining 10 percent can be allocated as a pool to other database instances collectively. The percentage assigned is only used as a maximum if I/O resources are oversubscribed. If other groups are not using their allocation, then it will be redistributed to the other consumer groups in the plan-specified ratios. This example is shown here:

```
BEGIN
DBMS_RESOURCE_MANAGER.CREATE_PENDING_AREA();
DBMS_RESOURCE_MANAGER.CREATE_PLAN('CONSOLIDATION','Consolidation
plan for our three applications');
DBMS_RESOURCE_MANAGER.CREATE_CONSUMER_GROUP('ORDERENTRY',
'OrderEntry Database App');
DBMS_RESOURCE_MANAGER.CREATE_CONSUMER_GROUP('REPORTING','Reporting
Database App');
DBMS_RESOURCE_MANAGER.CREATE_CONSUMER_GROUP('MARKETING','Marketing
Database App');
DBMS_RESOURCE_MANAGER.CREATE_PLAN_
DIRECTIVE('CONSOLIDATION','ORDERENTRY','OrderEntry allocation',
MGMT_P1=>65);
```

```
DBMS_RESOURCE_MANAGER.CREATE_PLAN_DIRECTIVE('CONSOLIDATION',
'REPORTING','Reporting allocation',MGMT_P1=>15);
DBMS_RESOURCE_MANAGER.CREATE_PLAN_DIRECTIVE('CONSOLIDATION',
'MARKETING','Marketing allocation',MGMT_P1=>10);
DBMS_RESOURCE_MANAGER.CREATE_PLAN_DIRECTIVE('CONSOLIDATION',
'OTHERS','Others allocation',MGMT_P1=>10);
DBMS_RESOURCE_MANAGER.SUBMIT_PENDING_AREA();
END;
/
```

In this example, we are calling the DBMS_RESOURCE_MANAGER PL/SQL package to create the CONSOLIDATION plan. Then we create consumer groups within that plan and then assign each a percentage of the I/O. The resource plan is now created but not active. In order to activate this plan, you will have to issue the following command:

```
ALTER SYSTEM SET RESOURCE_MANAGEMENT_PLAN='CONSOLIDATION';
```

Where you want to consolidate two significantly different I/O-intensive database instances onto the same physical storage cell, you can leverage an interdatabase plan on the Oracle Exadata Database Machine storage cells directly. In this example, you can consider an OLTP database instance that is highly sensitive to the latency of physical I/O requests. You will also consider a data warehousing database instance called DW that issues larger I/O requests but is more sensitive to throughput. In order to consolidate these two very different databases onto the same physical Oracle Exadata Database Machine storage cell, you must be able to prevent the DW from slowing down the OLTP database, yet allow the DW to open up on the storage cells when the OLTP database is no longer performing physical I/Os (because it is being satisfied from main memory or from the secondary flash memory area). Directly activating an interdatabase plan on the storage cells themselves will provide a solution to this common historic problem.

```
CellCLI> ALTER IORMPLAN -
dbPlan=(                         -
        (name=OLTP,level=1,allocation=80), -
        (name=DW,level=2,allocation=80), -
        (name=other,level=3,allocation=100))
```

In this example, the OLTP database gets priority and can access 80 percent of the I/O resources. The DW can access 20 percent of the I/O resources when the OLTP database is actively running and using up its maximum allocation; otherwise, it can use 80 percent of OLTP's unused allocation. Other databases can get any unused I/O at 100 percent, respectively.

Quality of Service Management

To better ensure that SLAs are met in real time and assure predictable performance for consolidated workloads, Oracle recommends quality of service (QoS) management. Oracle QoS is a policy-driven architecture that includes instrumentation of the entire Oracle stack, end-to-end work classification, real-time generation of correlated performance and resource wait data, identification of bottlenecks and their causes, incremental recommendations and impact projections, responses with just-in-time resource allocations, and protection of existing workloads from memory starvation.

Enterprise Manager simplifies QoS management by providing wizards and dashboards that support the policy-driven architecture. Policies are defined and enabled through a policy definition wizard. Bottlenecks and alerts are monitored through an applications performance dashboard. Reallocation of resources in solving problems takes into account expert system recommendations. Historical views of applications metrics are maintained for audit purposes. QoS is described in more detail in Chapter 8.

Consolidation Design

Now that you have all the various pieces that are required to consolidate database instances onto the Oracle Exadata Database Machine, you can consider an end-to-end consolidation design.

RAC Considerations

Oracle RAC provides tremendous consolidation benefits to database instances and the applications that connect to them. The ability to provide out-of-the-box high availability to applications, coupled with the benefit to scale inside a node (scale-up) or scale across the RAC cluster (scale-out) or both is unparalleled for everyday applications. When you are migrating multiple applications to the Oracle Exadata Database Machine, one of the key decisions you will have to make involves how you isolate instances and clusters. You could use one large RAC cluster for all consolidated applications, which would reduce management overhead and give you the option of allocation of resources through services, described in the next section. You could also choose to migrate each database to its own RAC cluster, which in many ways is the easier path, but which loses some flexibility in allocating resources and a smaller ration of availability with fewer nodes.

Along this same line, if you are buying a Full Rack configuration, you could choose to go with 2 heavy nodes in the X2-8 or 8 smaller nodes in the X2-2. The heavy nodes also come with more processors and more memory, which make them a more preferable target for OLTP workloads.

Finally, you could decide to not use RAC at all, but simply migrate stand-alone instances. This approach may seem like easiest approach, but you will sacrifice both availability and I/O bandwidth, since each individual instance will not benefit from multiple nodes.

There may be situations where scalability across multiple nodes is not seen as necessary. RAC One Node can be deployed on individual nodes as an alternative and provides enhanced application upgrade, maintenance, and mobility, as well as extremely fast failover for a database server node and other applications-related critical failure modes.

Workload-Based Consolidation

In workload-based consolidation of database instances, you attempt to group together applications that have similar resource profiles. For instance, applications that use roughly the same order of magnitude of I/O and CPU (say, 0 to 150 small IOPs at two cores each) can be consolidated together onto a similar number of RAC-enabled database server nodes.

Traditionally, OLTP was separated physically from data warehousing platforms, but by using IORM, this scenario might be accommodated despite such applications sometimes having wildly different sensitivity to I/O latency and throughput. Since OLTP applications are typically highly sensitive to CPU availability, you might want to use instance caging to ensure that OLTP applications always get priority for the CPU and I/O that they need. You will probably want to group together database instances onto database server nodes based on their similar workloads, priorities, and SLA levels of availability. That way, administration, patching, and security can be adjusted for higher priority applications that can run on physically separate database servers.

For extremely risk-adverse and security-sensitive environments, corporate policies may dictate that database instances must be physically separate and the same for the database storage cells that perform the I/O. This is still possible using the Oracle Exadata Database Machine, though it is usually not the optimal approach, since segregating these resources eliminates the possibility of the increased bandwidth and CPU resources being shared between different instances, as well as reducing availability options.

Time Zone-Based Consolidation

An important and often overlooked opportunity for consolidation is when multiple similar local databases service different time zones and locations. Consolidating database instances separately servicing different time zones onto common database servers can be enabled through Oracle's granular security, control, and monitoring. Resource groups in Database Resource Manager can take into account the time of day, switching consumers from one group to another or, in cooperation with Oracle Scheduler jobs, switching resource plans based on times.

Another important consideration involves providing adequate time windows for patching. Although almost all maintenance operations for the Oracle Exadata Database Machine can be implemented through a process of rolling upgrades, there are always going to be some things that can potentially require some downtime or require running in a performance-degraded mode for an extended period. Of course, Oracle Data Guard or Oracle GoldenGate can be deployed to always ensure that a secondary Oracle Exadata Database Machine is available. If you cannot tolerate any performance degradation during the online day or any downtime, you might want to patch during a natural outage window (i.e., during the night when fewer users are online as opposed to during the active day).

By consolidating applications based on their end-user time zone, patching and maintenance can be scheduled during times that are not so busy and security can be enhanced significantly.

Overprovisioning Consolidation

You might decide to group lower-priority database instances and their respective application connections onto specific database servers. By overstuffing database instances like test, development, reporting, quality assurance, and installation onto specific database servers, you can maximize

Oracle Exadata Database Machine utilization rates and reduce costs. In cases where the database instances can still run satisfactorily within a minimum CPU quantity, both instance caging and IORM can help ensure that worst-case scenario outcomes, such as all database instances spiking their resources at the same time, can still be managed with predictable performance.

Tight SLA Provisioning

If you decide to not overprovision database servers, you might strictly allocate CPUs through instance caging on a 1:1 basis until the entire database server CPUs are allocated to instances exclusively. IORM can be used to define and enforce I/O priority scheduling or percentage sharing. Such a consolidation plan ensures that the applications will always have exclusive access to the CPU and I/O priorities that they need to optimally run, but the risk is that some resources will go to waste if they are not actively being used. Many take this option, as their database instances and their applications are particularly sensitive to response times and delivering to the SLA is critically important.

Testing

This chapter has outlined some of the strategies you can use when using the Oracle Exadata Database Machine as a platform for consolidation. These are approaches which will give you some good information on which to base your plan. But nothing substitutes for testing how multiple applications will interact on the target platform. You can perform testing pro-actively by using a tool like Real Application Testing, which can capture actual workloads on one machine and replay then on another. You could use other load testing tools, or run systems in parallel during initial deployment. Any of these tactics will give you a better chance of success than simply trying a bunch of applications together and hoping it works—especially since the competition for resources between potentially conflicting applications can be extraordinarily complex in the real world.

For many people, the best way to implement consolidation is to start with the largest or most crucial application running alone on a Database Machine, and then migrating other applications to the platform, using tools like IORM and instance caging to allocate resources where appropriate.

Although this approach may not limit your ability to properly predict the extent of consolidation on a Database Machine, it has the advantage of a greater likelihood of ongoing success and happier users.

Summary

This chapter provided an introduction to some of the unique aspects of consolidation projects building upon techniques for deploying single database solutions described elsewhere in this book. As you have seen, consolidation can take multiple forms on the Oracle Exadata Database Machine. Projected cost savings by reducing the number of servers and storage platforms and thereby reducing overall power usage, floor space required, or management personnel are likely driving you in this direction.

Given the options that you have in deploying and managing such an environment that were described here, you have a lot of flexibility and can be extremely successful. Careful planning is essential. Evaluate consolidation opportunities based on goals that you establish, such as achieving better processor or storage utilization, retirement of oldest platforms first, and/or improving performance of databases where faster delivery of data will have meaningful business impact. Meet or exceed SLAs by clearly mapping how you will manage, maintain, secure, and deliver solutions that are also highly available.

As with any project of this type, the best advice is to plan for eventual full deployment, but deploy incrementally. This will help you better mitigate risk in such projects. Of course, business users of individual applications and data warehouses may change their usage patterns when they discover the power of this platform. Addressing these changing demands in an incremental fashion is always the best road to success.

Consolidation can provide a significant return on investment. Besides providing cost savings, improved speed of deployment and simplified management can help your organization react to changes in business conditions and achieve top line business benefits sooner. However, some legacy platforms will be more difficult to include in such a consolidation strategy. As you plan your initiative, you should consider all of these aspects as you prioritize the platforms to include in your initial and longer term consolidation efforts.

CHAPTER
10

Migrating to the Exadata Database Machine

p until now, we've covered the features of the Oracle Exadata Database Machine and the best practices for using it. If you are creating and deploying brand-new databases on this platform, you would have all the information you need. But there are an enormous number of existing databases and applications that can benefit from the Exadata Database Machine, which means that you will have to perform a migration to this new platform.

This chapter discusses the best practices and methodologies for migrating from Oracle and non-Oracle relational database sources to the Exadata Database Machine. In general, the methodology and steps required for such migrations depend on the source database and version, the hardware platform, and the operating system. You should remember that the process for migrating to the Database Machine is no different from the process of migrating to a regular Oracle Database 11*g* Release 2 on a Linux x86-64–based or Solaris-based platform configured with RAC and ASM. There are no special steps in the migration process that are specific to either the Exadata Storage Servers or to the Database Machine.

Also, there are no special certifications or validation requirements for Oracle Database applications to run on the Database Machine. If the applications are validated or certified to work against a non-Exadata–based Oracle Database 11*g* Release 2 utilizing ASM as the storage, they will automatically work without any modifications against the database deployed on the Database Machine. The application will seamlessly be able to utilize the Exadata Storage Servers and reap the benefits of features like Exadata Smart Scans and storage indexes, out of the box and without any modifications. This benefit is achieved because connections to Oracle Database 11*g* Release 2 and the Exadata Storage Servers are only visible to the database server processes and transparent to the application.

When considering migrating Oracle Databases from non-Exadata platforms, the migration process will include a platform migration, and may also include a database upgrade based on the version of the source database. Often, multiple methods can be used to accomplish the migration, but you should evaluate each method and choose the one that fits your scenario and business requirements the best. Typically, the requirements for a migration are lower costs, quick implementation times, low manual conversion, and minimal downtime to the applications during the migration process.

On the other hand, migrating non-Oracle Databases from any platform is generally perceived as being complex and requiring substantial manual effort. This added complication adds to high migration costs and requires more resources. However, by following the best-practice methodologies listed in this chapter and automating many of the steps by using proven processes and software tools, you can drastically reduce the costs and timelines of such migrations. Automation is the key to lowering migration costs, and should be considered whenever and wherever the opportunity presents its use.

In addition, the power of the Oracle Exadata Database Machine means that some portions of a migration effort, such as loading data, can be accomplished in a much shortened time, given appropriate resource allocations.

Oracle platform migrations from Oracle and non-Oracle hardware platforms have been performed for decades and quite a bit of documentation is available on this topic, which should give you some comfort in dealing with these types of migrations. This chapter will help you define a migration strategy to the Database Machine from both Oracle and non-Oracle sources, and also compares and contrasts the different migration methods available, with the pros and cons of each.

NOTE
Migrating hierarchical databases like IMS-DB is not in the scope of this book. The steps involved in migrating non-relational databases to Oracle tend to be specific to the type of source and cannot be generalized in a short chapter.

Premigration Steps

Platform migration projects need proper planning in order to accurately estimate the resources, cost, and complexity of the migration, as well as the timelines for the effort. This exercise will set expectations and determine the perception of success on the project. Premigration steps also play a key role in choosing the right migration strategy, architecting the migration steps, determining the tools needed to perform the migration, and most importantly, estimating how much automation can be incorporated into the migration process.

The typical premigration steps are

- Discovering the current environment

- Database Machine capacity planning and sizing

- Choosing a migration strategy

NOTE
Most of the premigration steps discussed in this section are focused on migrating non-Oracle databases, since they are the most complex of migrations. Considerations specific to Oracle sources will be pointed out as relevant.

Discovering the Current Environment

Sessions focused on discovering the current source system are essential planning exercises in a migration project. The purpose of such sessions is to document as much information as possible about the source, which will help you plan an appropriate migration strategy. This information will also help estimate project costs, timelines, and resources.

The discovery sessions should be held with the subject matter experts and architects who can provide the level of detail needed, and the conversations should be focused on gathering an appropriate amount of detail so they don't drag on. The information captured as a result of these sessions provides details related to systems and network architecture, performance metrics, applications architecture, database architecture, and the backup and recovery architecture. Hopefully, the information provided in this section will guide you in asking the right questions while keeping focused on the right topics.

Before we talk about the environment discovery phase, we will first define a few terms that will be used in the later discussions.

- **Server platform** The *server platform* consists of the combination of the hardware and the operating system (OS). When we talk about migrating to a server platform, it usually means replacing the current hardware and the OS platform with a different hardware and OS, for reasons such as outgrowing the current hardware capacity or for implementing a technology refresh. In the context of database migrations, the platform migration could also involve a database software replacement or a version upgrade as well.

■ **Data model, stored objects, and database schema**   The *data model* includes the data storage structures such as tables and summaries, database views, keys, constraints, and the data access structures such as the different types of indexes.

The *database stored objects* are mainly the procedures, functions, triggers, object types, and methods that are stored in the database. The stored objects incorporate some sort of processing logic and are usually implemented using database vendor–specific structured programming languages such as Oracle PL/SQL.

The *database schema* is the data model and the database stored objects, combined.

■ **Server-side scripts**   *Server-side scripts* are the OS scripts or commands that interact with the database using SQL queries or with database-specific OS commands and utilities to perform certain functions. The scripts can be written using utilities such as Shell scripts, Perl, or batch programs, or may be stand-alone scripts invoking database commands. Server-side scripts need not necessarily reside only on the database server platform, but can also reside on other servers and be connected to the database server remotely. A few examples are scripts that perform backups, data archiving, data loads, or data dumps, or scripts that simply run SQL commands.

■ **Surrounding applications**   *Surrounding applications* are the applications that connect to the database servers from other hosts. These applications may be resident on application servers, or reporting servers, or ETL (Extract, Transform, and Load) servers— basically any server with software components that initiate database connections and run SQL and other commands on the database servers.

■ **Source environment metrics**   *Metrics* that are associated with a server platform are a measure of some property or state associated with a software or hardware component. Some examples of metrics associated with hardware are CPU specifications, total memory, and hard disk specifications.

Metrics related to performance of the current system play an important role in sizing the Database Machine. Some examples of performance metrics are the CPU utilization rates, disk I/Os per second, and disk MBs scanned per second. You need to utilize the current system's built-in methods and tools for capturing performance metrics. The best practice for capturing performance metrics is to capture peak and average values, as both values play an important role in sizing the destination system.

Source code metrics are related to the software code that is associated with the database being migrated. The source code metrics of interest in this chapter would be the total number of lines of code (LOC) that have database-specific calls, and the complexity of the code categorized as low, medium, or high. The level of complexity will depend on the use of source database-specific features and functions, or features that do not have a one-to-one translation to the Oracle components.

Consider the following example for calculating source code metrics for a server-side script. Say, for example, part of the server-side script interacts with the database by creating a database connection and executes SQL statements that are specific to the database technology. The rest of the script has logic that processes the results of the SQL and does additional processing that is non-database related. For calculating the source code LOC metric, you can count, either exactly or approximately, the total lines of code of the script that have database-specific interactions. For calculating the source code complexity metric, you need to approximately determine the complexity of such calls and categorize the script as a whole to be of low, medium, or high complexity.

The source code metrics should be calculated for the surrounding applications, server-side scripts, database stored objects, and any other code that runs some processing logic on the database.

Discovering Current Systems Architecture

The architecture of the current systems helps in defining the appropriate Database Machine architecture that can support the same or better levels of SLAs, the disaster recovery requirements, and the network connectivity requirements to the external applications and systems. This information can be captured easily using the system administration tools and the OS-level monitoring commands of the current systems.

Capture the systems architecture by focusing on the following details:

- Server architecture, platform specifications, and hardware details.

- High availability (HA), disaster recovery (DR) architecture of the current system, and application-level service agreements.

- Components used in DR and HA. These are third-party proprietary technologies, active/passive or active/active HA, and failover times.

- Network diagrams depicting applications, external storage, and systems connectivity.

- Network throughput, latency, and bandwidth requirements for all connections going in and out of the source systems.

Discovering the Non-Oracle Database Environment

When performing a migration of non-Oracle databases to the Database Machine, the majority of the work involved is in migrating the data, database schema, and the server-side scripts. Hence, it is important to discover what resides on the source platform and identify the components that will be migrated over. This discovery step will also identify the components that are candidates for automated migrations and the components that can be grouped together for phased migrations.

This step is focused on gathering source code and performance metrics that are related to the source database platform, database schema, and the server-side scripts. This information can be gathered from the source database monitoring tools, administration tools, or by using SQL scripts.

A few high-level pointers on capturing these metrics are

- Capture the source database versions, the OS platform, and the availability of the JDBC, ODBC, and native drivers for connecting into the database.

- Investigate the use of different types of database structures in the source database, the use of complex data types, and features that are specific to the source database technology.

- Investigate if database-specific access structures have been defined for speeding queries. For example, the Teradata database has the capability to create join indexes for speeding up queries that involve joins. Join indexes in Teradata can be translated to Oracle Materialized Views. If such straight translations to Oracle-equivalent objects exist, the objects will be the candidates for automated migrations. The objects that are proprietary to the source database technology and for which an equivalent object does not exist on Oracle will need to be manually analyzed and migrated.

- Document the use of procedures, functions, triggers, complex types, and methods. Also gather the source code LOC metrics and the complexity metrics that categorize the object into low, medium, or high.

- Analyze the use of non-ANSI SQL implementations for DML (Data Manipulation Language, or write operations) and queries. This usage makes the SQL hard to translate, so it is important to document such occurrences.

- Analyze the use of server-side scripts, their purpose, the scripting languages used, and all the source code–related metrics that are associated with it.

- Capture the performance metrics of the database server—the I/Os per second (IOPS) for short I/Os and the MBs per second (MBPS) for long I/Os.

- Calculate the disk space utilization of the current database. The space used by data, indexes, summary tables, staging schemas, and projected growth requirements for the next three to five years should be estimated. Also incorporate nonlinear growth requirements that arise in order to support ad hoc growth.

- Capture the database authentication requirements—mainly the administrator and user authentication and the requirement of LDAP-based authentication mechanisms.

- Capture the security authorization requirements of the database schema—mainly the database roles, users, and privileges.

IOPS and MBPS

IOPS (input/output operations per second) and MBPS (megabytes per second) are the metrics that measure performance of storage devices. IOPS measures the small I/O performance, which is a typical characteristic of OLTP workloads. The objective of measuring IOPS is to see how fast the storage is capable of writing (or reading) transactions that span a small number of disk blocks. IOPS can be measured for reads, writes, or mixed read/write transactions, with a typical 4K or 8K block size.

The MBPS metric measures the storage bandwidth utilization, which is the total number of bytes flowing through the storage device or the network per second. The MBPS metrics are associated with large I/Os that prevail in data warehousing and reporting environments. These environments have workloads that scan large volumes of data from the storage.

Discovering the Oracle Database Environment

Capturing performance and capacity information from Oracle Databases is easy when compared to non-Oracle databases. The Automatic Workload Repository (AWR) contains all performance-related metrics for the database instance, as well as the CPU utilization metrics of the database server. The AWR report should be run against two points in time of peak system activity, and the results of these AWR reports will be used to calculate the current database performance numbers.

The metrics that you need to derive from the AWR reports are the storage performance metrics and the IOPS and MBPS the current storage is able to deliver. You will use these metrics later to calculate the right-sized Database Machine configuration that will provide an equivalent or better performance than the current source system.

In order to calculate these numbers from the AWR, locate the instance activity section and look up the "per second" column of the following metrics:

■ Physical read total bytes

■ Physical write total bytes

■ Physical read total IO requests

- Physical write total IO requests

- Physical read total multiblock requests

- Physical write total multiblock requests

Since multiblock requests are associated with large I/Os, they need to be subtracted from the total IO requests in order to get the IOPS for short I/Os. Use these formulas for calculating MBPS and IOPS:

MBPS = (physical read total bytes) + (physical write total bytes)

IOPS = (physical read total IO requests) – (physical read total multiblock requests) + (physical write total IO requests) – (physical write total multiblock requests)

In addition to these calculations, you should:

- Capture the database feature usage from the current system, mainly the use of partitioning, OLTP compression, SecureFiles compression, and the use of LOB segments, if any. If the current database does not use partitioning or compression options, then you have the opportunity to gain their benefits by introducing these features as part of the migration. Also, the best practice is to convert LOBs to the SecureFiles storage. Some of the migration steps discussed later in this chapter will take care of these types of conversions, so you should decide if you want to implement the best practices during the migration process so the appropriate method of migration can be narrowed down.

- Calculate the metrics related to disk space utilization from the database instance. These metrics are easily available through Oracle Enterprise Manager or the database dictionary views. The metrics of interest are

  - The total space allocated for all the tablespaces and percent of this space utilized

  - Space utilized by compressed objects (if any)

  - Total SecureFiles storage space (if any)

  - Total LOB segment space (if any)

■ Capture the source database platform specifications, mainly the details on the database versions, use of ASM, ASM allocation unit size (AU_SIZE), ASM diskgroup redundancy levels, and the database extent sizes. These values will help determine the right migration strategy in the later stages.

> **NOTE**
> *The Oracle IO Numbers (ORION) tool can be used to calculate performance metrics of the source database storage subsystem. The metrics captured by ORION mimic the actual Oracle Database I/O performance, since ORION uses the same I/O libraries and kernel code as the Oracle Database software. The ORION tool does not need the Oracle Database software to function and can be installed on both Oracle and non-Oracle source systems, provided it is certified on the platform.*

ETL, Data Loads, and Extracts Environment

Capture all ongoing data loads and extracts occurring on the source system, whether they are file-based or have other databases as direct sources or destinations. Capture the tools and processes used to perform these loads and extracts, whether they are packaged ETL tools or custom scripts. This information is needed to estimate the effort needed to refactor these processes to work against the Database Machine.

When capturing this information, you should:

■ Identify the sources for the data loads and destination systems for the extracts and their connection methods into the database, whether through SQL*Net, JDBC, or ODBC.

■ Identify any replication tools used either to feed into the source system or to replicate changes from the source to external systems. Investigate the current replication tool's support for Oracle Databases.

- Capture the source code metrics for the custom scripts used for loads and extracts. Document the tools or scripts used to perform the loads and extracts and whether they are proprietary to the third-party source technology.

- Capture the ETL tools used for loads, extracts, or ongoing ETL; their complexity; connectivity and driver requirements; source database-specific features used in ETL; and the tool support for Oracle databases.

Surrounding Applications Discovery

It is critical to discover the applications that will be affected when the source database is migrated to the new platform. The number and types of applications affected and the degree of the impact will determine the applications migration strategy. Once the applications and their details are known, the level of effort involved in modifying these applications to work with the Database Machine can be estimated. To collect this information, you should:

- Capture the complexity of the applications connecting into the source system, whether they are using database- and vendor-specific technologies, and the support of these tools and applications with Oracle Database 11g Release 2. Focus on capturing source code metrics on the portions of code that comprise database-related logic.

- Capture the use of vendor-specific SQL functions or logic within the application code. The more complex the vendor-specific SQL being used in these applications, the harder the translation becomes.

- Document the drivers used for connectivity—native, JDBC, ODBC and versions—and any specific requirements for running with particular drivers and versions.

- Identify the application servers connecting to the source database, whether they are based on Java or .NET, application server connection pools and mechanisms used, and Oracle Database 11g Release 2 support provided by the application servers.

- Capture off-the-shelf reporting and business intelligence tools used, along with the tools' support for Oracle Database 11g Release 2 and any custom SQL statements used within or generated by the tool that are proprietary to the source database.

Backup and Recovery Architecture

Although you may end up using different tools and techniques for performing backup and recovery of the Database Machine, you have to capture the backup and recovery architecture, methods, and SLAs from the current environment to ensure that you do not lose any existing capabilities in this area. Whether the current strategy is to back up to tape directly or to disk or you are using a hybrid disk and tape strategy, the idea should be to utilize the existing policies and infrastructure when configuring backups in the Database Machine environment.

To collect this information, you should:

- Capture the recovery time objective (RTO) and recovery point objective (RPO) from the current SLAs.

- Consider the requirement to connect external tape drives or disk-based backup storage systems to the Database Machine. The Database Machine connects to the outside world using the built-in InfiniBand and Ethernet ports.

- Investigate if third-party snap mirroring technologies are used to perform backups and also to stand up test or development environments. These technologies will not work on the Database Machine, as the third-party vendors cannot directly access the Exadata Storage Servers and there is no support for hardware RAID. Therefore, it is important to have an alternative solution to the snap mirror if this capability is needed on the Database Machine.

- Oracle RMAN is the only tool capable of performing backups of the databases residing in the Database Machine. For further details on this topic, refer to the section on backup and recovery best practices in Chapter 6.

Database Machine Capacity Planning and Sizing

The topic of capacity planning is huge in itself, so we will focus on a few important considerations that will help size the Database Machine. The best practice for sizing systems is to size for performance and then for capacity. Sizing for capacity is easier when compared to sizing for performance and more commonly practiced in the real world. Most people do not go the extra mile to size for performance, and this oversight is a major cause of performance issues that arise in the field deployments.

The metrics of the current system obtained through the discovery process will provide the information needed to size the Database Machine. As mentioned earlier, it is quite essential to have the discovery phase done right, since all the activities, including the migration methods and sizing, are dependent on the metrics captured in this process.

The process of sizing a Database Machine is focused on sizing the Exadata Storage Servers and the database nodes for capacity and performance. Once you have the sizing metrics that you need, you will match them against Tables A-1 and A-2 from the appendix and come up with the flavor of the Database Machine that will satisfy the capacity and performance requirements.

Sizing for Capacity

The metrics of the current system that will help size the destination system for capacity are mainly database space utilization metrics. These metrics include data and index space utilization, the planned growth (linear), and unplanned growth (nonlinear) metrics. Determining unplanned or nonlinear growth is a bit tricky, since the Database Machine is a consolidation platform and the rate at which an enterprise chooses to consolidate multiple databases and applications to the new platform may be unknown. Once multiple lines of business (LOBs) start seeing benefits, the rate of consolidation to the Database Machine can grow rapidly.

Once the capacity data is obtained, you can use it to calculate the rack size of the Database Machine that satisfies the capacity requirements. The Database Machine comes prebundled with one of two flavors of hard drives, the 600GB High Performance SAS (HP-SAS) or 2TB High Capacity SAS (HC-SAS), and by choosing one of these flavors of drives in a full-rack Database Machine, you can get a total raw space of 100TB or 336TB, respectively. However, this is the raw capacity, and the advertised usable data capacity (uncompressed) of the full rack, after taking out ASM mirroring and other system overheads, comes down to 45TB for HP-SAS and 150TB for HC-SAS. Use Table A-1 to match the total space you need against the capacity of each configuration to come up with the Database Machine of the right size that satisfies the capacity requirements.

Since you cannot mix and match HP-SAS drives and HC-SAS drives in the same Database Machine, the decision on the flavor of drive to use should be based on performance specifications of the drives and not just capacity. We will discuss this topic in the next section.

When factoring OLTP compression into the space requirements, you might be able to get a twofold to threefold savings on storage for OLTP compressed data. Exadata Hybrid Columnar Compression (EHCC) query compression can potentially give about a 10-fold savings, and EHCC archive compression about a 15-fold savings. The actual savings are, of course, dependent on the data repetitiveness and proximity of repetitive values in each compression unit (CU) of a table. It is a best practice to implement compression on the Database Machine, and if you like to implement this best practice, then consider compressing during the migration process. Otherwise, compressing it once the data has been loaded will require a data reorganization operation on the designated tables, which may incur additional outage.

The DBMS_COMPRESSION package supplied with Oracle Database 11g Release 2 can be used to estimate compression ratios achievable by OLTP and EHCC methods prior to actually compressing the data. The package will estimate compression ratios by sampling the data being compressed. For estimating compression ratios on databases versions 9i through 11g Release 1, you can use the Oracle Advanced Compression Advisor package with its DBMS_COMPRESSION procedures. More detail on Advanced Compression Advisor is available on the Oracle Technology Network.

Another way to reduce the storage footprint if you are using large objects is to take advantage of SecureFiles compression and deduplication, which is a feature available with the Oracle Advanced Compression Option. You should be able to get two- to three-fold compression for large objects (LOBs) that are stored using this feature. If you are using LOBs (non-SecureFiles based) in the current database, you should definitely consider converting them to SecureFiles. The deduplication, compression and other new features deliver storage savings as well as performance improvements, as compressed objects require less I/O and some internal improvements also contribute to better performance.

In order to estimate compression ratios on non-Oracle databases before actually migrating them over to Oracle, consider loading a sample of the source data into an Oracle Database 11g Release 2 and running the DBMS_COMPRESSION package. You do not need to load the complete table, but only enough to estimate the compression ratio.

Sizing for Performance

The performance metrics of the current system that helps size the Database Machine are mainly the I/O per second (IOPS) and the MBs per second (MBPS). The IOPS are typically used for sizing OLTP workloads, whereas the MBPS measurement is used for sizing data warehousing workloads. The Database Machine has sufficient CPU cores to handle all types of real-world workloads; however, if for any reason the application loads demand the need of more cores than what come preinstalled in the flavor of the machine, then the CPU sizing should also be taken into consideration. This might be the case with applications that perform extensive processing on the database using PL/SQL or server-side programs, or databases that have ongoing high-volume data loads coming in through the InfiniBand network. Data loads coming in through high-speed networks are generally known to bottleneck the CPU.

Keep in mind that when you size for all these metrics, you need to match up with the flavor of the Database Machine that will satisfy *all* four metrics we discussed so far (not just one or two), mainly the IOPS, MBPS, CPU, and storage requirements. For example, based on your IOPS, storage capacity, and CPU requirements, you have determined that a Database Machine X2-2 Half Rack is enough to cater to your needs. However, if you determine that in order to satisfy the MBPS requirements you need an X2-2 Full Rack, then the choice should be to go with the Full Rack and not the Half Rack.

Considerations for choosing a High Performance SAS– or a High Capacity SAS–based Database Machine will depend on the performance specifications of the drives and the storage requirements of the database. The performance of an HP-SAS drive is, for the most part, twice as fast as an HC-SAS drive, although your mileage may vary, based on the particulars of your workload. Remember that there is more to I/O performance than simply the seek times to retrieve data from disks.

Use Table A-2 from the appendix to match up your IOPS, MBPS, and CPUs to come up with the right-sized Database Machine to fit your performance requirements. The last step will be to compare the Database Machine configuration you select when sizing for capacity, with the configuration needed to achieve the required performance, and use the bigger machine of the two to provide you both the performance and the capacity that will be required from the Database Machine.

Exadata Flash Cache Considerations in Sizing

OLTP workloads have a concept of active data, or the working set, which basically is the portion of the data that will be actively accessed for the majority of the time, as opposed to the size of the entire data stored in the database. If this working set can be stored in some sort of cache or main memory, then the I/O performance will be extremely fast, since the data is accessed from the cache. Depending on the underlying technology used for the cache, the speed-up can be 20 to 100 times faster than fetching the same data from the hard disks.

As discussed in Chapters 3 and 5, the flash cards in the Exadata Storage Servers are configured as Flash Cache by default. The Exadata Flash Cache is utilized by the sophisticated, database-aware, LRU-like caching algorithm, which results in the most-used blocks staying pinned in the Flash Cache. The total uncompressed usable data capacity available in a full rack containing HC-SAS drives is about 45TB, and the total capacity of Flash Cache is 5.3TB, which translates to about 12 percent of the user data capacity. Based on this calculation, if the working set of an OLTP system is less than 12 percent, most of the working set can potentially be stored in Flash Cache. When the read I/O requests are targeted on the working set, the Exadata Storage Servers will perform the I/O using the Flash Cache rather than the hard disks. Exadata Flash Cache IOPS performance is 20 times faster than hard disks and MBPS performance is 2 times faster than hard disks, which will enable the Exadata Storage Servers to deliver extreme improvement in performance when the data is accessed from the Flash Cache.

> **NOTE**
> *The effective capacity of Flash Cache can be increased tremendously by using EHCC or OLTP compression. For example, an EHCC compressed table with a 10x compression factor will store about 53TB of uncompressed user data into 5.3TB of Flash Cache.*

The benefits of Flash Cache can be factored in when sizing for performance. However, this is not an easy task, since the size of the working set is hard to calculate and you can only go with assumptions. A few studies suggest that the typical working set for OLTP systems is about 10 percent of the total data size, and if you go with this, the Exadata Flash Cache should be able to hold a typical working set quite comfortably.

Choosing a Migration Strategy

Once the right information is gathered from the current source systems in the discovery sessions, the appropriate migration strategy can be chosen. Typically in a situation dealing with large and complex database migrations, a single migration strategy may not be the best option, but rather a combination of multiple strategies that best suits the specific platform being migrated should be considered.

The following sections discuss a variety of database platform migration strategies that can be used in real-world migration projects.

Replatform with Refactoring Strategy

A replatform migration approach for databases is usually focused on replacing the existing database server platform with a bigger and faster platform like the Exadata Database Machine. This replacement is done while keeping the surrounding applications and their interfaces with the database system intact. In a replatform of non-Oracle databases to the Database Machine, the legacy database software will be replaced with the Oracle Database software.

When you replatform the database server from a non-Oracle source system, you need to modify the surrounding applications, the database stored objects, the server-side scripts, and the database schema in order to make them functional against the new environment. These modifications are called refactoring.

The refactoring strategy can approach the task at different levels. The level with the least amount of intervention would be to make the minimum number of changes to the application and the code in order to make them function just like they did before. The next level would be to make additional changes that will implement the best practices of the new environment. Another level would be to implement or fix any code inefficiencies so that the code is more optimized and performs with higher efficiency. Other higher levels of refactoring will start resembling the rearchitecting strategies, which are discussed in the next section.

Even when you are migrating from Oracle database sources, you might need some level of refactoring to the surrounding applications, the database schema, and the server-side scripts. The refactoring in this case will be to implement the best practices of the Database Machine and of the Oracle Database 11*g* Release 2. Although implementing best practices is not a requirement, the process is generally well worth the effort, as it can fully unlock the potential of the Database Machine environment and to get the extra improvements in performance.

Estimating the costs of refactoring will depend on the lines of code (LOC) or the number of objects considered for refactoring, along with the complexity of the changes. Generally, the higher the LOC and degree of complexity of the code, the more resource consuming and complex the refactoring will be. When moving from non-Oracle systems, refactoring of the database schema can be performed using automated tools, which will be discussed in the migration steps. Refactoring of other objects will be mostly manual, and the tools will be of little or no help.

Application Rearchitecting Strategy

Evolution of software is quite natural, and over time, a software technology or application will evolve either for maintenance purposes or to meet additional business requirements. Rearchitecting involves a rewrite of the application and other processes to either make them more maintainable and optimized or to be in sync with the latest and greatest technologies. Sometimes, rearchitecting becomes a necessary evil when either the technology in use is outdated or out of support, or if the application was badly designed to begin with, resulting in poor performance and low reliability, or to conform to enterprise-wide IT standards that have evolved over time.

Rearchitecting strategies are more complex than refactoring and require a thorough analysis of the systems and the applications. With refactoring, you are simply reorganizing existing components, while the rearchitecting process allows you to redesign and implement entire portions of functionality, potentially including new capabilities in the product. Businesses usually undertake rearchitecting projects when there is a renewed direction from upper management to implement a specific tool or technology, or as part of a platform migration project. Migration projects provide an opportunity to modify legacy applications when the organization budgets the resources, time, and the expense.

The process of rearchitecting an application involves manual conversion and is similar to a brand-new implementation in many ways. Rearchitecting an application requires exhaustive and time-consuming test cycles and is the most complex migration strategy when compared with replatforming and refactoring. Rearchitecture projects do not necessarily provide a rapid payoff, but can have a long-term return on investment that is best determined by the business and the IT departments.

Consider an example of a rearchitecture scenario for migrating Teradata BTEQ scripts to the Oracle-equivalent components. Teradata BTEQ is a type of server-side script and is mostly used for performing ETL into the Teradata environment. The appropriate technology to use in Oracle to perform ETL is Oracle Data Integrator (ODI). ODI provides point-and-click interfaces for creating data flows and mappings rather than hand-coding the ETL logic, which is what BTEQ essentially does. The benefit of using ETL tools for performing data transformations (as opposed to using scripts) are multifold, some of which are improved productivity and maintainability, better manageability of processes, easier configurability of ETL, and flexibility to changes. A rearchitecture of these server-side scripts might be a necessary component of a migration effort, but as you can see, will pay off with added benefits for the short and long term.

Phased Migration Strategy

A phased migration strategy is essential in large-scale migrations and a necessity that ensures a seamless transition to the new environment. This strategy uses a divide-and-conquer approach in which a large system is divided into smaller groups and the groups are migrated one or more at a time in a phased manner, resulting in incrementally enabling certain functionality on the new system. You would group components and applications together based on their self-contained nature, the degree of interdependencies between groups and within groups, sharing of common database objects, and the degree of impact and risk to the business during the migration. The order in which phases are executed should reduce the overall impact and cost of the complete migration.

With large database implementations, sometimes the business continuity and availability requirements require parallel runs of the legacy and the new platforms for a time until the new platform is proven to be ready for production.

During the parallel run period, the loads and the inputs will be dual-feeding the two systems, and full cycles of all processes need to run on both of the systems in parallel. This parallel-run strategy adds to the cost and complexity of the migration, but is sometimes a necessity when the business demands zero-downtime migrations and testing strategies require production-like loads.

Automated Migration Strategy

Automating the steps of the migration process using software-based migration tools is an important component for the overall migration strategy. Automation can help to bring down migration costs, and thereby help accelerate the return on investment of the Database Machine deployment. The steps that can be fully or partially automated in a refactoring methodology are the database schema migration steps and the data migration steps.

When automated migration tools are unable to convert the object to the equivalent target technology, then the tool will flag the object as fallout. The fallouts of automated migrations will have to be dealt with manually, which adds to the costs and the timelines. Hence, it is important to estimate the fallouts early in the planning phase. The best approach to accurately estimate fallouts would be to implement a proof of concept that would evaluate the migration tool against a subset of the source database environment and prove its effectiveness and capabilities against the schema that is specific to the source database system. The code complexity metrics captured during the environment discovery process are also useful in estimating automated conversion rates and fallouts at a high level.

If an automated migration is the most efficient way to proceed, then one should ask why not use automation in each and every migration project from the start? The answer depends on the migration tool's limitations for the types and versions of the source and destination databases and their capabilities to migrate the different types of components. For example, data models are the easiest components to automatically translate, and most tools can easily incorporate this translation. Stored objects and SQL are harder to migrate, and fewer tools will support such capability.

The Oracle tools that are useful in automating migrations are Oracle SQL Developer for database schema and data migrations; Oracle GoldenGate (OGG) for data replication; and Oracle Data Integrator (ODI) for data migration, transformations, and replication. We will discuss the capabilities of these tools in detail in the later sections.

Migration Steps for Non-Oracle Databases

As discussed earlier, the recommended approach for migrating non-Oracle systems to the Database Machine is by using the refactor-with-replatform strategy. The typical steps required to implement this strategy are outlined here:

- Database schema migration

- Server-side scripts migration

- Data migration and synchronization

- Using automated tools for migration

Database Schema Migration

Migration of data models from non-Oracle sources can be automated using software tools, and this step is usually the easiest in the migration process. The standard data types, data storage structures, and data access structures existing in the source databases can easily be translated on a one-to-one basis to the Oracle equivalent objects. Challenges exist when the source database uses advanced types and objects that are proprietary to the source vendor technology. These objects are prone to fallouts since the tool might not be able to translate to an Oracle-equivalent object.

There are two scenarios of fallouts in a schema migration. The first scenario is when the fallouts happen because the respective feature or type is not named the same in both environments. To fix the fallout, you would need to manually convert these objects, but there still would be a one-to-one conversion. An example of this scenario is the use of Teradata Join Indexes or DB2 Snapshot Views in the source systems. The equivalent technology in Oracle that provides the same functionality is the Oracle Materialized View object. If this translation is not programmed into the tool, it cannot perform the translation.

The second scenario is when the technology or feature used on the source system does not have a direct translation on the Oracle platform. In such a case, you need to investigate 1) how much work is involved in refactoring the object or the code to accomplish the same function on the

Oracle platform; and 2) the repercussions of not moving the object or the code over to Oracle. Depending on the outcome of this investigation, the work involved in fixing the fallouts can be estimated.

An example of the previous scenario is during migration of a Teradata database to an Oracle database and encountering a Teradata hash index on the source, which is an object that does not have an exact equivalent on the Oracle platform. The nearest equivalent on Oracle for hash indexes is the Oracle B-Tree index. However, the approach in this case should be to abandon the hash index altogether in the migration. Once the migration is complete and you are testing the migrated platform, you can use Oracle SQL Access Advisor (part of the Oracle Enterprise Manager Tuning pack) to analyze missing index structures that can be created on Oracle to improve performance.

Server-side Scripts Migration

Currently, the migration tools provided by Oracle do not support automated conversion of server-side scripts. You must convert them manually or investigate third-party tools that might be able to provide this functionality.

You should also consider rearchitecting the server-side scripts into a business logic layer that can be implemented using middleware tools or other best practices available for the tasks that the scripts perform. However, you need to evaluate the costs of a rearchitecture versus a manual conversion. Rearchitecting using ODI or other tools might be the way to go, especially when you consider long-term maintenance costs of custom scripts and the issues that arise for supporting manually written code.

The metrics captured in the discovery phases will determine the total lines of code of the server-side scripts and their complexity. This should give you a rough estimate of the rearchitecture or the manual conversion effort involved.

Data Migration and Synchronization

The source system requirements listed next help in determining the appropriate data migration strategy:

- The downtime admissible on the source database and the applications as per the current SLAs.

- The requirement to replicate data between the current source database and the Database Machine. This is required when the migration strategy dictates a phased migration of components or to run a parallel production environment on the Database Machine.

- The effective throughput of the network between the current source and the Database Machine.

- The total size of the source database that will be migrated to Oracle.

Based on these metrics and requirements, there can be two options for moving data to the Database Machine. The first option involves shutting down all the activity on the current source database, performing a data dump of the source database into flat files, and then loading the dump files into the Oracle database on the Database Machine. This method incurs downtime—how much will depend on how fast the data can move from the source to the destination system.

The second option is to replicate the data, in *real time* or in *near real-time,* from the current source database to the Oracle Database and essentially run a parallel production system on the Database Machine. The replication process can be performed using software tools or custom scripts. Migrating using this option incurs zero to minimal downtime, and it allows you to run parallel production environments, which are quite useful for testing and for phased migrations.

The migration strategy can also involve combining the two approaches, with each approach working on a different set of data, based on the method that works best for each set. However, both the options discussed previously have a common step—the initial data migration step. In the first migration option, the initial data migration would also be the final data migration. In the second option involving replication, the initial load will be the method used to instantiate the destination system with the initial copy of the source database before starting the incremental migration process.

Initial Data Migration

The initial data migration process will consist of two main steps. The first step is to extract the source database into a temporary staging area, and the second step is to load from the staging area to the Database Machine. In order to accelerate the overall data migration process, the extract and the load steps can be parallelized, as long as the steps work on different data sets and excessive parallelism does not throttle down the system or network resources.

In a real-world migration scenario, the flat file extracts from the source system tend to be the bottleneck and not the network throughput or the data loads. The bottleneck is mainly due to the performance limitation of the source database storage system, the CPU limitation on the source platform, or writes to the temporary staging location.

It is not easy to estimate the time it takes for the initial data load, since multiple components exist in the path of the data and each component will have different throughput. It is important to remember that the overall data transfer throughput is limited by the slowest link in the data flow. The best way to estimate data transfer times is to measure the actual performance of a test run on the subset of data, under similar network connectivity like it would be in production.

The initial data migration process will push large amounts of data over the network connecting the source and the destination systems, and in order to get the best possible throughput, it is important to factor in the network throughput. The best throughput possible is on the Database Machine side using the InfiniBand network. Refer to Chapter 4 for the different mechanisms available to connect the Database Machine to the outside world.

The best practice for extracting data from the source database is to utilize the data dump utilities that come bundled with the source database software installation. These utilities are the most efficient and supported methods to pull data out of the source system. The loads into Oracle should be performed using the best practices of data loading such as the external table load.

Initial loads can be performed by using custom extract and load scripts, and by using automated tools such as Oracle Data Integrator, Oracle GoldenGate, or Oracle SQL Developer. We will discuss these products and their capabilities in detail in a later section.

Incremental Data Migration and Replication

Incremental data migration is the process of synchronizing the source and the destination systems by moving only the changed data (instead of the complete set) since the last synchronization process. When the incremental data migration happens in real time, it is called real-time replication.

The key requirement of the incremental data migration is the ability to capture changed data from the source system using an appropriate *change data capture* (CDC) strategy. Some of the CDC methods that can be used for capturing changes are

- **Data model–based CDC**   In order for the source database to support a data model–based CDC, the tables on the source database should be able to capture the timestamp of all the DML activity as it occurs on the source system. This is usually accomplished by using a column that stores a *row modified* (or *inserted*) timestamp for every row. The incremental extracts can use this timestamp to pull out only the changed rows since the last synchronization process. However, deletes will have to be captured in a separate log table using mechanisms such as delete triggers.

- **Trigger-based CDC**   Triggers can be defined on the source tables to execute when insert/update/delete activity occurs allowing it to take further actions. The triggers can be programmed to capture changes in a separate log table, or even propagate the changes directly to the destination database using queuing-based mechanisms.

- **Log-based CDC**   Almost all databases have some sort of *journalizing* capability. Journalizing is the process of capturing database transactions (or modifications) in a log file, which is stored in a format that is proprietary to the database vendor. Most database vendors provide an interface to these log files using an Application Programming Interface (API). By mining the log files using the API, it is possible to re-create the SQL as it occurred on the source database and then execute it against the destination database, at the same time preserving the transactional integrity of the DML. Real-time replication tools are based on the ability to mine database transaction logs in real time.

Based on the CDC strategy chosen, the methods that can be used for performing the incremental loads can be determined. Broadly speaking, the incremental load methods can be categorized into *near* real-time and real time.

- **Near real-time incremental loads**   When the CDC is performed by using the data model approach, then the incremental loads can, at best, be done in near real-time. Each run of the incremental load process will synchronize a batch of transactions that will be queued up to be processed. How "near" to real time the loads are is determined by the time it takes the incremental load to synchronize a batch without causing a measurable impact on the source system. The methods available for performing near real-time incremental loads are using custom extract and load scripts and ETL tools like Oracle Data Integrator.

The custom scripts and ETL mappings created for performing initial loads can also be used to perform incremental loads by modifying the SQL to extract only the changed rows since the last run instead of the complete data.

■ **Real-time incremental loads**   Using the log-based CDC approach, changes can be replicated as they occur on the source system in real time to the destination system. The Oracle tools that support real-time replication using the log-based CDC approach are Oracle GoldenGate and Oracle Data Integrator. Both tools can perform replication from heterogeneous sources to the Oracle database. In the next section, we will discuss the capabilities and guidelines that will help you choose the right tool.

Using automated tools to perform real-time incremental loads is the most preferred method for performing real-time synchronization of data between the current source and the Database Machine. This method does not need the data model to support change data capture, as the tools are capable of capturing changes using built-in mechanisms. Also, the work involved in the setup and configuration of the tools is much less when compared to the custom scripts method.

Using Automated Tools for Migration

As mentioned previously, automating portions of the migration process can deliver a faster, smoother migration. This section will describe some of the tools that can be used for automating migration tasks.

Oracle SQL Developer

Oracle SQL Developer is a GUI-based tool that can be used for the purposes of database development against a variety of database sources. SQL Developer has support for many different SQL-based tasks, such as creating and browsing database objects, running SQL statements and scripts, and creating and debugging PL/SQL code. It has a data modeling component and provides the capability to migrate third-party databases to Oracle. SQL Developer also has the ability to create graphical reports based on the results of SQL statements. These features enable SQL Developer to perform a variety of tasks using point-and-click interfaces, which in turn will enhance user productivity.

In the context of migrations, Oracle SQL Developer has support for migrating non-Oracle database sources, including Microsoft SQL Server, Microsoft Access, IBM DB2, MySQL, Teradata, and Sybase. The tool allows you to perform automated migrations of database schema and the data. SQL Developer supports data migrations by creating data movement scripts for offline migration, and can also be used in data migration online by connecting into the source and destination systems simultaneously and perform a data move in real time.

More capabilities and features are continuously added to SQL Developer, so before you plan on using it for the migration, verify the up-to-date support for the source databases and versions and its capabilities, especially with respect to stored object migrations.

SQL Developer for Schema Migration   Migration of database schemas from non-Oracle databases can be performed using Oracle SQL Developer. Schema objects such as the data models, stored procedures, and triggers can be seamlessly converted to the Oracle-equivalent objects by a simple press of a button. SQL Developer supports a variety of third-party database sources, and the specific source object types that can be migrated automatically by the tool should be verified prior to performing the migration.

Oracle SQL Developer uses a database schema as a repository in which it will store all the source database schema definitions, the converted schemas, migration reports, and conversion logs. The database schema migration process in SQL Developer consists of the following steps:

- Capture the current model into the SQL Developer migration repository.

- Translate the captured source database model to the Oracle-equivalent model

- Generate the Oracle-equivalent Data Definition Language (DDL) statements from the model.

SQL Developer has a schema capture mechanism that can capture the source database schemas, either directly by connecting to the source (online) or indirectly by the use of source database-specific capture scripts (offline). The online method will capture the schema by reading the data dictionary of the source database. The offline method will effectively do the same thing and can be used when you do not have the privileges or the network access to connect to the source system. SQL Developer can generate source-specific capture scripts, which can be shipped to the source system and executed using appropriate credentials. The output generated by these scripts can be shipped back and loaded into the SQL Developer repository to create the source model.

SQL Developer has built-in reports that will display a summary of all the conversions it has performed, and it is able to do this by querying the migration repository. These reports can be run at the end of the conversion process to evaluate if there were any fallouts or warnings during the conversion. Also, at each step during the conversion, the fallouts and warnings will be displayed in the SQL Developer window. This will help you monitor the progress of the conversion and make appropriate decisions when encountering issues.

SQL Developer has built-in intelligence to handle a few types of fallouts. When it finds an object type on the source database that is not named exactly the same in Oracle but it functions similarly, it will translate it to the Oracle-equivalent object. A good example of this is when you have DB2 snapshot views on the source DB2 database. The equivalent of DB2 snapshot views in Oracle is Materialized Views, and SQL Developer will automatically convert DB2 snapshots to Materialized Views.

Oracle SQL Developer for Data Migration   Oracle SQL Developer is capable of creating extract and load scripts that can be utilized to perform the initial data migration. The scripts generated by SQL Developer will incorporate the source-specific utilities for performing extracts and the Oracle-specific utilities for performing the loads.

In the absence of SQL Developer support for the type of the source database or the version, the data extract scripts need to be created manually. The time and effort to create the scripts need to be factored into the migration process, and for the most part, this will be proportional to the number of source database objects being migrated. However, SQL Developer can still be used for creating the load scripts on the Oracle side, if the format of the data extracted conforms to the SQL*Loader control files created by SQL Developer.

SQL Developer can also be used for moving data *online* between the database systems it supports. It does this by connecting into the databases using the JDBC drivers and selecting the data out of the source and inserting it into the destination. However, using SQL Developer for performing online data moves is not efficient for migrating large data sets.

Oracle GoldenGate

Oracle GoldenGate provides real-time capture, transformation, routing, and delivery of database transactions between Oracle and non-Oracle databases. GoldenGate facilitates high-performance, low-impact data movement in real time to a wide variety of databases and platforms while maintaining transaction integrity.

Oracle GoldenGate supports a variety of use-cases, including real-time business intelligence; query offloading; zero-downtime upgrades and migrations; disaster recovery; and active-active databases using bidirectional replication, data synchronization, and providing high availability. In the context of migrations to the Database Machine, Oracle GoldenGate can be used to support the following use-cases:

- Synchronization of parallel production or dual-active environments

- Phased migration requirements in which portions of the database are made available on one or both systems, with single or bidirectional replication

- Zero-downtime migrations from both Oracle and non-Oracle source systems that are needed for applications requiring a high level of SLAs

- Instantiation of destination databases by performing initial loads from the source

Prior to starting a heterogeneous data replication project, verify GoldenGate's support for the non-Oracle source system and the specific version you are interested in migrating. If GoldenGate is selected as the tool of choice, refer to the best practices for configuring GoldenGate for the Database Machine as discussed in Chapter 6.

Oracle Data Integrator

Oracle Data Integrator (ODI) is a data integration tool that integrates heterogeneous systems and platforms using a web services–based architecture. It also provides E-LT capability by utilizing the source or the destination platform to perform the transformations, rather than using a separate transformation engine. ODI supports a variety of sources and destinations, and connects to the database systems using the native drivers or JDBC/ODBC.

ODI has a framework of *knowledge modules,* which are plug-ins that encapsulate the best practices for loading, transforming, and integrating data for a specific source or target. Using knowledge modules, ODI is able to integrate with a variety of sources and utilize the source-specific and optimized techniques that are efficient for performing E-LT on the source platform. This feature is useful in the context of data migrations because it provides a highly efficient data transfer mechanism by merely using point-and-click interfaces, thus eliminating the use of custom extract and load scripts. Prebuilt knowledge modules are available for a variety of source systems that help you perform tasks such as data extraction, loading, and change data capture (CDC).

ODI is also useful for performing incremental data loads in *near* real-time and replication in real time between the source and destination databases. The method of CDC used will determine how much in real time the modified data can be propagated. Following are the mechanisms available with ODI for change data capture:

- **Change data capture using the source data model** This method is appropriate if the tables involved in CDC have columns that store a timestamp of the changed row when it gets modified or inserted.

- **Change data capture using ODI Knowledge Modules** This method uses techniques such as triggers or mining of database logs to capture changes.

- **Change data capture using ODI GoldenGate Knowledge Modules** ODI and Oracle GoldenGate can be connected together to provide greater optimization and extensibility. Specifically, these Knowledge Modules will leverage the power of Oracle GoldenGate for its real-time, log-based CDC.

Once the changes are captured, ODI can use a publish-and-subscribe model for propagating changes to the destination database in real time or near real-time (based on the capture method). The CDC Knowledge Module support for non-Oracle sources and their specific versions needs to be consulted prior to deciding on using ODI.

Third-party Tools and Services

Third-party tools exist in the market and are capable of migrating database schemas, database stored objects, and server-side scripts from non-Oracle systems to Oracle. The effectiveness of these tools needs to be investigated thoroughly against your database environment. A tool should be evaluated for its support for the source database type, the object types it can automatically migrate, and its automated conversion rates.

You should remember that each database environment is different, and the success and automated conversion rates of these tools from one successful migration cannot be generalized, since you might not get the same results in your environment as have been achieved in other scenarios. Using advertised conversion rates and success stories as a guideline might help, but cannot be taken as accurate estimates and applied as-is to your migration project. The best way to get an insight into the effectiveness of the tool is to perform a proof of concept with the vendor on a sample representation of your environment and observe the results.

There are third-party vendors that provide end-to-end migration services that encompass the use of automated tools along with manual migration services. These vendors utilize the best on-shore and off-shore implementation models (sometimes referred to as *best shore*) to considerably lower the cost of manual migrations. This book does not discuss third-party service providers or third-party migration tools.

Migration Steps for Oracle Databases

This section will highlight the important methods and steps currently in use for migrating Oracle Databases residing on non-Exadata platforms to the Oracle Database 11*g* Release 2 on the Database Machine. These methods will be discussed at a high level; for detailed step-by-step instructions, refer to the Oracle Database documentation and the My Oracle Support portal.

The considerations that determine the selection of the right method are the need to migrate with zero-downtime, implementing best practices during the migration, performing a full database migration versus a subset, the current database version, the OS version, and the database platform being migrated.

The migration methods can be grouped under two main categories—*physical migration* methods and *logical migration* methods.

NOTE
At the time of writing this book, the Solaris-based Database Machine configurations were not offered by Oracle. Hence, the steps for migrating Oracle databases to a Solaris-based platform are not discussed in this chapter. However, the migration methods available to you in such cases are similar to the ones highlighted in this section. But you need to consider the special requirements for the Oracle Solaris 11 Express target platform. Refer to the Oracle Support notes and the Oracle Database 11g Release 2 documentation for further details.

Migrating Using Physical Methods

Physical migration methods will perform block-for-block copy of the database blocks from the source system to the destination Database Machine platform. By the nature of their definition, these options are more rigid and inflexible in modifying the data within the blocks during the migration process. Physical migration methods do not allow the implementation of Oracle Database best practices during the migration process. If your strategy requires you to implement best practices as part of the migration, consider using the logical migration methods.

The key characteristics of physical methods are

- Physical migration methods are generally faster than the logical migration methods, unless the logical method is moving far less data than the physical method.

- The physical migration is of complete databases and not subsets. Moreover, these methods are not capable of performing a database upgrade during the migration. The only exception to this is the Transportable Tablespace method, which in fact can upgrade the database during the migration.

NOTE
It is recommended that you implement the Oracle Database best practices to unleash the full power of the Database Machine. The important best practices are ASM allocation unit size of 4MB, the minimum 4MB database extent size, using SecureFiles for LOBs, table partitioning, and database compression technologies such as OLTP and EHCC.

Migrating Using ASM Redundancy

Using ASM, it is possible to add disks to an existing ASM diskgroup and ASM will automatically initiate a rebalance operation and redistribute the data blocks on the newly added disk. Similarly, when a disk is dropped from an ASM diskgroup, ASM will automatically re-create the data blocks that were on the dropped disk by copying them from the mirrored location (provided the ASM diskgroup is mirrored and enough space exists). These add and drop steps can be performed while the ASM and the database instances are online, without affecting the availability of data.

This capability in ASM can be used for migration of databases to the Database Machine. The migration process would start by adding grid disks on the Exadata Storage Servers to the existing ASM diskgroups configured using the non-Exadata storage. You would then drop the disks on the non-Exadata storage and initiate a rebalance operation that re-creates the blocks (using mirrored copies) that were originally present on the dropped disk on the Exadata Storage Servers. These steps are repeated until all diskgroups are migrated over to the Database Machine.

The considerations for using this method are

- The source system platform should be based on Linux x86-64, and the database and ASM version should be the same as the Database Machine (i.e., 11.2).

- The source system's ASM diskgroups must be configured with normal or high redundancy.

- Application impact can be controlled such that the rebalance happens with minimal impact. This can be adjusted with the POWER clause of the rebalance operation.

- Since ASM on Exadata needs to access the legacy storage, the legacy storage must be exposed to the Database Machine using NFS or iSCSI. If moving from a previous version of the Database Machine, then you should connect the two machines using the InfiniBand Network or the 10 Gigabit Ethernet.

- Although the migration itself will incur zero downtime, in reality, there will be a slight downtime incurred in order to switch the database and ASM instances from the non-Exadata platform to the Database Machine.

Migrating Using Partition Roll-in and Roll-out

A partition roll-in and roll-out strategy deals with deleting the old table partitions out of the database when they are no longer required (roll-out) and adding the new data that is loaded to new table partitions (roll-in). Using this strategy, you can load the new data on the partitions that reside on the Exadata Storage Server, while the old data on the legacy storage will be deleted over time, based on the roll-out criteria. This method does not incur a data migration from the source to the destination database.

However, the main requirement for using this method is that the data model should be designed for the partition roll-in/roll-out strategy. The requirement seems stringent for any realistic migration use-case to fit in, but it might be possible to use this method in conjunction with other methods, like the Data Pump, which will move part of the data that does not support the partition roll-in/roll-out rules. We will discuss the Data Pump method in later sections.

The considerations for using this method are

- The source system platform should be based on Linux x86-64 and the database should be 11.2.

- The use of ASM on the source database is optional. The new table partitions will reside in the ASM on the Database Machine.

- The legacy storage needs to be connected to the Database Machine using NFS or iSCSI.

- Data migration is not needed in this option. There will be a slight downtime associated in order to switch the database and ASM instances from the non-Exadata platform to the Database Machine.

- The source database data model should support partition roll-out and roll-in requirements as stated earlier.

- Smart Scans across the new partitions residing on the Exadata Storage Servers and the old partitions residing on the legacy storage are not possible.

- The legacy storage cannot be decommissioned quickly, and this could be an issue when justifying the purchase of the Database Machine.

Migrating Using Physical Standby Database

The Data Guard physical standby database is a block-for-block replica of the primary database. The Data Guard apply process is responsible for replicating the changes from the redo logs on the primary database to the physical standby database in real time, and it supports both synchronous and asynchronous mechanisms.

Physical standby databases can be used for performing database platform migrations. The method involves creating a Data Guard physical standby database of the current source database on the Database Machine and then performing a Data Guard switchover to the physical standby.

The considerations for using this method are

- The source system platform should be a Linux-based or Microsoft Windows–based database with versions 11.1 or 11.2.

- This method can incur less than a minute of downtime, which is required for performing a Data Guard switchover to 11g R2 database on the Database Machine.

- If the source database version is 11.1, then you need to perform an upgrade to 11.2, either at the source or at the destination. The upgrade process will incur additional downtime.

■   The network bandwidth and throughput between the Database Machine and the source system should be adequate to handle the peak transaction rates. Otherwise, the downtime will be greater than what was mentioned earlier.

■   Consider this method when migrating from the HP Oracle Database Machine. The source database can be upgraded to 11.2 after moving it to the Database Machine.

Migrating Using Transportable Tablespaces

A transportable tablespace can be used for moving (or copying) a database tablespace along with all the objects that reside in it from one database to another. Using this method, tablespaces can be migrated from Oracle Database versions 10.1 and later, residing on any platform, to the Oracle Database 11*g* Release 2 residing on the Database Machine. The major steps involved in this method are to modify the tablespaces on the source database to read-only mode, to copy the data files of the tablespaces from the source to the Database Machine, and last, to plug in the tablespaces into the destination 11*g* Release 2 database.

The considerations for using this method are

■   The source system can be on any platform and OS, and the database version can be 10.1 or later.

■   This method allows you to upgrade from older versions of the database and to move between platforms of different endian formats.

■   This method supports partial database migrations at the tablespace level.

■   The time-consuming part of this process is the copy of the data files from the source to the Database Machine, and the time it takes for the file transfer will determine the downtime needed for the migration process. To minimize the downtime, consider connecting the source database through the InfiniBand or the 10 Gigabit Ethernet network.

Platform Endianness

Endianness is the method of representing multibyte data by computer systems. The endianness of a platform can be of two types—*little endian* and *big endian*. Little-endian systems store the least significant byte of the memory in the lowest address, whereas the big-endian systems store the most significant byte of the memory in the lowest address. The lowest memory address of multibyte data is the starting address of the data. Some examples of little-endian systems are Linux and Windows, and big-endian systems are HP-UX and Sun SPARC.

When moving data between platforms of different endian formats, the data needs to be converted so that the data integrity remains preserved. This is not an issue with logical migrations, since the SQL layer will be performing the endian conversion. But in physical migrations, the data is migrated at the block level as-is, and there needs to be an additional step that performs the endian conversion. The RMAN CONVERT command can accomplish this conversion.

Migrating Using Transportable Database

Using the transportable database method, an entire database can be migrated from one platform to another as long as the source and destination platforms have the same endian format. The method involves transferring the data files to the Database Machine, performing the RMAN convert operation if there is a change in the OS, and running the transport script at the end, which opens the newly transported database.

Some key considerations of using the transportable database method are

- The source database version needs to be 11.2 and the source platform should be little-endian based.

- When the source is on a non-Linux–based, little-endian platform, an additional step of converting the database files to Linux format is involved. The RMAN CONVERT command is utilized to perform this operation.

- If using the RMAN CONVERT command to perform file conversion, then consider converting the files on the Database Machine after the transfer is complete. The conversion will be much faster because of the high performance and throughput of the Exadata Storage Servers.

■ The downtime with this method is dependent on how fast the files can be transferred to the Database Machine, the time to run the RMAN CONVERT command, and the time to execute the transport script.

Migrating Using Logical Methods

Logical migration methods will extract the data out of the source database and load it into the destination database, using utilities that interface through the SQL layer. Logical methods are more flexible than the physical methods, but generally require longer downtimes to perform the migration.

The main benefit of using logical methods is that they allow you to implement the Database Machine best practices during the migration process. If you implement the best practices after the migration, as the case will be when you use physical methods, the data needs to be reorganized using a process that could require another system outage.

The key characteristics of logical methods are

■ Logical methods enable migration of subsets of data and also allow you to implement the database best practices during the migration process.

■ Logical methods will allow you to perform a database upgrade during the migration process.

■ Logical migrations generally incur longer downtimes, with the exception of the GoldenGate and the Data Guard logical standby methods.

Migrating Using Logical Standby Database

The Oracle Data Guard logical standby database is a logical replica of the primary database, which is kept in sync using the Data Guard SQL Apply process. The SQL Apply process converts the transactions from the primary database redo logs to SQL statements, and the SQL is then applied on the logical standby database to replicate the transactions.

The logical standby database can have different physical characteristics than the primary database, and can even be on different versions. Using this capability, the source system can be migrated by creating a logical standby of the source on the Database Machine and then performing a Data Guard switchover to the logical standby database.

The considerations for using this method are

- The source database can be 10.1.0.3 or later on a Linux x86-64 platform.

- The outage time on the source database is the time it takes to perform a Data Guard switchover to the standby database.

- This method allows you to perform an upgrade of the database during the migration process.

- You can also use this method to upgrade from HP Oracle Database Machine to the Oracle Exadata Database Machine with minimal downtime.

- The SQL Apply process does not support all data types and objects. If you have unsupported objects and data types in your source database, you should consider using methods like Data Pump for migration of those objects. For a complete list of unsupported data types and objects, refer to the Oracle Data Guard documentation.

- Since the SQL Apply process requires more work on the target system than the Redo Apply used for physical standbys, you must make sure that the target machine can keep up with the changes sent to it, although with an Exadata Database Machine as the target, the chances of a failure in this area are slight.

Migrating Using Oracle GoldenGate

Oracle GoldenGate can replicate data between two Oracle Databases running on different versions and platforms. This feature allows you to migrate and upgrade a prior version of Oracle Database on any platform to the Database Machine and keep the databases in sync for a time, and then perform a switchover once the destination is ready to go live.

The benefits of using Oracle GoldenGate for migration are

- This method provides zero-downtime migrations. The only impact is for the applications to initiate a reconnection to the Oracle Database on the Database Machine.

■ There are no restrictions on the source platform or the database versions. The source needs to be 10.1 or later, on any platform. Even non-Oracle sources are supported with GoldenGate.

■ The initial instantiation of the database on the Database Machine will happen while the source database is online and with minimal impact.

■ There is no performance impact on the source database, since GoldenGate asynchronously mines the redo logs for capturing changes from the source.

As mentioned earlier, GoldenGate can be used to run a parallel production environment on the Database Machine. This is considered a huge feature for databases that require a zero-downtime migration with minimal risks.

Migrating Using Oracle Data Pump

If you can afford some downtime for performing the migration, then consider the Data Pump method. Some highlights and benefits of using Data Pump are

■ This is a simple solution, but needs downtime. The amount of downtime depends on the data volume and the effective network bandwidth available between the source database and Exadata.

■ The source database needs to be 10.1 or later on any platform.

■ If Data Pump is used in the network mode, there is a one-time data movement between the source and the destination, and there is no need for a temporary staging environment.

■ If you need the temporary staging environment, the capacity of the temporary staging location will depend on the amount of data being migrated.

■ Consider tuning the Data Pump jobs by using parallelism.

■ This method enables migration of subsets of data, including subsets of schemas and even portions of tables or partitions by using the QUERY clause.

Migrating Using Create Table as Select (CTAS) and Insert as Select (IAS)

This method is extremely flexible and supports all versions of Oracle Databases on all platforms. If you are considering a migration with this method, you would first create a brand-new database on the Database Machine with all the best practices in place, create a database link to the existing Oracle database, and last, you would start data migration using Create Table as Select (CTAS) or Insert as Select (IAS) methods.

- This method supports migration from any Oracle database version on any platform.

- It requires downtime, which for the most part depends on the time it takes to move the data through the network.

- CTAS and IAS methods are single threaded and are not automatically parallelized since the database link is inherently serial when used in a statement. However, you can manually parallelize the migration process by initiating multiple CTAS or IAS statements. But keep in mind that the overall throughput is limited by the available network bandwidth between the source and the destination.

- This method enables migration of subsets of data, including subsets of schemas and even portions of tables or partitions by using the QUERY clause.

- Consider routing the database links over the InfiniBand or the 10 Gigabit Ethernet network to improve the data transfer rate.

Summary

In this chapter, you have learned about the different migration methodologies for migrating databases to the Exadata Database Machine. These methodologies have been proven to be successful in real-world migrations that have complex requirements. In order for you to navigate a large migration project, the details listed in this chapter will help you plan the outcome that will be successful, the most cost effective, and the one that applies best in your environment.

APPENDIX

Exadata Capacity and Performance Specifications

efer to the tables provided in this section for the Database Machine capacity and performance specifications. Since the specifications are subject to change when new versions of the Database Machine are introduced by Oracle, refer to the latest Exadata Database Machine data sheet on Oracle.com for up-to-date numbers.

Exadata Database Machine Storage Capacity

	Full Rack X2-2 and X2-8 (HP-SAS)	Full Rack X2-2 and X2-8 (HC-SAS)	Half Rack X2-2 (HP-SAS)	Half Rack X2-2 (HC-SAS)	Quarter Rack X2-2 (HP-SAS)	Quarter Rack X2-2 (HC-SAS)
No. of database nodes	8	8	4	4	2	2
No. of Exadata Storage Servers	14	14	7	7	3	3
Flash Cache	5.3TB	5.3TB	2.6TB	2.6TB	1.1TB	1.1TB
Total storage capacity (base 1000)	100TB	336TB	50TB	168TB	22TB	72TB
Total storage capacity (base 1024)[1]	92TB	306 TB	46TB	153TB	20TB	65TB
Usable capacity (uncompressed)[2]	45TB	150TB	22.5TB	75TB	9.25TB	31.5TB

[1]The storage capacity has been rounded to the nearest decimal and is based on base 1024.

[2]Usable capacity is calculated after accounting for ASM mirroring of normal redundancy and protection from one disk failure.

TABLE A-1. *Exadata Database Machine Storage Capacity*

Exadata Storage Server Performance

		Full Rack X2-8	Full Rack X2-2	Half Rack X2-2	Quarter Rack X2-2
Raw disk data bandwidth[1][3]	HP-SAS	25 GB/s	21 GB/s	12.5 GB/s	5.4 GB/s
	HC-SAS	14 GB/s	12 GB/s	7 GB/s	3 GB/s
Disk IOPS[2][3]	HP-SAS	50,000	50,000	25,000	10,800
	HC-SAS	25,000	25,000	12,500	5,400
Flash IOPS[2][3]		1,500,000	1,500,000	750,000	375,000
Raw flash data bandwidth[1][3]		75 GB/s	75 GB/s	37.5 GB/s	16 GB/s
Total database CPU cores		128	96	48	24

[1]The bandwidth is peak physical disk scan bandwidth, assuming no compression.

[2]IOPS—Based on IO requests of size 8K.

[3]Actual performance will vary by application.

TABLE A-2. *Exadata Storage Server Performance*

Index

A

ACS (Advanced Customer Services),
137–140, 150
Active Data Guard, 65–66, 212, 213
active requests, 191–192
ACTIVEREQUEST object, 122
activerequest object, 191–192
adaptive parallelism, 57
ADDM (Automatic Database Diagnostics
Monitor), 8, 269
administration tasks, 162–178
ADR (Automatic Diagnostic Repository), 120
adrci (Automatic Diagnostics Repository
Command
Interface), 164
ADRCI interface, 120
Advanced Compression Option, 67, 99,
104, 136, 278
Advanced Customer Services (ACS),
137–140, 150
ALERTDEFINITION object, 122
alerts
acknowledging, 188
clear, 183
critical, 182, 188
described, 181
history, 188
informational, 183
monitoring, 180, 181–183, 187–189

Oracle Enterprise Manager, 199–202
propagating via SNMP/SMTP, 189
stateful, 182
stateless, 182
threshold, 189–190
warning, 182
allocation directives, 114
ALTER command, 119
ALTER SESSION command, 54, 56, 96
ALTER SYSTEM command, 96
ALTERHISTORY object, 122
analysis capabilities, 72–73
analytic functions, 73, 271, 272
analytics, embedded, 271–275
analytics extensions, 271
API (Application Programming
Interface), 368
appliance-like computing solutions, 5–7
Application Programming Interface
(API), 368
application servers, 142, 354
applications
consolidating, 340
OLTP, 339
rearchitecting strategies, 361–362
surrounding, 347, 367
tuning, 318
upgrades, 229–230
archive compression, 102

389

Join the World's Largest Oracle Community

GET YOUR FREE SUBSCRIPTION TO *ORACLE MAGAZINE*

Oracle Magazine is essential gear for today's information technology professionals. Stay informed and increase your productivity with every issue of *Oracle Magazine*. Inside each free bimonthly issue you'll get:

- Up-to-date information on Oracle Database, Oracle Application Server, Web development, enterprise grid computing, database technology, and business trends
- Third-party news and announcements
- Technical articles on Oracle and partner products, technologies, and operating environments
- Development and administration tips
- Real-world customer stories

If there are other Oracle users at your location who would like to receive their own subscription to *Oracle Magazine*, please photocopy this form and pass it along.

Three easy ways to subscribe:

① Web
Visit our Web site at **oracle.com/oraclemagazine**
You'll find a subscription form there, plus much more

② Fax
Complete the questionnaire on the back of this card and fax the questionnaire side only to **+1.847.763.9638**

③ Mail
Complete the questionnaire on the back of this card and mail it to **P.O. Box 1263, Skokie, IL 60076-8263**

Want your own FREE subscription?

To receive a free subscription to *Oracle Magazine*, you must fill out the entire card, sign it, and date it (incomplete cards cannot be processed or acknowledged). You can also fax your application to +1.847.763.9638. **Or subscribe at our Web site at oracle.com/oraclemagazine**

O **Yes, please send me a FREE subscription** *Oracle Magazine.* O No.

O From time to time, Oracle Publishing allows our partners exclusive access to our e-mail addresses for special promotions and announcements. To be included in this program, please check this circle. If you do not wish to be included, you will only receive notices about your subscription via e-mail.

O Oracle Publishing allows sharing of our postal mailing list with selected third parties. If you prefer your mailing address not to be included in this program, please check this circle.

If at any time you would like to be removed from either mailing list, please contact Customer Service at +1.847.763.9635 or send an e-mail to oracle@halldata.com. If you opt in to the sharing of information, Oracle may also provide you with e-mail related to Oracle products, services, and events. If you want to completely unsubscribe from any e-mail communication from Oracle, please send an e-mail to: unsubscribe@oracle-mail.com with the following in the subject line: REMOVE [your e-mail address]. For complete information on Oracle Publishing's privacy practices, please visit oracle.com/html/privacy/html

X _____

signature (required)   date

name   title

company   e-mail address

street/p.o. box

city/state/zip or postal code   telephone

country   fax

Would you like to receive your free subscription in digital format instead of print if it becomes available? O Yes O No

YOU MUST ANSWER ALL 10 QUESTIONS BELOW.

① WHAT IS THE PRIMARY BUSINESS ACTIVITY OF YOUR FIRM AT THIS LOCATION? (check one only)

- □ 01 Aerospace and Defense Manufacturing
- □ 02 Application Service Provider
- □ 03 Automotive Manufacturing
- □ 04 Chemicals
- □ 05 Media and Entertainment
- □ 06 Construction/Engineering
- □ 07 Consumer Sector/Consumer Packaged Goods
- □ 08 Education
- □ 09 Financial Services/Insurance
- □ 10 Health Care
- □ 11 High Technology Manufacturing, OEM
- □ 12 Industrial Manufacturing
- □ 13 Independent Software Vendor
- □ 14 Life Sciences (biotech, pharmaceuticals)
- □ 15 Natural Resources
- □ 16 Oil and Gas
- □ 17 Professional Services
- □ 18 Public Sector (government)
- □ 19 Research
- □ 20 Retail/Wholesale/Distribution
- □ 21 Systems Integrator, VAR/VAD
- □ 22 Telecommunications
- □ 23 Travel and Transportation
- □ 24 Utilities (electric, gas, sanitation, water)
- □ 98 Other Business and Services _____

② WHICH OF THE FOLLOWING BEST DESCRIBES YOUR PRIMARY JOB FUNCTION? (check one only)

CORPORATE MANAGEMENT/STAFF
- □ 01 Executive Management (President, Chair, CEO, CFO, Owner, Partner, Principal)
- □ 02 Finance/Administrative Management (VP/Director/ Manager/Controller, Purchasing, Administration)
- □ 03 Sales/Marketing Management (VP/Director/Manager)
- □ 04 Computer Systems/Operations Management (CIO/VP/Director/Manager MIS/IS/IT, Ops)

IS/IT STAFF
- □ 05 Application Development/Programming Management
- □ 06 Application Development/Programming Staff
- □ 07 Consulting
- □ 08 DBA/Systems Administrator
- □ 09 Education/Training
- □ 10 Technical Support Director/Manager
- □ 11 Other Technical Management/Staff
- □ 98 Other

③ WHAT IS YOUR CURRENT PRIMARY OPERATING PLATFORM (check all that apply)

- □ 01 Digital Equipment Corp UNIX/VAX/VMS
- □ 02 HP UNIX
- □ 03 IBM AIX
- □ 04 IBM UNIX
- □ 05 Linux (Red Hat)
- □ 06 Linux (SUSE)
- □ 07 Linux (Oracle Enterprise)
- □ 08 Linux (other)
- □ 09 Macintosh
- □ 10 MVS
- □ 11 Netware
- □ 12 Network Computing
- □ 13 SCO UNIX
- □ 14 Sun Solaris/SunOS
- □ 15 Windows
- □ 16 Other UNIX
- □ 98 Other
- 99 □ None of the Above

④ DO YOU EVALUATE, SPECIFY, RECOMMEND, OR AUTHORIZE THE PURCHASE OF ANY OF THE FOLLOWING? (check all that apply)

- □ 01 Hardware
- □ 02 Business Applications (ERP, CRM, etc.)
- □ 03 Application Development Tools
- □ 04 Database Products
- □ 05 Internet or Intranet Products
- □ 06 Other Software
- □ 07 Middleware Products
- 99 □ None of the Above

⑤ IN YOUR JOB, DO YOU USE OR PLAN TO PURCHASE ANY OF THE FOLLOWING PRODUCTS? (check all that apply)

SOFTWARE
- □ 01 CAD/CAE/CAM
- □ 02 Collaboration Software
- □ 03 Communications
- □ 04 Database Management
- □ 05 File Management
- □ 06 Finance
- □ 07 Java
- □ 08 Multimedia Authoring
- □ 09 Networking
- □ 10 Programming
- □ 11 Project Management
- □ 12 Scientific and Engineering
- □ 13 Systems Management
- □ 14 Workflow

HARDWARE
- □ 15 Macintosh
- □ 16 Mainframe
- □ 17 Massively Parallel Processing

- □ 18 Minicomputer
- □ 19 Intel x86(32)
- □ 20 Intel x86(64)
- □ 21 Network Computer
- □ 22 Symmetric Multiprocessing
- □ 23 Workstation Services

SERVICES
- □ 24 Consulting
- □ 25 Education/Training
- □ 26 Maintenance
- □ 27 Online Database
- □ 28 Support
- □ 29 Technology-Based Training
- □ 30 Other
- 99 □ None of the Above

⑥ WHAT IS YOUR COMPANY'S SIZE? (check one only)

- □ 01 More than 25,000 Employees
- □ 02 10,001 to 25,000 Employees
- □ 03 5,001 to 10,000 Employees
- □ 04 1,001 to 5,000 Employees
- □ 05 101 to 1,000 Employees
- □ 06 Fewer than 100 Employees

⑦ DURING THE NEXT 12 MONTHS, HOW MUCH DO YOU ANTICIPATE YOUR ORGANIZATION WILL SPEND ON COMPUTER HARDWARE, SOFTWARE, PERIPHERALS, AND SERVICES FOR YOUR LOCATION? (check one only)

- □ 01 Less than $10,000
- □ 02 $10,000 to $49,999
- □ 03 $50,000 to $99,999
- □ 04 $100,000 to $499,999
- □ 05 $500,000 to $999,999
- □ 06 $1,000,000 and Over

⑧ WHAT IS YOUR COMPANY'S YEARLY SALES REVENUE? (check one only)

- □ 01 $500, 000, 000 and above
- □ 02 $100, 000, 000 to $500, 000, 000
- □ 03 $50, 000, 000 to $100, 000, 000
- □ 04 $5, 000, 000 to $50, 000, 000
- □ 05 $1, 000, 000 to $5, 000, 000

⑨ WHAT LANGUAGES AND FRAMEWORKS DO YOU USE? (check all that apply)

- □ 01 Ajax
- □ 02 C
- □ 03 C++
- □ 04 C#
- □ 13 Python
- □ 14 Ruby/Rails
- □ 15 Spring
- □ 16 Struts
- □ 05 Hibernate
- □ 06 J++/J#
- □ 07 Java
- □ 08 JSP
- □ 09 .NET
- □ 10 Perl
- □ 11 PHP
- □ 12 PL/SQL
- □ 17 SQL
- □ 18 Visual Basic
- □ 98 Other

⑩ WHAT ORACLE PRODUCTS ARE IN USE AT YOUR SITE? (check all that apply)

ORACLE DATABASE
- □ 01 Oracle Database 11*g*
- □ 02 Oracle Database 10*g*
- □ 03 Oracle9*i* Database
- □ 04 Oracle Embedded Database (Oracle Lite, Times Ten, Berkeley DB)
- □ 05 Other Oracle Database Release

ORACLE FUSION MIDDLEWARE
- □ 06 Oracle Application Server
- □ 07 Oracle Portal
- □ 08 Oracle Enterprise Manager
- □ 09 Oracle BPEL Process Manager
- □ 10 Oracle Identity Management
- □ 11 Oracle SOA Suite
- □ 12 Oracle Data Hubs

ORACLE DEVELOPMENT TOOLS
- □ 13 Oracle JDeveloper
- □ 14 Oracle Forms
- □ 15 Oracle Reports
- □ 16 Oracle Designer
- □ 17 Oracle Discoverer
- □ 18 Oracle BI Beans
- □ 19 Oracle Warehouse Builder
- □ 20 Oracle WebCenter
- □ 21 Oracle Application Express

ORACLE APPLICATIONS
- □ 22 Oracle E-Business Suite
- □ 23 PeopleSoft Enterprise
- □ 24 JD Edwards EnterpriseOne
- □ 25 JD Edwards World
- □ 26 Oracle Fusion
- □ 27 Hyperion
- □ 28 Siebel CRM

ORACLE SERVICES
- □ 28 Oracle E-Business Suite On Demand
- □ 29 Oracle Technology On Demand
- □ 30 Siebel CRM On Demand
- □ 31 Oracle Consulting
- □ 32 Oracle Education
- □ 33 Oracle Support
- □ 98 Other
- 99 □ None of the Above